HISTORY OF CIVILISATION

The Golden Age of Persia

The Golden Age of Persia

The Arabs in the East

RICHARD N. FRYE

AGA KHAN PROFESSOR OF IRANIAN, HARVARD UNIVERSITY, AND PRESIDENT OF THE ASIA INSTITUTE, PAHLAVI UNIVERSITY, SHIRAZ

WEIDENFELD AND NICOLSON

LONDON

Weidenfeld and Nicolson
11 St John's Hill, London SW11

ISBN 0 297 76871 9

Printed in Great Britain
by Ebenezer Baylis and Son Ltd
The Trinity Press, Worcester, and London

To Jeff, Becky and Bob

CONTENTS

	Preface	xi
1	Past, Present and Future	1
2	Sasanian Iran	7
3	Central Asia before the Arab Conquests	27
4	The Arab Conquests in Iran	54
5	The Islamic Conquest of Central Asia	74
6	The 'Abbasids and Western Iran	104
7	Heresies and the Oecumene of Islam	126
8	Iranian Contributions to Islamic Culture	150
9	Arts and Crafts	175
10	The Iranian Dynasties	186
11	Turkish Ascendancy	213
12	The Heritage of the Arabs	231
	Maps: Iran in the Seventh Century	237
	Iran in the Tenth Century	238
	Appendix 1 PERSIAN WORDS IN ARABIC	239
	Appendix 2 TABLES	241
	Caliphs	241
	Minor Iranian Dynasties	241
	Umaiyad Governors of Khurasan	242
	Arab Tribal Alignments under the Umaiyads	243

Glossary of Terms 245
Notes 248
General Bibliography 268
Primary Sources 270
Index 272

LIST OF ILLUSTRATIONS

Between pages 114 and 115

1 Bronze censer from Armenia, Sasanian style (Hermitage Museum, Leningrad. Photo: Asia Institute Archives)
2 Early Islamic silver plate (Hermitage Museum, Leningrad)
3 Transcaucasian stone plate, Islamic period (Asia Institute Archives)
4 Sixth-century Hephthalite silver bowl (Samarqand Museum)
5 Sasanian silver bowl (Private Collection, Tehran)
6 Late Sasanian silver bowl (Asia Institute Archives)
7 Islamic silver bowl (Hermitage Museum, Leningrad)
8 Boyid gold medal (Freer Gallery of Art, Smithsonian Institution, Washington D.C.)
9 Folk art decoration, West Persian painted ware, ninth century (Asia Institute Archives)
10 Recent pottery from Afghanistan (Photo: R.N.Frye)
11 Brass candleholder, 1225 (Boston Museum of Fine Arts. Photo: Asia Institute Archives)
12 Qajar tile work from Isfahan (Photo: Asia Institute Archives)
13 Shield from Panjikant (Photo: from A.Yu.Yakubovskii, ed., *Zhivopis Drevnego Pyandzhikenta*, Moscow 1954, plate 5)
14 Head from wall painting, Bust, Afghanistan (Photo: from D. Schlumberger, 'Le palais ghaznevide de Lashkari Bazaar', *Syria*, vol. 29, Paris 1952, plate XXXII)
15 Sasanian textile from a tomb in the Caucasus (Hermitage Museum, Leningrad)
16 Silk caftan, north Caucasus, eighth century (Hermitage Museum, Leningrad)
17 Islamic textile from Khurasan, tenth century (Louvre Museum, Paris)
18 Coat from Qajar Iran, eighteenth century (Yale University Art Gallery, Hobart Moore Memorial Collection)
19 Cloth tomb covering, sixteenth century (Cincinnati Museum of Art)

20 South-west Persian architecture: Imamzadeh Ja'far (Photo: Asia Institute Archives)
21 'Daniel's tomb' at Susa (Photo: Asia Institute Archives)
22 Ruins of a *chahar taq*, third century (Photo: Asia Institute Archives)
23 Tomb tower of Lajim in Mazandaran, 1022 (Photo: Asia Institute Archives)
24 Tomb tower of East Radkan, thirteenth century (Photo: Asia Institute Archives)
25 Ruins of *madrasa* at Chisht, twelfth century (Photo: R.N.Frye)
26 Ruins of mosque at Chisht, twelfth century (Photo: R.N. Frye)
27 Central courtyard – main mosque of Shiraz (Photo: Asia Institute Archives)
28 The city walls of Yazd (Photo: Asia Institute Archives)
29 Sasanian bridge at Shustar (Photo: Asia Institute Archives)
30 Safavid bridge at Isfahan (Photo: Oleg Grabar)
31 Sasanian column base (Photo: Rostamy)
32 Islamic stucco, Sasanian tradition (Photo: Asia Institute Archives)
33 Islamic stucco revetment, Damghan (Photo: Asia Institute Archives)
34 Islamic *mihrab* with old Iranian motifs, seventeenth century (Photo: Asia Institute Archives)
35 Timurid shrine near Herat (Photo: R.N.Frye).
36 Qur'an dated 1050, copied in Iran (Metropolitan Museum of Art, New York. Photo: Asia Institute Archives)
37 The oldest manuscript in Persian (Vienna Nationalbibliothek, Cod. A. F. 340, 447/1055. Photo: Asia Institute Archives)
38 Miniature from the *Shahname*, fourteenth century (Fogg Art Museum, Harvard University – Sachs Bequest)
39 Page from *Shahname*, 1482 (Fogg Art Museum, Harvard University)
40 Fifteenth-century miniature (Fogg Art Museum, Harvard University – Sears Collection)
41 Qajar miniature, calligraphic picture of 'Ali (Fogg Art Museum, Harvard University – Chester A.Priest Bequest)

PREFACE

The purpose of this volume, a sequel to *The Heritage of Persia*, is not to retell the story of the Arab conquests in Iran and central Asia and their aftermath, for this has been done. Rather the viewpoints of the conquered peoples in regard to the Arab conquerors, and to Islam in general, are the *leitmotif* of this work. It is concerned also with the fate of the Arabs and of Islam in the east, including the reasons for the fall of the Sasanian empire. The transition in Iran and central Asia from a variety of cultures to a united Islamic society is also examined. It must be remembered that in the east the Arabs conquered more than Iran, more than the Sasanian empire. Central Asia became part of the caliphate and the Iranians of central Asia became united with their western cousins under one state for the first time since the Achaemenids *by virtue of the Arab conquests*. Consequently central Asian and east Iranian influences must be taken into account when assessing the legacy of ancient Iran on Islamic culture. Furthermore, in my opinion, the Arab conquests were primarily responsible for the spreading of the Persian language in central Asia and throughout the east, where before Islam various Iranian languages and dialects were spoken, whereas the written languages were Khwarazmian, Sogdian and Kushan-Bactrian. Much attention has been directed up to now to the spread of Arabic in the east, but side by side with it, and by no means in opposition to Arabic, went a spread of the Persian language. Everyone knows that many Iranians (Persians, Sogdians, Khwarazmians, etc.) learned to speak and write Arabic, but those Arabs who settled down in the east had to communicate with the mass of local people who did not learn Arabic, and for this purpose they used, for the most part, the former 'official' spoken language of the Sasanian court which they called Dari, i.e. simply Persian without Arabic borrowings. Modern Persian is a continuation of this tongue, later embellished with countless Arabic words and expressions to form a new ornate style called Farsi, in contrast with the simpler Dari.

While I wish to stress Iranian continuity, on the other hand to ascribe every Islamic feature or custom not found in the Qur'an to pre-Islamic survivals is surely folly. Iranians certainly retained their past cultures, but they also did accept Islam, which became for them much more than a legalistic religion, and they contributed to it a good deal which was not just ancient survival. Furthermore, to eliminate Arabic words from modern Persian would be as difficult as trying to remove the French or Latin contributions of the Normans from the English language. Iran not only became a part of the Islamic world but it was the leading part for a long time, and one might say that the Iranians were the first who broke the equation 'Arab equals Islam', and made of the latter a truly universal culture and religion. Therefore one must not ignore the contributions of Iran to Islam, any more than one should minimize the overwhelming contribution of the Arabs to Islam.

Another topic which needs to be examined is the rise of the New Persian language and poetry in Transoxiana rather than in Fars province. The former had not been Sasanian territory, and its inhabitants, like the famous al-Biruni, had to learn both Persian and Arabic after the Islamic conquests. The eastern Iranians saw the need of fusing the two, and as a result an arabicized, Islamic New Persian language was created. In western Iran Arabic and Persian were also spoken, but Persian was not written since it was still attached to the formalized Pahlavi language, vehicle of Zoroastrianism, while Arabic was the parallel Islamic tongue, and the two written languages remained apart. Furthermore, the east fell under a local Iranian dynasty, the Samanids, whereas western Iran was closer to Baghdad. When the Seljüks united Iran and then invaded Anatolia, they carried everywhere with them the New Persian language and culture, which had evolved in the east under the Samanids. Paradoxically the New Persian language thereafter became more arabicized, because most Iranians everywhere had become Muslims with a common Arabic vocabulary, whereas various Persian dialect words could only be understood in limited areas. Therefore, in my opinion, the history of the rise and spread of New Persian should be studied with the historical developments in the background, and with the relations between 'official' written, 'official' spoken languages and dialects in mind. The division between western and eastern Iran, of course, is of prime importance. I use the term 'Iranian' for all Iranians everywhere and restrict the word 'Persian' to the west Iranians, the descendants of the Sasanians.

A book which is not a monograph must of necessity present general viewpoints. At the same time, details and sometimes even minutiae cannot be ignored where they have relevance to a larger problem. I have tried to avoid the mere listing of names or the accumulation of facts taken from other secondary sources which are readily available, and the notes or bibliographical references should help the reader to the further investigation of matters of interest to him. This work was begun over a decade ago, but it was abandoned when my attention was turned to pre-Islamic Iran. This is a long overdue obligation and probably my last work on the Islamic period or on Islamic subjects. On the other hand, I do believe that one must change what is almost an Islamic dictum, namely that history really begins with the Prophet. History must be understood as a continuity, and certainly we find it in the Islamic part of the history of Iran. Not only were the Persians, under the Sasanians, in many senses the heirs of the ancient Near Eastern world, but later under the Timurids and Safavids they became the heirs of classical Islamic thought, philosophy, literature and art. In many respects they were truer heirs of the classical Islamic tradition than the Ottoman empire. If I have managed to convey this sense of continuity in Iran I shall feel well rewarded.

In this hectic world it is difficult to secure the aid of a colleague in reading a long manuscript. If it had been possible undoubtedly many errors would have been avoided, especially in areas where my competence is wanting. I have tried my best to ensure accuracy but beg the indulgence of readers if slips should be found. Errors in theories or interpretations are another matter, but I hope I can convince the reader of the viability of those which I have proposed in this book. I have not burdened the reader, or the printer, with diacritical points in the text but have sought to reduce to a minimum such technicalities which do not have a bearing on any argument. In the index, appendices and notes the correct forms of a transliteration of the Arabic alphabet are given, but the reader is asked to remember that living languages such as Arabic and Persian need transcription of sounds rather than the close transliteration which is necessary for dead languages. Some inconsistencies inevitably will occur for which the author begs the reader's indulgence.

My secretary at Hamburg University, Frau J.Dannenberg, typed several of the chapters. Mrs Barbara Henson of the Middle East Center and Miss Carole Cross of the Department of Near Eastern Languages, both of Harvard University, typed the rest. Mrs Janet Bolandgray of Shiraz typed various pages of corrections. Dr Richard Bulliet of Harvard read the first part of the manuscript and gave me several welcome suggestions. To all of these persons I am most grateful. This book was brought to its final form in voyages between Cambridge, Mass., Hamburg and Shiraz, and the author hopes merely that it will stimulate thought and be of some value to seekers after knowledge in this vast field.

Richard N. Frye

CHAPTER 1

PAST, PRESENT AND FUTURE

Of all of the lands of the Middle East, Iran is perhaps both the most conservative and at the same time the most innovative. Whereas Egypt and Syria, for example, underwent great changes in the course of two millennia of history, Iran seems to have preserved much more of its ancient heritage. The christianization of the eastern Mediterranean world brought a profound break with the past for both Egypt and Syria; for history began with the coming of Christ, and all that happened before was simply a prelude to the appearance of the Messiah. Remembrance of the age-old succession of pharaohs in the land of the Nile was no longer significant for the Egyptians, who looked ahead to a new destiny under the aegis of Christianity. And so it was also for the Fertile Crescent, north Africa and Anatolia. Iran, however, retained its ancient Zoroastrian faith, together with customs and practices, unchanged by allegiance to a new religion.

Politically, too, Iranians never forgot the glories of imperial rule even though in time they would forget even the name of the Achaemenids. Empires and kingdoms might come and go, but the memory of a unified great state not only continued to inspire folk bards and poets but also to motivate political action. The end result was a restoration of imperial ideals in the Sasanian state of the third century of our era, which state resuscitated the past as nowhere else in the Near East. A foreign yoke, the Roman empire, had replaced ancient and traditional allegiances of all peoples around the Mediterranean Sea. The Romans may have been the heirs of the Greeks but hardly of the Egyptians or Syrians, whereas the Sasanian Iranians were definitely heirs of the Achaemenids, who in turn had been the summation of the traditions of Assyria, Babylonia and pharaonic Egypt in the Near East. For had not the Achaemenids fused the art and architecture as well as the religions and cultural traditions of the ancient Near East, and from the political and legal heritage created an international state which ruled the entire Near East for more than two centuries? Had not the Achaemenids created a universal law, the *data*, or law of the great king, which was applied to the entire empire impartially over the local laws and traditions which in turn had been put in order and codified at the command of Darius, who in Egyptian sources is called the last great lawgiver of the land of the Nile?

Then came Islam, and yet a new revelation replaced the old one of Christianity. The bedouins of the Arabian desert brought their language, as well as their religion, to the entire Near East and only Iran, together with Anatolia, escaped from becoming an Arabic-speaking land. For Islam was more than a religion. It was a way of life and a complete culture and civilization which erased the past, the age of ignorance; it proclaimed that real history began with Muhammad the Prophet of God. Iran was converted to the religion of Islam, but what happened to the culture and civilization of Islam is discussed in later chapters. The concept of a land of Iran continued through the Arab conquests down to the sixteenth century where the national state of the Safavids upheld by the Shiʿite state religion re-created, in many aspects, the Sasanian state of pre-Islamic Iran. The continuity of ancient Iranian traditions down to the present is impressive. For example, the main day of celebration of the Persians today is not an Islamic holiday but rather the ancient *noruz*, New Year's Day on the spring equinox, the 21st of March.

The conservatism of the Persians can readily be seen in the repetitive character of their history. One may be tempted to see in this a reflection of an ancient Indo-Iranian cyclical theory of history, perhaps as opposed to a linear view of history held by Semitic peoples of the Near East. Or more illuminating is the view that some people are very strongly conditioned by their past, to such an extent that they act in patterns imposed by the past, and they then interpret their history as what should have happened rather than what actually did happen. Elsewhere I have indicated the persistence of recurring motifs in the stories of the rise of dynasties throughout the history of Iran.[1] One may ask the question whether Ismaʿil, the founder of the Safavid dynasty at the beginning of the sixteenth century, consciously acted out his drama of manifest destiny by following the traditions of Cyrus the Great and Ardashir the Sasanian ruler. Or did later historians force the story of the rise of Ismaʿil into well-known patterns and motifs so as to conform to the popular conception of the founder of a dynasty in Iran? The ancient Persian concern with rectitude and the evil of lying is found again and again throughout the history of Iran, but the question of just what truth is has also exercised the minds of Persians throughout time. Surely the aphorism of the thirteenth-century poet Saʿdi, that the little white lie which causes pleasure is better than the truth which causes pain, is one which had its roots in hoary antiquity. For Herodotus leaves no doubt in the reader's mind that the ancient

Persians were very much concerned about the lie, and this is confirmed in the Old Persian cuneiform inscriptions.

The conservatism of the Persians in preserving ancient beliefs and customs can be seen in many facets of their culture. Today the landscape is dotted with shrines, *imamzades*, or the tombs of children of religious leaders of the Shi'ite persuasion of Islam. One would hesitate to speculate on how many of them were simply continuations of Zoroastrian shrines, but of course not Zoroastrian tombs. This is a subject as yet little studied but with fascinating ramifications, not to mention stories preserved from olden times.[2] Further enumeration of survivals from the pre-Islamic past would only emphasize the continuity of traditions in Iran and the conservatism of the people in this respect throughout history.

Paradoxically from the earliest times we find what seems at first glance to be just the reverse. Herodotus (I.135) said that no people were so prone to accept foreign habits as the Persians. Anyone who has walked the streets of new Tehran can see all kinds of styles of architecture and the latest women's dress styles from Paris and elsewhere. One need not fear a lack of variety or adaptation in many if not most of the facets of culture in the history of Iran. Unlike China which accepted and then absorbed foreign influences, Iran has adapted them to her own genius with no premium on the blind retention of native features if something more interesting appeared on the scene. One simile which can perhaps elucidate the seeming paradox between Iran's capacity to endure and the alacrity with which the people accept new customs, styles or the like, is the oft-quoted cypress tree of Persian poetry. Unlike the mighty oak which may be broken if hurricane winds blow, or the tumble-weed which is moved every way by the wind, Iran's symbol is the cypress which has deep roots. When fierce winds blow the cypress may be bent to the ground but, returning to its original position after the storm, it survives the gales.

The Persian's view of the history of his own country follows this pattern: Iran first came into history by the creation of the Median, followed by the Achaemenid empire. This world state, with its adaptability, its tolerance and its universal laws gave the Persians a model to follow ever afterwards. The model was changed, romanticized and even made into an epic of Iran, but it continued to exert a powerful influence, one might say an abiding interest and attraction, throughout history. After Alexander the Great's conquest of Iran, dark ages came over the land, ended by the resurrection of the imperial ideal in the form of the Sasanian state. Then came the Arabs who conquered Iran as Alexander had done, but now the new ideology and religion of Islam came to stay. Iran accepted Islam but changed it by making of it an iranicized, international religion and culture not wedded to Arab or bedouin customs and beliefs. Just as the English language bloomed after the Norman conquest when Latin and French words enriched the rough Anglo-Saxon tongue, so did the Persian language soar to unprecedented heights after enrichment by an enormous Arabic vocabulary, as well as by such features as the rules of Arabic prosody. Few peoples have produced the variety and beauty of poetry as the Persians with Sa'di, Hafiz, Rumi and a host of others. Mystical poetry, love poetry, the epic are all ornaments of the Persian language, and one might truthfully say that the glory of Persian genius is best revealed in poetry.

To return to the Persian's view of his own history, the golden age of Islam was followed in the twelfth and thirteenth centuries by Turkish and Mongol invasions which devastated Iran. True, the cultural flowering in these centuries, catalysed by contact with Far Eastern examples, is not to be denied. None the less Iran was torn by internal struggles until the sixteenth century, when again, as under the Achaemenids and the Sasanians, Iran rose to imperial greatness – this time not so much in foreign conquest but in the unification of Iran politically, culturally and religiously under the Safavids. Just as Cyrus founded the Achaemenid empire but Darius put the stamp on it for the future, and just as Ardashir had founded the Sasanian dynasty but Chosroes I had stabilized and adorned it, so Isma'il founded the Safavid state and Shah 'Abbas made of it a household word for splendour and luxury. In his capital of Isfahan Shah 'Abbas presented a new Iran to the western world, with Persian carpets, tilework, and all the concomitants of the arts and crafts which tourists imagine. 'Half the world is Isfahan' was a saying attributed to the proud Isfahanis of the time.

Just as the Achaemenids ended with the foreign conquest of the Greeks, and the Sasanians with the Arabs, so the Safavid state fell to invading Afghans from the east. In the middle of the eighteenth century the meteoric career of Nadir Shah restored an Iranian empire even greater than that of the Safavids, but only for a few years. This was followed by the sympathetic rule of Karim Khan Zand in Shiraz and then by the Turkish Qajar dynasty of the nineteenth century. The Qajars were not well prepared for the impact of Russia and the West, and the prestige of Iran and its place in the world sank until the 1920s when Reza Shah reversed a trend towards stagnation and set the nation on the road to reform and material progress. In the last ten years the reforms of the present monarch Mohammed Reza Pahlavi, which are conveniently called the 'White Revolution', have produced a rocket-like development of economic prosperity and progress. Such is the Iran of today.

Even this bird's-eye view of the history of Iran reveals a kind of rhythm in the rise and fall of dynasties, but this views history only from the court and from a political angle. The cultural continuity has been mentioned and will be constantly reappearing in the chapters which follow. There is also an institutional continuity, best revealed perhaps in the persistence of bureaucratic organization and methods from the earliest times. It almost seems as though the remarkable bureaucracy created by the Achaemenids propagated itself throughout history down to the present time, a noteworthy testimony to a remarkable survival power through changes in dynasties and religions. For example, the Achaemenids had a double bureaucracy with some scribes conversant with cuneiform and others with Aramaic alphabetical writing. The early Muslim period in imitation saw Arabic and Persian followed by Turkish and Persian, and today English and Persian. The permanent insecurity, with a subordinate official not only dependent on the one above him but acting as his slave in a sequence up the hierarchy to the ruler on top, is a constant feature of bureaucracy in Iran. The game of musical chairs among the higher bureaucracy which one sees today is thus a constant feature of bureaucracy in Iran – another heritage from the past. At the same time we find in classical Greek authors down to the present the observation that the Persians are fond of titles and of excessive politeness. One might add that hospitality is also an age-old trait of the inhabitants of this land. One could continue to multiply examples, but, in short, few nations of the world present more of a justification for the study of history than Iran.

It is therefore hoped that in the pages to come the reader will keep these general remarks in mind when we follow the sometimes tedious analysis of that period which represents the greatest change in the history of Iran, and indeed of the entire Near East, the coming of Islam. Never before or since has this part of the world been so profoundly shaken by the message of a simple merchant from Mecca in the Arabian peninsula. Much more than industrialization and western influences today Islam changed the entire course of Iran's history. Just how the Persians and their cousins, other Iranians on the plateau, in central Asia, the Caucasus and down to the plains of the subcontinent of India, reacted to the Arab expansion is the story told in the following pages.

The so-called scientific method is no secret confined to the physical sciences, but, I believe, is merely an approach to knowledge which all domains of learning should share. Data must be assembled before theories can be formulated and questions asked. Just as in the sciences when new data are forthcoming old theories give way to new hypotheses so, in our endeavour here, new discoveries of archaeology, new manuscripts or other sources may well change completely our views of the past. Many scholars in the humanities or even in the social sciences feel that they are writing the ultimate truth for all time, something which a physical scientist, even uncharacteristically arrogant, would never assume. The story which follows is merely an attempt to bring some order into the information assembled, with the full realization that much, if not all, may be outdated sooner than one likes to think. Nevertheless the task is well worth the undertaking, and if further stimulus is provided to the reader in this area the author will be well rewarded; for what is told is very much abbreviated, and very far from all.

CHAPTER 2

SASANIAN IRAN

The heritage of Sasanian Iran which was transmitted to the Arabs was enormous, for the Arabs conquered the entire Sasanian empire, whereas they took possession of only outlying provinces of the Byzantine empire. A complete model of imperial rule was thus presented to the Arabs by the Persian realm, and the Arabs borrowed from Sasanian Iran more than from any other source. One cannot enumerate the borrowings or influences, many of which will be apparent in the body of the book, but a survey of Sasanian Iran on the eve of the Arab conquests may indicate the nature of the later borrowings into Islam better than an examination of details.

The Sasanian state was ruled by the king of kings, a title which had become almost hallowed in Iran by traditions of over a millennium. The rulers of the house of Sasan succeeded one another rapidly in the last half-century before the Arab conquests, but tradition was strong enough to maintain a prince of the royal family as the sole candidate for the throne in the face of rebels. The ruler presided over a court which once had been not only splendid in richness, and in some ways glamorous, but also a centre of power and authority. By the seventh century, however, provincial capitals had acquired some of the authority formerly vested in the court at Ctesiphon, as well as the splendour. The change in the power structure of the Sasanian empire from the third to the seventh century can be characterized as the difference between the earlier period of a ruler supported by sub-kings and great feudal lords, and later a ruler supported by a court and bureaucracy together with a large number of small aristocrats (*dihqans*). By the seventh century the great families of Karen, Suren, Mihran, Zik and others had lost their pre-eminent positions, and the sub-kings had all but vanished. Even the Arab buffer state of the Lakhmids in Iraq had been absorbed into the centralized, bureaucratic Sasanian empire.

The prestige of the throne, in spite of a loss of authority, did none the less command a general loyalty among the common people. The dating of documents and inscriptions was made from the accession year of the last Yazdegird, and this dating continued in use among Zoroastrians after Yazdegird's death, although another era, beginning with the death of Yazdegird in AD 651, gradually replaced the former dating. The ruler possessed a special quality in the eyes of his subjects which was called *farn* or *farr* in New Persian, *farrah* in Middle Persian, *xvarəna* in Avestan. Originally meaning 'life force', 'activity', or 'splendour', it came to mean 'victory', 'fortune', and especially the royal 'fortune', the *kavaem xvarəno* of the Avesta.[1] From an early period the special position of 'the King of Kings of Iran and non-Iran' had been established among the traditions of the Iranian people. By Sasanian times the land of Iran, *Iranshahr*, had become identified as the domain of the *shahanshah*, the area where the religion of Zoroaster held sway. Iran was not just the land where Iranian speakers lived, but something more abstract which we should examine. We can reconstruct the extent of *Iranshahr* from brief accounts of the area in Pahlavi and Arabic books of the Islamic period, and then we shall have a better conception of the Sasanian state and society.

Iraq with its capital of Ctesiphon (Middle Persian: *tyspwn*) was called by the Sasanian kings the 'heart of *Iranshahr*'.[2] The capital was actually a complex of seven towns called 'the cities' by the Semitic-speaking inhabitants of the land, who also called it *Mahoze* 'metropolis', and the Arabs took over this designation, and called the complex al-Mada'in. Here was built the famous court of the Sasanian kings known in Islamic times as the *Aiwan Kisra*, called today the *Taq* of Kisra or Chosroes. The traditional number of settlements, seven, may not be historically accurate, but there seems to have been a group of several towns forming the capital.[3] The ruler spent most of the year in this capital, only moving to cities of the highlands of Iran for the summer. By the end of the Sasanian empire those provincial cities which had each in turn served as a capital in the early Sasanian period, such as Bishapur in Fars province, had declined considerably, and they were little, if at all, frequented by the court. The cities of Hamadan and Istakhr, though still important centres, were no longer officially 'summer capitals'. After the extensive economic and social reforms of Chosroes I Anushirvan (531–79), not only had the power of the old nobility been reduced, but the aristocracy itself had been much changed. The great feudal families in the early Sasanian empire, such as the Karen, Suren, Varaz, Spahbad and others, had not only lost much of their influence and position at court, but their land holdings had been reduced. The nobility of service which Chosroes I had established maintained the power and prestige of the court for some time after the death of that sovereign, but after the devastating wars with the Byzantines the lower orders of aristocracy began to assert their independence of the central government.

The contrast between the group which wielded authority and power at the beginning of the empire and that class of local aristocracy which was strong at the end of Sasanian rule is instructive. From the trilingual inscription of Shapur I (*c.* 240–72) on the Ka'ba of Zardusht at Naqsh-i Rustam in Fars, we see that local kings of Kirman, Georgia, and outlying areas had parallels in the great feudal lords of the court.[4] The only local officials administering territories under direct central control seem to have been the satraps of such cities as Isfahan and Hamadan, which incidentally shows a decline in importance of the title of satrap from Achaemenid times. It is true that there are many titles in the inscription, such as the important *bitakhsh* (Arabic: *fattash*) a kind of vice-regent whose authority is uncertain in the sources. None the less the overall picture is clear, for we can follow a continuation of the power of local Parthian noble families into Sasanian times. More than three centuries later, however, the Sasanian empire had changed and become much more bureaucratized than formerly. New titles have appeared and old ones have vanished. What was the situation on the eve of the Arab conquest?

Perhaps the most frequent title we find in Arabic sources on the conquest of Iran is *marzban*, or 'warden of the marches'. This title may have replaced the *bitakhsh*, for the first *marzban* we find in the sources was assigned to Armenia in the year AD 430, where formerly the *bitakhsh* had held sway.[5] In the time of Chosroes I the *marzban* was what his title meant – a military governor of the frontier – and theoretically there were four of them, corresponding to the four points of the compass.[6] Soon afterwards, however, the title of *marzban* was used in the sources to mean just governor, or even as al-Ya'qubi said, a regional chief (*ra'is al-balad*).[7] In Khurasan the east Iranian counterpart of the *marzban* was called the *kanarang*, a title originally used by the Kushans presumably with the same meaning as *marzban*. Another military title, borne by a military governor and sometimes confused with the *marzban*, was the *padgospan* (*al-fadhusban* in Arabic). By the seventh century the *marzbans* seem to have taken the place of the *satraps* of the earlier Sasanian empire, for they are little more than mayors of cities although some of them controlled two or more cities. To clarify this we must examine the provincial division of the Sasanian state at the time of the Arab conquest.

The general name for 'province' in the inscription of Shapur at the Ka'ba is *štry* in Middle Persian, *xštr* in Parthian, and *ethnos* in Greek, whereas in the inscription of Kartir on the same structure from the same period, the word used is *nsng* in Middle Persian (Armenian *nahang*).[8] It would seem that in the third century there was no organized division of the empire or standard nomenclature for local government.

By the end of the empire, however, there is a systematic division into provinces or regions, *balad* in Arabic and probably *štry* (*shahr*) in Middle Persian, although the latter term later was confused with its capital the *sharistan*, the city proper, or Arabic *madina*.[9] The province was subdivided into *kura* (from Greek *khora*), which latter term, however, is sometimes called *shahr* in New Persian, with no distinction from the word for 'province'. But the *kura* is also equated with *ostan* or even *bum*.[10] A *kura* was divided into *rostaks* (Arabic: *rustaq*) or *tasugs* (Arabic: *tassuj*). It is uncertain how large these subdivisions were, for some later geographers in Islamic times said that the *tassuj* was a subdivision of a *rustaq*, and the *tassuj* was further composed of villages.[11] Unfortunately, we do not have contemporary writings in Pahlavi on the Sasanian subdivisions, and it would seem that conditions in Fars province, for example, were not duplicated in Khurasan.

We know more about Fars than about other provinces in the pre-Islamic period. It was divided into five *kuras* designated by the major cities in them, Istakhr, Arrajan, Bishapur, Ardashir-Khwarra and Darabjird. The first was the largest and seems to have extended far to the east including Yazd. Sometimes Istakhr was called simply Fars, for the entire name may have been Istakhr-i Fars, or 'the fortress of Fars'. Arrajan was also called Veh az Amid Kavad, or Wamqubad in Arabic sources, originally meaning 'better than Amida has Kavad (built this)'. Coins with the legend *Biramqubad* in Kufic script should be read as *Bizamqubad*, a contraction of the Middle Persian. Bishapur was the smallest of the districts in the province, and the main city Ardashir-Khwarra was later called Gor, and then in the time of the Boyids or Buwaihids, Firuzabad. Darabjird was an old name which has persisted to the present in a shortened form Darab. Fars province, however, as the Sasanian homeland, was probably better organized and with clearer divisions and subdivisions than other provinces.

Khuzistan (al-Ahwaz in Arabic) was a rich lowland agricultural province divided into at least seven *kuras*, the largest of which was called Hormizd Ardashir or Hurmizshahr, called Suq al-Ahwaz by the Arabs, present-day Ahwaz, capital of the entire province at the time of the Arab conquest. Another *kura* was 'Askar Mukram, which was the name of the Arab camp or cantonment near the old Sasanian town called Rustaqubad, arabicized from Rustam Kavad, according to Yaqut.[12] Shustar, or as the Arabs called it, Tustar, was the chief city of another *kura*, and the nearby Shush (Arabic: al-Sus) was another, also called Iran Khwarra Shapur 'Shapur (has made) Iran glorious'. Not far from these two was Jundisabur of the Arabs, derived from the original Veh Andiokh Shapur, 'the better Antioch of Shapur', settled by Shapur I with Roman war prisoners. It was called Beth Lapat in Syriac sources. Ramiz was a sixth centre, its name derived from a

Middle Persian form Ram-Hormizd-Ardashir, while a seventh was Surraq, with the principal town called Dauraq. Other lists of the *kuras* of Khuzistan are given by various geographers, so it is difficult to know which districts were in existence in the seventh century.[13] Idhaj, for example, is mentioned both as the chief town of a *kura* of the same name, or as part of the *kura* of Ramiz. Two other names which occur in lists of *kuras* are Nahr Tira and Manadhir, north of Ahwaz, but it is impossible to determine which, if any, may have been the chief city of a *kura*. There were, of course, other important cities in the province, such as Karkha de Ledan, the Syriac name for the Middle Persian *Iran asan kard Kavad*, present Aiwan-i Karkha. The subdivisions of Khuzistan may have changed from time to time, but the picture at the end of the Sasanian empire must have been approximately what has been outlined above.

The large province of Media may have been divided into at least two parts by the seventh century, but in origin it was the ancient land of the Medes in the mountains extending from the plains of Mesopotamia to the central deserts of Iran.[14] It was also sometimes called Kuhistan by the Persians and al-Jibal by the Arabs. Ibn Khurdadhbih lists six *kuras* for the province, Masabadan, Mihrijanqadaq, Dinawar (also called Mah al-Kufa), Nihavand (also called Mah al-Basra), Hamadan, and Qum.[15] It seems that Isfahan (Arabic: Isbahan), Raiy and Azerbaijan (Arabic: Adharbaijan) were in early times included in the province of Media (Mad, May and Mah, according to different Iranian dialects), but in early Islamic times, as reported by Ibn Khurdadhbih, they were separated from it. Inscriptions on Sasanian seal impressions in clay indicate that Isfahan and Raiy did not belong to the province of Media at the end of the Sasanian empire. As a matter of fact, several such inscriptions indicate that provincial boundaries were ignored in the combination of new administrative districts. For example, an agate seal found in the present town of Rezaiye lists three cities together under one administration, Jundisabur, Susa and Mihrijanqadaq.[16] So one cannot be rigid in delimiting the provincial boundaries since changes did occur. All the names of the chief cities of the *kuras* listed above are old, pre-Islamic names, most indeed pre-Sasanian in origin. Qum probably was originally Godman, pronounced Goman, later shortened to Gom and arabicized to Qum. It was also called, for a short time, *Iran-vinard-Kavad*, 'Kavad put Iran in order'.[17]

Isfahan was always an important centre, sometimes considered part of Fars province and at times part of Media, or even alone by itself. It was also called Gay, older Gava.[18] On a seal from the *Bibliothèque Nationale* in Paris we find the legend in Middle Persian *spx'n plm't'ly w'spwxlk'n* 'Isfahan, the executive officer (of) Vaspuhrakan'.[19] The translation 'executive officer' is a generality for the word literally means 'order carrier'. He was probably a representative of the central government, but his powers and authority are unknown. The epithet Vaspuhrakan seems to have been applied to the Isfahan district, and it may have indicated the apanage of the crown prince at some period during Sasanian rule. The word also was used to mean 'noble', or 'special, particular', so it is sometimes difficult to decide in Middle Persian texts whether it is used as a common or proper noun.[20] Isfahan, centrally located on the plateau, was an obvious goal for the first Arab conquerors, who concentrated their efforts on taking the city after the battle of Nihavand.[21]

Azerbaijan, the old Atropatene of the Greeks and Romans, was probably a special province of the Sasanian empire since the inhabitants were Armenians and Kurds, as well as Persians and others, and also because it was a frontier province against the Byzantines and the peoples of the Caucasus. We do not know the extent of the province to the north. The Mughan steppe, Albania (Arran) and Derbend (Arabic: Bab al-Abwab) were probably under a special military governor in the time of the Sasanians, while Armenia and Georgia were separate kingdoms allied to Sasanian Iran, but not part of *Iranshahr*. One of the important military governors of the Sasanian state ruled the province of Azerbaijan, the Fadhusban (in Arabic), who was mentioned above. The boundaries of Azerbaijan varied considerably throughout history, and we have no information on the subdivisions of the province. The capital, at the time of the Arab conquest, was the city of Ardebil, an ancient settlement.[22] In the time of Harun al-Rashid the town of Maragha became the capital. One has the impression that Azerbaijan was not as populous or important at the time of the Arab conquest as it became later, for we do not hear much about this province in early Islamic times. Even less is known of the inaccessible Caspian Sea coast, a world of jungles far removed from the arid plateau. In any case, the people of the Caspian coast were not touched by the initial Arab invasion.

Raiy, ancient Raga, between the Elburz mountains and the central salt desert, was the last large city in western Iran on the road to the east. It was also an emporium for the Dailamites, people of the mountains, who fought together with the people of Raiy against the Arabs when they approached the city.[23] Raiy was the centre of the strip of land on the plateau from Qazvin in the west to Qumis in the east, the province of Komisene of the Seleucids. The principal city of the latter, as usual, was called after the name of the province by the Arabs, but it was replaced later by Damghan. The city of Qumis was probably the site of Hecatompylos, the ancient capital of the Parthians.[24] This was the last district in western Iran, before the border of Khurasan, the centre of eastern Iran and a new cultural area.

Khurasan, meaning 'land of the rising sun', was called the 'upper provinces' by the Seleucids and Parthians, which was probably borrowed from the designation 'the upper satrapies' of the Achaemenid empire.[25] Its boundaries were imprecise because they varied with the extension and contraction of political frontiers in the east. The military centre of Sasanian power in the east was the oasis of Merv (Arabic: Marw; Old Persian: Margu). Three other large cities, Nishapur, Herat and Balkh, were not under the jurisdiction of Merv. The last two were frequently in Hephthalite hands and thus even outside *Iranshahr*, and reckoned as irredenta lands. The jurisdiction of Merv probably did include Marw al-Rud and Taliqan in the district of Juzjan.[26] Merv was surnamed al-Shahijan 'the royal' to distinguish it from the southern town of the same name. Merv was also a trade centre, with merchants from all over central Asia coming to Sasanian Iran through this city. Inscriptions in many languages have been found in the oasis attesting its cosmopolitan character from early times. At the time of the Arab conquests Merv was ruled by a *marzban*, while the nearby city of Tus had a similar official called the *kanarang*, suggesting that Tus at one time had been a Kushan or Hephthalite outpost on the west. It seems that the River Murghab was the primary frontier of *Iranshahr* in the east, and Taliqan in Juzjan represented a military outpost to the east of the river at the time of the Arab conquests. Balkh, the ancient Bactra, surnamed 'mother of cities' by the Arabs, had been only sporadically under Sasanian rule, and at the time of the Arab conquests the Kushan-Bactrian language was still written, and probably also spoken there, although the Hephthalites probably had brought some changes to the spoken language of the area. Herat, ancient Haraiva which the Greeks called Aria, was the centre of a district including Bushanj or Fushanj and Badghis, similar to the modern province. Whether Herat was governed by a *marzban* or not is uncertain, but Ibn Khurdadhbih's assertion that all Khurasan in Sasanian times was governed by an Isbahbadh (Persian: *spahbad*) called *badhusban* (i.e. *padgospan*) who had four *marzbans* under him, is unattested elsewhere.[27] On the other hand, as a frontier province against central Asia and the east, Khurasan at times could have been united under a military viceroy. At the time of the Arab conquests, it is unclear how much territory was Sasanian and how much was under local, mainly Hephthalite, princes. The importance of Khurasan under the caliphs is due probably in large measure to the unification of Transoxiana with Sasanian Khurasan, added to the Hephthalite domains north of the Hindu Kush mountains into a great reservoir of manpower and resources which persisted in its importance down to the Mongol conquests in the early thirteenth century.

Seistan (Arabic: Sijistan), the land of the Sakas, lay around the lake formed by the drainage of the River Hilmand, just as the Merv oasis was formed by the drainage of the River Murghab, and it also had imprecise boundaries. In the Sasanian period the eastern frontier was sometimes pushed far up the River Hilmand, while at other times it did not encompass more than the lake at present called the Hamun. Its capital city was Zaranj (Old Persian: Zranka) and the province apparently was governed by a *marzban*. In Parthian times the Suren feudal lords ruled Seistan but by the end of the Sasanian empire the province had become a subdivision of the central administration as a separate province. Turan and Makran (Arabic: Turan, Makuran) were included under the governor of Seistan. In fact, like Khurasan in the north, Seistan in the south extended as far to the south-east as Sasanian authority was accepted, which frequently varied. Makran was the coastland, and in the interior was Paradene, which name may have survived to the present as Pahra, in modern Baluchistan.[28] To the east was Turan, probably modern Kalat, and beyond Turan was Hind or the Indus valley. The identification of the land Turan, inhabited by Dravidian Brahuis, as the abode of the enemies of the Iranians living in Seistan, has been suggested by several scholars, but it remains only a surmise.

One should not fail to mention Gurgan (Arabic: al-Jurjan), ancient Hyrcania, a fertile province to the east of the Caspian Sea, where from ancient times settled Iranians had to defend their lands against nomads from the northern steppes. One of the great fortification walls, or *limes*, was built here, extending from the Caspian Sea eastward almost two hundred kilometres. Traces of the wall still exist, called locally *Sadd-i Iskandar* 'Alexander's barrier', or *Qizil Yilan* 'the red snake'.[29] The time of construction is unknown, but most probably it was late Sasanian just as the nearby wall of Tammisha (Arabic: Tamis) east of the modern town of Sari. Arabic geographers attribute the latter wall to Chosroes I (531–79) who built it as a defence against the Turks.[30] It was called *al-khandaq* or 'ditch' by Tabari, and probably there was a moat on the eastern side. In essence there were thus two defence systems, one protecting Gurgan and the second wall protecting Tabaristan from raids from the east.[31] The extensive walls on the frontiers of the Sasanian empire were built probably as part of an overall defensive policy implemented for the most part under Chosroes I.

The most famous of the Sasanian defensive walls was at Derbend between the Caucasus mountains and the Caspian Sea. Although this wall was really outside the boundaries of *Iranshahr*, it was of importance for the defence not only of the Sasanian empire but also of the Byzantine empire. The latter frequently paid large sums of money to Iran as part of the cost of maintaining the forts and fortifications in the Caucasus against inroads of Huns, various Turkic peoples and the Khazars. The

Arabs were impressed with the Sasanian walls and fortifications, and later rulers sought to emulate their pre-Islamic predecessors.

There was also a *limes* in Iraq against the bedouin Arabs (Arabic: *khandaq Sabur*). This was similar to the others mentioned above, and was designed to protect al-Hira and other areas of Iraq from hostile raids from the desert.[32] Yaqut says that Shapur II (309–79) dug it (the moat with a wall) between Iran and the Arabs after being frightened by their attacks. He built frontier watchtowers to protect whatever was near the *Badiya* (desert), and he ordered a *khandaq* to be dug from the lower region of the *Badiya* 'to what is before Basra and is joined to the sea'. There he built towers and forts and arranged frontier watchtowers, so that it (the *khandaq*) was a barrier between the inhabitants of the *Badiya* and the (people of) al-Sawad.[33] Others ascribed the digging of a moat to Chosroes I, but this may represent the common tendency in Islamic times to ascribe an unknown ancient monument to Kisra, which became a generic word for all Sasanian kings among the Arabs.[34] Baladhuri adds that the Arabs who lived by the *khandaq* guarded it and had the use of the land as a fief without paying a land tax. With the absorption of the Lakhmid state into the Sasanian empire about 602, the Sasanian defences against the Arabs fell apart, which created a hole in the defences into which the forces of Islam moved.

We have described the Sasanian empire in general terms and may say that *Iranshahr* was that territory ruled by the Persians and which was predominantly Persian or Sasanian in culture. There were Iranians who lived outside the boundaries of the Sasanian state such as the Sogdians in central Asia and the Alans in the north Caucasus. There were, of course, non-Iranians within *Iranshahr*, primarily the Semitic-speaking people of Iraq. Yet they were considered as part of Iran; other peoples were in non-Iran (*Aneran*) as the Sasanian inscriptions have it. We cannot tell always which areas were considered part of Iran and which were designated non-Iran in the empire, but it would be a good guess that Azerbaijan, for example, was in *Iranshahr* while Georgia was not. Khuzistan was probably regarded as part of Iran but Adiabene, or the north-west frontier region, or the domain of the Lakhmids, was not. In other words the concept of *Iranshahr* was not conterminous with the Sasanian empire, but it probably varied throughout history. When the dynasty of the Lakhmids was ended and the kingdom was incorporated into the empire, al-Hira hardly became thereby a part of *Iranshahr*. For the latter was basically an amorphous concept which probably came to signify the area where the Persian language and culture was *dominant*. This does not mean, however, that all the people inside *Iranshahr* spoke Persian, for the linguistic situation was undoubtedly complex within the Sasanian empire.

One may divide the various languages used within any given area into four categories. First, the 'official' written language; second, the 'official' spoken language; third, a dialect spoken at home; and fourth, the religious or 'ritual' tongue. They may be identical languages, or close to one another, or completely different. From the geographers who wrote in Arabic, especially Muqaddasi, we see that dialects were spoken in many towns of Iran. Let us take several cities of Sasanian Iran and determine their four-fold linguistic situation. In Ahwaz, for example, the 'official' written language was Pahlavi with its cumbersome Semitic masks or heterograms. The 'official' spoken language was probably Persian, or what was later called Dari, the court language, evolving from a Middle towards a New Persian stage. At home most people spoke an Aramaic dialect. The religious language was Avestan, although Pahlavi was the language of commentaries or interpretation of the sacred text. In Merv the 'official' spoken and written languages were the same as in Ahwaz, but in one quarter of Merv the Sogdian merchants spoke one or more Sogdian dialects, while others spoke a Kushan-Bactrian dialect, or some other tongue. After the reform of language in the bureaucracy of the Umaiyads by the action of the caliph ʿAbd al-Malik in 78/697, in Merv the 'official' written language became Arabic, the 'official' spoken languages were Dari and Arabic, and dialects continued to be spoken at home (as well as Arabic and Persian), a complicated situation. The religious languages were Arabic for Muslims and Avestan with Pahlavi for Zoroastrians. It is necessary to keep this four-fold division of languages in mind when discussing problems of language. As we have mentioned, the four at times might coalesce, and an inhabitant of Basra in Islamic times might claim Arabic for all four. Yet even then, the Arabic written, and that spoken on the *minbar* of a mosque, or the dialect spoken at home were not identical. Yet language was very important in determining a man's allegiances and his culture.

We have mentioned Sasanian influence on later Islamic institutions and culture, and this should be elaborated. One interesting detail is the use of titles and honorifics by the Persians, which had an influence in the Umaiyad and especially ʿAbbasid caliphates. Classical authors reported the fondness of Persians for titles, and the frequent confusion of Persian names and titles in Greek sources indicates the complexity of the matter.[35] There were many titles in the court, and others at provincial centres, but we are concerned with those which the Arabs encountered rather than a complete list or a theoretical reconstruction of the structure of the Sasanian state and society based on the titles. For titles change their significance in history and what applied to the third century would not apply to the seventh.

The prime minister of the Sasanian state was called the *vuzurg framadar*, literally 'the great commander', and we know of the existence of many ordinary *framadars* from inscriptions and seal impressions. The functions of a *framadar* are unknown, although one might suppose that he was an executive officer of the court. Mihr Narseh, the famous *vuzurg framadar* of the first half of the fifth century, also carried the title of 'great' *hazarbad* or *chiliarch* in Armenian sources.[36] One would surmise from the latter title that he also held a military position, rather than assume that the two titles were strict synonyms. In later Sasanian times we are told that the commander-in-chief of the armies, the *Iran spahbad*, was a separate person from the prime minister. At the end of the Sasanian empire, in any case, the religious, military, and administrative institutions are in theory distinct from each other.

Under the *vuzurg framadar*, the titular head of the secular administration, was the important chief of scribes, the *dipiran mahist* or the *dipir-i vuzurg*, the actual head of the bureaucracy. Just how much the religious institution and the administration overlapped is unclear for the *mobads* or Zoroastrian priests performed certain functions which required the co-operation of the scribes. The activities of the *mobads*, however, were for the most part judicial, since the religious institution was concerned primarily with legal affairs. We find many seal impressions of the *yatakgov* 'attorney' combined with the office of judge (MP: *d'twbly*), frequently a judge of the poor (MP: *dlgwš'n*), as well as the *andarzbad* or councillor (MP: *'ndrčpty*), both offices, it would seem, held by priests. The duties of both are uncertain, but they performed various functions in the religious-judicial institution. The Muslim *qadi* was the equivalent of the Sasanian *mobad*, which title itself had replaced an earlier *magus*, one of the magi. The Arabic title *qadi al-qudat* was probably a calque on the Sasanian title *mobadan mobad*, 'priest of priests', or 'chief priest'. Many administrative activities were directed by the *mobads* as they were later in Islam directed by the *qadis*. The system of Islamic *waqfs* (Arabic plural: *auqaf*) or pious endowments was similar in many ways to the Zoroastrian fire temples, or rather to the endowment of fires. Al-Khwarazmi distinguishes between the *atash hamar difira* or the 'office of the accounts of fires', and the *ruwanikan difira* or the *auqaf*, making a distinction between endowments of fires and endowments established for the dead, but they were both endowments similar to general *waqfs*.[37] Let us return to the scribes.

The scribes and other members of the secular administration were very influential, especially at the end of the Sasanian empire when the frequent change of rulers enhanced the importance of the stability of the bureaucracy. Also the religious institution had declined, indeed one might say decayed, since lengthy rites, rituals and ceremonies had alienated many Persians from the Zoroastrian religion. The Christians were certainly increasing in number at the end of the empire, which further weakened the Zoroastrian state church. Many *mobads* had become civil officials, thus entering and strengthening the ranks of the scribes, the bureaucracy. From earliest times of course the accountants or record keepers of the finances were important. In Middle Persian they were called *hamarkar* (*xm'lkly*), frequently mentioned in Syriac and Armenian sources as the tax collectors. It is possible that this is the Middle Persian equivalent of the Arabic *jahbadh*, the first part of which may go back to Akkadian *gittu* 'document, account', although the Old Persian form is lacking.[38] The most important official of the 'Abbasid caliphatew as the vizier (*wazir*) or prime minister, equivalent to the *vuzurg framadar* described above. There has been much controversy over the origin of the word, whether Arabic or Persian. The institution, of course, is age old, for rulers always have needed executive officers or assistants. The word itself would seem to be a mixture of the Arabic word with a Middle Persian word *vičir* 'decision' (see below) attested as an official in Syriac *gezira*, in Aramaic of the Talmud *gezirpat* and in Armenian a *gzir* 'village headman'.[39] Titles usually decline in importance with the passage of time but some increase, and such is the case here, where the Islamic vizier replaces the *vuzurg framadar* of Sasanian times.

The rise in importance of the scribal class at the end of the Sasanian empire was another result of the reforms of Chosroes I, surnamed Anushirvan, 'of the immortal soul'. Whereas heretofore the three classes of society in Iran had been the priests, the warriors, and the peasants together with artisans; after Chosroes, the scribes, i.e. the bureaucracy, became a fourth class between the warriors, or the nobility, and the common folk. With the fall of the Sasanian empire, and with the consequent loss in importance of the nobility and the Zoroastrian religion, the scribes were exalted even more than previously. This was primarily the class to whom the Arabs turned to find qualified people to administer the conquered territories. Later, after the formation of Islamic Sunni orthodoxy, the '*ulama*', or learned men of Islam, began to challenge the scribes, the *kuttab*, and eventually the religious institution became much more influential than the scribes. This change will be discussed later.

There were many features of Sasanian rule and organization taken over by the Arabs. The postal system of the Persians had been famous since the days of Darius the Achaemenid king and the Sasanians had revived a more modest postal system. The officials or couriers were the *parvanak* (Arabic: *farwaniq*), which al-Khwarazmi tells us is to be read *barwana* in Persian, or *khadim* (literally 'servant') in Arabic.[40] Documents were sealed with special seals or seal rings, MP *mwdr(k)* (Arabic: *al-muhraq*).[41] The practice of carrying seals or wearing seal rings, of which great numbers have been preserved from Sasanian times, was continued under Islam even to our day. Although we have no definite information about the Sasanian postal routes, from the ancient Greek work of Isidore of Charax on the Parthian postal stations, and other indications in Arabic authors, we may conclude that a road network, with rest stations (Arabic: *ribat*), existed in Sasanian times, and it was later taken over and utilized by the Arabs.

One could discuss many such institutions, but an account of each would require a monograph. In this general book one must concentrate on the patterns of continuity from the past and borrowings into Islam. We have only briefly mentioned the institutions of the Sasanian government which influenced the Arabs after their invasion of Iran. In the intellectual sphere the influences were not only overwhelming, but we have copious evidence for them in many Arabic sources. One may well ask why we do not have Middle Persian sources as evidence for Persian influences on Islam. There are at least two reasons why the extant Middle Persian literature in Pahlavi books which has survived is scant and scholastic in nature, if one may use this latter term in the context of Sasanian Iran. First, the Pahlavi script, and system of writing with Aramaic heterograms or masks, was so cumbersome and difficult to learn that many Persians welcomed Arabic, and they then accepted the Arabic alphabet for writing Persian, inadequate though it was, as a great advance over the past. Secondly, after many Pahlavi works were selected and translated into Arabic, no one needed the originals or sought to copy and thus preserve them. Pahlavi remained the province of the Zoroastrian priests. Only the *mobads* sought to preserve the ancient writings for religious reasons, hence the overwhelming predominance of religious books among the preserved Pahlavi texts. If the Zoroastrians had not gone to India, and maintained themselves as a separate community – the Parsis – much more would have been lost. The loss of ancient writings is, for the most part, the result of lack of interest and any desire to preserve them, rather than any deliberate attempt to destroy or extirpate them. Writings may have perished in the burning of Persepolis by Alexander, or in the conquest of Alexandria in Egypt by the Arabs, but stories of the deliberate destruction of unique manuscripts must be regarded with scepticism. For the literature of Sasanian Iran, however, we are fortunate in having much preserved in Arabic translation, even if a large part of it is fragmentary and re-worked in an Islamic frame. At least one can form an idea of Sasanian literature from the Arabic sources.

Just as I have suggested that one may divide the languages used in any place into four categories, so one may describe literature under three headings. This division is not based on genre or types of poetry or prose, but on social distinctions and the audience for whom the writing was intended. Just as in the case of language and dialect, here too the lines dividing the categories are difficult to establish. The first category I call 'high literature' commissioned by the court or intended for the nobility and educated persons. The second is folk literature, unwritten stories, tales and sayings usually couched in a rustic tongue, or even in dialect. The third group is learned literature, strictly speaking not literature but technical writing. This last was by and for intellectuals. Obviously all three groups overlapped and were mixed, but one might say that the first category was intended for the edification and pleasure of the rulers and the warriors, while the second was for the common folk, and the third was the product of men of the pen, the religious class and the bureaucracy. Let us examine Sasanian productions of all three groups, which we know primarily from Arabic sources.

The major works of the first category are found in the counsels (*andarz*) frequently addressed to aristocrats or to rulers, and in the genre called 'mirrors for princes'.[42] There is not space to discuss the contents of any of the Pahlavi *andarz* or *pand* works preserved to our day, except to note that all have been copied and re-worked by Zoroastrian priests, so that religious and ethical details are prominent.[43] Similar to the *andarz* literature are the special books of advice to kings, the 'mirrors for princes', which have not survived in Pahlavi, but had an enormous influence on Arabic *adab* literature. In almost every Arabic book of *belles lettres* are stories of the wisdom of Chosroes Anushirvan, or of the sage advice of Ardashir, the first Sasanian king. For court practices and rules of conduct for the caliphs the Arabs had nowhere to turn save to Sasanian examples. The Caesars still ruled in Constantinople but the mantle of the Kisras had fallen on the successors of the Prophet, first in Damascus and then in Baghdad. The Arabic word *adab* can be considered a parallel, if not a direct translation, of Middle Persian *frahang* and might best be translated as 'culture'. This does not mean that the Persians taught the Arabs the fundamental principles of *adab* 'good conduct', with its social and ethical norms. Rather the secondary and later meaning of *adab* as humanistic learning, an intellectual view of culture, was established primarily by the Iranians in the time of the 'Abbasid caliphate. The ancient education of the Persians reported by Herodotus, which consisted of learning how to 'ride a horse, shoot a bow and speak the truth', had become very sophisticated by Sasanian times. Women and children, it seems, were also taught in pre-Islamic Iran. That women as well as children were supposed to be educated in Sasanian times is clear from one Pahlavi passage which has it, 'do not withhold your wife and child from culture, so that trouble and great sorrow does not reach you, and you may not be regretful'.[44] The important position of women in pre-Islamic Iran is also attested by the

Sasanian law book the *Datastan namak* which has survived in a later Pahlavi recension called the *Madiyan-i Hazar Datastan* 'Book of a thousand laws'. It is not possible here to discuss detailed questions regarding the position of women in pre-Islamic Iran, mainly because of the ambiguity of the very few source materials. The use of the veil and the existence of harems, on the other hand, were general oriental customs, concentrated for the most part among the aristocracy.

Real folk literature did not survive in Pahlavi writings, which is understandable in view of the fate of Pahlavi in the hands of priests. There are, however, many survivals in Islamic literature of the folk literature of the past. The mere existence of the epic, not only in Firdosi's rendering of it in the *Shahname*, but other 'epics', or parts of the same cycle, such as the *Garshaspname*, *Burzuname*, and others, attest to the vitality of the epic genre among the people. Likewise the existence of a large body of rustic poetry, which did not follow the rules of prosody of Arabic, or New Persian poetry, hardly can be denied. All recent histories of Persian literature discuss folk poetry, frequently in dialect, which had previously been ignored by scholars. Folk poetry was neglected in great part because it was almost always simple in style, perhaps beneath the dignity of poets well trained in Arabic and New Persian literature. We have one Iranian language today the literature of which is almost wholly derived from folk stories. This is the literature of the Ossetes in the Caucasus. This literature is important because it is in an Iranian language little influenced by Islam, or even by Zoroastrianism, which, of course, coloured most pre-Islamic Iranian literature.

Stories (Persian: *dastan*), or folk romances, certainly existed in Sasanian times, and continued into Islam, frequently with an Islamic re-working. Indeed Herodotus and other Greek writers reveal the existence of a flourishing folk literature even in Achaemenid times. It is interesting to try to reconstruct some of the old tales, and trace elements in them down to the present; but this is not our task here. One may in brief postulate the existence of at least three general Iranian folk literatures, an eastern, a western and a northern. The first is characterized primarily by those cycles which have survived in Firdosi and other epics. Western Iranian folk literature apparently was not as rich as in the east, and did not survive as well, probably because of the more prosaic life in the Achaemenid and then the Sasanian empires, as compared with the more feudal and chivalric modes of life in the east, including central Asia. The northern branch, which we have mentioned as surviving only among the Ossetes, was probably quite different from the other two, since the history of the Scythians, Sarmatians, Alans and their descendants the Ossetes, was different from that of the peoples in the lands to the south and east of the Caspian Sea. Suffice it to say that the heroic or popular tradition seems to be characteristic of, or dominant in, eastern Iran and central Asia, whereas the religious tradition of Zoroastrianism appears dominant in western Iran.

It was probably in western Iran also that the bulk of learned literature in Pahlavi was composed. This literature, as always, was of concern only to a small group of intellectuals, or to the scribal class, which latter prepared the way for the Islamic *kuttab*, or scribes, who also translated and wrote much if not most learned Arabic literature in the first three centuries of Islam. As we have mentioned, this category of literature was under the patronage of the ruler and the nobility, as was 'high literature'. There were a number of centres of learning in western Iran where there was intellectual activity in Sasanian times, the most important of which was the city of Jundisabur.

The Persian centre of learning at Jundisabur impressed the Arabs, even though perhaps it had passed its prime by the middle of the seventh century. It was especially famous for medicine; even Greek neoplatonist philosophers, driven from Athens in 529, had taken refuge there for a few years. The school or university continued to flourish under Islam, and Ibn Bukhtishuʿ, a famous doctor of the time of al-Mansur, was head of the medical school until his death in AD 771. There and elsewhere many books were translated from Greek, Sanskrit and Syriac into Pahlavi in late Sasanian times. It is significant that a number of Syriac and Greek works were translated into Arabic not from the original languages but from Pahlavi, an indication of the importance of Iran as the transmitter of ancient knowledge to Islam.[45] It should be remembered that Sasanian Iran was on the whole a city-centred culture even if the towns were small compared with the later megalopolis of Baghdad or even Islamic provincial centres such as Nishapur. The growth of cities in Iran may have been responsible for the decline of the great nobility at the end of the Sasanian empire, as mentioned above, but the growth of cities did parallel an expansion of agricultural land as well.

Two archaeological surveys, in the Diyala river basin north-east of Baghdad and in Khuzistan, have both established the great extent of cultivated land under the Sasanians. The results of the survey in Khuzistan led the investigator to declare, 'There is both archaeological and documentary evidence that the agricultural and commercial development of Khuzistan was accompanied by the multiplication of urban settlements on an unprecedented scale.'[46] The same could be said of land on the Diyala plain. We do have one similar survey on the Iranian plateau from the districts of Fasa and Darab in Fars province and this unpublished survey indicates that the development which took place on the plains of Mesopotamia was paralleled on the plateau. This same tendency continued into Islamic times until the rise of

Baghdad, which in some measure brought about an impoverishment of the countryside by the influx of peasants into the huge metropolis. Unfortunately archaeologists have not yet excavated a large Sasanian city, and we have little information about the size, organization or character of such a settlement. One might suppose that Sasanian cities were not greatly different from later Islamic counterparts, which means they were on the whole collections of settlements. Greater Baghdad in essence followed the pattern of Sasanian al-Mada'in, although the original round city may have been copied from Sasanian settlements such as Firuzabad. On the Iranian plateau the oasis nature of settlements determined the nature of cities. Isfahan, for example, was the most important settlement in the oasis bearing the same name. Naturally settlements grew around the castles of the ruler or governor, and one may conjecture that the urban development of Sasanian times, while widespread and numerous, was still rudimentary. The traditional division of an Iranian Islamic town into fortress or citadel, the city proper, and the suburbs was probably not so generally characteristic of Sasanian cities as it was later under Islam. On the other hand the widespread use of walls as a means of protection surely applied to the Sasanian cities and their citadels, especially on the frontiers. In the central part of the Sasanian empire the Arabs did not find massive fortifications in the towns they took, again testifying to the concentration of Iranian military forces on the frontiers. Yet the use of walls to enclose gardens, houses and even hunting preserves is an ancient practice in Iran, not just for privacy or defence, but to restrain the ever-encroaching desert or steppe.

Undoubtedly Sasanian art and architecture made a great impression on the Arabs, for long after the conquests geographers such as Ibn Khurdadhbih, Ibn Rusta, Istakhri and others speak of impressive Sasanian buildings and ruins.[47] We cannot be concerned here with the Iranian origins of the *aiwan*, the wonder of the enormous arch at Ctesiphon, or other architectural features which survived the fall of the Sasanians to influence later architecture. The characteristic square courtyard flanked by four *aiwans* (livan) of later Iranian mosques was probably pre-Islamic in origin, for even in distant Tajikistan this form has been found in a Buddhist monastery at Adjina tepe near Dushanbe.[48] Much has been written about Sasanian influences on Islamic art and architecture and the general lines of such influence are fairly clear. But such influences spread far beyond Iran. We have Japanese silks, ewers and glass bowls from the Shosoin collection in Nara, dated in the seventh and eighth centuries AD, copied from Sasanian originals.[49] Sasanian motifs may be found on medieval European textiles and rugs, and indeed diffused all over the Eurasian continent.[50] Many Sasanian influences on Islamic art are too obvious and well known to require elaboration here.[51] Persian rugs, crafts and a host of other features of Islamic and modern Persian life are in large measure pre-Islamic in origin. Again, we can not be concerned with such matters here, but must examine general features of Sasanian art as a background for our study of Iran under Islam.

Sasanian art, as well as Sasanian political, religious and other institutions, summed up the long past of the Near East. In many senses Sasanian Iran was the heir of the ancient Near East while the Byzantine empire was the heir of Greece and Rome. It is no longer possible to speak of Sasanian art as a 'degeneration of Hellenistic art', for the ever-growing discoveries of influences which Sasanian art seems to have exercised in the Eurasian continent alone contradict such a narrow view of the nature of Sasanian art.[52] It is true that the Sasanians tried to imitate their predecessors the Achaemenids, in this as well as in other domains, but Sasanian culture, including art, cannot be dismissed either as a degenerate hellenistic or as only a pale reflection of a mixture of Achaemenid and hellenistic culture. Sasanian art combines many ancient traditions of human and animal representation, with geometrical and plant forms, as a prelude to Islamic art. One might continue with an examination of the decorative nature of Sasanian art, with aesthetic judgements and other matters, but this would be an enormous task. Suffice it to conclude that Sasanian culture and art have been grossly underestimated and neglected in the past, but future archaeological discoveries, one hopes, will reveal the immense diversity and richness of the material culture of Sasanian Iran.

To turn to another question, that of the relations of the Arabs to Iran and Iranians before Islam, we find even more of a vacuum in our knowledge than in other domains. Let us turn to the Iranian name for the Arabs. The name 'Arab' was not applied to all desert bedouin by the Sasanians, for the province Beth 'Arbaya in Syriac was the group of districts between the upper Tigris and Euphrates rivers, of which Nisibis was the chief city. This designation probably corresponded to a Middle Persian *Arabistan* or 'land of the Arabs', as one may reconstruct from traces of letters of the end of the word in the Parthian version of Shapur's great inscription at Naqsh-i Rustam, line 1. The Sasanians probably used this designation for the northern desert area not only as a continuation of the Achaemenid province of Arabaya (in Old Persian), but also because of the migration of the Tanukh and Asad tribes into Mesopotamia about the time of the beginning of the Sasanian empire.[53] The Asad moved into the Harran area followed by other tribes. Some Arabs were quickly absorbed by the local population, especially in southern Mesopotamia, but those in the north maintained their identity and their nomadic habits. The origin of the name ʿArab is uncertain, as is its relations with the Aribi of pre-Achaemenid times. The name ʿArab is found, however, in Pliny, Strabo and other classical authors. For the early Sasanians the various tribes were not called by a generic name ʿArab, which term was reserved for the northern Mesopotamian area, but some time later, probably towards the end of the Sasanian empire, a generic term for the Arab tribes did emerge. This was the word *Tačik*, derived from the name of the tribe Tayyi'.[54] The later history of the word is interesting, for it came to mean in eastern Iran also those Iranians converted to Islam who in the eyes of their contemporaries had 'become Arabs' by accepting the religion.[55] When the Turks spread over western central Asia they used the term as a synonym for 'Muslim', and, since the Arabs were soon absorbed into the local population, the word Tajik came to mean the local, settled Iranian population, all Muslims of course. Today the Tajiks inhabit the Republic of Tajikistan, as the last Persian speakers in central Asia, an island among the Turkic Uzbeks, Kirghiz and others.

To discuss the history of the Lakhmids, the Kinda confederacy of inner Arabia, or the Sasanian occupation of south Arabia, would require another book. It is relevant to our theme only to show that pre-Islamic Arabs were in contact with the Persians in many areas and in many capacities. Arabs were not only neighbours of the Persians but Arabs had been exiled by the Sasanian government to various parts of the Sasanian empire, including the east. The practice of deporting entire cities or districts which were rebellious was an ancient one in the Near East and the Sasanians simply followed the old practices. The spread of Nestorian Christianity to such places as Merv and Herat may have been primarily the result of the deportation and settlement of Semitic peoples to the eastern frontiers of the Sasanian empire.[56] According to al-Thaʿalibi, after the massacre of rebellious Arab tribesmen by Shapur II, he transplanted his captives to various parts of Iran, the Bakr b. Wa'il to Kirman, and the Bani Hanzala to Fars.[57] Tabari has the same account, but adds that parts of the Taghlib and ʿAbd al-Qais were sent with the Bakr to Kirman.[58] This does not mean, of course, that the Muslim Arabs at the beginning of their conquests in Iran found fellow countrymen all over the country. Such early deportees, for the most part, had been absorbed by the local population. But it does indicate that the Arabs were by no means complete strangers to Iran. Because of trade, and the Sasanian practice of moving officials as well as rebellious tribes or groups to various places in the empire, Arabs must have been acquainted with Iran and Iranians in their homeland.

One may mention Arab officials, for which our sources do give information. A number of Arab poets lived at the court of the Lakhmids at al-Hira, including al-'A'sha and 'Adi b. Zaid. The grandfather of the latter was the secretary of Nu'man the Lakhmid king and a friend of a Persian governor called Farrukhmahan who took Zaid into his house. 'Adi's father grew up with the children of the Persian noble and learned to speak Persian. He was proposed to Chosroes I for the position of postmaster, usually reserved for Persian nobles, since 'Adi was a scribe in Pahlavi as well as a poet in Arabic.[59] Al-'A'sha too spent some years at the Sasanian court. We have already mentioned the Sasanian troops stationed on the *limes* or the Syrian desert, most of whom were Arabs.[60] There is no doubt that both in the military establishment and in the bureaucracy of the Sasanians Arabs were to be found, which is not unexpected.

The Prophet attacked a certain Arab al-Nadr b. al-Harith for telling stories in Mecca about the Persian heroes and kings, which drew people away from Muhammad and his message. (See Sura 31, verses 5–6, which is said to have been directed against al-Nadr.) Some Arabs also were Zoroastrians, especially in areas under Sasanian rule, such as Bahrain and Yemen.[61] Among the tribes, too, such as the Tamim, there apparently were fire-worshippers, which, however, does not necessarily mean they were Zoroastrians.[62] Although Zoroastrianism was never a missionary religion, before the spread of Islam it was neither restricted to Iranians nor as exclusive as it later became; so the existence of Zoroastrian Arabs is plausible. On the other hand the use of the term 'fire worshipper', or even '*majus*', by Arabic authors was by no means reserved solely for Zoroastrians. Fire played a role in many ancient rituals, and the term *majus* was even applied to the Vikings by Arab authors.[63]

It is clear that the Sasanian empire exercised a tremendous influence on the Muslim Arabs, the fruit of which appeared in the time of the 'Abbasids. Likewise the contacts between Iranians and Arabs were not few and slight but many and profound. The Sasanians ruled Iraq and the eastern coast of Arabia called Bahrain (not just the island), as well as Yemen, for a time. The extension of Sasanian political hegemony to Medina or over the Hijaz, on the other hand, is not likely, but influences were extended where military conquests did not reach. Finally, much which was Iranian passed to the Arabs through Syriac or other intermediaries. Thus the picture of Arab-Sasanian relations before the expansion of Islam is fairly clear, and, needless to say, a good deal has been written about them as may be seen from the bibliography. What is not so well known is the area east of the central deserts of modern Persia, what I call the east Iranian cultural area. Since Khurasan became a great centre of Islamic learning under the 'Abbasids, after they launched the revolt which overthrew the Umaiyads, it is necessary to examine central Asia and Khurasan before the coming of Islam.

CHAPTER 3

CENTRAL ASIA BEFORE THE ARAB CONQUESTS

The area of eastern Iran and central Asia, or *l'Iran extérieur* as French scholars call it, was Iranian in languages and cultures long before the advent of Islam, but it was different from Sasanian Iran. One may say that the greatest discoveries in Iranian studies since the Second World War have been made by Soviet archaeologists in the central Asian republics, and by the French in Afghanistan, in effect opening a new field of study. Among the discoveries two new Iranian languages, Khwarazmian and Kushan-Bactrian, have been brought to light by archaeological excavations.[1] What had hitherto been a virtual *terra incognita* has now emerged from the unknown as a great cultural area with a long history. The future undoubtedly will bring new discoveries and new vistas of our knowledge of the past of the enormous territory between China and the Near East, together with eastern Europe.

There are three parts of this large area which concern us, Chinese Turkistan (*Tsentralnaya Aziya* of the Russians), Russian Turkistan (*Srednyaya Aziya*) and eastern Iran, the territory east of the central deserts and south of the River Oxus, the present Amu Darya. All three were inhabited primarily by Iranians in ancient times, but the first area, Chinese Turkistan, seems to have been an outpost of Iranian culture, which by the time of the Islamic conquests was undergoing turkification. It was closely connected with Russian Turkistan, and certainly cannot be ignored in considering the east Iranian cultural domain, but it cannot be discussed here. The distinction between the other two, Russian Turkistan and eastern Iran, in antiquity, however, was much less than today and in the present publication the two are considered as one, for the political boundaries of recent times did not then apply. One could further divide this large territory, of course, into smaller units, cultural as well as geographical subdivisions.

Perhaps the most important part of the east Iranian cultural area in antiquity was Sogdiana, the Sug^{u}da of the Old Persian inscriptions. The fertile valley of the River Zarafshan at the time of the Arab conquests had three main oases from west to east, Bukhara, Samarqand

and Panjikant. In addition the Sogdians had expanded to the east where they occupied Chach, present Tashkent and the Ferghana valley. A commercial folk, Sogdian colonies were to be found in Semirechiye, in Chinese Turkistan, in Mongolia and in China.[2] The Sogdians were in origin probably an Iranian tribe like the Persians, the Parsa of the Old Persian inscriptions, who settled in the east. Recent archaeological excavations indicate that Sogdiana, not long before Islam, had developed a local school of art, related to but distinct from the art of its neighbours. Likewise the dominant religion at the time of the Arab conquests seems to have been a local form of Mazdaism. Manichaeans, Nestorian Christians and Buddhists were also to be found there, but local cults seem to have been predominant. Perhaps a special cult devoted to the Iranian mythical hero Siyavush prevailed in certain areas of Sogdiana. Siyavush was a kind of Adonis figure who apparently held the imagination of many people in the east.[3]

Soviet excavators in Varakhsha, and elsewhere in the oasis of Bukhara, as well as in Afrasiyab (old Samarqand), in Panjikant, and in various sites in the western part of the Ferghana valley, medieval Ustrushana, have recovered Sogdian documents and inscriptions as well as wall paintings, art objects and objects of daily life. From these it is now possible to reconstruct the life and culture of the ancient Sogdians, who were an enterprising and cultured people.[4]

On the lower River Oxus and around the Aral Sea lived the Khwarazmians whose language was related to Sogdian. As the Sogdian merchants dominated trade with China, so did the Khwarazmians engage in trade with eastern Europe. Their caravans ventured far up the Volga in search of furs, honey, amber, walrus ivory and other articles of trade. Later the Russians were to borrow the Khwarazmian form of the word 'Musulman' for Muslim, and with an initial change of *m-* to *b-*, Basurman/Besermen entered the medieval Russian chronicles.[5] The Khwarazmians probably had moved into the delta of the Oxus from the south in ancient times, but by the seventh century of our era they were concentrated around the Aral Sea. Like the Sogdians the Khwarazmians seem to have been mostly followers of local Mazdaist cults, though not necessarily the same as in Sogdiana. The art, such as has been recovered by archaeologists, appears similar to but not identical with Sogdian art. The Khwarazmians evidently had a long tradition of local rulers, for their calendar was dated by an era beginning some time in the first century AD and lasting at least until the ninth century AD, a situation unique in eastern Iran.[6] Perhaps the beginning of the era coincided with the independence of Khwarazm from Parthian rule.

In any case the Khwarazmians are to be distinguished from other Iranians whom the Arabs met, as the great savant al-Biruni tried to show in his writings. The Soviet archaeologist Sergei Tolstov devoted his life to Khwarazm, and because of him such names as Toprak kale and Janbas kale have become famous in archaeological circles.[7]

A third centre of east Iranian culture was Bactria or Tokharistan, subdivided into northern Bactria to the north of the River Oxus and southern Bactria to the south. The name Bactria originally may have been a river name and was then used to designate the Iranians who settled there. The main city was Bactra, later Balkh, called by the Arabs 'mother of cities' because of its antiquity. In tradition the field of activity of Zoroaster the prophet, Balkh still awaits extensive excavations. The name Tokharistan came later to designate the area to the east of Balkh, although it was at times used in a wider context for most of ancient Bactria. Presumably the name Tokharistan dates from the time of the nomadic invasions of Bactria towards the end of the second century BC when various tribes from the east and north put an end to the Greco-Bactrian kingdom. The identity of the Tokharian people is much disputed by scholars, but most agree that the name 'Tokharistan' was brought to Bactria by a nomadic tribe, which if not originally Iranian in speech, soon must have been iranicized after settling down in Bactria. Some scholars believe the Tokharians spoke the Centum Indo-European language which has been found in documents unearthed in Chinese Turkistan but, as mentioned, if this is true they probably soon afterwards adopted an Iranian tongue in their new homeland. To use the ancient term Bactria for the land, the northern part was and is further divided into a series of river valleys which descend from the Hissar range, marking the border with Sogdiana, south to the Oxus. To the west was the river called today the Kashka Darya with its most important city Nakhshab or Nasaf, south of Samarqand. Although a part of Bactria, undoubtedly many Sogdians also were to be found here. To the east of the Kashka Darya is the Surkhan Darya flowing south to Termez through the land called Chaganiyan, the Saghaniyan of the Arabs, while to the east the Wakhsh Darya flowed through the land known as Khuttal to the Arabs. Further valleys to the east were not so populous or important in history. Southern Bactria was composed of valleys of streams flowing north from the Hindu Kush mountains. These valleys were neither as wide nor as fertile as in northern Bactria, the three most important being the Balkh river valley from the direction of Bamiyan to the plain of the Oxus; second, the main valley and route over the Hindu Kush mountains, where the modern towns of Kunduz and Baghlan are located, and third, the eastern valley leading to the Pamirs, in modern Badakhshan.

The cultural unity of southern and northern Bactria was assured by the common dominant religion of Buddhism with a similar Buddhist art, and a common written language, Bactrian, written in a modified

Greek alphabet. It is clear from archaeological investigations that the Oxus was not a cultural frontier or barrier, but rather that the mountain ranges to the north and south were far more formidable for the movement of peoples and ideas. Excavations at such sites as Airtam and Kara tepe near Termez, Adjina tepe south of modern Dushanbe in northern Bactria, and Surkh Kotal in southern Bactria have shown the overwhelming influence of Buddhism on the art and material culture of both territories.

Two places have served as border areas between east and west Iran, Merv and Herat. These already have been briefly mentioned but further discussion of them in an east Iranian framework might be useful. The first area was a strategic oasis in the desert between the Oxus and the plateau of the present-day province of Khurasan. Whether Old Persian Margu meant 'meadow' or 'plain' we cannot be sure, but the meaning would have fitted well the geography of the district. Antiochus I is said to have built walls around the oasis of Merv (Strabo XI.516), and we may presume that the oasis later was well fortified since it was the military centre of the Sasanians in the east. Merv was in Sasanian territory, but on the frontier it undoubtedly served as a point of contact between east and west.

Herat was similar to Merv. Probably named after the river of the same name, it too was located on a crossroads. Whereas Merv was the meeting point of central Asia and the Sasanian empire, Herat was a gateway to India far to the south-east. It was much easier for tribes and even merchants coming from central Asia to India to pass through Herat over the desert to Seistan or directly to Qandahar, and then to India, rather than to go from Balkh over the Hindu Kush and down the River Kabul to India. Herat was an Iranian city, but farther up the Hari Rud, the River of Herat, were probably Dardic speakers and perhaps farther east Indians, even as late as the time of the Islamic conquests. In other words the population of the Hindu Kush mountains in the seventh century was probably predominantly non-Iranian, although to the south Iranians had made considerable progress in establishing settlements.

In both Merv and Herat the predominant religion was probably Sasanian Mazdaism or Zoroastrianism. The art of both areas too was undoubtedly more Sasanian in inspiration than anything else. Few excavations have been carried out in Merv and none in the Herat oasis. In the valley of the Hari Rud near Chisht one finds caves which may have served as Buddhist sites, similar to Bamiyan, so one may infer an extension of Buddhism to the Herat area.[8] Excavations in the Merv oasis have unearthed a Buddhist Sanskrit book and other objects testifying to the existence of a Buddhist monastery there in the late Sasanian period.[9]

The Hindu Kush mountains have been mentioned as the home of Dardic speakers, now pushed back to present Nuristan in Afghanistan and in north-west Pakistan. It is probable that the mountain areas were predominantly occupied by them, whereas the lower cities such as Kabul, Ghazna and others had large Indian populations. The heart of this cultural area was probably the Koh-i Daman and Kabul valleys or plains. In the seventh century we must not only reckon with Buddhism here but also with Hinduism and, of course, with local cults. Indian influences were strong in the arts and crafts as witnessed by objects from excavations in Begram and smaller sites near Kabul and Ghazna. Whereas the area north of Ghazna was predominantly Indian, it is difficult to determine how far the iranification of the southern part of present Afghanistan had progressed by the seventh century of our era. Probably the ancestors of the present Afghans or Pathans were in occupation of the area from Qandahar to Ghazna, if not more territory, by the time of the Arab conquests at the end of the seventh century. In any case one may presume that the southern part of present Afghanistan had been iranicized by the end of the Sasanian empire.

The ancient history of the Brahui speakers in present-day Kalat and surroundings is unknown and conjecture is wide open. Probably the Brahuis, Dravidian speakers, were in Baluchistan before Islam, and, as mentioned, they might have been opponents of the Iranians in the traditional epic opposition of Iran and Turan. Unfortunately our knowledge about their early history is a blank. Further to the east came the plains of the Indus valley where various Indian peoples lived.

In this general survey of the eastern Iranian cultural area much has been omitted, some of which may appear again in a later more detailed discussion of particular places. A general historical background is necessary, however, before we can consider the Arab conquests.

For the people of Egypt and the Fertile Crescent and those of Greece and Rome, the vast land mass of central Asia was an unknown and even frightening area. Consequently the various peoples there within the ken of the ancient world were usually subsumed under a general designation, perhaps in an attempt to simplify the unknown by giving one overall term for the inhabitants. In Greek sources we first hear of the Cimmerians, possibly related to the ancient Thracians and even to the Centum speakers, the Tokharians of Chinese Turkistan. According to Herodotus (IV.5) they were replaced by the Scythians who expanded from central Asia into the south Russian steppes in about the eighth century BC. He further stated that the Persians called the Scythians by the name Saka. Pliny too (VI.50) reported that the Persians called all the Scythians Sakas. This is not the place to discuss the etymologies of the words Saka and Scythian, nor to speculate whether originally the latter were a sub-tribe of the former, or whether both were variations of the same name which came to be used as a general designation for all peoples to the north. Suffice it to say that both Persians and Greeks had a general name for the peoples of central Asia.

Archaeologists, however, reveal a more complex situation and not one dominant culture over all the steppes. Again the details are not important for our purposes, but one may assert with confidence that Cyrus did not find a vacuum with only a few nomadic tribes when he conquered central Asia. The oases were occupied and irrigation systems existed from early times, while the material culture of the area was certainly far from primitive. We know next to nothing about this area in Achaemenid times. Classical sources report the transportation to the east of some rebellious Ionians, as well as other subjects of the Achaemenid great king, the descendants of whom Alexander is said to have found; but until the coming of Alexander the Great we may speak of the prehistory of the east rather than its history.[10] One may, however, study the legacy of the Achaemenids in the east, for certain features of administration and culture were surely the result of inclusion of much of the eastern area in the Achaemenid empire.

The Achaemenid bureaucracy was based upon the Median, which in turn inherited older Assyrian and Babylonian practices. Under the Assyrians the Aramaic language and script flourished as a *lingua franca* of the Near East, if not even then as an official language beside cuneiform written on clay tablets. We know that the Achaemenids used Aramaic as a bureaucratic language all over the empire, from papyri found in Egypt to inscriptions in Anatolia and on the frontiers of India. This bureaucracy was most probably a continuation of Assyrian and Median organization and practices, presenting strong 'caste-like' or closed 'trade-union' features to the outside world. It was not an easy task to master writing in the ancient world, and the scribal class seems to have closely controlled entry into its own ranks. Obviously on the outskirts of the empire, in India, for example, the influence and activity of the bureaucracy was less than in the centre where the government exercised more control.

If we use the four-fold division of language proposed in the last chapter and apply it to the Achaemenid empire, we find interesting results. First, we have the 'official' written language which was Aramaic all over the empire. In Ionia, however, side by side with Aramaic the local Greek language was a second 'official' tongue, in Egypt Egyptian, and so forth. Second, there was an 'official' spoken language. In parts of Mesopotamia the 'official' spoken language, Aramaic, might have been very close to the 'official' written language, although never exactly the same everywhere or at any time. Surely the 'official' spoken language in much of Iran and in the quarters of the Achaemenid army and bureaucracy throughout the empire was Persian, hardly the Old Persian of the Achaemenid inscriptions, but probably a tongue well on the way to a Middle Persian stage where many grammatical features had been simplified or had fallen away. The 'official' spoken language in eastern Iran may well have been Persian rather than, or possibly as well as, any of the local tongues such as Old Sogdian or Old Khwarazmian. Again we can only surmise, for the sources are not at hand to draw clear conclusions. Third, there were local dialects, which may have been close or far from the other two languages mentioned above; or the three may have been entirely different languages. Finally the religious language of much of Mesopotamia was Akkadian, while in most areas of Iran Avestan was probably employed for theogonies recited in the east as well as in the west.

In considering eastern Iran or central Asia, one may thus postulate that the 'official' written language in that area was Aramaic, the 'official' spoken language may have been Persian, while various dialects and languages were spoken locally. The conquests of Alexander changed this picture with the addition of Greek. Again the parallel with Arabic later might be kept in mind. The Seleucids, heirs of Alexander in the east, retained the Achaemenid bureaucracy with Aramaic, while Greek was added as another 'official' written language. The 'official' spoken language too probably became Greek, but Persian may have been maintained in a special position for many years. In the Indian domains of the Seleucids conquered by the Mauryas much of the imperial style and art of the Achaemenids was borrowed, but the use of Aramaic was not, for the Indians wrote their own languages in alphabets derived from Aramaic. Especially significant was the Kharoshthi alphabet of northwest India, but more important for later history was the Brahmi alphabet. The Indians who had been under Achaemenid rule did not continue the use of Aramaic but went their own way, whereas the Iranians continued to live under the traditions of the ancient Near East, at least in the domain of writing.

With the break-up of the Seleucid state in the second century BC, and the fall of the Greco-Bactrian state to nomadic invaders from central Asia in about 130 BC, changes began to occur. It seems that for a time the Parthians continued to follow the Seleucid practice of two 'official' languages. It would be interesting to know whether there were in effect two bureaucracies, one writing in Aramaic and another in Greek, but most likely they were combined in one, and probably many scribes could write in both Greek and Aramaic. In time, knowledge of both Aramaic and Greek in eastern Iran suffered a decline, probably Greek first in the Parthian homeland and contrariwise Aramaic first in Bactria, where the Greeks had settled in significant numbers. One may further suspect that Greek had replaced Aramaic in Bactria at an early date.

In any event an interesting development took place in Bactria where the Greek alphabet was adapted for the local Iranian language, which scholars today call Bactrian or Kushan-Bactrian, probably initiated by the great Kushan king Kanishka in the second century AD.[11] Meanwhile in the Parthian domains, in Khwarazm, and in Sogdiana, Aramaic was dominant, but it was a changed Aramaic. Naturally Iranian words had entered the scribal repository, but it is a disputed question just how much Aramaic the scribes in Parthian Iran knew. Certainly from Achaemenid times onwards the scribes had not read their Aramaic texts to princes, generals and others in authority in spoken Aramaic, which the soldiers and rulers did not understand, but rather they translated the texts in the 'official' spoken language which was Persian, or after the Achaemenids, probably into a local dialect. In Parthia the documents written in Aramaic were orally translated into Parthian, in Sogdiana into Sogdian and in Khwarazm into Khwarazmian. At least this is the most likely theory of what happened. The question arises of when the oral translation of Aramaic so influenced the scribes that their written Aramaic ceased to be Aramaic and instead became Parthian. When did similar processes take place in other Iranian languages, which were then written with Aramaic 'masks'? This is the stage familiar to students of early Sasanian inscriptions written in Parthian and Middle Persian.

In short we may say that the Avroman documents in Parthian, from the first century AD, are written in an Aramaic which a literate inhabitant of Mesopotamia could understand as Aramaic, albeit defective Aramaic.[12] Shortly thereafter, possibly in a movement to iranicize the Parthian state, the nature of the Parthian writing changed from defective Aramaic with Parthian loan-words, to Parthian with Aramaic 'masks'. This was probably a long process, but one cannot say definitely because we have no documents from the period after the first century to the third century AD. In the middle of the third century, from Sasanian times, in Dura Europos on the Euphrates, and of course in the royal inscriptions, we find Parthian with Aramaic 'masks'. It is easier to assume a gradual development on the part of the scribes, rather than a royal decree, or an order to change the writing at one time, although this is an alternate hypothesis. The question remains as to whether the Aramaic 'masks', or what is called heterographic writing, for example writing *MLK'* but pronouncing it *shah*, were *ever* pronounced in their Aramaic form. The scribes may have pronounced *MLK'* as *malka* among themselves, but hardly for the officials for whom they wrote. Later Ibn al-Nadim tells us that in Pahlavi, the Zoroastrian book form of Middle Persian writing, words were written in Aramaic but pronounced as Persian.[13] We may assume that this was true also in Parthian.

This extended discussion on the script and scribes was necessary to show the conservatism and also the continuing influence of the bureaucracy in Iran before the Islamic conquest. For long training was necessary before one could master the intricate writing system, and the caste of scribes, if one may use the term caste, seems to have been quite important under the Sasanians, forerunners of the *kuttab* of Islamic times. As mentioned, the traditions of the scribes developed in different ways in various parts of the Iranian domain. In Fars province, in Parthian times, local rulers prepared the stage for the rise of the Sasanians with their special form of writing which became Middle Persian or Pahlavi, the official script of the Sasanian empire. In Khwarazm and in Sogdiana the archaism of both languages *vis-à-vis* Middle Persian may have helped influence the cultural and even political separation of these lands from the south, such that local forms of writing developed. Here the ideographic form of writing with Aramaic 'masks' was less suited to the grammatical complexities of both Khwarazmian and Sogdian than was the case with Middle Persian. Consequently the number of such 'masks' in both languages is small. Kushan-Bactrian, on the other hand, continued to be written in Greek characters without the problem of Aramaic 'masks'. Thus the writing systems in the various Iranian domains reflected the political and cultural peculiarities of those territories. There may have been some small areas where other local developments occurred, but these 'aberrant' writing systems had little influence elsewhere or have not survived.

The history of eastern Iran or central Asia has been dominated by the recurring invasions of nomads from the north and east. It is true that the massive Turkish movement of later times did change most of Russian Turkistan from an Iranian to a Turkish land, but Iranian culture greatly influenced the conquerors. Nomads did invade eastern Iran before the Arab conquests but on the whole they accepted the local culture and bureaucracy which they found and instituted little change. The picture which has been presented above probably was little changed from the first centuries of our era until well into Islamic times. So to repeat, Merv and Herat were first Parthian and then Sasanian in culture, while the Hindu Kush area, with Kabul and Ghazna, may be considered an offshoot of the Bactrian Iranian area, but both were situated in a predominantly Indian cultural area. Qandahar was probably the same as Kabul, but with Parthian, followed by Sasanian, influence more important than Indian influences, although it must be stated that we are not well informed about this large territory.

The reader may object to the use of the word 'influence', used in such a broad manner, but because of a paucity of sources one is obliged to speak in general terms. Furthermore, we cannot be concerned with details, for this chapter is only intended as a background for the Arab conquests, where fortunately we do have sources.

The date of Kanishka, the most important ruler of the Kushans, is still disputed, but most scholars now uphold a date in the beginning of the second century AD.[14] A century before this period the local Khwarazmian era apparently was introduced in Khwarazm, possibly marking the accession of a new dynasty which was to rule for many centuries. So, cautiously and tentatively, one may suggest that the foundations of the later Khwarazmian, Sogdian and Bactrian states were being formed in the first two centuries of our era. Perhaps it would be better to say that the first two centuries witnessed a consolidation of these areas into separate cultural (and political, although this is uncertain) units. This consolidation is perhaps more important than the question of whether Khwarazm was included in the Kushan empire, or whether later all or part of the Kushan domain was included in the Sasanian empire. Regardless of whether or not the political boundaries were altered for a time the cultural and linguistic units mentioned above did survive political changes. The only two major problems of change in the period from the second century down to the Arab conquests were the expansion of the Sasanians from the west, beginning in the third century, and the Hunnic invasions from the north, beginning in the second half of the fourth century.

We cannot follow the fortunes of the Sasanians in the east because there is not sufficient information to reconstruct the history. Tabari says that the king of the Kushans submitted to Ardashir I, but the significance of this act is open to question.[15] The great inscription of Shapur I (*c.* AD 240–72) at Naqsh-i Rustam says that he ruled the *Kushanshahr* up to Pashkibur and further to Kash, Soghd and the border of Chach.[16] The fact that Shapur mentions these borders of the Kushan kingdom would indicate that he wished the uninitiated reader of his inscription to know how far that great Kushan realm extended, perhaps indicating a note of pride that such a great domain now owed allegiance to him. Beyond this allegiance one cannot go, for there is no evidence that the Sasanian armies marched through the Kushan kingdom destroying cities and winning battles. Rather it seems that the Kushan kingdom merely paid tribute and gave its allegiance to Shapur. The inscription seems to mean that the Kushan kingdom, which was in submission to Shapur, claimed that its boundaries extended as far as the plains of the sub-continent, wherever Pashkibur may be located, and in the north to the borders of the states of Kashgar, Sogdiana, and the Shash of the Arabs, or the Tashkent region. This I interpret to mean that Shapur's claimed suzerainty reached to the borders of these three small central Asian states, which borders could have extended to the Hissar range of today, if we take Sogdiana as the western, Shash as the central, and Kashgar as the eastern neighbours of the Kushan kingdom at this period.

There is no evidence of change in the status of Kushan-Sasanian relations under the immediate successors of Shapur I, including Narseh (293–302), but we do not know whether perhaps some of the Kushans did secure complete independence from the Sasanians. Some time, at the end of the third or during the fourth century, Sasanian princes became rulers of the Kushans, according to the coins issued by them, carrying the titles 'king of the Kushans', 'great king', or 'king of kings of the Kushans'. It seems that most of these coins were issued during the rule of Shapur II (309–79) and his immediate successors.[17] Just how far the Sasanians replaced the Kushans in the east is impossible to tell, but they probably laid claim to the land between the Hissar mountains to the north and over the Hindu Kush to the south, although they may not have exercised rule south of the Hindu Kush where the Kushan-Sasanian coins are rare. But we simply do not know. One may consider the rule of Shapur II the high point of Sasanian rule in the east, for soon after him the Hunnic invasions changed the picture.

Although the Altaic-speaking peoples had probably moved quite early from the forests of Siberia south on to the steppe lands, where they learned the arts connected with horse riding from the Iranian nomads, from those generally called Scythians or Sakas, the expansion of Altaic-speaking peoples towards the west took place only at about the beginning of our era. Contacts with Iran, as with Europe, came even later as part of a great wandering of the Huns from east Asia, interestingly coming at about the same time as the expansion of the Germanic peoples.

The westward expansion of the Huns ended at Chalôns in 451 with the defeat of Attila, but how did the Huns fare in the part of the world that we are discussing? From the fourth century until the defeat of the Hephthalites by both the Sasanians and the Turks in 557, we may reckon with about two centuries of apparent Hunnic rule in eastern Iran. The history of this period in eastern Iran is complicated by a mass of different coins which cannot be fixed to any absolute chronology. R.Göbl has tried to bring order into the coins, and it would seem that the Sasanian governors in the east were followed by rulers called Kidarites, after the name of a ruler which appears on the early coins of this group.[18] We cannot tell who the Kidarites were, but they considered themselves heirs of the Kushans, and sometimes they are called little Kushans by present-day scholars. The continuity of traditions and of a culture fashioned by the Kushans seems most likely, and nomad invaders from the north may have influenced but hardly changed these traditions. The Kidarites themselves may have been nomadic invaders from the north, but there is no evidence for this.

When we come to the coins with a legend *Alkhon* we probably do find true Huns. Just what relation the authors of these coins had with the Chionites, mentioned by Ammianus Marcellinus (XVI.9.4 and XVIII.6.22) and others, is not easy to determine. One may suggest that the Chionites were Hunnic invaders, and the Alkhon were a tribe, or leaders of a part or all of them. It also cannot be determined if the Hephthalites were a later and different invasion, or essentially a tribe of Huns who followed the first wave of Chionites almost a century later. What is important for the later post-Islamic history, which we shall investigate below, is that the Iranian *nomads* of central Asia had been replaced by Altaic-speaking nomads, the Huns, followed by the Turks, also an Altaic-speaking folk.

The Chionites, the earliest Huns (Khiyon = Hun) to come to eastern Iran, as we have noted, were mentioned by Ammianus Marcellinus during the years of the 350s. They do not appear again on the pages of history, but Bahram v (421–39) was victorious against unknown opponents, perhaps Chionites, in eastern Iran. His victories must have been impressive for the rulers of the oasis of Bukhara copied the coins of Bahram, at first with Pahlavi legends, and then with the special Aramaic alphabet of Bukhara and the legend 'king of Bukhara' (βωγ'r γωβ).[19] Probably a short time after Bahram v the Hephthalites appear on the scene. At the present state of our knowledge it is impossible to solve problems of the sure identification of such names as Alkhon and Walkhon mentioned in the Armenian geography of Moses of Chorene, and the Οὐαρχωνῖται of Byzantine authors, plus other stray names which appear in scattered sources.[20] Names on coins cannot be assigned yet to definite time periods with assured sequences. Likewise the identification of words as proper names or as titles is frequently most uncertain. Such is the case with Khingila, which title or family name appears on many coins, while Toramana and Mihirakula appear to be the proper names of specific leaders of the Hunnic invaders of India. We can say that, according to many sources, King Peroz (459–84) was the *first* Sasanian to fight against the Hephthalites. Whether the Hephthalites were basically a Hunnic people or an indigenous folk from the mountains of modern Badakhshan is at present impossible to determine, but suffice it to say that they appear in the Hunnic phase of the history of central Asia, and they utilized the existing Iranian language in modified Greek script as their written language. We may safely infer that there were Hunnic elements among the Hephthalites, if not just the ruling class, but the Hephthalites adopted the predominantly Iranian culture of their predecessors the Kushans. Further, it would seem, from Chinese sources, that the name

Hephthalite came from a personal name of a chief, Habtal or Hephtal, which could be etymologized in several ways. This is more or less the extent of our knowledge.

The supremacy of the Hephthalites in eastern Iran was assured by their victories over Peroz, followed by later alliances with the Sasanian kings Kavad (488–531) and Chosroes I (531–79). Under the last, however, the Turks appeared in Russian Turkistan, and about 557 the Hephthalites were defeated by the Turks in alliance with the Sasanians. Henceforth various small Hephthalite principalities existed as vassals of the Turks, or in independence. In spite of invasions from the north and east the cultural life of eastern Iran seems to have continued from earlier times, perhaps not in a straight line, but for the most part at least unbroken. Such was the situation on the eve of the Arab conquest.

Perhaps one should distinguish between the Hephthalite, or rather the Hunnic, and the later Turkic phase of the expansion of Altaic-speaking peoples. For after 557, a full century before the Arab conquest of Russian Turkistan, the Turks were present, and if not in control of all of the territory, at least some of them had wandered south of the Hindu Kush mountains. The later Turkish tribe of Khalaj were said to have descended from the Hephthalites, although they may have been simply a Turkish tribe which occupied territory once held by the Hephthalites.[21] In spite of the Turkish intrusion the settled Iranian aristocracy surely continued to play the leading role in the rule of eastern Iran.

One should emphasize the point that linguistic criteria are being used for terms such as 'Turkic' or 'Turkish', and not anthropological or even cultural criteria. This is, of course, inadequate and general, and may lead to misunderstanding. It may be inaccurate to speak of 'Altaic' or 'Turkic' peoples, for we know that such peoples were highly mixed, imbued with various external influences and cultures, and without unity. But there are, unfortunately, no other satisfactory terms to use for peoples, confederations or the like, and a linguistic designation such as 'Turkic' must be understood as a general term to designate the language spoken by the leaders of the group or the people. Obviously 'Turks' living near the borders of China had become sinicized whereas those near Sogdiana became iranicized, and the two may have borne little resemblance to one another save in the everyday language of the ruling group. But the concepts 'Chinese' people and culture and 'Iranian' peoples and culture also can be misleading if we think of both concepts as unified or monolithic. These *caveats* must be mentioned when we, of necessity, speak in general terms. Let us return to central Asia.

Archaeological surveys and excavations in the central Asian republics of the Soviet Union have revealed the existence of extensive walls and fortifications around oases, for example around Bukhara, Merv and Shahrasiyab (medieval Kish south of Samarqand). While these great walls were built at enormous expense and labour primarily to ward off attacks by nomads, they also served as a barrier against the sand and the encroachment of the desert. The walls enclosed the irrigated land and if they were allowed to fall into ruins, the desert would soon hold sway. For example, today land to the west of the city of Bukhara is now desert whereas in pre-Islamic times irrigation had made the area around the ruins of Varakhsha habitable.[22] So the 'great wall' pattern was widespread in central Asia in the pre-Islamic period. Within the walls were not only villages and towns but also many fortified villas or castles of the landed aristocracy. Outside the oases, especially on trade routes, and wherever water was found, there might be fortified villages, castles or simply towers. Many of the villages and castles were occupied by the local aristocracy, and all indications point to a great extension of the landed nobility at the expense of central authority. The same was true in western Iran, but to a lesser extent, where at the end of the Sasanian empire the *dihqans*, the local, landed aristocracy, had assumed powers and influence formerly held by the crown or the court nobility. If we may assume an overall, though loose, Turkish central authority in Russian Turkistan in this period, it was certainly weak and merely nominal, for the local princes seem to have maintained a great measure of independence everywhere. In the small, local courts traditions of chivalry and old tales of heroes were better preserved than in western Iran where the central bureaucracy of the Sasanians and the Zoroastrian priesthood, supported by the central government, exercised more control against such feudal tendencies. It is safe to say that the stories of ancient Iran were more popular in the castles of the *dihqans* of central Asia than in western Iran. In general terms we can contrast the more knightly court of a *dihqan* in his castle in eastern Iran, and his troubadours, with the more prosaic *dihqan* of western Iran who had a Zoroastrian priest and a scribe, tax-collector and other agents of the central government with him. Furthermore, in many cases it seems that in western Iran the *dihqan* was himself appointed by the government whereas in the eastern lands, outside of the rule of the Sasanians, the *dihqan* himself was the government, although perhaps with a feudal obligation to a higher lord.[23]

From the extensive excavations in Panjikant, Sogdiana, it seems that merchants were an important and powerful segment of the population. Whether this was true all over eastern Iran is questionable, for land was surely more important than trade in areas other than Sogdiana, although trade must have been significant in Khwarazm and Merv as well as in Sogdiana. Undoubtedly local patterns varied, but the overall picture was none the less different from western Iran where land holdings were paramount. The majority of houses excavated in Panjikant had wall paintings, evidence of the wealth of the community. Many of the scenes depicted are nobles drinking wine, the hunt, religious iconography, but especially scenes from heroic stories or from the epic, which was to be recorded later by Firdosi. Panjikant was certainly not unique in Sogdiana, for wall paintings in Afrasiyab, or old Samarqand, reveal similar conditions, and as archaeologists extend their work undoubtedly more sites similar to Panjikant will be found. A word may be said about the wall paintings and other art remains of central Asia from the artistic point of view.

Christianity and Buddhism both had an iconography and what might be called a distinctive Christian or Buddhist art. The Manichaeans were proud of the artistic abilities of their founder Mani, but a special iconography, as among Christians and Buddhists, does not seem to have developed. Zoroastrianism, one may surmise, was almost iconoclastic for there are no cult pictures or statues typical of that religion. Likewise the local variants of Mazdaism in the east do not appear to have developed any religious art. Therefore one might generally characterize Iranian art, both west and east, as secular, and in the west with a tendency towards geometric forms, emblems and heraldry in decoration. The overall predominance of decoration over meaning or content has been a hallmark of all Iranian art through the ages. Perhaps the strong influence of Buddhist art in eastern Iran gave the artists of the east, such as at Panjikant, more of an impetus to portraiture, or at least to the representation of humans, while the west Iranian artists turned more to abstract designs and patterns which could be reproduced in clay, on stucco or on textiles. One should not overemphasize such differences, but none the less the artistic emphasis of central Asia seems to have been different from western Iran.

It also seems to have been the custom all over the Iranian world, if not elsewhere as well, to drink wine from bowls; these were somewhat flatter than those in use among the ancient Greeks. Such drinking bowls are seen in the wall paintings of Panjikant and many silver bowls exist in the museums of the world from this period of history and from this area. Silver always has been the coinage of the steppes, and nomads have sought to accumulate silver objects as sources of wealth, as well as for the artistic qualities of silverwork which they also valued. We can now make distinctions among the various silver objects formerly all described as 'Sasanian' or 'early Islamic on a Sasanian model'. Art historians can begin to assign such objects to a Khwarazmian, Sogdian or Bactrian school. There is no longer any doubt that by pre-Islamic Iranian art one must include far more than Sasanian art. It is true that at the end of the Sasanian empire Sasanian influence in art had expanded not only into central Asia but also into the Byzantine empire and eastern Europe. The garments of the nobles depicted on the walls of Afrasiyab show distinct Sasanian motifs on the cloth, and one can find Sasanian influences far into Chinese Turkistan. Just as Greek influences were spread in the Achaemenid empire even before Alexander the Great, so were western Iranian influences active in central Asia before Islam. But just as Alexander's conquests gave a tremendous impetus to the spread of Hellenistic influence in the east, so the Arab conquests not only extended Arabic, but also the Persian language and west Iranian culture into the east. This will be discussed later.

One should try to be more precise in regard to religion, for the Arabs were carriers of a new religion and in eastern Iran they did not encounter the Zoroastrian 'state religion' of the Sasanian empire, but rather Buddhism, Manichaeism, and local cults, Mazdaist and others. The situation of Buddhism, however, to take one example, had greatly changed from earlier times and by the seventh century it had lost much of its influence. Let us turn to religions in eastern Iran in the various areas mentioned above.

To begin with Merv, the military headquarters of the Sasanian forces in the east, one may assume that the official state religion of Zoroastrianism was present there. Barbud, the famous musician of the court of Chosroes II (591–628), was said to have come from Merv, and it would seem that Merv was perhaps a centre of learning at the end of the Sasanian empire. The discovery of potsherds with Sogdian and Pahlavi writing on them indicates that Merv was also an international entrepôt.[24] Since it was a frontier city and a crossroads of trade, one would expect a variety of religions and from all evidence, albeit fragmentary, such is the case. A Nestorian Christian bishopric existed as early as the fourth century, and we know that the Christian bishop of Merv recovered the body of the murdered last Sasanian ruler Yazdegird III (632–51).[25] There were different Christian sects, but we cannot discuss the conflicts between Nestorians and Jacobites here. It is highly probable that Merv was the centre for Christian missionary activity in central Asia and the Far East. One may doubt whether Buddhism had any adherents left in Merv by the time of the Arab conquests. The existence of a Buddhist monastery in earlier times in the Merv oasis has been revealed by excavations which *inter alia* produced an extensive Sanskrit Buddhist text, on rules for the monastic life, written on palm leaves.[26] The date of the monastery cannot be determined with precision, but coins of Chosroes I dated 549 were found in the excavations, implying the existence of the Buddhist establishment at least until the middle of the sixth century, but there is no evidence for Buddhists there in later times. There is also a lack of evidence for Manichaeans although one might presume their existence in Merv. Since archaeological traces of Manichaeism would be difficult to identify, we must rely on written sources which unfortunately tell us nothing of Manichaeism in Merv. Local cults cannot be excluded but again there is no evidence.

Khwarazm was the homeland of the great Islamic scholar al-Biruni and we might expect to find some evidence of the pre-Islamic religions of Khwarazm in his writings, but those writings on such matters are lost. He does tell of the existence of Malikite Christians in Khwarazm, which is somewhat unexpected.[27] According to him, the *magi* of Khwarazm were like those in Sogdiana, but apparently unlike those of Sasanian Iran.[28] Ancient beliefs and practices, such as rites with incense to keep away the demons, may have been more important to Khwarazmians than any formal, organized religion.[29] The persistence of ancient rituals and folk beliefs, however, is a phenomenon which can be observed almost everywhere in this part of the world. If Zoroastrianism, as known from Sasanian Iran, was not widespread in Khwarazm, however, what was in its place? At present there is no direct evidence of an organized Mazdaism in central Asia which was basically different from the Zoroastrianism of Sasanian Iran, and the use of two terms, Mazdaism and Zoroastrianism, is here a purely arbitrary one, simply to distinguish between the two, the Sasanian and central Asian forms of the same religion. All evidence points to one overall religion, differing only in that in the Sasanian empire the religion was supported by the state, probably with certain rites not found in central Asia. Furthermore, there were probably more and varied local practices in the Mazdaism practised in central Asia, while from the Arabic sources one would gather that the priesthood was small and weak in central Asia compared to the Sasanian clergy. Burial customs, incidentally, are a difficult subject which must be used with great care to determine religious differences. In central Asia various methods of interment were practised and at present there is no instructive pattern discernible in them.

Jewish colonies existed in almost all trading centres in eastern Iran as did Christian, but other sects such as the Sabians, Samaritans, Marchionites and the like are unattested. In Khwarazm al-Biruni was able to obtain information on Judaism from local Jews, but as elsewhere in the east Jews do not seem to have played an important role in the overall life of the communities. They did, however, cause problems for 'orthodox' Judaism, for such sectarians as Hivi from Balkh and others indicate an inclination to heterodoxy in the east. These people, however, are from Islamic times and will be discussed later.

In Sogdiana local Mazdaism, as in Khwarazm, was more important than other religions. We know, however, that Samarqand became a Manichaean centre and Christian Sogdians have left their writings found in Chinese Turkistan.[30] Local practices, such as the making of clay idols or statues, attested by archaeology and by a number of writers in Islamic times, seem to have been more in the nature of old folk beliefs than part of an organized religion. The goddess Nana or Nanai was widely revered in Sogdiana but cult practices or temples definitely dedicated to her remain unknown. The identification of Nana as a mother goddess, however, represented in Sogdiana and Khwarazm as a four-armed deity, is probable.[31] Further archaeological excavations may bring new evidence to substantiate this view. Cults of the mother goddess were widespread throughout the orient and local forms of rites and rituals probably varied greatly, partly depending on influences from the great organized religions. To return to the *magi*, or priests of Mazdaism, it is probable that they chanted much the same theogonies as in Sasanian Iran, but without much of the secondary literature or interpretations of the Avesta familiar to us from the Pahlavi writings of the ninth century from Fars or elsewhere in western Iran. The existence of a literature separate from the Avesta and other writings of the west Iranian Zoroastrians in the east is attested by a reference of al-Biruni to a book of the *magi* of Sogdiana. Therefore, one may conclude that in Sogdiana, at least in the eastern parts on the upper River Zarafshan and in Ferghana, many ancient beliefs and rites existed, nominally Mazdaist or Zoroastrian, but in some cases even indicating pre-Zoroastrian survivals from the Aryan pre-history of this area.

Northern and especially southern Bactria, as we have mentioned, were flourishing Buddhist centres, but the invasions of Huns, and also probably the Sasanians, had undoubtedly harmed the expansion of Buddhism. Yet the Chinese Buddhist pilgrims Hsüan Tsang and Huei Ch'ao report active Buddhist monasteries in the seventh and early eighth centuries, especially in what is today southern Tajikistan and northern Afghanistan.[32] The new Turkish rulers who had established themselves there were apparently adherents of Buddhism. Although Hinayana Buddhism at that time was predominant, there are signs that Mahayana and syncretic forms of Buddhism also existed. Undoubtedly Manichaeism and Christianity also had adherents in Balkh and other towns of Bactria, but there are no records of them. Another religion, Hinduism, may have existed in Bactia, although if so it was probably limited, for the most part, to Indian immigrants.

To the south of Bactria was the mountain area of the Hindu Kush, the Paropanisadai of Ptolemy and other classical authors, from Iranian **uparisaina*: 'above the eagle', a most apt name for the high mountain masses. This was, as noted above, the western boundary of the Indians and the eastern frontier of the Iranians, but the cultural influences from India were especially strong in this region. The most important sub-regions of this area were the valley and plain north of present Kabul called today Koh-i Daman with the ancient site of Begram, and the Kabul valley including the present Wardak and Logar valleys. To the east were the lowlands of India beginning with the present-day Jalalabad valley, ancient Nangarhar. The mountain area, like the eastern lowlands, had been a centre of Buddhism, as the many remains of *stupas* and other Buddhist monuments testify. By the seventh century of our era, however, Buddhism had lost much of its strength especially in the lowlands to the east where a resurgent Hinduism mostly in the form of Śaivaism had replaced Buddhism as the dominant religion. None the less in the mountains in Bamiyan and other isolated valleys Buddhist monks continued to live and expound the law of their master. In Bamiyan, according to Islamic sources, a Buddhist monastery was pillaged by Ya'qub b. Laith in 870, evidence of the continuing activity of Buddhists there.[33] We do not have comparable evidence for Hinduism, at least in the archaeological remains, but the Hindushahi dynasty of Kabul, which we shall meet again in a later chapter, is evidence enough for the existence of Hinduism in this area, and Muslims later had to combat Hinduism or various forms of it rather than Buddhism in the Kabul and more eastern areas.

The Upper Hilmand valley and the highland plains leading from Qandahar to Ghazna and Gardez may be considered as one geographical area, for the desert to the west, between Herat together with Seistan and the River Hilmand, was a considerable obstacle to movement, although not of course to be compared with the mountains in the centre of present-day Afghanistan. None the less it did separate this easternmost Iranian land, ancient Arachosia, from areas to the west. In Qandahar Indian influences were strong and this frontier region passed back and forth from Iranian to Indian political control from the time of the Achaemenids and the Mauryas to the Moghuls and the Safavids. The land from the Hilmand basin to Ghazna and Gardez underwent too many invasions and cross-currents of merchants and others to have had the same history as the mountain valleys to the north. The religious picture also does not appear as simple as in Buddhist dominated lands to the north. Buddhism certainly existed south of the Hindu Kush mountains, but from Chinese Buddhist pilgrims it would seem that local cults were especially strong. One Chinese text says that there were many heretics in this land who followed the cult of the god Su-na.[34] Much has been written about the deity Shun, Zun or Zhun in the vicinity of Ghazna. More will be said about this later in regard to the raids of 'Abd al-Rahman b. Samura in the middle of the seventh century. The name of the god has often been discussed, and a suggestion has been made that it should be read as Zur rather than Zun. The god moreover has been identified as Zurvan, an Iranian time deity, or even as a sun god, either local or brought to Zabul by nomadic invaders after the fall of the Kushans. Others suggest that Zun was an Indo-European deity, perhaps related to Imra of the Kafirs or Śiva of the Indians. Whatever the answer to this question, it is sufficient to note that many local cults existed in the east of which we have few records. In the case of Zun, the story of a great mountain where the main temple or sanctuary of the god was located was evidently not a fairy tale, and it was only one detail of an interesting religion. The multitude of deities mentioned on the gold coins of the great Kushans, long before this period, should be enough to indicate a most varied religious picture in the entire east Iranian area. The ultimate success of the great 'literary' religions has perhaps blinded us to the existence of many sects and religions which played a role on the stage of history and then vanished. Further archaeological excavations will probably elucidate many of the problems which we now find in the pre-Islamic history of east Iran.

To turn briefly to the political history of central Asia and the east in the seventh century AD, there is unfortunately little which can be reconstructed. We should try, however, to determine the eastern frontier of the Sasanian empire at this time and, as far as possible, the situation prevailing in the small states outside that empire. We should begin with the Sasanian military centre of the east Merv, where a *marzban*, who was at the same time probably one of the great army commanders of the Sasanians, held sway. The River Oxus was the usual boundary of the Sasanians in the north-east, some 120 miles from Merv. At times the Sasanians crossed the river to invade Bukhara and perhaps farther east, but, at the end of the Sasanian empire, to the north and east of the Oxus was Sogdian land, including the land under the rule of the Bukharan oasis. Amul, on the south bank of the river, may have been nominally under Sasanian rule, but if not, surely Persian influence was strong and we may assume that many Persians were settled there.

Khwarazm was not under Sasanian rule but, as mentioned, was ruled by a local dynasty which had long ruled over the land. If we believe al-Biruni, the most significant ruler in the history of the dynasty was a certain Afrigh who was a builder of castles in the land and who started a new era of time reckoning from his rule perhaps in the second or third century AD, according to al-Biruni.[35] This is probably not to be accepted literally, but we may believe al-Biruni when he names the ruler of Khwarazm at the time of the prophet Muhammad as Arthamukh, and a subsequent ruler at the time of Qutaiba b. Muslim called Askajamukh b. Azkajawar. Just how far the land of Khwarazm was under one central government is difficult to determine. Because of its geographical position alone, it was probably more unified than Sogdiana. We cannot say whether some of the towns of Khwarazm were almost independent, although it is not impossible that some were under direct central control while others were not. Khwarazm does not seem to have been under Turkish rule at any time in the pre-Islamic period, and there is no evidence of any vassal status to any other state, so we may conclude that the land was ruled by an independent dynasty up to the coming of Qutaiba b. Muslim. Tabari says that just before the Arab conquest a certain Khurzad, the brother of the reigning shah of Khwarazm, seized power and deposed the ruler in favour of another member of the family, and this was the situation when Qutaiba arrived on the scene.[36]

Sogdiana was divided into a multitude of independent city states, but there was some sort of hegemony of the large cities over the surrounding small ones. The existence of confederations of small states is not directly attested but we may presume the existence of some kind of union among many of the states. Thus the lower or western Zarafshan valley was under the influence (if not direct rule) of Bukhara, the main city of the area. The rulers of Bukhara bore the Sogdian title of king γωβ, which was later changed into Persian *khuda* 'lord' by Muslim writers who sought to find a comparable word intelligible to their readers. We have the name of one pre-Islamic ruler of Bukhara whose name appears on a silver vessel in the Hermitage Museum in the Bukharan variant of the Sogdian alphabet as *dzwy* or *dnwy*, but he cannot be identified elsewhere.[37] Other names of other rulers in the oasis of Bukhara suggest that the ruler of Bukhara was only the nominal overlord of the others. The use of the Bukharan alphabet on coins of the ruler of Baikand, south-west of Bukhara and outside the oasis, is an indication of the extent of Bukharan influence if not of political control. We also learn that there was a lord of Vardana in the northern part of the oasis, and the historian of the city Narshakhi says that the town of Ramitin was once the capital of the oasis. Furthermore excavations have revealed the palaces of the rulers of Bukhara in the site called Varakhsha, at present in the desert to the west of the oasis. This indicates a fluctuation in the seat of the rulers, not to mention sub-rulers. At the time of the Arab conquest, however, Bukhara was the main city of the oasis, which also had many castles or villas of the aristocracy on the land outside of the metropolis.

Samarqand, ancient Marakanda, was undoubtedly the main city on the upper Zarafshan, with a local ruler called the *ikhshid*, in Sogdian *'γšyδ*, a title probably derived from the Old Iranian root 'to rule', hence 'king'. This title was also used for the rulers of Ferghana, so it probably was a general Sogdian title for ruler. Samarqand was the main city of the upper Zarafshan river valley and Panjikant to the east was under the sway of Samarqand. Just how far the rule of Samarqand extended or was recognized is unknown, but it probably fluctuated greatly at different periods. One cannot tell from chance coin finds whether the ruler of Samarqand ruled all sites where coins which originated in Samarqand were found. The pre-Islamic rulers of Sogdiana left a series of copper coins, but beyond the names, which are written in a difficult cursive Sogdian, they give us no information. Some of the names of the rulers from the end of the seventh century were *šyšpyr*, *βrγwm'n*, *twk'sp'δ'k*, and then about the year 700, with the Arab conquests in full swing, we find *trγwn*, a name found in Arabic sources as Tarkhun.[38] Panjikant, though nominally under the rule of Samarqand, had its own local rulers who struck copper coins for local use. As in the case of Khwarazm, where the name Khusrau was recorded as a princely title by some Arabic writers, so Tarkhun came to be regarded as the title of the local ruler of Samarqand.

South of Samarqand is the Kashka Darya, on the banks of which the two towns of Nasaf and Kish (present Kitab area, Uzbek SSR) played an important role in the history of the Arab conquests in central Asia. We might assume that there was a confederation of the towns of the Kashka Darya under the leadership of Kish but unfortunately information is lacking. Archaeological excavations in this area have begun only recently, and one must await the results of further work before any progress in elucidating the pre-Islamic history of the Kashka Darya valley can be made.

The continuation of the Sogdian cultural domain to the east included the large and rich Ferghana valley. To the west of the Ferghana valley lay the principality of Ustrushana, present-day Shakhristan in the Uzbek SSR. The Arabs dropped the 't' in the name, so we find Usrushana in Arabic sources. Archaeological surveys in this area have revealed that between the Turkistan mountain range to the south and the River Jaxartes (Syr Darya) to the north the land was heavily cultivated and densely populated in this period. The main city of Ustrushana was also called Panjikant or Panjikat, the Bunjikath of Arabic authors, which name was to be found in many places elsewhere. The name of the ruler of Ustrushana, in Arabic sources *afshin*, has not been found in Sogdian documents or on coins, and it may be either a name or a general word for 'ruler' or 'lord' picked up by Arabic authors and used as a specific title for the ruler of Ustrushana. Later the name of al-Afshin Haidar was to become famous at the 'Abbasid court. Again it is uncertain how far the domain of the ruler of Ustrushana extended. Most of Ferghana to the east, in any case, was under various independent princes.

The Ferghana valley, according to Arabic authors, was ruled by an *ikhshid*, as in Sogdiana, but in Sogdian the title is expressed by an Aramaic mask *βrγ'nk MLK'*.[39] At the time of the Arab conquests in the beginning of the eighth century the name of the ruler of Ferghana as reported in Arabic was al-Tar.[40] The local dynasty was replaced by Turkish rule in 739, although in the seventh century it seems that the land for a time had been under a Turkish ruler who was followed for a short interval by the local native dynasty. Perhaps the local Iranian dynasty ruled continuously, though at times under Turkish overlordship. We have no information about Ferghana but one may conjecture that the local dynasty came to the fore when the Arabs advanced and the Turks retreated, but a discussion of this will follow in a later chapter. The capital of Ferghana seems to have shifted between Akhsikath, perhaps the main city for the local dynasty, and Qasan, perhaps a capital of the Turks. Or the first town, in Sogdian *'γsyknδh* 'white city'?, may have been the main city for all, while Qasan to the north could have been a more fortified centre of government.[41] Our information does not allow a decision.

Chach, or as the Arabs called it Shash, was probably changed by the Turks into Tashkent 'the stone city', although it is not on the same spot as the modern city. Chach had been conquered by the Turks as early as *c.* 565 when the first Turkish empire of the Altai region had expanded into western Turkistan. As suggested above, the suzerainty of the Turks over the city states of Transoxiana was probably only nominal most of the time. With the division of the Turkish Khaqanate into an eastern and a western part at the beginning of the seventh century, the position of the Turks in central Asia was weakened. It is impossible here to discuss developments among the Turkish tribes in the steppes of Mongolia and central Asia. Suffice it to say that when the Arabs appeared on the scene at the end of the seventh century the west Turkish Khaqanate had fallen into various parts. Turkish tribes, however, as indicated above, had penetrated and remained in eastern Iran although we have no information about them. At the same time that the west Turkish Khaqanate fell in 659, the Tibetans and the Chinese under the Sui and then the T'ang dynasties rose in power and influence. Although the history of Chinese Turkistan and the Far East cannot be our concern here, these factors must not be forgotten in any discussion of eastern Iran and central Asia at this time.

After the fall of the west Turkish Khaqanate the westernmost Turkish power was that of the Türgesh, and these were the Turks who took over the role of Turkish protectors of the Sogdian city states against the Arabs. But the Türgesh were to suffer from the expansion of a new grouping of Turks from the River Orkhon, the new Khaqanate of the Gök Turks. In 710 the Türgesh were defeated by the new Turkish empire in Semirechiye, north-east of Tashkent. The new state, however, did not long survive its founder and internal struggles kept it from playing a decisive role in the affairs of Transoxiana. The latter, however, was not free from the infiltration of Turkish tribes from the north and east, and the Arabs had to contend many times with Turks in their advance into central Asia.

Al-Biruni calls the ruler of Chach Tudun, either a widespread Turkish title, possibly derived from Chinese, or perhaps we have a confusion of this title with an earlier Sogdian military title attested as *twttk*. Since the flat Chach area was easily open to invasion, Turkish tribes probably had infiltrated into the area from early times. Beyond Chach or Tashkent was Turkish land. To the east of Ferghana lay Kashgar and the states of the Tarim Basin which Sogdian traders visited on their way to China. Again it is impossible to discuss the past of the city states of Chinese Turkistan where Buddhist documents in the Khotanese Saka language, an Iranian tongue, and in 'Tokharian', with its two dialects, a western Indo-European language have been found, not to mention Turkic, Tibetan, Chinese and some western Iranian languages. The history of these states along the 'Silk Road' from China did not have such a direct influence on Russian Turkistan and eastern Iran to warrant a long digression. We need only say that the southern towns such as Khotan and Yarkand were strongly Buddhist with Indian cultural influence, while the northern cities such as Kucha and Turfan had Buddhists but also had numerous followers of Manichaeism, while the Sogdian or other Iranian cultural influences were strong. The political history of Chinese and Tibetan expansion, followed by the Turks who ultimately turned the land into a Turkistan, lies beyond the limits of the present work. The Arabs, however, were to meet the Chinese in battle on the River Talas in 751 and defeat them. China was far from the city states of Transoxiana, but none the less her influence was far reaching and cannot be forgotten in recounting the history of the Arab expansion in central Asia.

The bewildering variety of titles and names which appear in the Arabic chronicles and geographies when speaking of Bactria and the Hindu Kush region make any reconstruction of history extremely difficult. Presumably many, if not most, of the small principalities of northern Bactria, present Tajikistan, owed a nominal allegiance to the Turks when the latter were united and strong, but when weak and divided their rulers, such as the lord (*khuda*) of Chaganiyan, were independent. At the beginning of the eighth century the *sher* of Khuttal, as the ruler was called in Arabic sources, was perhaps the chief sovereign of the entire region. Khuttal was one name for the land of the Wakhsh valley and other valleys to the east. The title *sher* was analogous to *ikhshid*, meaning 'ruler', although Tabari mentions a ruler of Khuttal which has been restored as Tudun Tarkhan.[42] Khuttal seems to have been the ancient indigenous name of the territory of northern Bactria, in Sogdian *γwttwrstn* or Khuttulstan.[43] Other petty dynasts such as the prince of Shuman and the ruler of Termez (Arabic: Tirmidh) are briefly mentioned in the sources.

South of the Oxus was the great city of Balkh, presumably the chief city, if not always the capital, of greater Tokharistan. Later Tokharistan was restricted and divided into upper and lower parts with Taliqan the capital of the former, while at this later time Balkh lay to the west of both parts.

Frequently the Turkish titles of *yabghu* and *shad* are mentioned in the Arabic sources referring to the ruler of Tokharistan and his viceroy respectively.[44] Many scholars have considered the Turkish dominion in this part of the world as a parallel to the early Arab conquests. The local dynasts continued to rule in both cases, while submitting to either Turkish or Arab overlords whose rule at times was very lax. This point of view seems reasonable although it is not easy to document at all times. Although information is not available, the city of Balkh may have been an independent city without a prince ruling it. It is possible that a Buddhist official was the chief person in the city, the head of the large *vihara* or Buddhist monastery establishment; this person as reported in Arabic sources was called *barmak*.[45] Even if this is true the city none the less must have come under foreign domination at times, as we shall see later when Tarkhan Nezak captured the city shortly before 663. The capital of Nezak was farther west in the town of Badhgis. Between Balkh and Badghis was the land of Gozgan (Arabic: Juzjan) ruled by a lord (*khuda*) according to the Arabic sources. Perhaps originally Nezak was this ruler. In the Hindu Kush mountains we find the *sher* of Bamiyan, the *shar* (variation of *sher*) of Gharchistan, who was also called Varaz banda, which seems to have been an appellative or family name rather than a title. According to the *Hudud al-ʿalam*, the chiefs of Manshan in the southern Hindu Kush were called Baraz banda, while the name Varaz appears in connection with Herat and other districts of the east, perhaps the name of a princely Hephthalite family.[46] The Kabul shah with the eponymous title of Khingila has been mentioned and will appear later. There apparently was also a *shar* of Ghur, although this may have been an extension of the title from Gharchistan into the south. In any case, we may assume that the mountain areas had many petty chiefs who receive various titles in the sources.

Ghazna, meaning the 'treasury', was the chief city of Zabul or Zabulistan where the ruler was called by the title *zunbil* or *zhunbil*. The extent of his domains is unknown but from various indications in the Arabic sources, and from geographical realities, one might deduce that he ruled also Arachosia (Qandahar), the al-Rukhkhaj of the Arabs. It is likely that his sway extended westwards to the River Hilmand, for the Arabs had to fight the *zunbil* in this region. This ruler was the most important opponent of the Arabs in the lands south of the Hindu Kush and he caused much trouble for them for many years. To the south and east of present Qandahar there was a forbidding desert which was also the frontier of Iranian-speaking peoples. Presumably at that time, as today in Kalat, the population was Dravidian, composed of Brahui speakers. The lack of sources again permits only conjecture. The nature of the land, as well as the absence of any great state in the Indus valley, would lead one to suppose that the sparsely settled and inhospitable area was composed of many independent tribes and oases. There is no evidence of large organized resistance to the Arabs in their raids to the River Indus, and there are no reports of the existence of extensive settlements before reaching the Indus valley. Once in the Indus valley the Arabs were in a new world of the plains of India, which is beyond the scope of the present work.

The eastern Iranian world into which the Arabs came when they first penetrated Khurasan was variegated and with many distinctive local cultural features, as we have seen. The west Iranian culture of the Sasanians, in the last century of the empire and probably most strongly in the reign of Chosroes II, had passed far beyond the confines of Merv in the east. Although evidence is lacking, a reasonable surmise would have the spoken Middle Persian language understood in the markets of such cities as Balkh, Bukhara and Samarqand even before the Arab conquests which spread this language farther to the east and north. Sasanian motifs may be seen in profusion on the garments worn by Sogdian nobles, as depicted on wall paintings in Afrasiyab and Panjikant. This extension of Sasanian influence in the east is what one would have expected, since the great empire, as a neighbour of the small principalities in central Asia, would inevitably exercise a great attraction, especially in cultural matters, for the aristocracy of adjoining smaller states. None the less the long-held view that all art and civilization in the east was merely a provincial and pale reflection of Sasanian Iran is now universally discredited. The past of this large area, as reconstructed primarily by archaeologists, shows a long and independent tradition separate from western Iran. Whether, however, one should place all these local cultures together in one eastern Iranian as opposed to Sasanian tradition is another question. Only the future work of scholars in this field will enable us to answer many questions and to gain new perspectives in this history.[47]

Later the interaction and the unification of the western and eastern Iranian cultural spheres under the oecumene of Islam brought to pass a unity which had not existed since the time of the Achaemenids. Even then the extent of the Achaemenid unity was hardly comparable to the all-embracing Islamic unity so many centuries later. It was only under

Islam that the general Iranian epic, fusing eastern heroic stories with the more prosaic western Iranian history, was formed. It was only under Islam that a realization of Iranian unity and identity, as distinct from the Arab, came into existence. One may suppose that in the fifth century AD an educated Persian living in Fars regarded a Sogdian from the Ferghana valley as quite 'foreign'. Five centuries later an educated Persian living in Fars probably felt that the person from the Ferghana valley was quite akin to him whereas the Arab was not.

The tremendous impact of the new ideology of Islam on the ancient world has been underplayed or neglected recently in the emphasis on economic, social and political factors in the expansion of the Arabs. The power and impact of the new religion of equality did exist, however, and perhaps far more than other factors the revolutionary idealism of Islam was responsible for the success of Islam among non-Arabs. In spite of excesses, abuses of power and the human failing of blaming an entire people or nation for the wrongs of individuals, Islam as a religion and ideology brought by the Arabs transformed the entire Near East, including Iran, probably more than any other event in the past millennia of this part of the globe. We must turn to the Arab conquest of Iran to follow the events and reconstruct the changes which followed.

CHAPTER 4

THE ARAB CONQUESTS IN IRAN

It is not the intention of this book nor is it in the competence of the author to discuss the internal relations between Arab Muslims, Arab non-Muslims, non-Arab Muslims, groups such as 'people of the book', and others. We are here concerned only with Iran and not with events in Arabia. None the less certain general considerations about Islam and its influence on Arab society must be mentioned before the story of the conquests in Iran can be told.

Islam was undoubtedly the most profound social and religious revolution to take place in the history of the Arabs, if not in the entire Near East. The Arab tribes were shaken as never before or since, for the Arab Muslim in theory after Islam was no longer bound to his tribe with its common property and tribal obligations; rather, personal duties and rights were to replace the tribal solidarity, and the individual Muslim was obligated to defend the entire Islamic community (*'umma*), if necessary by war (*jihad*). The individual Muslims, called *mukallaf* in the sources, were equal before the law, and each was responsible for fulfilling the five duties imposed by Islam: the profession of faith (*shahada*), prayer (*salat*), fasting in the month of Ramadan (*saum*), alms, theoretically a tenth of one's property (*zakat*), and the pilgrimage to Mecca (*hajj*). Sometimes, in the history of Islam, *jihad* is mentioned as another pillar of the faith equivalent to the others mentioned above. This was the theory of the religion, but in practice, as might be expected, much was not observed. For example, the collection of alms in Umaiyad times became a state responsibility, a kind of tax limited to Arabs, a tax on all their property. More important for Iran, however, were the new conceptions of society developed under early Islam.

In the *shari'a* or Islamic religious code the community of Islam was made distinct from non-Muslims, and in later tradition the community was defined as composed of the aristocracy (*al-khassa*) and the common folk (*al-'amma*). There was, however, another basis of classification, which might be called a social division, between, first, free Arab

Muslims, secondly, non-Arab Muslims (*maula*), who in the beginning of the Arab conquests were attached as clients to Arab tribes, thirdly, the non-Muslims (*dhimmi*), and, finally, slaves (*'abd* or 'personal' and *mamluk* or 'state', also purchased).[1] This division of society was not propagated as a religious dogma, but it was none the less real and operative. The social theories as well as the realities of Islam encountered in the east the class structure of Sasanian Iran, which was one of a traditional caste division into priests, warriors, scribes and artisans. The result of the meeting of the two was not so much a collision as an accommodation, for in some ways Zoroastrian social beliefs paralleled the Islamic; in the former people were divided between followers of the 'good religion', as Zoroastrianism was called by its followers, and all others. It should be noted that the Iranian social class divisions did not vanish but continued into Islamic times, and both Nasir al-Din Tusi and Nizam al-Mulk upheld the correctness of this division of society in their writings.[2] That such conceptions could be accommodated to Islam indicates the power of tradition in Iran, even though the religion had changed. We will return to general considerations of Iran under Islam, however, in a later chapter, after a survey of the conquests and the establishment of Islam in western Iran and in central Asia.

The reasons for the fall of the Sasanian empire to the Arabs are varied, and they have been enumerated many times by historians. The exhausting wars with Byzantium, and the consequent turmoil in the succession to the throne of the king of kings, have often been cited as the prime reason for the inability of the Sasanians to resist the Arab armies. The new strength in unity of the Arab tribes under Islam is usually mentioned as being of equal significance. But even without Islam, the victory of a short-lived union of Arab tribes over a Sasanian army at Dhu Qar some time around the turn of the seventh century had indicated that a unified group of nomads could overcome an army of settled folk. The impetus of the new religion of Islam, however, should not be under-rated in the brilliant victories of the Arabs, for it did provide the unity as well as the inspiration and drive to conquest.

In any event the Arab army sent by the Caliph Abu Bakr to conquer Iraq, just after the death of Muhammad, marched against al-Hira, the old capital of the Lakhmids, which was still an important centre in the eyes of the Arabs.[3] Furthermore, the city was strategically located to the north of the great swamp of lower Iraq, on the edge of the desert, and it was the military centre of the Sasanian defence against the nomads. For invaders coming from the desert the city was thus a key to Iraq, and it was inhabited for the most part by Christian Arabs. Shortly after the first raids into Iraq the famous Arab general Khalid

b. al-Walid took charge of all the forces which assembled about al-Hira in the usual manner of bedouins gathering from all sides. This was early in the year 12/633 and the Persians apparently were unprepared to meet such a challenge. There is no evidence that the Arabs in the town, from the tribe of Bakr b. Wa'il and others, made common cause with the Muslim invaders. On the contrary, they defended al-Hira against the Muslims after the Persian troops had been driven from the town and defeated, which does not mean, on the other hand, that they were pro-Sasanian.[4] They defended themselves against any outsiders. The town was taken by the Muslims, however, in the summer, probably in Rabiʿ al-awwal 12/June 633.

The Arabic sources do not always coincide; indeed many times they are contradictory about the course of events of the conquests. It is not our task in this work to attempt to harmonize the different accounts of the same affairs in the sources, which, of course, is an important task in Islamic history, but rather we must concentrate on those matters which are relevant to Iran. The general course of events can be surmised by a comparison of the sources, even though details present many problems. It is uncertain, for example, how many forts or castles were taken by Khalid b. al-Walid or other Muslim detachments before the conquest of al-Hira, or whether any battles were fought before the capture of the city. Certain traditions of large-scale fighting before the submission of al-Hira seem to be apocryphal, but the tradition that al-Hira sent the first tribute from the Sasanian empire proper to Abu Bakr in Medina seems to be correct. The amount of the tribute, as reported in various later sources, is so varied that no reliance can be placed on any of the traditions.

After the capture of al-Hira there were probably raids elsewhere in Iraq, but all indications point to a conflict of Muslim Arab against Christian or pagan Arab, or settled Aramaean inhabitant of the land, rather than against the Persians. The main military force of the Muslims under Khalid, however, was ordered to the west to aid in the invasion of the Byzantine empire, and only al-Hira and surrounding territory remained in the hands of the Muslims under the command of al-Muthanna b. Haritha al-Shaibani.

The Persians had probably regarded the Muslim advance on al-Hira as another annoying raid of the bedouins. For ages it had been the practice of bedouins from the desert to obtain booty or to levy tribute on towns, so the initial advance of the Muslims cannot have frightened the Persians too much, although some later sources speak of great alarm in Ctesiphon as a result of the early Arab raids. Since the Muslims remained in al-Hira, however, it was obviously a continuing threat to Sasanian supremacy in Iraq, so the Persians prepared for a counter strike against al-Hira. The Muslims, meanwhile, were busy in Palestine and Syria when the caliph Abu Bakr died in the year 13 on 21 Jumada al-thani/22 August 634 and was succeeded by 'Umar. Some Arabic sources assert that Yazdegird had not yet succeeded to the throne of the Sasanian empire and that the Persians were involved in problems of succession, but in reality the last ruler of Iran had assumed power before the fall of al-Hira. This is not to deny possible discord at the beginning of Yazdegird's reign, and even disunion and strife among the Persians, but the new ruler was surely acknowledged by this date. As mentioned above, many sources are contradictory and it is frequently difficult to arrange various skirmishes or conquests of towns in a proper chronological order. The number of warriors involved in the early raids is usually also exaggerated in the sources as is the amount of booty taken, but in a general account these details are not significant.

The motives behind this first invasion of Iraq also cannot be investigated here. Suffice it to say that there was no apparent plan of conquest and rule, but the booty obtained, either by tribute levied or by plunder, stimulated other Arabs both in Arabia and in Iraq to join the Muslim forces. The Muslim Arabs, however, had at first little thought of making conversions to the faith; rather they thought only of booty, but this was to change later. The complicated unions and then separations of various Arab tribes during the conquests cannot be discussed here. Perhaps pagan members of the Bakr tribe at the beginning, for example, did join the Muslim Arabs against their tribal compatriots, Christian members of the Bakr tribe in Iraq, but inter-tribal conflicts of the Arabs during the early raids were on the whole sublimated until most of Persia had been conquered. These internal tribal questions, however, are very complicated.

The Persians prepared to re-take al-Hira and the new caliph 'Umar sent reinforcements under Abu 'Ubaid al-Thaqafi to the Muslim garrison of the city. The Muslims advanced over the Euphrates and met the Persians in battle. At the 'battle of the bridge' over the river the Muslims were disastrously defeated and Abu 'Ubaid was slain; this battle took place towards the end of the year 13/634. The Persians, however, did not advance directly upon al-Hira, perhaps because of internal quarrels or fear of the bedouins, but they did re-occupy al-Hira in the following year. The caliph was upset by the news of the defeat at the bridge and sent new recruits, especially from Yemen, to raid Iraq. The former Muslim 'governor' of al-Hira, al-Muthanna, took the initiative and defeated the Persians in a battle called al-Buwaib, possibly in the month of Ramadan 13/November 635.[5] The Persian commander Mihran was killed and the Muslims re-occupied al-Hira. During this same period Muslim Arabs seem to have occupied lands in southern Iraq around the future city of Basra. More important for the Muslims were the conquests in Syria and the victories against the

Byzantines. After the victory on the River Yarmuk in Palestine the caliph ʿUmar sent Saʿd b. Abi Waqqas, a companion of the prophet, against the Persians with a larger body of troops than had been gathered at any of the previous raids against the Sasanian empire.

The Persians were now fully alive to the danger and assembled an imperial army under the command of their top general Rustam. Again the sources are contradictory, but it would seem that the Arabs retired before the Sasanian army and awaited reinforcements from Syria. The numbers of troops on both sides cannot be established, but the unequal numbers on the two sides is certainly exaggerated. The Persians probably had more troops than the Arabs, but not many more, and the numbers involved were probably not more than twenty-five to thirty thousand men altogether. The battle took place at al-Qadisiyya to the west of al-Hira, possibly on Jumada I, 16/June 637, and when Rustam was killed in the fighting the Persians broke and fled. It is difficult to accept the claims of Arab poets and other authors that the Muslims before the battle had called on Yazdegird and the Persians to adopt Islam. Many stories are told, the reliability of which is difficult to determine. The war elephants of the Persians seem to have caused great trouble for the Arabs, while the Arab reinforcements from Syria probably turned the tide in favour of the Muslims.

After the battle of al-Qadisiyya the Muslims were able to advance into the heart of Iraq to the River Tigris opposite Ctesiphon, also called al-Mada'in. They met with some resistance on the way, but the Sasanian capital could not be defended, and after a short siege and the flight of Yazdegird towards the east, the Arabs occupied the complex of towns probably a month after their victory at al-Qadisiyya. The booty seized by the Muslims was great and it undoubtedly induced many pagan or Christian Arabs who had joined the Muslim army to be converted. The Persians, however, gathered at a site called Jalula' north-east of Ctesiphon and near the Zagros mountains. There the Arabs again defeated the Sasanian force, possibly in December of the same year 16/637. It seems clear that once the imperial army was defeated at al-Qadisiyya no important force could be assembled in Iraq, especially during the summer, to stop the victorious Arab forces. It is reported that the Sasanian king waited at the town of Hulwan to hear the results of Jalula', and then he fled into the highlands of his native land.[6] Iraq was lost to the victorious Arabs and they were not slow in occupying all of it.

The resistance of the local people to the Muslims after the Sasanian defeats was neither strong nor prolonged, and detachments of Muslim Arabs occupied most of the plains within several years. New groups of Arabs from the peninsula moved into the fertile lands of Mesopotamia. In many cases the tribute levied on the settled population was less than their former taxes paid to the Sasanian government. On the whole the number of Muslims was swelled by recruits from the peninsula, rather than from the conquered local Arab or Aramaean population of Iraq, much of which was Christian. The Muslim Arabs were in Iraq to stay, since they now settled down to rule the land. The military camp (*misr*) of Basra was probably founded shortly after the battle of al-Qadisiyya by an Arab leader 'Utba b. Ghazwan who came from Medina as an independent leader to southern Iraq, and not as a subordinate to Sa'd b. Abi Waqqas, the victor of al-Qadisiyya.[7] Once a base was established in the south, it was easy to raid to the east into the rich province of Khuzistan. Shortly after the foundation of Basra, Sa'd b. Abi Waqqas was probably ordered by 'Umar to leave Ctesiphon and establish a centre for central and northern Mesopotamia near the desert. Thus not far from al-Hira was founded Kufa, the sister camp of Basra.

From 17 to 21/637–41 the Arabs slowly conquered Khuzistan, which offered more local resistance than any other area in the lowlands of Mesopotamia. The resistance was not centrally organized even though some Arabic sources give great prominence to the activities of the governor of the province, al-Hurmuzan. He gave resistance to the Arabs, however, not as the leader of any central provincial force, but rather as an organizer of successive local resistances to the Muslims. Suq al-Ahwaz was taken early but other towns near to or in the mountains held out longer. About 19/640 the Arabs invaded Fars province by sea from Bahrain, and their raid was successful in that many towns submitted and paid tribute, but the Arabs soon withdrew from the highlands to the coastal plains. In 21/641 al-Hurmuzan was captured by or submitted to the Arabs and was sent to Medina.[8] Yazdegird, meanwhile, was not idle but had gathered a large army on the Iranian plateau with the hope of defeating the Arabs and reconquering Iraq. The Arabs learned of these preparations and 'Umar ordered troops from the new military centres of Kufa and Basra to prepare for war with the Persians. The new force was placed under the command of a certain al-Nu'man b. Muqarrin.

The Muslim army which advanced into Persia to fight the Sasanian army was different from the forces which had defeated the Persians at al-Qadisiyya. The *diwan*, or roll of the Arab warriors (*muqatila*) had been instituted, the military organization of the tribesmen had been improved, and great numbers of bedouins had migrated from the Arab peninsula to the military camps of Basra and Kufa to participate in the wars of conquest, which had now become holy wars of Islam (*jihad*) rather than mere raids for plunder. In other words the Muslims were stronger and better organized than a few years before the battle of Nihavand. One might surmise that the press of immigration of the tribesmen from all over Arabia, south as well as north, catalysed the further Arab conquests in Iran as well as elsewhere.

It seems probable that the Arabs took the offensive to destroy Persian resistance before it became stronger. Al-Nuʿman had been active in the conquest of Khuzistan, so he was an experienced warrior. Various Persians are mentioned in different sources as the leader of Sasanian forces, including one Mardanshah b. Hurmuz, a high-born Sasanian noble, who was killed in the battle. Again traditions of the battle of Nihavand are contradictory.[9] It is certain, however, that this was the most difficult battle of all those which the Arabs had to fight against imperial Sasanian forces. The losses on the Arab side, including the commander al-Nuʿman, indicate the severity of the battle. Whether the Muslims drew the Persians by a ruse from their fortified positions and then defeated them, or if other strategems were used, is unclear. In any event this battle sealed the fate of the Sasanian central authority, but not of local forces in Iran. Henceforth the Arabs had to deal with local resistance, sometimes extremely obstinate, but the central authority of the Sasanian state was effectively destroyed. After the battle, which took place in the spring or summer of 21/642, the forces from Kufa and from Basra separated in their plans for further conquest, the Kufans responsible for the north and the Basrans for the southern part of Persia. The great losses in the battle of Nihavand restrained the Arabs who advanced cautiously and slowly after the battle. There was no doubt, however, that the organized resistance of the central government of Sasanian Iran was ended. Once the central authority was gone resistance was of necessity local, which nevertheless did not always reduce its severity.

The city of Nihavand was taken and Arab forces advanced to Raiy. Once on the plateau, of course, the Arabs had no severe geographical obstacles to retard their expansion. In the following year 22/642–3 Azerbaijan, the cities of Hamadan, Qum and smaller towns elsewhere were conquered. The chief source for these and later conquests in Iran is the work of al-Baladhuri, himself of Persian origin, and other authors serve to complement his observations. Once the Arab forces had spread over the Iranian plateau, the conquest proceeded swiftly, but we must ask if the policy of conquest there was different from that which governed the earliest raids outside the Arabian peninsula. It would seem that in Iran there was a plan of conquest. From the sources one has the impression that the earliest raids into the lowlands of Mesopotamia were unplanned and in the nature of forays for booty, as had been the custom of the bedouins for centuries. The first two caliphs realized that the Muslim bedouins could not change their natures simply by the adoption of Islam. On the other hand, the desire of the bedouins to raid could be coupled with the missionary zeal of the

Muslim leaders around the caliph to further the expansion of the faith. It has been the fashion recently to deny any religious motivation behind the Muslim conquests. This is at the other extreme from the picture of the Arab from the desert with fanatic zeal to convert or kill those who refused. Both religious and economic motives were present in the conquests, as well as a desire to conquer, which latter was neither solely bound up with religion nor just with the hope of booty. It is impossible here to discuss the various motives which stimulated the Arabs to conquest, for they were not only many and varied but also of different importance at different times. Rather one may ask how an inhabitant of Iraq, for example, Arab or Persian, became a Muslim or joined the Muslim forces.

As we have mentioned, Persians were known to the Arabs in their homeland of the Arabian peninsula, and in Mecca itself there were probably Persians, other than Salman al-Farisi, who became a Muslim before the expansion of the Arab armies into the Fertile Crescent. What was the status of such non-Arab Muslims? The term *maula* appears many times in the sources as one who joined Islam in the early days of the conquests, and this term must be examined. There was a change from the Qur'anic meaning of 'helper' or 'patron', and also from the presumably pre-Islamic significance of the word among the tribes meaning one who became a relative or associate of a tribe. In the very early conquests non-Muslims were simply made prisoners of war or slaves, but obviously with swollen numbers of subject peoples other mechanisms were needed to integrate conquered peoples into the Islamic community. So the old Arab tribal system of *maula* (pl. *mawali*), usually translated as 'client', came into force. One may suppose that in Iraq many officials of the defeated Sasanian regime joined the Arab Muslim forces; for example, ʿAmr the son of ʿAdi b. Zaid, the famous Christian poet in Arabic at al-Hira, may have joined the Muslim forces as an interpreter without becoming a Muslim. Baladhuri tells us that after the battle of al-Qadisiyya, some 4,000 troops of the imperial guard, the *jund-i shahanshah*, joined the Muslim army.[10] He also tells an interesting story of the conversion of a large group of Sasanian cavalry, the *asawira* (pl. of *suwar*), who settled in Basra but chose to associate themselves with the Tamim tribe rather than with the Azd whom they had at first considered joining.[11] This indicates that the prospective clients were by no means subjugated and at the mercy of their masters, but could even choose their patrons. Obviously other cases were different, which reveals the variety of relationships in the early Islamic period. After the battle of Jalula' many Persian troops who realized the hopelessness of the Sasanian cause joined the Muslim armies.[12] There is no evidence of religious proselytizing in this early period; rather, conversion to Islam was more for political or military than for religious reasons. Most Arabs and Persians seem to have viewed conversion to Islam in this light. Basra and Kufa grew in size as people flocked to the two military camps to join the Muslim cause. While there is no evidence that the Muslim armies actively tried to make conversions, it appears that the caliph 'Umar was already seeking to restrict conversions to Islam only to the Arabs. One tradition claims that he stopped the victorious Arabs from invading the Iranian plateau after the battle of Jalula' because he did not wish to convert Persians to Islam.[13] Often one cannot trust later tradition, but certainly the practice of dividing booty among the Muslim warriors after a battle or after the conquest of a town must have caused the Muslim leaders to have second thoughts about conversions. At first the Muslim armies apparently needed and welcomed extra support, but it is difficult to believe that they welcomed swollen ranks after the battle of Nihavand. For one thing, new converts meant additional pensions to be paid. The system of pensions, the '*ata*', deserves a few words of comment.

If a slave were captured in battle by a Muslim Arab, he usually remained a slave in the service of his new master as part of the booty. Prisoners of war who were not slaves might ransom themselves or be reduced to slavery. By accepting Islam the slave was not thereby freed. His master had to free him, which was regarded as a meritorious act in Islam. We have seen that enemy forces which surrendered could become attached to an Arab tribe as *mawali*. Could they, however, participate fully in the prerogatives of Arab Muslims, especially in regard to the division of the spoils of war? This question caused difficulties for the caliph 'Umar who had to concern himself with this problem. It is clear that there was no uniform system or practice of tribute or taxation in the Arab Muslim empire in the process of its formation. Indeed in most regions agreements between the conquering Arabs and the local people seem to have been almost ad hoc arrangements. The '*ata*', or pension system, was instituted by the caliph 'Umar to systematize the rewards and pensions from the great amount of spoils which came into the central coffers during his reign. As Claude Cahen well describes the system,

> according to a hierarchic order which took into account kinship with the Prophet and especially seniority as regards admission to Islam, graduated pensions were distributed to the whole Muslim population which had been displaced from its homes by the holy war, women, children, slaves and clients (still not numerous and not by definition foreigners), but excluding, of course, the bedouins and others who remained in Arabia and elsewhere, unaffected by the military expansion of Islam.[14]

The *diwan*, or bureaucracy for the records, was instituted through necessity, and it was not without a Sasanian prototype as a model. The pension system was open to abuse, and many complaints were raised that pensions were used as rewards, or were raised, lowered or transferred at the whim of the caliph or of any army commander. At first the assignment of pensions was on a tribal basis, but soon it became a more local affair, which meant that certain revenues from a locality were assigned to persons settled there. In his discussion of the pension system Baladhuri describes how pensions were assigned to Persian *dihqans*, the landed aristocracy, such as al-Hurmuzan, who had surrendered to the Arabs and embraced Islam.[15] He further relates that the caliph 'Umar wrote to the commander of the Arab armies to give *mawali* or client status to foreign freemen who had accepted Islam. So we may conclude that most Persian soldiers entered the ranks of Islam as slaves who were captured, or as freed slaves, although some of the aristocracy or soldiery became clients of their own free will. Some non-Muslim Persians of course joined the army as camp followers or as scribes, tax-collectors or the like. Some Muslim Persians were apparently assigned pensions individually, though most received their pay through the tribes to which they were attached as clients. The numbers of foreigners who joined the Muslims of course increased as the conquests expanded. Whence came the money to pay for the pensions and the expenses of the new state in formation? We must turn briefly to the thorny problem of taxation.

It is now generally accepted that taxation was by no means uniform throughout the lands conquered by the Muslims. Likewise the terms of capitulation of various towns and districts were by no means uniform, but as a general practice the terms of surrender, either peacefully (*sulh*) or by warfare (*'anwatan*), provided a source of revenue for the Muslims until a regular system of taxation replaced the treaty. This process usually took time and a new system of *jizya* 'poll or head tax' and *kharaj* 'land tax' was not instituted from the beginning, as the interpretation of some later sources would have it. In all probability no new system was in fact introduced but only a reform of the pre-Islamic Sasanian system of taxation. In this sense the statement of Yahya b. Adam al-Qurashi is probably correct:

> The Muslims, when they defeated the Persians, left the Sawad (southern Iraq), and those of the Nabat and *dihqans* who had not fought the Muslims, in the same position (as previously). They imposed the *jizya* on the heads of the men, surveyed the land in their possession and charged *kharaj* on it. Any land not possessed by anyone was seized as *sawafi* (state land).[16]

The last, mostly former imperial land of the Sasanians, presented problems for the new caliphate, and much discussion and controversy has existed about the actual practices of administration and about later theories projected back to the time of the conquests.

To summarize the situation in the lowlands of Mesopotamia: those towns which had surrendered and made treaties with the Muslims were permitted to continue to pay the agreed tribute, collecting such money in the manner that the local officials wished. On land outside this category the caliph 'Umar imposed a tax, probably the same as under the Sasanians and collected by the local *dihqans* as previously, although it is probable that adjustments were made in it in later years. The caliph dealt with *sawafi* land as he pleased since it was land formerly belonging to the Sasanian government or to nobles who had been killed or had fled. Under 'Uthman and his successors much of this land was given to favourites as fiefs. Some sources, such as Ya'qubi, say that only under Mu'awiya did his famous governor of Iraq, Ziyad b. Abihi, establish the fixed administration of the province, which until that time had followed various arrangements established at the time of the conquests.[17] It seems clear that Iraq presented problems for the conquering Arabs, for fellow tribesmen as well as settled Arabs and non-Arabs were present; some towns submitted to the Arabs before being attacked, whereupon they made treaties stipulating a fixed yearly tribute. Some lands were abandoned by their owners and the administration of these fell to the conquerors. Likewise, problems of new Arab Muslims, of non-Arab Muslims, slaves and clients had to be met by the conquerors.

On the Iranian plateau the situation was simpler, since the Arab Muslim armies were faced with a non-Arab, completely non-Muslim population which had to be subdued. Unfortunately, sources for the Arab conquests on the Iranian plateau are few, and, unlike Iraq, we may assume that there was a greater uniformity in the conditions imposed by the conquest of, and submission by, the local people. On the plateau the Arabs made treaties with each town they captured, which treaties included the villages and surrounding countryside which depended on the town.

The Arabs knowingly and purposefully spread over the plateau to conquer and to expand their power. As noted, after the battle of Nihavand an Arab army took the cities of Dinawar and Masabadan and then proceeded to Raiy where the local forces were defeated. According to Baladhuri the defeated people made peace with the Arabs on the same terms as the people of Nihavand.[18] It is interesting to note that Raiy, as well as other places, revolted against the Arabs after making peace, possibly in protest against later attempts to obtain more money from them.

The Arab forces which conquered the northern part of Iran were mainly under the aegis of Kufa, whereas those who moved against Isfahan and the south were from Basra, although in the beginning they sometimes operated together. At the conquest of Qum and Kashan, however, the forces of Basra were paramount. In both towns severe fighting preceded the capitulation of the local people. Because of the protest of the Basrans that the Kufans were obtaining more returns from the conquests than they were, the caliph 'Umar divided the conquests on the plateau between the two cities. In this division the city of Nihavand was called the Mah (Media) of Basra while Dinawar received the designation Mah of Kufa.

Azerbaijan was the next goal of the Muslims and the *marzban*, the supreme governor of the province rather than just a military leader, assembled forces to meet the invaders. After heavy fighting the invaders were again victorious, and terms were made which indicate the overwhelming interest of the Muslims in obtaining booty. As Baladhuri and others report the terms of settlement, in addition to a large yearly tribute in *dirhems*, the leader of the Arab army, Hudhaifa b. al-Yaman, undertook 'not to kill or enslave any of the (population of Azerbaijan), nor raze any fire temples, nor expose them to danger from the Kurds, nor to hinder the people of Shiz in their religious practices'.[19] The wide depredations of the Muslims in Azerbaijan were noted by Sebeos, an Armenian historian who confirms and complements the Arabic sources.[20] It seems that these early conquests did not really mean the definitive subjugation of an area but rather the payment of tribute after the conclusion of a pact which was probably regarded as a temporary measure by both sides, at least in the beginning.

Azerbaijan seems to have remained more loyal to the Arab Muslims than other provinces, especially Fars, which were in frequent rebellion. Baladhuri tells of the rapid progress of Islam in Azerbaijan and, although this must be taken with a grain of salt, the fact that both the local population and the missionary oriented Arabs in the army of conquest were more inclined to accept the new situation, cannot be excluded as the possible basis for Baladhuri's statement.[21] Furthermore Azerbaijan was exposed to raids by Kurds and Khazars, from north of the Caucasus, while Byzantine and Armenian territories were adjacent. So Azerbaijan as a frontier province may be considered atypical of the land on the Iranian plateau. Minor revolts against Arab Muslim rule are reported there for the years 25/645 and 30/650, but on the whole the province remained peaceful. Many Arabs were settled in Azerbaijan since it was a frontier province against the Byzantines and against the Caucasus mountains. The actual extent of Arab rule in Azerbaijan is uncertain because of the lack of information in the sources, but we may assume that the Arabs reached the famous Sasanian frontier fortress of Derbend and obtained the submission of the Persian forces there.

Meanwhile the conquest of Fars province began in earnest, for the earlier invasions from across the Persian Gulf had been mere raids for plunder. By 23/643 Tawwaj in Khuzistan had been captured by 'Uthman b. Abi'l-'As after a severe battle with the governor of Fars at Rishahr. After this 'Umar ordered him to invade Fars with the aid of Abu Musa from Basra. Most of the towns of the province capitulated and agreed to pay tribute to the Arabs, although some broke their treaties after the Arabs left. It is impossible to follow the events with any certainty, but the stronger resistance of the inhabitants of Fars, as compared with other provinces, seems certain. Istakhr, the capital, was particularly obstinate in resistance. It was apparent to the Arabs that especially strong measures were needed to hold this province since the initial advances were more like raids than actual conquest. It was not until the caliphate of 'Uthman that a concerted effort was made not only to subdue but also to hold the province. The caliph sent the governor of Basra, 'Abdallah b. 'Amir b. Kuraiz, with a large army, probably in 29/649, to subdue and hold Fars. It seems that Darabjird was surrendered by a *herbad* or Zoroastrian priest who was in charge of the city.[22] Istakhr was taken after heavy fighting and many of the nobility were killed. The towns of Fars, after a series of revolts, were apparently finally conquered by the Arabs under 'Abdallah, which may be considered as a turning point from raids to permanent occupation.

Although our information is sparse and uncertain, it appears that Yazdegird had taken refuge in Istakhr after the battle of Nihavand and, with the advance of the Arab armies in Fars, had fled to Kirman. 'Abdallah apparently sent a strong detachment in pursuit of Yazdegird, but the latter fled farther to Khurasan, leaving Kirman to the Arab conquerors. 'Abdallah b. 'Amir was persistent and sent one of his lieutenants with a force into Seistan in 30/650. In the same year 'Abdallah turned his attention to Khurasan and the fleeing Sasanian monarch. The Arab vanguard under al-Ahnaf b. Qais was sent across the central desert through Tabbas to Kuhistan, south of Khurasan, some sources claiming Isfahan as his point of departure while others claim Yazd. The goal of his expedition, however, seems to have been the fertile oasis of Nishapur which was taken by the Arabs. It is interesting that Baladhuri says that the *asawira*, the Persian cavalry mentioned above, went with Ahnaf to Khurasan, an indication of the growing importance of the *mawali* in the armies of Islam.[23] The *asawira* continued to be favoured people under Islam as they had been under the Sasanians, for they did not pay taxes when they joined the Arab forces.[24]

Nishapur, or Abrshahr as it is called in early Arabic sources, was not taken without a fight. After the conquest of Nishapur a treaty was made stipulating the payment of a tribute of a million *dirhems*, but all figures of tribute paid to the Arabs from various towns in Iran are uncertain. One may infer from the amounts of tribute mentioned by Baladhuri and others little more than the relative prosperity or wealth of one district as compared with another. Such well-known towns of today as

Herat, Nishapur and Tus (*hodie* near Mashhad) were apparently also city centres at the time of the Arab conquests. ʿAbdallah b. ʿAmir was the Arab conqueror of Khurasan, but the dates of his various exploits are uncertain. Likewise, the movements of Yazdegird are uncertain, but it seems that after the capture of Istakhr he fled to Seistan and then to Khurasan. Whether the Arabs were deliberately pursuing him is also difficult to determine, but it is possible. In any case, both Yazdegird and the Arabs would head for Merv, the Sasanian army stronghold of the east. That he crossed the Oxus and then recrossed it to Balkh is most unlikely; his murder in the Merv oasis is much more plausible, although legends probably grew up about his end.[25] The death of Yazdegird III, the last Sasanian ruler, was thus similar to the end of the last Achaemenid, Darius, and it occurred in 31/651.

With Yazdegird in his flight to the east went many followers, especially from among the Persian nobility. Nothing is told of their fate, but we may assume that many of them fled farther to the east, and some, like Peroz, son of Yazdegird, died in China. Although Sui China was interested in events in central Asia, there was little hope of Chinese aid for the descendants of the Sasanian kings. With the death of Yazdegird and the capitulation of Merv, Sasanian resistance was practically at an end. Later attempts to restore the Sasanian dynasty were really without hope of success, although at the time the defeat and retreat of the Arabs from Iran must have seemed a real possibility to many Iranians.

Just as Merv had been the military capital of the Sasanians on the frontier with Transoxiana, so the same oasis became the centre of Arab military operations in the east. The *marzban* of Merv made peace with ʿAbdallah b. ʿAmir for a large tribute, variously reported but apparently the largest amount from all the districts of the east. Baladhuri says that in the original treaty it was agreed that the Arabs should receive living quarters in Merv and that the collection of the taxes was the responsibility of the local population and not of the Arabs.[26] This implies that in other cases the Arabs themselves collected the taxes, although this is uncertain. In the early years of the conquest the taxes or tribute, for they were at that time identical, were collected mostly in kind not in coin, and slaves were one of the important commodities in the payment of tribute. Again there is a problem with the chronology of events since the subsequent raids to the east and north by Muslims from their main base in Merv apparently date from after the time of ʿAbdallah b. ʿAmir.

It would seem that the treaty with Merv was concluded in the year 36/656, about four years after the death of Yazdegird and in the same year as the death of ʿUthman. By this time the purely Arab nature of the Muslim armies in the east was a myth, for strong detachments of Sasanian soldiers as well as individual Persians had joined the forces of Islam with or without conversion to Islam. We must examine this process of the growth of Islamic armies.

One must distinguish between the early armies of Islam and the situation under the Umaiyads. We have mentioned that Persian soldiers joined the Arab armies early in the capacity of auxiliaries, or more often either as personal *mawali* of prominent Arabs or simply as general *mawali* of a tribe. In both cases, of course, tribal responsibility for the newcomers was assumed. The *mawali* received no pay or part of the booty since their patrons were supposed to take care of them and allocate rewards.[27] The *mawali* at first generally accepted this, but later they were to demand equal rights with Arab Muslims.[28] Slaves were not expected to fight, although they frequently followed their masters on campaigns and took care of the camps. Even with the influx of Persian *mawali* into the armies of Islam, however, the expansion of Islamic domains into central Asia required ever greater manpower, and under the Umaiyads it was not at all unusual to find many 'people of the book', the *dhimmi*, performing military service.[29] Later, under the Umaiyads, some governors had to threaten the *dhimmis* with a loss of their rights in order to keep them in the army.[30]

Obviously many problems beset the Umaiyads in their attempts to maintain adequate military forces, especially on the frontiers, but the enmities within the Arab camps were the most difficult of all for them to surmount. These resulted in the almost exclusive use of Syrian troops, plus some Arabs from Oman and Hadhramaut, as the core of the Umaiyad armies. The Umaiyads were also not above using paid mercenaries instead of Arab troops whom they frequently could not trust. Sometimes, because of difficult fighting especially in central Asia, the Umaiyad state was very hard pressed to raise money as well as equipment and men to meet the needs on the frontier. On one occasion, it came to such a crisis that Junaid b. ʿAbd al-Rahman, governor of Khurasan, was obliged to promise their freedom to all slaves who fought with the Muslims against the Turks.[31] This was exceptional but indicative of the length to which an Arab commander would go in order to secure a victory.

It should be clear that by the Umaiyad period the Muslim armies had ceased to be purely Arab armies, even though the Arab contingents remained the core of the fighting forces. Much has been written about the dominant role of the Arab tribes, and their conflicts, in the history of the Umaiyad caliphate. The Arabic sources quite naturally stress the importance of tribal and personal struggles in history, and the *mawali* were also brought into these struggles. The fall of the Umaiyad caliphate, which was characterized as an Arab kingdom by Wellhausen, has been traditionally ascribed to the Arab tribes in Khurasan, which finally united against Umaiyad attempts to establish central authority over the provinces and brought down the government in Damascus. This view is too simple, for it would be more true to say in the same simple way that the Umaiyads fell because they failed to expand the equation 'Arab equals Islam' into a universal brotherhood with an oecumenical culture. It is true that the Umaiyads failed to reconcile the feeling of superiority of the Arabs with the contention that all Muslims were equal. But even that is not a completely adequate answer to the question of the fall of the Umaiyads, for many factors were involved of which Arab tribal rivalry was only one. We should return, however, to the process of the conversion to Islam.

It would appear that there was no master plan to settle the Arabs permanently in Iran before the time of Mu'awiya, the first Umaiyad caliph. Rather, the presence of any Arab troops at all was to ensure the collection of tribute and the observance of treaty terms. There was indeed a system of replacement and transfer of Arab tribesmen under their chiefs. Sometimes a commander would be chosen by men from various tribes, or the commander would be appointed by the governor of Basra or Kufa. This leader would usually divide his jurisdiction among tribal chiefs under him, but he was responsible for the collection of tribute and the division of booty with the traditional one-fifth going to the caliph through the governor. So the Arab *muqatila* were rotated and were bound to the garrison cities of Iraq, either Basra or Kufa. This necessitated a system of rolls, the above-mentioned *diwan*. The book-keeping was done by former Sasanian scribes in the east now part of the caliphate, writing in Arabic as well as in the Pahlavi language.

On the whole it was to the advantage of the caliph and the central government that the opponents of the Muslims should surrender rather than offer resistance, for the Arabs were supposed to remain warriors and not to interfere with the local people who paid tribute. Land and property conquered by force was to be divided among the Muslim warriors, but this of course eliminated the tribute (later the taxes, *kharaj*) which was renewable annually by treaties made when a locality surrendered. Naturally it was to the interest of the caliph to terminate the treaties and to have taxes paid on a regular basis. It is impossible to discuss here the involved problems of taxation in Iran in early Islamic times. Much has been written about it though all problems regarding the taxes are far from being solved. It is clear that conditions of taxation were different in Egypt, Iraq and Khurasan, but a general summary may suffice here.[32]

Tribute in kind on subject peoples in early times seems to have been called indiscriminately *kharaj* or *jizya*. Later *kharaj* came to mean land tax, while taxes on movable property and persons were called *jizya*. Later the word *jizya* came to be used for a poll tax on non-Muslims.

Other taxes on markets, customs duties and the like were called *maks* (pl. *mukus*). By the fourth century of the *Hijra* the tax system had become 'de-islamicized', and only the *jizya* remained as a religious institution. For by that time the *zakat*, or alms, which had been instituted as a state as well as religious obligation, had become a personal rather than a public matter. Responsibility for paying the land tax under the Sasanians had been a collective matter of a village or town, and the Arabs at first simply took over the Sasanian system, first as tribute and then as annual taxes. Consequently, the conversion of one man or family in the village to Islam did not lessen the taxes of the village. At first the new convert would usually join the Arab army and leave his village, so he gave up any land holdings he had. Obviously, as more people became Muslims and remained where they were, all sorts of difficulties arose. Usually they were solved by the central government supporting the local authorities in Iran; i.e. requiring the new convert to contribute his share of the land taxes. So gradually the poll-tax came to be the main distinction in tax obligations between Muslim and non-Muslim. Later new problems arose when many Muslim converts in villages and towns left their abodes to go to Baghdad or other large centres, leaving their lands uncultivated. This of course resulted in a tax crisis. The famous governor of Iraq, Hajjaj b. Yusuf, is said to have sent new converts back to the land and even to have forbidden conversion to Islam.[33] None the less, if a person became a Muslim to escape paying the *jizya*, he would then have to assume a new tax, the *zakat*, so the state in the end did not lose much revenue.

At first, after the conquest of Iran, the town of Kufa was made the revenue gathering centre for Azerbaijan and al-Jibal (ancient Media), while Basra received the revenues from Khuzistan, Fars, Kirman, Seistan and Khurasan. Afterwards when the Umaiyads came to power, Arabs, mostly from Basra, were settled in Merv, and that city became a revenue centre. So the process of conquest, on the economic side, is clear – from the status of tribute to regular channels of taxation. Ya'qubi says that Ziyad b. Abihi, the Umaiyad governor of Iraq, in 45/665–6 re-established 'the ancient administration of the east', including the collection of taxes.[34]

If Muslim troops were stationed in a town on the Iranian plateau, the military ruler of the place would be an Arab *amir*, while the tax collector could be a non-Muslim *dihqan*, or a Muslim *'amil*, or the two offices could be combined in one person. Finally the representative of the Muslim legal authority would be a *qadi*. The three important offices, military, financial and legal, were the bases of Muslim rule in the east, but, except for the *qadi*, they did not have to be Muslims.

Relations between Arab Muslims and non-Muslims were regulated by religious decrees, but difficulties arose between Arab Muslims and non-Arab Muslims, the *mawali*. Theoretically under Islam all Muslims were equal, but obviously there were many sources of conflict. Some Arabs believed that non-Arabs should not clothe themselves as Arabs, and many other forms of discrimination existed.[35] On the whole, however, the discontent of the *mawali* as second-class Muslims was mainly on social grounds, and among other groups in the caliphate there was little, if any, anti-Muslim activity, and actually relatively little anti-Arab reaction. The fact that the conquered population was at a higher level of education and general culture, dominating the bureaucracy and learning, was also a sore point with many Arabs. This antagonism was to culminate in the *Shuʿubiyya* movement of ʿAbbasid times which will be discussed later.

Where did the Arabs settle in Iran? It seems clear that they followed much the same pattern as the Greeks under Alexander and others who sought to control the plateau. Fars and Media were not heavily settled since these provinces, especially Fars, remained both quiet and also predominantly non-Muslim, once the revolts had been crushed and treaties established, for a long time. In the north Qazvin, on the Khurasan road, needed a garrison to fight the Dailamites, mountaineers of the Elburz range to the north. Ardebil, the capital of Azerbaijan, an outpost against the Caucasus, was also a centre of Arab settlement. Presumably many towns on the Khurasan road to the east had Arab garrisons, but the great military centre of the Arabs in the east was Merv. Seistan was also a frontier province and Arabs were settled there to protect the hinterland as well as to extend the frontiers of Islam to the east. We must return, however, to chronology.

By the time of the murder of the caliph ʿUthman in 656, Iran had been conquered by the Arabs and garrisons had been settled in a few places to ensure the collection of tribute. The Arabs who had settled in Basra were primarily the Tamim, a north Arabian tribe of the Rabiʿa group of tribes. These were also the tribes which went to Khurasan. Later in Basra and in Khurasan they were joined by the Azd, a south Arabian or Yemenite tribe. In Kufa the leading tribes were Qais, of the Mudar group, and Kinda, a Yemenite tribe. It is not possible to follow the shifting tribal allegiances and alliances, except to remark that the tribes looked after their own interests and little else. The death of ʿUthman, however, led to the first civil war in Islam when tribal enmities and new religious oppositions were mixed in bloody conflict. This conflict, though momentous for the Arabs and for Islam, had few repercussions among the Persian population. The aftermath of the battle of Siffin in 657, however, did have consequences for Iran, for the Muslim rebels against ʿAli, the Kharijites, moved into Persia after defeats in Iraq at the hand of the caliph. A certain Kharijite leader called al-Khirrit b. Rashid raised some Persian Muslims as well as

Christians against ʿAli. This revolt in Khuzistan and Fars may have been more than just another Kharijite revolt; rather it may have had elements of a general anti-Islamic movement on the part of certain non-Muslim Arab bedouins with Persian support. Unfortunately the sources are not clear. The revolt was suppressed and the leader killed in 38/658.

The local population of Fars and Kirman had refused to pay taxes to ʿAli, so he sent Ziyad b. Abihi as governor (*amir*) of the two provinces. Ziyad was able to pacify the area and establish his headquarters near Istakhr.[36] Elsewhere it seems that Arab rule was not contested in this period. At least we hear of no great uprisings on the Iranian plateau. It is highly probable that there was really very little Arab control save for the collection of taxes. The situation was changed, however, with the assassination of the caliph ʿAli at the hands of a Kharijite on the 17th of Ramadan in the year 40 or 25 January 661. Shortly afterwards Muʿawiya received the allegiance of Ziyad, governor of southern Iran, and a few years later the caliph extended Ziyad's jurisdiction by making him governor of Basra and viceroy over all of the domains of the Muslims in southern Iran to the River Indus. Other parts of Iran, however, did not accept Umaiyad rule easily.

From a study of the coinage compared with literary sources, one can reconstruct the ebb and flow of personal politics plus the usurpation of certain areas, usually for short periods, by rebels against the central government. It is, of course, almost impossible to differentiate between uprisings motivated by religious or political reasons, for in Islam it is difficult to distinguish between the two. The internecine struggles of the Arabs, however, cannot be our main concern, since the local population, while sometimes involved in these struggles, on the whole continued their lives much as they had done for centuries.

It is difficult to realize that even during the civil war the Arab conquests proceeded on the frontiers. For example, some Armenians submitted to the Arabs in 40/660, and in the following year one army under ʿAbd al-Rahman b. Samura was sent to Seistan while another under Qais b. al-Haitham, governor of Khurasan, subdued Balkh. Kufa became the centre for the operations in the east, for it had been ʿAli's capital, and under the Umaiyads, whose capital was Damascus, Kufa remained the centre for the eastern part of the caliphate.

Muʿawiya died in Rajab 60/April 680 after twenty years of rule which saw campaigns launched against the Byzantine empire, a fleet created, and expansion of the frontiers of Islam in the east and to some extent in the west also. A new policy of consolidation of rule as well as the extension of frontiers came into being. In Iran the Umaiyad period saw the extension of Islamic frontiers across the River Oxus and into the mountains of Afghanistan. This is the subject of the next chapter.

To recapitulate the Arab conquests: after the battle of Nihavand the central Sasanian government was finished, although Yazdegird tried to rally local support against the Arabs. As the Arabs advanced in Iran, their armies were increased by Persian adherents. As long as Yazdegird was alive there was frequently strong and bitter local resistance to the Arabs, and some towns or districts revolted several times before they were subdued. Sometimes large forces were gathered which proved formidable foes to the Arabs. For example, a nobleman of the Karen family (Arabic: Qarin) gathered an army of some 40,000 from Herat, Badghis and Kuhistan in the year 32/652, but he was killed and his army scattered.[37] Throughout the caliphates of ʿUthman and ʿAli local uprisings, or most frequently simply the refusal to pay taxes, brought swift retribution. According to the *Fars name* of Ibn al-Balkhi, a revolt of the city of Istakhr was bloodily crushed in the caliphate of ʿAli.[38] So the apparent ease of conquest of Iran by the Arabs is misleading.

Although a centralized resistance was gone local forces continually caused great difficulties. On the other hand from the sources one gains the impression that by the time of the Umaiyads, in spite of the local uprisings, Iran was not in danger of breaking away from Muslim rule. Furthermore the number of local people who had joined the ranks of Islam and had made its cause their own almost precluded any 'Zoroastrian' attempt to regain their land. One has the impression that Zoroastrianism really was bankrupt and hardly in a position to oppose the 'holy war' of the Muslims. From the religious side there was hardly any opposition in Iran; rather, economic and social factors dominated the resistance. Since the Arabs for the most part left the finances and local administration in the hands of the local *dihqans*, many of the small revolts against Muslim rule were against local oppressors rather than against the Arabs. The old conception of Arabs pouring from the desert with the Qur'an in one hand and a sword in the other is gone for ever. It never existed, and the realities are much clearer today.

CHAPTER 5

THE ISLAMIC CONQUEST OF CENTRAL ASIA

When the Arab armies reached Khurasan they must have realized that they were far from the heartland of the Sasanian empire, indeed on the frontiers of another world, that of central Asia. It has been mentioned that the Arabs, after the initial conquests, settled in strategic towns to control the lines of communication to the east, in Qazvin, Qum, Qumis, Merv and Seistan. That all except the first were relatively warm, and in or near deserts, hardly was important, for the geographical or strategic importance of them all, and especially of the oasis of Merv, was undeniable. The conquest of central Asia began with the surrender of Mahoye the *marzban* of Merv to ʿAbdallah b. ʿAmir, governor of Basra, probably in the year 32/652, shortly after the death of Yazdegird, if the treaty reported by Baladhuri refers to this date and not to ten years later.[1] A preliminary agreement was probably made at that time, and then reaffirmed in 36/656, according to Tabari.[2] Apart from tribute to be paid in kind, Muslim troops were to be quartered in the town, a practice followed in Qum and elsewhere.[3] With the occupation of Merv a central point for further conquests in central Asia was secured, but it took time to build this centre.

It is probable that even if the Umaiyads had not won the civil war with ʿAli, the conquest of central Asia still would have occurred. For the practice of yearly raiding had changed to one of conquest and the yearly collection of taxes, the demand for which became insatiable. But central Asia was to prove more difficult to hold than western Iran for a variety of reasons, primarily because the political, social and religious structure of the Sasanian empire made a surrender and terms of peace easier to maintain by virtue of the unity of an hierarchically ordered and well-organized society, which was not the case in the east. The Zoroastrian state religion had not extended into central Asia, and the border towns of Merv, Herat and others did not have the same history of peace and order as those in the interior of the empire. As in all border areas in central Asia, rebels were at hand who would not accept peace terms made by the local authorities with the Muslims. Furthermore any desire to convert non-Arabs to Islam, however weak it may have been in western Iran, was almost non-existent in central Asia at the beginning. On the contrary, conversion to Islam was discouraged, if not actually forbidden, in order to preserve the revenues coming to the state. The Umaiyad caliphate was not a brotherhood of the faithful but almost a business enterprise. Many writers, medieval and modern, have condemned the Umaiyads for abandoning the ideals of the early Islamic community, supposedly upheld by the first four caliphs, and perhaps, in comparison with them, this is true. The new empire, however, had to be managed in an 'imperial' manner, and the ideals of a small, closely knit community of the faithful were insufficient to run an empire.

During the civil war between 'Ali and Mu'awiya some towns of Khurasan threw off their allegiance to the Muslims, so 'Abdallah b. 'Amir, who had been reappointed governor of Basra by the first Umaiyad caliph, sent first Qais b. al-Haitham in 41/661–2 and later 'Abdallah b. Khazim to pacify Khurasan. The cities of Herat, Badghis and others were at that time brought under Umaiyad control.[4] It is possible that only at this time, and not earlier, substantial Arab colonists were settled in Merv. The first task of the forces in Merv was to pacify the land south of the River Oxus, which took a number of years. We hear of the invasion of the mountains of Ghur, south-east of Herat, by a governor of Khurasan al-Hakam b. 'Amr al-Ghifari in 47/667, however without lasting results.[5] Kuhistan and the territory around Balkh also had to be pacified. It was not until 51/671, when al-Rabi' b. Ziyad al-Harithi was sent to Merv as governor of Khurasan with 50,000 men of Basra and Kufa plus their families, that a permanent base for further expansion was established.[6] This meant that Merv had become a 'Basra' of the east with settled Arabs who became a power factor in Umaiyad politics.

Tribal identity was very important, especially for those Arabs who settled in the east, but Mu'awiya's policy was to move the centre of authority from the tribes to the caliphate, which brought opposition from the tribes. Mu'awiya wanted a special '*amil* or tax collector to handle the '*ata*' or pension system instead of the tribal chiefs. This naturally was opposed by the tribal chiefs who had profited in the past from collecting tribute from the local aristocracy which apportioned the taxes and collected them. The newcomers to Merv were settled according to tribal divisions and each group was distinct in regard to the payment of the pensions, which practice perpetuated the tribal divisions. So the desired centralization of the caliphate was more theoretical than practical. As mentioned, most of the Arabs sent to Khurasan were from the Tamim tribe of the Mudar confederation and from the Bakr of the Rabiʿa group, with the Azd of Yemen coming later. Tribal strife, however, did not end with the settlement of the tribes in the east. In the year 64/683 of the *Hijra* there was a regular war between the Bakr and Tamim, with the result that many of the Bakr were driven into Herat and other parts of present Afghanistan.[7]

The Arab tribes fought among themselves for many reasons other than personal animosities. The ancient rivalries of the Arabs of Qahtan (south Arabs) and ʿAdnan (north Arabs) were reaffirmed in the east.[8] New alignments of the Rabiʿa and Yemenite tribes, plus later the Azd from Oman, against Qais and Tamim in the Mudar union, brought serious conflicts in Khurasan which, however, were not identical with tribal conflicts in Syria, where Qais and Kalb were in frequent clashes. One should not discount economic reasons for the tribal conflicts in Khurasan, for the Azd, as we shall see, were very involved in local trade and business with the native peoples. Obviously as the years passed the Arabs settled in Khurasan not only mixed more with the natives but their interests coincided more with local interests. We must return, however, to the conquests.

Further raids began again in earnest after the Arab families were settled in Merv and after ʿUbaidallah b. Ziyad had become governor of Khurasan in 54/673. Although he was in this post only a little more than a year before he left for Basra and greater assignments, none the less he started the invasion of Transoxiana by crossing the River Oxus into the oasis of Bukhara. Unfortunately the accounts of ʿUbaidallah in Bukhara, found in several Arabic and Persian sources, are a mixture of fact and fiction. The story of his defeat of the army of Bukhara and his relations with the woman ruler of the oasis city, Khatun, has many legendary features. It is impossible to disentangle the chronological inconsistencies of the account, and one may only conclude that ʿUbaidallah was successful in obtaining tribute and slaves whom he took with him to Basra and settled there.[9]

He was followed by Saʿid b. ʿUthman b. ʿAffan who raided not only Bukhara but Samarqand in 56/676, where, following the example of his predecessor, he obtained hostages.[10] This son of the caliph ʿUthman was later killed in Medina by some of his Sogdian slaves.[11] There were no more great raids during the caliphate of Muʿawiya, who was much concerned with the Byzantine frontier and with Kharijite disturbances in Iraq and western Iran. After the death of Muʿawiya in 680, the death of Husain at Kerbela and the subsequent revolt of Ibn Zubair in the Hijaz overshadowed events in Khurasan, although disturbances broke out there, as usually happened at the death of a caliph. With caliph Yazid's death in 683, however, Umaiyad rule in Khurasan fell apart and the governor, Salm b. Ziyad, had to leave the province.[12] Consequently the Arab tribes fought among themselves, an indication of the stronger tribal loyalties in Khurasan than allegiance to Ibn Zubair or to the Umaiyads. The victor in the tribal struggles was ʿAbdallah b. Khazim al-Sulami, a Qaisite and leader of the Mudar, who with the help of the Tamim defeated one group of Bakr after another.[13] Then, however, wishing to be free of the Tamim, ʿAbdallah turned against them. This move weakened him, so he advised his son to cross the Oxus and take refuge with a local dynast, while ʿAbdallah himself marched against Nishapur to put down an uprising of the Tamim. Meanwhile ʿAbd al-Malik had succeeded to the caliphate and was restoring order. He offered ʿAbdallah the governorship of Khurasan, but the latter refused to acknowledge ʿAbd al-Malik as caliph. The result was the defeat and death of ʿAbdallah in 72/691 while trying to join his son in Termez.[14]

There is no doubt that the internal quarrels and civil wars of the Arabs weakened their general position in Khurasan. This was also true of the other Arab centre in the east, Seistan, for the various tribes had settled in and around Zaranj, the capital of Seistan, as they had in Merv. In 43/663 the governor of Seistan, ʿAbd al-Rahman b. Samura, had raided Bust, and according to several sources had advanced as far as Ghazna.[15] The raids into Sind seem to have followed a more southern route than Seistan, and some of them may even have come by sea. The most formidable opponent of the Arabs in what is today Afghanistan was the ruler of the Ghazna area, Zabulistan, called the *zunbil*, whom we met in the last chapter. A number of scholars have proposed that this title means something like 'the leader for (or servant of) the god Zun', and this may be accepted in lieu of a better explanation.[16] In the lands under the rule of the *zunbil*: al-Rukhkhaj, Zamindawar, and Zabulistan, from south-west to north-east, the Arabs found considerable opposition to their expansion. In spite of raids by al-Rabiʿ b. Ziyad al-Harithi, successor of ʿAbd al-Rahman, and ʿUbaidallah b. Abi Bakra, who replaced al-Rabiʿ in 51/671, the lands from present-day Qandahar to Kabul remained outside Arab control. After the death of Muʿawiya revolts also broke out in the areas east of Seistan and the Arabs suffered reverses, which were not repaired by the new governor of Seistan Talha b. ʿAbdallah al-Khuzaʿi who was appointed in 63/682.[17] Although Seistan may have been more important than Khurasan at the time of the early conquests, after the advent of the Umaiyads the latter province was clearly much more in the foreground, not only because of the threat from Turks expanding from central Asia, but also because of the importance of Khurasan for trade both with the Far East and with eastern Europe.[18]

Kharijite revolts in Seistan characterize the history of this province more than the Arab inter-tribal warfare. Ibn Zubair's appointee, ʿAbd al-ʿAziz b. ʿAbdallah b. ʿAmir, in 66/685 restored order in the province and won over the allegiance of many of the Arabs settled there. He was able to defeat the *zunbil* who had extended his power at the expense of the Arabs, but in 72/691 caliph ʿAbd al-Malik was able to restore Umaiyad authority over the province, and Umaiya b. ʿAbdallah b. Khalid, the new governor of Khurasan and Seistan, appointed his son ʿAbdallah to be his regent in Seistan.[19] The situation in both Seistan and Khurasan and indeed throughout the entire caliphate changed with the coming to power of ʿAbd al-Malik's viceroy of the east, al-Hajjaj b. Yusuf, in 78/697 which inaugurated a new era of the Arab conquests.

The dynastic conception of rule and the supremacy of Syria were promoted during the reigns of ʿAbd al-Malik and his successors. Likewise it would seem that further conquests were needed by the new caliph to supply more money to the central government, for the economic situation of the caliphate after the many rebellions, especially in Iraq, was deplorable. Khurasan had always remained under the jurisdiction of Iraq, even though Merv had developed a certain autonomy. Consequently Khurasan was exploited by the Umaiyads to support Iraq, and the local aristocracy, which collected taxes for the Arabs, was supported by the Umaiyad government as long as revenues were forthcoming. It is clear that by the time of Hajjaj many Arabs were working together with the local aristocracy for the joint exploitation of the province. This was not unexpected, for the settled Arabs would in time naturally engage in trade and business in co-operation with local merchants, and one of the exponents of this co-operation was the governor of Khurasan, al-Muhallab b. Abi Sufra.[20]

The caliph ʿAbd al-Malik had sent Umaiya b. ʿAbdallah b. Khalid as governor of Khurasan to replace ʿAbdallah b. Khazim who had supported Ibn Zubair. According to Baladhuri the chief men of the province had requested someone from the Quraish tribe as governor to prevent a continuation of the civil war among the Arabs of Khurasan.[21] ʿUmaiya proved ineffectual, however, both in trying to defeat Musa b. ʿAbdallah b. Khazim in Termez, and in raiding across the River Oxus. Indeed, Turks and other peoples from beyond the Oxus had been sufficiently emboldened by the inter-Arab strife to raid south of the river. Furthermore Umaiya had great difficulties with the Arab tribal chiefs, so it was only natural that Hajjaj, after the rebellion of the Kharijites in Fars and Kirman had been suppressed, sent the victorious general al-Muhallab as the new governor of Khurasan. Al-Muhallab was head of the Azd of Oman and he brought many of his tribe with him to Khurasan, thus introducing a new tribal factor into the existing enmities. The Azd supported the Rabiʿa group with Bakr against Mudar comprising Tamim and Qais. The new governor crossed the River Oxus and laid siege to the town of Kish. He also secured tribute from other towns in central Asia, but the rebel Musa b. ʿAbdallah b. Khazim secured new support from Arabs who deserted al-Muhallab, so the position of the Azdite governor was weakened. Muhallab died in 82/702 and was succeeded by his son, Yazid. Tabari has an interesting remark about one of the Arab chiefs who joined Musa; he says that Thabit b. Qutba al-Khuzaʿi was highly honoured and beloved by the Iranians who swore oaths by him.[22] This is one of several indications that some Arabs were highly regarded by the natives. Musa, although he opposed the official government of the province of Khurasan, was also able to defeat Turkish and local forces which sought to dislodge him from his secure position on the River Oxus.

Yazid, although he raided Buttam (present area of Dushanbe, Tajik SSR) and elsewhere, was unable to defeat Musa. He then raided Khwarazm at the request of Hajjaj but he showed himself not to be as competent or as compliant as the viceroy of the east wished, so Hajjaj secured the caliph's approval to dismiss him in 85/704. Afterwards, not particularly to Hajjaj's liking, the caliph appointed his half-brother al-Mufaddal b. al-Muhallab as governor of Khurasan. The latter sent an army against Musa who was finally defeated and killed the same year. Hajjaj, however, now secured caliphal approval to appoint Qutaiba b. Muslim, a man who would carry out his wishes and who was a proper lieutenant for the strong man of Iraq.

Qutaiba b. Muslim belonged to a small tribe, the Bahila, which stood aside from the quarrels of the larger tribes. The advantage of being an outsider enabled Qutaiba to unite a motley group of Muslims whom he led to conquests in central Asia. The disadvantage of belonging to a small tribe was apparent in his downfall, when everyone abandoned him. Qutaiba had shown his abilities before he became governor of Khurasan, for in 83/702 he had driven a rebel from Raiy.[23] Qutaiba became governor of Khurasan in 86/705 and at once began to raid across the River Oxus. He first raided northern Bactria, two of the river valleys running from the north to the Oxus, probably the present Surkhan and Kafirnigan rivers, the medieval lands of Akharun and Shuman. The prince of Chaganiyan to the west had asked Qutaiba for help against the ruler of these two lands and Qutaiba was able to secure the submission of the area with tribute.[24]

Qutaiba's conquests have been described many times, but it should be emphasized that his new policy was to encourage a large and active participation of the local population in further conquests. Previously raids had left no permanent settlements of Muslims on the other side of the River Oxus, but Qutaiba left prefects and garrisons in the conquered places. Furthermore Qutaiba goaded the settled Arabs to action, although he had to incite them with the promise of rich booty. For the now settled Arabs did not wish to engage in further fighting, being content to reap the fruits of commercial co-operation with the natives in Merv and elsewhere. None the less the conquests of Qutaiba must have seemed a good business venture to many Arabs and natives, as well as a religious duty for those who were good Muslims.[25]

Before advancing on Bukhara Qutaiba made a treaty with Nezak, Hephthalite prince of Badghis, and an influential man among the natives. Nezak, with many soldiers, accompanied Qutaiba on his expeditions, for Yazid b. al-Muhallab had already secured the submission of Nezak in 84/703.[26] In 87/706 Qutaiba took Baikand, a large trading town on the edge of the oasis of Bukhara, where he obtained much booty including several large pearls which he sent to Hajjaj.[27] The following year he entered the oasis of Bukhara and subdued several towns including Numijkath and Ramitin, but Bukhara itself, which was probably the fortified centre of the oasis, resisted him, calling on Sogdians and Turks for aid. The latter attacked the rearguard of Qutaiba's army commanded by his brother ʿAbd al-Rahman, and the latter was very hard pressed until Qutaiba came to his help and defeated the enemy, in which battle Nezak showed considerable bravery on the Muslim side.[28] This victory seems to have discouraged his opponents, for in the next year Qutaiba was again victorious in the oasis of Bukhara although he could not take the capital until, according to some sources, Hajjaj suggested a successful strategy after studying a plan of the city.[29] In 90/709 Bukhara was taken after a fierce struggle and Qutaiba imposed severe terms on the defeated. As formerly in Merv, Muslims were quartered on the populace, but many of the local aristocracy preferred to leave the city and to build new houses outside. The Arabs remained in the city since Qutaiba intended that Bukhara should become a base for further operations to the east. The local population, of course, had to pay tribute as well as provide for the conquerors in the city, all of which imposed a heavy burden on them.[30]

The ruler of Samarqand, Tarkhun, was one of those who had fought unsuccessfully against Qutaiba and now the turn of his city came. Rather than oppose the large Muslim force, Tarkhun elected to make peace and to seal it by sending hostages to Qutaiba.[31] The pact with the Muslims led to his fall, for in the following year Qutaiba sent his brother ʿAbd al-Rahman to Samarqand to collect the promised tribute. Tarkhun paid it but his people revolted and deposed him, whereupon he either committed suicide or, according to Yaʿqubi, was killed by his successor Ghurak.[32] Qutaiba, however, was not able at the moment to interfere because of the revolt of Nezak.

After his return from Bukhara Nezak had left Qutaiba, probably in protest against some insult to himself or a slight to his followers in the distribution of booty, although the reason is not known to us. Certainly Qutaiba took an enormous booty, including great numbers of slaves, in his campaigns in Transoxiana, and he was well known for his strong, oppressive policies. In any case, Nezak went to Tokharistan where he formed a coalition of the local princes of Taliqan, Marw al-Rud and others, against Qutaiba. The latter sent his brother to Balkh with a large force to counter any move of the allies. In the next year 91/710 Qutaiba occupied Marw al-Rud, Taliqan and Faryab. Nezak himself was besieged in a castle but escaped. He was persuaded to surrender to Qutaiba who promised to spare his life, but the former broke his word and put him to death together with his followers.[33] Qutaiba then conquered Kish and Nasaf, but was called away from Transoxiana by Hajjaj to Seistan to fight against the *zunbil*, who soon submitted, at least temporarily, allowing Qutaiba to return to his tasks beyond the River Oxus.[34]

There followed an expedition in 93/712 against Khwarazm. The Khwarazmshah had fled to Qutaiba after his brother Khurzad seized power. Qutaiba supported the fugitive, conquered Khwarazm, and then captured the chief rebels whom he turned over to the Khwarazmshah who promptly executed them. At first the Khwarazmshah submitted and paid tribute, but then when Qutaiba withdrew the Khwarazmians revolted, either under the leadership of their *shah*, or, according to Baladhuri,[35] after having killed him. In any case Khwarazm was ravaged by Qutaiba to such an extent that al-Biruni, writing many years later, claimed that Qutaiba had destroyed the ancient books as well as the scholarship and the scholars of Khwarazm.[36] Qutaiba certainly was severe in regard to Khwarazm, and afterwards he divided the land between a Khwarazmshah called Askajamukh, son of the former Khwarazmshah, whose capital was in Kath, and an Arab governor who made his capital in the town of Gurganj.[37]

Qutaiba had also regulated the succession of the kings of Bukhara by appointing Tughshada, presumably the son of the queen who had ruled Bukhara before Qutaiba's conquests. Qutaiba was then able to turn his attention to Samarqand and Ghurak.[38] The latter sent to Ferghana and to the Turks for aid, but these troops were defeated by Qutaiba and Ghurak was obliged to capitulate. Again much booty was secured by Qutaiba and Arab troops were stationed in the city of Samarqand, primarily to oversee the collection of tribute.[39] Here Qutaiba is said to have plundered local temples and destroyed idols, which does not mean, however, that he did not do the same elsewhere. In 94/712 a Turkish army came to the rescue of Samarqand but they found no support among the local population and had to retreat. The danger from a Turkish invasion, however, was great and we must devote a few words to it.

In spite of extensive research on the relations between the Turkish states on the Orkhon as well as in Semirechiye, and the Arabs, it has not been possible to establish a clear historical picture.[40] We cannot discuss the history of the western and eastern Khaqanates of the Turks in central Asia, but suffice it to say that bands of Turks had penetrated south to Transoxiana even before the Arab conquests. Just as the Arabs raided from the south, so did the Turks at times establish short-lived hegemonies over some of the city states of Transoxiana after raids from the north. During the governorship of Qutaiba the eastern Turks had succeeded in defeating the western Turks and uniting a large domain under themselves. In 94/712 it was an army of the eastern Turks which came to the aid of the Sogdians. An alliance between Ferghana and the Sogdians was formed and this worried Qutaiba considerably. After his defeat of the allies before Samarqand and his occupation of the city, Qutaiba raided into Shash and Ferghana with the purpose of destroying the coalition.[41] Most of the Turks in this part of the world were Türgesh, although it is difficult in the Arabic sources to determine the tribal affiliations of Turks who are called only by this generic name. Not only did the Arabs have to contend with Turks in Transoxiana, but also in Tokharistan and in areas of present Afghanistan.

The eastern Turks had extended their power to the west after 710 by subduing the western Turks, but on the death of their *khan* in 716 the kingdom fell apart and the Türgesh became the dominant power with which the Arabs had to contend; although this was after the death of Qutaiba.[42]

Qutaiba received news of the death of his patron Hajjaj while on a campaign in Shash in 95/714, and he returned at once to Merv, but, assured of his continued occupation of the post of governor, he set out again for the east. It was in Ferghana, however, that the news of the death of the caliph al-Walid in 96/715 reached him. Qutaiba had supported al-Walid's son ʿAbd al-ʿAziz for the succession but instead the caliph's brother Sulaiman became ruler, and he lost no time in removing Qutaiba from his post. The latter, however, raised a revolt against Sulaiman, but the Arabs deserted him and his fate was sealed when the leader of the *mawali*, Haiyan al-Nabati, abandoned him and only a few Sogdians and others remained to help him and his family.[43] He was killed and his head sent to Sulaiman. It was not surprising that Qutaiba lost all support when he turned against Sulaiman. Not that anyone had any particular regard for the new caliph, but it was an opportunity to turn against a hard and even cruel, though capable, leader. Haiyan, whom Qutaiba expected to support him, had on occasion been badly treated by Qutaiba, while many Arabs had reasons for various grudges.[44] The fall of Qutaiba, however, marked the end of Muslim advances in central Asia for a long time, and the situation in Seistan and Sind was similar.

The conquests in central Asia under Hajjaj were matched by the success of Muslim arms in Sind. Muhammad b. al-Qasim, son-in-law of Hajjaj, in 92/710–11 advanced through Makran and Baluchistan to the seaport of Daibul in Sind which he conquered. As in Transoxiana Arabs were now settled down in conquered cities to maintain Muslim authority and collect the taxes. Here, as in central Asia, local people joined the army of Muhammad.[45] In the following year he took Multan where much booty, including large quantities of gold, was obtained. At the death of Hajjaj, Muhammad left Multan and, with the accession of Sulaiman to the caliphate, he was removed, like Qutaiba, from office and sent in chains to Iraq. Thus did the appointees of Hajjaj suffer for their patron who had died before them. One may pause to assess the policies which led to the conquests of Qutaiba, as well as those of Muhammad b. al-Qasim, for both were directed by one man, al-Hajjaj b. Yusuf, viceroy of the east under ʿAbd al-Malik and al-Walid.

The policies of Hajjaj are interesting to study, for his actions were calculated to strengthen the position of the Umaiyads in the east and ensure a prosperous rule for the dynasty. In 83/702 the city of Wasit was built by him between Basra and Kufa as a strong point and garrison town for Syrian troops. These were the only reliable soldiers for the Umaiyads and Wasit, rather than Basra or Kufa,was from this time the point of departure for troops going to the east. The importance of this move cannot be underestimated, for henceforth Syrian soldiers rather than the *muqatila* of Basra or Kufa were to be the backbone of Muslim armies in the east. It should be mentioned in passing, although it does not directly concern us, that Hajjaj also sponsored the conquest of Oman by Mujjaʿa b. Siʿr, a parallel to Qutaiba and Muhammad b. al-Qasim. Hajjaj spent a lot of money on the campaigns of his commanders, and they were well equipped; on the other hand the investment paid off well, for the booty sent back from Transoxiana and Sind more than repaid any expenses and filled the treasury of Iraq, which was badly in need of funds. For Iraq, more than any other province, had suffered greatly from the Kharijite civil wars and from the revolt of ʿAbd al-Rahman b. Muh. b. al-Ashʿath who, before he fled to Seistan, had taken both Kufa and Basra, and had posed a grave threat to Hajjaj and the Umaiyads. Lest one conclude that Hajjaj was only a great military organizer, some of his other activities should be mentioned, for they influenced Iran as well as Iraq and the rest of the caliphate.

Perhaps the most famous reforms which occurred during the governorship of Hajjaj were the transfer of the records of the *diwan* from Pahlavi to Arabic and the striking of Islamic silver *dirhems* with Qur'anic texts on them, instead of the traditional Sasanian silver coins. Both of these reforms probably had an influence on trade and business in Iran where conservative practices were generally upheld. The dismay of the scribes at the change from Pahlavi to Arabic, on the other hand, probably had less effect than we suppose, although the story of Zadanfarrukh, his son Mardanshah and Salih b. 'Abd al-Rahman, a *maula* of the Tamim, as has been recorded in many sources, would lead one to believe that it caused great unemployment.[46] Actually it would seem that this reform applied mainly to Iraq for it was not carried into effect in Khurasan until the time of the governorship of Nasr b. Saiyar, the last Umaiyad governor, and although there is no evidence in the sources we may believe that the transfer of the language of records from Pahlavi to Arabic was slow throughout Iran. Many of the scribes probably could write in both languages and Arabic was certainly easier to write than Pahlavi, so the opposition to such a change was probably minimal and due more to lethargy in regard to change than to deliberate opposition. The change in currency must have been more striking than that in writing since coins were in common use. Byzantine gold coins quite naturally set the standard for the reformed gold *dinar* of 'Abd al-Malik, on which was only Arabic writing and no figures. The earliest of these gold coins which has been preserved is dated from 77/696 or 7. Gold coins were struck only in Syria and not in Iraq or Iran. In the east, where the Sasanian silver *dirhem* held sway, it of course set the standard for the Islamic *dirhem*, the earliest of which is dated 79/698 or 9. The relation of the *dirhem*'s weight to the gold *dinar* weight of the *mithqal* was set at seven to ten, but in practice the weight correspondences were two to three.[47] There is no record of the reception of this coinage in Iran, but we may assume a long period of mixed use of old and new coins, for there is numismatic evidence that the old coins were still struck in Fars as late as 83/702, and as late as 84/703 in Khurasan. This is not surprising for in any case the silver content of coins in early times was usually more important than any figures or legends depicted on them.

Hajjaj was also well known for his promotion of agriculture, of drainage and of irrigation. He also tried to keep peasants from migrating from the countryside to the cities because of the consequent fall in revenues. Although his harsh measures roused opposition there is no question that his efforts increased the amount of land under cultivation and eventually the prosperity of the peasants. In this he was following, unconsciously no doubt, ancient Zoroastrian admonitions to make the land prosper, whereas Muslims on the whole, following the Prophet, were more interested in trade and industry. Unused lands were given to those who would cultivate them and the result, especially in Iraq, was an increased prosperity which had its effects in the east.[48]

As already mentioned, the various conquests initiated by Hajjaj, during his governorship of Iraq, were intended to replenish the empty coffers of the treasury in Iraq which had been devastated by the Kharijite wars and rebellions. Hajjaj also sought to recapture the flavour and spirit of the early years of the Arab conquests, for during the conquests begun by Hajjaj there was perhaps a greater desire to convert and to spread the *dar al-Islam* than ever before. ʿAbd al-Malik, the caliph himself, had been raised as a pious Muslim and, even though politics overshadowed all else in his reign, his wars with Byzantium were motivated by religion as well as by the political interests of the caliphate. The spread of Islam would have fitted the ideas of the ruling caliph. ʿAbd al-Malik, however, did more than his predecessors in changing the caliphate from a brotherhood based on bedouin mores into an Arab kingdom. His reforms all pointed to a stricter and better organization of the empire, for that is what the caliphate had become. In addition succession to the throne was to be from father to son, as in the Byzantine empire not as in an Arab tribe, although ʿAbd al-Malik could not openly flout the time-honoured customs. The identification of Islam with Arab, and the tendency to make Islam the national religion of the caliphate, was intensified under his son and successor al-Walid, and this must have influenced Hajjaj and his lieutenants. It should be added that it was probably Hajjaj who ordered a re-edition of the Qur'an as assembled in the time of caliph ʿUthman. The introduction of vowel signs in the text of the Qur'an is also attributed to him. Although he had various motives in ordering a new edition of the Qur'an, his desire to establish a uniform text and settle disputes can hardly be denied a religious motivation. Unfortunately the sources are so much concerned with personal and tribal rivalries of prominent Arabs that the overall effects of caliphal ideas or policies can scarcely be determined. It is also unwise to project the situation in Syria, or even Iraq, on to the plateau of Iran, for circumstances were different in all three areas. Let us turn, then, to the effects of Hajjaj's policies in the east.

There is much evidence that Hajjaj drove his lieutenants hard; in fact his severity is said to have resulted in the uprising of al-Ashʿath, mentioned above. This rebellion is fully described by Wellhausen, and need not be repeated here except to note the sentiments of the soldiers in the army. At the beginning of the revolt in Seistan in 81/700 a certain ʿAbd al-Mu'min b. Shabath of the Tamim said to the troops that if they obeyed Hajjaj's orders they would remain in this land and never see their loved ones in Iraq.[49] From this and other sentiments expressed it seems clear that al-Ashʿath's rebellion was primarily an Iraqi Arab versus Syrian Arab struggle, as seems clear from Tabari, who also speaks of this enmity elsewhere.[50] The fact that many noble Arabs but only one *maula*, a certain Firuz Husain from Seistan, were mentioned as participating in this revolt indicates that it was by no means the result of the discontent of the *mawali* which sparked the revolt. In fact it is difficult if not impossible to find any great *mawali* movements against Arabs in this period. The reason seems clear, for the *mawali*, as non-Arab Muslims, were bound to their Arab patrons and thus apart from their non-Muslim native compatriots. Their numbers were still small *vis-à-vis* the native population as well as the Arabs, so that they could only act through or with their patrons, and hardly in opposition to them. This did not mean that the *mawali* had no grievances; quite the contrary, but they had no power as a separate group. The Shi'ite revolt of al-Mukhtar in Kufa at the beginning of 'Abd al-Malik's reign, wherein the *mawali* were promised full equality with the Arabs, indicates that a rebellion could not hope for success with only the support of the *mawali*, although al-Mukhtar, of course, had more than that.[51] If the non-Arab Muslims had played a more important role in the history of this period than the sources tell us, then we should find at least some clues to this, but it seems that, although the numbers and strength of the *mawali* were ever growing, their influence was still bound to their Arab patrons. A change in high policy came, however, with the caliphate of 'Umar II, but before examining his policy we must return briefly to Khurasan and central Asia.

With the death of Qutaiba not only did further conquests come to a halt but a Turkish counter thrust developed. During Sulaiman's two-year reign, after briefly appointing as governor a Tamim Arab called Waki' b. Abi Sud who had raised the opposition against Qutaiba, he then appointed Yazid b. al-Muhallab, the Azdite, in 98/717 to the governorship for the second time. Yazid left his son Mukhallad as his lieutenant, and another son Mu'awiya to govern Bukhara, Samarqand, Kish and Nasaf in his absence, while he undertook an expedition to the west where he conquered Gurgan. He also fought against the Ispahbad of Tabaristan but made peace with him after being unable to subdue him. As usual, natives of Khurasan supplied Yazid with troops for his campaign.[52] A revolt in Gurgan was suppressed with great severity. The road to Khurasan from the west, which had been secured by Qutaiba when he was governor of Raiy and then of Khurasan, now by Yazid's campaign was made even more secure. Yazid, however, was not overly conscientious in sending booty to the capital where 'Umar II had been hailed as new caliph at the death of Sulaiman in 99/717, and 'Umar removed him from his post and had him arrested and imprisoned. 'Umar did not, however, follow a policy of favouring one tribal group over another; rather he wished to appoint reliable and righteous men to positions of authority.

'Umar II is known in the sources as a pious and even fanatical caliph. His aim in his reforms was to reconcile the financial and political needs of the state with the Islamic religion. As far as Iran and central Asia are concerned, the main effect of 'Umar's policy was a proclamation of the equality of Arabs and *mawali* in Islam. 'Umar said that no Muslim, Arab or not, should pay a land or head tax, but conquered land should belong to the community.[53] After the year 100/718 no Muslim was to be allowed to purchase land which had a tax upon it. None the less several devices, such as a Muslim renting the land, were found to obviate many problems which arose.[54] Such a reform was impossible to realize without great losses to the treasury, and the later solution was to consider the *kharaj* as a tax on the land, no matter who owned it, and the *jizya* as a head tax on non-Muslims, whereas Muslims were supposed to pay *zakat* or alms.[55] In regard to central Asia 'Umar hoped for a peaceful conversion of the non-Muslims to Islam instead of the holy war, which brought more booty than conversions. According to Baladhuri some of the princes of Transoxiana accepted the invitation of 'Umar and became Muslims while the *mawali* were rewarded for their services and theoretically made equal to the Arabs.[56] We cannot discuss further 'Umar's fiscal measures, or his actions against Christians and non-Muslims, save to remark that he always sought to follow the prescriptions of Islam in all cases.[57] Unfortunately 'Umar did not have time to gain support for his policies, which might have eventually saved the Umaiyad caliphate for after his death in 101/720 affairs reverted to their former practices.

In central Asia 'Umar's first governor Jarrah b. 'Abdallah al-Hakami believed that the east could only be held by rough and forceful measures, so 'Umar dismissed him. He was followed by 'Abd al-'Aziz, appointed by Yazid II in 102/721 after the death of 'Umar. Meanwhile the Sogdians had not been idle. After the death of Qutaiba Tughshada, the ruler of Bukhara, and Ghurak, the ruler of Samarqand, sent letters to China seeking aid against the Arabs.[58] It should not be forgotten that princes of the Sasanian family were in China and in small states along the Silk Road hoping for a chance to regain some measure of lost power. This rather forlorn situation continued throughout the Umaiyad caliphate and then all hope was abandoned. Attempts were made by the Sogdians also to form an alliance with the Turks, and during the governorship of 'Abd al-Rahman a revolt broke out, possibly upon news of the death of 'Umar. In any case many Sogdians decided to leave Samarqand and other towns and go to the Ferghana valley where they thought they could escape Muslim control. The position of Ghurak was uncertain, so it seems that in the years 720–1 a prince or *dihqan* of the town of Panjikant, on the upper Zarafshan river, was made ruler of Samarqand, or, as Sogdian documents call him, *sγwdyk MLK'* 'Sogdian king' and *sm'rkndc MR'y* 'lord of Samarqand', Devashtich by name.[59] Sa'id b. 'Abd al-'Aziz, nicknamed derisively by the local inhabitants *khudaina* 'the woman' (Sogdian *γwt'ynh* 'queen'), was unable to prevail over the rebels and the Turks, so Sa'id b. 'Amr al-Harashi was appointed and moved energetically against the rebels. Ghurak made peace with the Muslim forces, but Devashtich apparently made common cause with the rebels and withdrew to his principality of Panjikant. Sa'id himself went against one group of Sogdians who had fled to Khojand in the Ferghana valley while he sent a *maula*, Sulaiman b. Abi'l-Sari, against Devashtich. Both Muslim forces were successful and many captured Sogdians were executed including Devashtich.[60] When strong Muslim forces appeared on the scene the king of Ferghana, to whom the Sogdian migrants had turned for aid, refused to support them. For a time the Muslims were successful, but in 106/724 the Turks defeated a Muslim army in Ferghana and unrest continued among the natives.

The policies of 'Umar had perhaps raised high hopes among many of the subject peoples, as well as the *mawali*. During 'Umar's reign the people of Samarqand had requested Sulaiman b. Abi'l-Sari for permission to send a deputation to Damascus to complain of the injustices they had suffered from the time of Qutaiba who had driven them from their lands. It was impossible now to dispossess the Arabs in Samarqand although 'Umar recognized the justice of the complaints of the natives.[61] Later such complaints were unavailing, for the policies of 'Abd al-Malik and Hajjaj returned. With the return of the old policies revolts and anti-Umaiyad conspiracies flourished.

In 102/720 Yazid b. al-Muhallab, who had risen against the caliph Yazid II, was defeated and killed in Iraq and consequently members of the family of the Muhallibids were hunted down everywhere and killed. It meant also a coming to supremacy of the Qais tribe, and more tribal enmities. When the new governor of Khurasan Muslim b. Sa'id al-Kilabi prepared a campaign against the Turks in Ferghana, members of the Azd and Rabi'a tribes in Tokharistan revolted and made 'Amr b. Muslim, a brother of Qutaiba, their chief. Nasr b. Saiyar was put at the head of troops of Mudar and was sent against the rebels whom he defeated at al-Baruqan near Balkh, but discontent still smouldered.[62] Muslim b. Sa'id was defeated by the Turks in Ferghana and escaped with great difficulty, for the Azdites in his army had deserted him before his encounter with the enemy. (This indicates the instability of the Muslim forces in Khurasan through Arab tribal quarrels.)[63] With the accession of Hisham b. 'Abd al-Malik to the caliphate a certain measure of order was restored, and the new governor of Khurasan, Asad b. 'Abdallah al-Qasri, brother of the viceroy of Iraq Khalid, reconciled the Azd as well as the local population. He was replaced, however, in 109/727 by Ashras b. 'Abdallah al-Sulami, a Qaisite. During the governorship of Asadi Shi 'ite missionaries arrived in Khurasan but they were caught and executed. Likewise the first missionary for the 'Abbasids, Ziyad Abu Muhammad, was caught and put to death.[64]

Ashras tried to appease the restless Sogdians by promising them remission of the *jizya* if they converted to Islam. Many flocked to the emissaries sent by Ashras to become Muslims. The local princes, however, protested strongly to Ashras, pointing out that they could not maintain the level of tribute if so many were converting to Islam and thus escaping the head tax. Ashras had to renege on his promise, and he reimposed the head tax on new converts. As a result some 7,000 Sogdians left Samarqand and called on the Turks to come to aid them.[65] Ghurak, prince of Samarqand, also joined the Turks, and Ashras had to fight several severe battles. Ghurak later returned to his allegiance with the Arabs, although his son remained with the Turks. But Ghurak was besieged, together with the Arabs, now his allies, at a small town near Samarqand in 110/728. According to the sources, in addition to the Turks and Sogdians and other peoples of central Asia besieging the Arabs, there was Khusrau, a descendant of the last Sasanian king Yazdegird.[66] The Muslims were able to escape from this siege but their problems in the east were not at an end.

By 110/728 the situation in Transoxiana was desperate for only Samarqand, where Nasr b. Saiyar was the governor, and a few other towns were in Muslim hands. Not even Bukhara remained loyal. A new governor, Junaid b. ʿAbd al-Rahman, a former governor of Sind, in 112/730 gathered a force and attacked the Turks near Samarqand. The situation, however, was so bad that in an exceptional move he promised all slaves their freedom if they would fight against the Turks.[67] Junaid was successful, and later even Bukhara was retaken and Qatan b. Qutaiba installed there as his lieutenant. The Turks, however, controlled the countryside and famine conditions prevailed not only in Transoxiana but also in Merv and in other parts of Khurasan on the south side of the Oxus. The Turks, though once beaten, recovered and besieged both Bukhara and Samarqand, so the caliph Hisham had to raise 20,000 men, divided between Basra and Kufa, and equip them with lances and shields to go to Samarqand.[68] In the next few years the Arabs had to fight a good deal in Transoxiana and they were hard pressed by the Turks and the native Iranians. With the death of the head of the Turks about 738, however, the situation improved.

Asad b. ʿAbdallah al-Qasri had returned as governor of Khurasan in 117/735, and a conciliatory policy towards the natives was again in force. But before this, during the governorship of ʿAsim b. ʿAbdallah, a Qaisite, a revolt had occurred in Transoxiana which was a forerunner of the ʿAbbasid uprising. For the first time, as far as the sources tell us, a revolt of the *mawali* for their rights broke out in Khurasan, but it was led by an Arab commander, al-Harith b. Suraij al-Tamimi. It was ironic that such a revolt continued even after Asad came back as governor, for according to one source he was a generous man, who held in esteem the nobles of both the Arabs and the natives.[69] It is noteworthy that al-Harith, an Arab, led the revolt for equal rights for the *mawali*, an indication of the mixed situation in the east, which subject will be discussed later. Al-Harith in many respects was continuing the policies of 'Umar II, and the previous treatment of Sogdian converts to Islam prepared the way for his uprising. Once his revolt gathered momentum, of course, many Arabs joined him simply in opposition to the government and not with any sympathy for the *mawali*. He moved to Tokharistan, where he received support from a Turkish ruler in the area, and then to Balkh which he captured. Finally he appeared before the gates of Merv itself, the Umaiyad capital of the east. He was repulsed, however, and had left for the city of Termez to the east when Asad b. 'Abdallah became governor.

The revolt of al-Harith prompted others to rebel and Asad had difficulty in subduing the various rebels, so he moved his capital to Balkh in order to be closer to the rebels in the hills and valleys to the north. Not only did he move to Balkh but he also rebuilt much of the city and the old mosque, for a large part of the city had fallen into ruins, since the Arab centre until then had been at Baruqan rather than at Balkh.[70] In the work of rebuilding Balkh Barmak, who was in charge of the famous Buddhist temple or monastery of Naubahar in Balkh, was the leading local spirit, and was supported by Asad. In the winter of 118/January 736 Asad was able to surprise the Khaqan of the Turks, who was with al-Harith in Guzgan, and he roundly defeated the allies. Iranians fought on both sides, one group for the Turks, and another for the Arabs. As already mentioned, the Khaqan was killed in about 738 and the Turks fought among themselves, leaving the Muslims in peace for a number of years. Unfortunately Asad was not able to take advantage of the strife among his adversaries, for he died the same year, 120/738. His successor was an old veteran of wars in central Asia, Nasr b. Saiyar of the Kinana tribe allied to the Mudar, who had been a lieutenant of Asad in Sarakhs.

Nasr, the last of the Umaiyad governors of Khurasan, put his friends or members of his tribe in various minor posts in Khurasan, but al-Harith was still at large among the Turks and other rebels were stirring. Nasr moved the capital back to Merv and prepared an expedition against the Turks. In Samarqand an event occurred which indicates the close co-operation of the Iranian chiefs with the Muslim government. In an audience which Nasr held together with Tughshada, the ruler of Bukhara, and the Arab tax collector or governor of Bukhara, Wasil b. 'Amr, two Bukharan nobles, converts to Islam, complained to Nasr of the injustice of the local government and, not finding any response, they attacked Wasil and Tughshada, killing both, before being killed themselves.[71] This again reveals the co-operation between the Umaiyad government and the local dynasties, although to be sure Nasr had special, close connections with the king of Bukhara.

Nasr's campaigns against the Turks were highly successful. Ustrushana, Ferghana and Shash submitted to him and paid tribute, while the chief of the Türgesh, who had gained power in this area after the death of the Khaqan, was captured and put to death. Al-Harith was not taken, however, and remained a thorn in Nasr's side.[72] Nasr also permitted the Sogdians who had fled to Ferghana and elsewhere in the time of Asad to return to their homeland without fear of punishment or hardship. On the whole Nasr had a high opinion of the natives, which feeling was reciprocated by many of them. In Nasr's governorship Arabic was finally introduced into the chancelleries of Khurasan and the east; although this was later than elsewhere in the caliphate.

The inner Umaiyad strife in Syria after the death of Hisham in 743 also finally reached Khurasan. Under Hisham the Umaiyads had reached a pinnacle of power, yet the caliph had done little to reconcile either the *mawali* or the Arabs, especially in Khurasan. Furthermore the expansion of the empire in north Africa and Spain had imposed immense demands and strain on Syria, so even though Hisham during his relatively long reign established some stability this feeling was unfortunately only on the surface. His successor, al-Walid b. Yazid II, was a dissolute person who, to raise money, sold the governorship of Iraq to Yusuf b. ʿUmar, a Qaisite, who turned and killed the previous governor Khalid b. ʿAbdallah al-Qasri, a Yemenite Arab, under torture, which, of course, again roused tribal passions. Al-Walid was probably the builder of Mshatta, an Umaiyad palace complex in the Syrian desert.

Revolts broke out everywhere and al-Walid was killed in 126/744. A rebel against al-Walid, Yazid III, ruled for a very short time, professing to follow in the footsteps of ʿUmar II, but he looked for support to the Yemenite Arabs, especially Kalb, which tribal favouritism again aroused great opposition among other tribes. In any event he lived but a short time and was followed by his brother Ibrahim b. al-Walid. But many people had been spurred to revolt and this was now not easily stopped. Marwan b. Muhammad, governor of Armenia and Azerbaijan, had marched to Harran in Mesopotamia after the death of al-Walid, uncertain whether to recognize the new caliph or not. Members of the Qais tribe joined him and he decided to advance to revenge the death of al-Walid. After some fighting he was proclaimed caliph in Damascus in 127/744. Because there was still considerable opposition to him in Syria, he moved his capital to Harran in the heart of the area of the Qais tribe. This move emboldened the opposition in Syria to revolt and Marwan had to return to put down the uprising. He was successful and was again hailed as caliph in Damascus. Still more revolts broke out but were put down until finally Syria was fully under his control by 128/746.

In Mesopotamia Shiʿites had risen in Kufa and seized the city, but were driven out late in 127/745. Their leader was a certain Ibn Muʿawiya, and after the defeat in Iraq he went to the Iranian plateau where he gathered support and was able to usurp the rule in Fars, Kirman and al-Jibal. Kharijite uprisings also took place in Iraq during the uncertain atmosphere of the times, and they made considerable progress until Marwan, finished with his task in Syria, in 127/746 defeated an army of them and drove them again eastward. Ibn Muʿawiya was killed and the Kharijites scattered. It seemed as though Marwan had finally settled with his enemies in Syria and Iraq and was victorious. But a more powerful foe had appeared in the east who was to bring down the Umaiyad dynasty. This was Abu Muslim, a *maula* who in many respects represented the victory of the *mawali*, as well as that of the ʿAbbasids, over the house of the Umaiyads.

In Khurasan Arab tribal conflicts broke out again following the struggle for the succession in Syria. The Azd and Rabiʿa tribes revolted under an Azdite called al-Karmani, and declared that they sought revenge for the murders, long past, of the Muhallabites at the hands of the Umaiyads.[73] Nasr b. Saiyar thought of obtaining support against al-Karmani from the rebel al-Harith who had been in exile among the Turks. The latter returned to Merv in 127/745, but instead of joining Nasr he made common cause with al-Karmani, bringing many of his fellow Tamim tribesmen, as well as other supporters, to the side of al-Karmani. Together they took Merv while Nasr retreated to Nishapur. The allies soon began to fight among themselves and al-Karmani was killed. Nasr regained Merv for a time but the sons of al-Karmani, at first willing to deal with Nasr, were persuaded by Abu Muslim, the ʿAbbasid rebel, to join him, as was also a Kharijite leader, Shaiban b. Salama, with his following. This was too much for Nasr, who for a second time abandoned Merv after fighting in the streets, and in Rabiʿ II, 130/December 747 Abu Muslim took over Merv as Nasr fled again to Nishapur. Umaiyad rule in Khurasan and in the whole of Iran came rapidly to an end. Before turning to internal conditions in Iran and the east under the Umaiyads, we should direct our attention briefly to Seistan, the other centre of Arab control in the east.

The province of Seistan, with its capital Zarang, or Arabic Zaranj, served the Muslims in the same capacity as Khurasan with its capital Merv, for both had to contend with strong opposition to Arab expansion on the eastern frontiers. One reason for the long and resolute resistance of the *zunbils* to Islamic expansion was surely the fierce tribesmen, ancestors of the Afghans or Pathans, who supplied troops to fight against the Islamic invaders. Just as Transoxiana was for a long time enemy territory, *dar al-harb*, so the southern part of present Afghanistan remained an obstacle to the success of Arab arms over a long period. We have mentioned how the governors of Seistan sent one army after another to the east, and then how the Kharijites gained influence in the province. The city of Bust became the outpost of the governor of Seistan in the east, much as Bukhara and then Samarqand in Transoxiana was for the governor of Khurasan. Unfortunately there is much less information in the sources about the Umaiyad governors of Seistan than there is about Khurasan so one must piece together the fragments which exist and seek to reconstruct a history of the province.

The *zunbil* had already ceased to pay tribute to the Muslims in the reign of ʿUmar II, but with the accession of Yazid II he declared his independence outright. The Umaiyad government was unable to bring him back to obedience mainly because of the Kharijites. They kept the province in turmoil and prevented the Umaiyad governors from consolidating their power. Not only did the Kharijites cause trouble in Seistan but their raiding expeditions on several occasions extended to Herat.[74] Finally in 108/726 an army was prepared under a new governor al-Asfah b. ʿAbdallah al-Shaibani not only to crush the Kharijites but also to bring the *zunbil* back to submission. If the governor had concerned himself with the former first and then carefully prepared a campaign against the *zunbil* his army might have accomplished its mission. It was, however, ambushed in winter and destroyed by the *zunbil*'s forces. The governor himself was killed (729) and new officials had to be sent to the province. The next governors left the *zunbil* alone and concentrated on internal matters, but the Kharijites were not subdued even though their activities diminished. The tribal enmities in Syria and Iraq at the end of the Umaiyad caliphate also had their echoes in Seistan in the frequent change of governors. Finally the struggle between the Tamim and Bakr b. Wa'il tribes brought chaos to Seistan. More Kharijites gathered and then a Shiʿite force under ʿAbdallah b. Muʿawiya came to Seistan in 129/747, although the latter shortly passed on to Herat. The Umaiyad government had already ceased to exercise any effective rule outside the capital Zaranj, and this province shared the same fate as the rest of the caliphate.

We must now survey Khurasan, central Asia and Seistan under the Umaiyads. Why was it that western Iran posed few problems for the conquering Arabs whereas the east was not only more difficult but became the centre from which the Umaiyads were overthrown? Why does one not hear of any Zoroastrian revolts under the Umaiyads, whereas under the ʿAbbasids one heretical movement after another gained adherents? What happened to the Arab tribes whose conflicts during the Umaiyad caliphate dominate the pages of Tabari and other historians, whereas under the ʿAbbasids they vanish from Iran and the east? Finally, what happened in the east which later made Khurasan and Transoxiana important centres of Islamic learning? The rest of this chapter will be devoted to these questions.

Many cities in Iran have local histories, in Arabic or Persian, for the most part written four, five or six centuries after the Arab conquests. In these histories there is usually a section on the coming of Islam to that city, and some details are interesting for the picture they give of the early relations between Arabs and Iranians. Some towns and even villages, although they have no local histories, may preserve documents written much later yet purporting to tell of the Arab conquests. I have reported on one of these from the Biyabanak area of the central deserts of Iran and have heard of others.[75] From these documents, as well as from Tabari, Baladhuri and other sources, we may deduce several hypotheses. First, the Arab conquests loomed very large in the minds of the people, at least in later times when the histories were written. Secondly, the treaties or documents themselves were important for later tax questions and served as a basis for the legal operation of the local government. Finally, most small towns and villages in Iran and central Asia were relatively untouched by Islam in the Umaiyad period, and their populations were converted only several centuries or more after the Arab conquests. Frequently a town or village will have preserved the names of Muslim martyrs who were killed in their area fighting infidels. Naturally many if not most of such names are either borrowed, to enhance the reputation of the locality, or are simply fictitious. None the less the desire to have local Islamic martyrs, or saints, indicates the feelings of the populace, and some grains of history may be contained in these usually fanciful local reports. This is true of central Asia as well as Iran, but central Asia presented problems for the Muslim armies which were different from those in Iran.

One problem in dealing with Khurasan is that the main source, Tabari, reports only the tribal narratives about the conquests. Thus the accounts of battles, as reported by the members of the Tamim tribe, or the 'Bahili' tradition of the conquests of Qutaiba are all we have; one must be careful in drawing conclusions from material which was composed to glorify or at least to tell the story of members of the tribe. None the less many details or brief notices can be assembled to give us a picture of the east which, contrary to the main concern of the histories, is not dominated by tribal affairs. In several places notice has already been taken of the *asawira*, or elite Persian cavalry corps, of the *jund-i shahanshahi*, or imperial guard, as well as prominent individual Persians who converted to Islam, primarily to be on the winning side and to escape paying the *jizya* or head tax. Baladhuri reports that some nobles of Isfahan converted to Islam because they disdained to pay the poll tax, as did some Persian troops in Qazvin.[76] But the conversion of members of the nobility to Islam in western Iran was not usually followed by that of the common folk. Although one must be careful of making too sweeping a generalization, it seems as though this western Iranian pattern was not followed in Khurasan or in central Asia. The reasons for this are obvious. First, by the time the Arab conquerors reached Merv, and even more so after they crossed the River Oxus, they were not interested in acquiring *mawali*, or new converts to Islam. The Arabs at first needed their help, but later, after the death of Yazdegird, any augmentation of the ranks of the Muslims meant more hands for the division of spoils in future conquests, and, more important, a loss in revenue to the state because of the diminution of the poll tax. The conquests in central Asia were quite frankly intended to raise new revenues, and conversion to Islam was a secondary factor. Naturally the native population did not appreciate this exploitation. Their treatment at the hands of the Arabs, much more severe than, for example, that of the people in western Iran, surely helped to bring an end to the ancient Sogdian, Khwarazmian and Bactrian cultures, which will be discussed briefly later.

The medieval world was a brutal world, but the conquests in central Asia seem to have been exceptionally rough. One finds many notices in the sources about the harsh treatment of the local people. For example, Yazid b. Muhallab, on an expedition to Khwarazm, removed the clothes from his prisoners so that they froze to death.[77] The harshness of Qutaiba is amply reported, and his son in the year 90/708 crucified thousands of the inhabitants of Taliqan who had revolted, the length of the row of poles on which the people were fixed extending four *farsakhs*.[78] Captured soldiers (*asara*) could be killed and frequently were in central Asia, whereas non-combatant captives (*sabi*) were enslaved but not killed. The slave markets, not only of Kufa and Basra but also of Balkh and Merv, were swollen by the conquests of Qutaiba, and a constant supply from central Asia continued throughout the Umaiyad caliphate. Indications of different treatment of captured Arab and captured *mawali* rebels abound in the sources. For example, at the end of the Umaiyad caliphate when ʿAbbasid forces captured Nihavand after a siege, the *mawali* were killed but the Arabs were allowed to go free.[79]

Fighting in Transoxiana was often not only brutal but fierce, for the local nobility lived a more militant, chivalrous and independent life than did their colleagues, the *dihqans* of western Iran.[80] The Arabs had to concentrate their forces on the frontiers and the interior of the caliphate saw few garrisons, as mentioned above. Where strong Arab garrisons existed in the east, relations between the conquerors and the native people were strained. On one occasion in Seistan the Arabs were characterized as followers of Ahriman, at other times Muslims and non-Muslims fought each other, as in Bukhara.[81] This does not mean that in western Iran everything was always quieter and easier, for in Qum, for example, there were many fights, and at one time the Arabs are reported to have cut off the heads of prominent Zoroastrians.[82] On the other hand the greater martial spirit of the populations in the east led to more uprisings and we hear of defeats of Arab armies by the natives, while such defeats were rare in western Iran. Sometimes too the Iranian converts to Islam in the east turned against the Arabs in support of the natives.[83] The conquests in the east were for many reasons more difficult than they had been in western Iran.

During the Umaiyad caliphate many Persians fled to Transoxiana to escape the Arabs and their rule. They joined fellow countrymen who had come there after the death of Yazdegird and still others, primarily merchants, whose families had settled in central Asia in pre-Islamic times. We hear of people, probably mostly from the upper classes, fleeing from Isfahan to the east, from Merv to Bukhara, and from Kabul and from Termez in 720.[84] The flight of Zoroastrians to Makran and over the sea to India is too well known to need repeating here.[85] Other Persians went north to Tabaristan, or to the Caucasus.[86] We have already mentioned those Sogdians who migrated to Ferghana rather than submit to heavy taxation, so the movement of peoples eastward during the Umaiyad period helped to spread western Iranian culture (i.e. Sasanian) to the frontiers of China. Direct evidence exists for the presence of Persians in Transoxiana and China.

In the Sogdian documents from Mount Mugh a Persian army commander is mentioned though not named, evidence for a continuing participation of Persians from west Iran in the struggle in Transoxiana against the Arabs.[87] This Persian may have been connected with the forces of Khusrau b. Yazdegird mentioned by Tabari as an ally of the Turks against the Arabs in 110/728–9.[88] On the other hand Devashtich, the Sogdian local lord of Panjikant, certainly had Arabs in his service, an indication of the mixture of peoples and loyalties in central Asia in this period.[89] The Arabs were called Taziks by the Sogdians, a term later extended to all Muslims, and as the Arabs were absorbed by the local population it came to mean the local population, today called Tajiks. Further east, in China, Persians who had fled from the Arabs were also to be found, as attested by a Middle Persian inscription from Shansi province.[90] Naturally, as has been mentioned, the Arabs brought with them to central Asia many Persians as *mawali* or simply as camp followers, and undoubtedly they helped to swell the numbers of Persians in central Asia.[91] The fact that the cities of Iraq were filled with Persians, many of whom were drafted into the armies for service in the east, also contributed to the 'persianization' of central Asia, which was not unexpected in view of the prestige and the weight of numbers of Persians from the Sasanian part of the Iranian plateau. There was, of course, a feeling of difference between the Iranian peoples of Transoxiana and the Persians from the west, a difference, however, sometimes confused in the sources.[92]

We have spoken of the opposition of the Iranians to the Arabs, while at the same time mentioning that some Arabs and Iranians did work together from the earliest period of the conquest. Indeed Arabs relied heavily on the west Iranians, Muslims or not, to help them in their further conquests among the small Iranian principalities of central Asia. At first the *mawali* were not well treated; for example, they were not supposed to be addressed by their *kunyas* (Abu) as were the Arabs, for this was a term of respect. Rather the *mawali* were called by their personal names (*ism*) or by their family or trade names.[93] The qualities of the Iranians, however, could not be ignored even by an Arab government in Damascus, so many were appointed governors of provinces and to other high positions.[94] In 743, for example, a Sogdian Muqatil b. ʿAli, was appointed governor of the city of Amul in Tabaristan.[95] Not only *mawali* but also Zoroastrians or other non-Muslims were appointed to important positions. It was reported that a certain Bahram Sis was made a *marzban* by the governor of Khurasan, Muslim b. Saʿid al-Kilabi, in 105/723, and years later in 121/738, Nasr b. Saiyar complained how Bahram Sis, in his position, had favoured the Zoroastrians and had transferred their loads to the backs of the Muslims.[96] Even though non-Muslims could rise to high places, they were still under the control of Muslims and the Islamic regulations applied to them. That is, they were obliged to support the government, not to offend Muslims and to pay the *jizya*. Although they were governed by the rules of their own religious community, the Islamic law, the *shariʿa*, was above those rules. The non-Muslim, or the *dhimmi* 'people of the book', had no personal rights but only community rights, and the *jizya* was collected by the community. At the time of the rise of ʿAbbasid propaganda in 744 it was feared by the Umaiyad government that the Christian and Jewish communities in Khurasan were strong enough to throw the balance of power in favour of Arabs revolting against the state.[97] This fear, however, was hardly justified.

The process of assimilation between Arabs and local Iranians was well advanced by the end of the Umaiyad caliphate. One could collect many examples of persianized Arabs, those who spoke Persian, wore Persian clothes or adopted Persian customs and manners, but they would only present individual or family details and would not give a statistical picture of the general trend of Arabs in the east, which is impossible to recover.[98] Furthermore, during the ʿAbbasid caliphate the process of assimilation was completed and we cannot recover the stages of this process in the preceding caliphate. The son of Salm b. Ziyad, who was born on the north side of the River Oxus received the nickname al-Sughdi, and other Arabs were named after their birthplaces in Iran (as al-Karmani) or elsewhere in the east.[99] The reverse also applied, for Salm was so well liked that, according to one source, 20,000 children of local people in Transoxiana were named after him.[100] And, as is well known, Iranians adopted Arab names with Iranian endings, almost as nicknames, such as Hasanoe, Fazloe, and the like, further evidence of mutual assimilation. On the other hand for many people sharp distinctions remained. As late as 729 in Bukhara when a local noble converted to Islam it was said that he became an Arab.[101] This points up the differences between the Arabs and local Iranians, but it also indicates that the designation 'Tajik' in the local tongues did not only mean Arab but also Muslim, which is significant for the later history of the word. As already mentioned, individual Arabs made themselves well liked by the native population, for example, the governor of Khurasan Asad b. 'Abdallah al-Qasri received gifts from the *dihqans* and local nobility because of the high regard they held for him.[102] There was another domain in which the Arabs co-operated with the natives which has been little investigated – and this was in trade and industry.

In a famous passage in Tabari we are told that in the year 77/696 the governor of Khurasan, Bukair b. Wishah, wished to make a raid in Transoxiana, but he had to gather horses and weapons to equip his troops and there was no money available for this. So he had to raise a loan from Sogdian merchants, who were willing to invest in a profitable raid.[103] The fact that the Sogdian word for debt *pwrc* was borrowed into Turkish *borch* indicates the role of the Sogdians as middlemen not only between the Arabs and the Turks but also in China. The city of Baikand in the oasis of Bukhara was very active in the China trade, according to Narshakhi, and that the Sogdians had settlements all over central Asia and in west China is well known. Undoubtedly Qutaiba and other Arab commanders, when they raised troops for expeditions further east, also obtained money from Sogdian merchants, but loans for raids were not the only commercial relations between the Arabs and the natives. A recent study has suggested that the advent of the Azd tribe in Khurasan headed by the Muhallabid family should be examined in the light of commercial connections between the Azd and the natives.[104] Furthermore the importance of Sogdiana in the weaving industry is well known and need not be elaborated here. For example, Zandaniji from the Bukharan oasis was famous throughout the caliphate, according to Narshakhi and other sources.[105] One group of the Azd had been noted for their weaving in Arabia on the highlands of 'Asir and later when they came to Basra. Although there are no direct statements about the collaboration of members of the Azd tribe in Merv and local weavers, it would not be making wild assumptions to guess that the Azd brought their weaving and trading skills with them to Khurasan and participated in the local weaving and trading activities. This would explain the reluctance of some Arabs to engage in further raiding in Transoxiana, preferring rather to reap the rewards of the weaving industry and of commerce. It should be noted that whereas in Sasanian Iran the landed aristocracy, the priests, scribes and common folk comprised the four traditional classes or castes, in Transoxiana the society seems to have been divided instead between the aristocracy (Sogdian *''ztk'r*), the merchants (*γw'kr*) and the ordinary folk (*k'ryk'r* 'workers')[106] The more important position of the merchant in central Asia as compared with Iran corresponded to the more significant role which he played in the society of the small central Asian city states, a society which was based on trade. The enormous number of wall paintings in the houses of Panjikant, unearthed by Soviet archaeologists, indicates that no town based solely on the surrounding agriculture could have afforded such expensive decorations in so many houses, or would have been interested in such luxuries. Only a trading centre, such as Panjikant seems to have been, would have produced the material culture revealed by the spade of the excavator. It is not at all difficult to believe that many Arabs were impressed with the prosperity and culture of the city states of central Asia, and joined them willingly. The Arabs, as well as west Iranian Persians, contributed also to the spread of west Iranian (Sasanian) culture to central Asia. Many words and terms were brought from western Iran to Transoxiana at the time of the Arab conquests.[107]

One should not forget that Arabic was not introduced into the chancelleries of eastern Iran and central Asia before the time of Nasr b. Saiyar, in 742. The question of which official spoken and written languages were used by the Arabs in Bukhara and Samarqand in, say, the year 725 might be raised. When the Arab armies occupied Transoxiana during and after the time of Qutaiba they must have kept the records, the *diwan,* in Pahlavi, since this had been the custom in Iran, and the armies were composed of many Persians as well as Arabs. The Sogdians used their own language to communicate among themselves, but when Devashtich wrote to an Arab official he had a scribe, presumably an Arab, who wrote for him a letter in Arabic. Pahlavi and Sogdian both gave way to Arabic as the written language of the government, but what of the spoken language? As we have noted, one must be careful in interpreting the word 'Persian' in the sources, because it could be used for Sogdian, Khwarazmian, or another Iranian language. When it is recorded, however, that Arabs or non-Arab Muslims spoke Persian one should accept this as it stands. For Persian or Dari, the Persian spoken at the Sasanian court and by the bureaucracy, undoubtedly continued to be a *lingua franca* in the eastern part of the Iranian world, and with the Arab conquests in central Asia this tongue, Dari, became even more widespread in the east at the expense of local tongues such as Sogdian. The Arabs united almost all Iranians for the first time since the Achaemenid empire, but it was under the banner of Islam and with Persian as the *lingua franca* of the east. This explains how the people of Tajikistan today speak a Persian rather than a Sogdian or Bactrian dialect. The rise of a New Persian literature in Transoxiana rather than in Fars province is another problem which will be discussed later.

It is interesting to note that during the Umaiyad caliphate we hear of no religious revolts in Khurasan or Transoxiana, whereas in the succeeding 'Abbasid period there are many, as we shall see. The answer to this lies, I suggest, in the synthesis of Islamic ideas and local beliefs, which did not manifest itself until the end of the Umaiyad or beginning of the 'Abbasid era. Transoxiana had many religions, Buddhism, Manichaeism, Nestorian Christianity and local Zoroastrianism, not to mention small colonies of Jews and Hindus. Consequently Islam made more progress on the frontiers than in western Iran where the Zoroastrian state religion maintained more of a unity in its community than was the case in central Asia, which had no universal state church of Zoroastrianism. The advent of another religion, Islam, into central Asia had much less of a disturbing impact in the order of society than elsewhere. Since Zoroastrianism, as we know it, was not a strong missionary religion, and furthermore was generally optimistic and positive in its outlook, one would hardly expect a Zoroastrian religious crusade or holy war against Islam. The latter religion was perhaps more concerned with 'orthodoxy' rather than with 'orthopraxy', whereas Zoroastrianism, at least in Islamic times, was more concerned with orthopraxy among its adherents. Khurasan of the Arabs was much larger than in ancient times since the Arabs included central Asia beyond the Oxus in their province of Khurasan. Such cities as Nishapur, Balkh and Merv were closer to Bukhara and Samarqand than to Isfahan or Shiraz. Nishapur, for example, with its many revolts, should be considered part of eastern rather than western Iran. It should be remembered that Zoroastrianism in central Asia was called in Sogdian the religion of the Magi (*mwγ'nc dyn*) and, with its many local features, is not to be identified with the Zoroastrianism of Sasanian Iran.

One feature of the religious life of central Asia which aroused the curiosity of the Arabs was the many idols of clay or wood which were 'worshipped' by the local people.[108] Soviet archaeologists have unearthed thousands of clay statuettes of different styles from various sites in central Asia, so many indeed that different schools of glyptic art can now be assumed on the basis of these clay figurines. Furthermore it seems that these figurines were a general feature of central Asian society and not of Iran, since archaeological excavations on the Iranian plateau have failed to uncover them. One may suggest that the idols were an ancient practice of the peoples of central Asia which continued under Buddhism, local Mazdaism, and possibly even Manichaeism and Christianity. In other words I suggest that the practice of making clay figurines was not bound to any one of the major religions which we know. The conventional theory that such figurines were of Buddhist inspiration is refuted by their widespread provenance throughout central Asia, a great number from places where there were hardly any Buddhists, and by the absence of Buddhist iconographic features. Rather, survivals from an ancient mother goddess cult and other local cults would seem to be the best explanation for the large number and varied place finds of such objects. In any case many folk beliefs and non-religious practices must be taken into account in assessing the religions of central Asia in this period. The pre-Islamic customs, holidays and usages which were adopted, adapted or at least tolerated by the religion of Islam were legion and it would require another book to investigate them. Suffice it to say that many practices of Zoroastrianism, such as prayer five times a day, were so similar to those of Islam that an identification of the two religions was not only possible in the minds of many, but the similarities must have made it easy for many to convert, especially from an 'orthopraxy' oriented religion to one more concerned with 'orthodoxy'.

One might object that the Arab tribesmen were not particularly interested in formal religion, but by no means were all the Arabs who came to Khurasan simple camel riding warriors. We have seen how one branch of the Azd which came to the east was noted for its trading and weaving abilities, and undoubtedly there were others with other specializations. In the garrison cities of Khurasan the Arabs soon intermarried with the local population and engaged in local activities. It is true that new infusions of Arab troops from Basra and Kufa, or later from Syria, kept the tribal spirit alive, but more as a tradition of the past than as a true reflexion of the real situation. As already mentioned, the Arab armies soon became Muslim armies, and even when one hears of Arabs being sent to the east in the latter half of Umaiyad rule, one wonders how many Arab bedouins there were in these armies. After the time of Abu Muslim the Arab tribes vanish from the pages of the history of eastern Iran and central Asia. This does not mean that there were no Arab tribes settled as tribes here and there in the east, but their numbers were negligible and their influence practically nil. Some Arabs, how many we do not know, left the east with the decline and then fall of Umaiyad power and authority in Khurasan, but the main reason for the disappearance of the Arab tribes of the east from the pages of our sources was that they were absorbed into the greater Islamic oecumene which was being formed at the end of the Umaiyad caliphate. The *mawali* had by then won, for the most part, the rights of equality with Arab Muslims.

This process took place in Khurasan, and to a lesser extent in Seistan, rather than in western Iran, and thus in the east a basis for a future flowering of Islamic culture was laid. One reason for this, of course, was the settlement of more Arabs on the frontiers than in the interior, and the consequent greater mixture. Furthermore, as we have emphasized, the frontier areas were more free and open and prone to the mixture of cultures than the hinterland. Finally, in Khurasan and Transoxiana a trading and commercial society flourished which had analogies with the Hijaz, homeland of the Prophet Muhammad. Shiraz and Isfahan were noted more as centres of agricultural areas than of trade, and Sasanian Zoroastrianism recommended the cultivation of land and the extension of cultivation above other activities, whereas Sogdiana flourished as a nation of tradesmen. It is small wonder that the background for a successful co-operation between Muslims and non-Muslims was laid in the east, whereas in western Iran the lines dividing peoples into communities, or ghettos, were more strictly drawn. The future flourishing of an oecumenical Islamic culture in eastern Iran and Transoxiana was laid in the Umaiyad period.

When one searches for reasons for the fall of the Umaiyads, especially in our area of Iran and the east, they are not difficult to find. The discontinuity in government and in policies is observable in the changes in governors, a change even more rapid than that in caliphs. In fact when the Umaiyad caliph designated his son as his successor, the opposition of a brother or other member of the family would not be unexpected. When Sulaiman replaced Walid and then removed the successful governors and army commanders of his predecessor, he was laying foundations on sand for the future. Tribal factionalism and the spirit of revenge dominated the politics and indeed the whole history of the Umaiyads. 'Umar II's policies served only to arouse hopes in the non-Arab Muslims for equal treatment with the Arabs, which hopes were dashed at the end of his reign. The various tax measures, principally those regarding the *jizya* in Iran and the east, from 718 to 729 also caused great unrest. In 728 in Bukhara the *dihqans*, who collected the taxes, asked the government in despair from whom should the *kharaj* be taken. Ashras the governor replied that the *kharaj* should be taken from those who had previously paid it, while the *jizya* should be put back on the heads of those recently converted to Islam.[109] Perhaps rather than ask why the Umaiyad caliphate fell, one might question why it lasted as long as it did. Or one almost might say that Islam spread in the east in spite of the Umaiyad government rather than because of it. In any case the picture we have of Umaiyad rule in Iran and the east is more complicated than the simple picture of continual Arab tribal conflicts as gleaned from the tribal narratives in Tabari, and as masterfully reported by Wellhausen so many years ago.[110]

CHAPTER 6

THE 'ABBASIDS AND WESTERN IRAN

The victory of the 'Abbasids runs parallel with a marked decline in the influence of the Arab tribes in Khurasan. They did not all leave the east by any means, for much later we hear of Arab tribes in Seistan in Juzjan (modern north-west Afghanistan), and elsewhere.[1] The role of the Arab tribes, as tribes, in the fall of the Umaiyad dynasty has been exaggerated in my opinion. One cannot deny the importance of the Arabs in the overthrow of the Umaiyads, or the existence of tribal loyalties in Khurasan. The tribal organization in Khurasan, however, was unlike that in the Arabian peninsula, for the tribesmen in the east were settled, and by the time of the 'Abbasids they had become part of the local scene, if not yet fully assimilated into the mass of the Iranian population. In any case the tribal structure had surely changed: the septs or subdivisions of the tribe which camped together, called *haiy* by the Arabs, had given way to the *dar* or the settled sept. The extended family or Arabic *'a'ila*, the descendants of a tribal patriarch, had become even more scattered in Iran after the Islamic conquests. The most important change which occurred, however, was the freeing of the individual Muslim from a servitude to and an economic dependence on the patriarch of the tribe. Many would argue that from the beginning Muhammad had this social change in mind, but it happened only after the expansion of the Arabs from the peninsula.

The settling of the Arab tribesmen after the rapid conquests and their organization into *dars* brought a great increase in concubinage and the growth of large harems with intermarriages between Arab warriors and local women. This undoubtedly contributed to changes in Islamic society, and especially to the dominant and special position of the Arabs in that society. Under the 'Abbasids the word *maula*, in the sense that it had under the Umaiyads, finally goes out of existence. If one tries to compare the theoretical basis of Islamic society and of taxation, as found in Arabic books, with the realities of the various provinces of the caliphate, many exceptions to and variations on the theory become apparent. It is impossible to give an overall estimate of the realities of the islamicization of Iran, but let us briefly examine the social situation, the tax structure, and finally the administration under the ʿAbbasids.

As we have mentioned in the previous chapter, there were strictly speaking only two classes of people in the ʿAbbasid caliphate, Muslims and non-Muslims, although a social classification differentiated the Arab Muslim freeman (*mukallaf*) from the convert (*maula*), and further the non-Muslim freeman (*dhimmi*) and the slave (*ʿabd* or *mamluk*). There is no doubt, however, that from the beginning of the ʿAbbasid caliphate the distinction between Arab and non-Arab Muslim became blurred and the later literary movement emphasizing a distinction between the two, called the *Shuʿubiyya*, was not a widespread popular movement but rather limited to literati and scholars mostly at the caliphal court in Baghdad.

The question of taxation under the ʿAbbasids is much more involved, and at the present there is still a lack of clarity regarding taxes in various parts of the caliphate. It will be recalled that the tax in Khurasan, and in the east in general, was based primarily on individuals, probably because the local rulers had practised this before Islam. This practice caused great unrest under the Umaiyads, since theoretically if a man converted to Islam his taxes were lightened and the tax load was then increased among the remaining non-Muslims. To recapitulate briefly: the *kharaj*, which in the beginning meant tribute, was 'on the heads of individuals' in Khurasan.[2] Frequently, however, if a local Zoroastrian in Khurasan became a Muslim he did not escape paying his former taxes but was even fined additionally. Nasr b. Saiyar tried to change this situation but it was too late for the Umaiyads. Under the ʿAbbasids taxes were more stabilized. The *kharaj*, which together with the *jizya* had been indiscriminately considered as tribute in the Prophet's time, was now reserved for the land tax, the most important and stable source of revenue in the caliphate. The tax on people (and on movable property) came to be called *jizya*, and then it became under the ʿAbbasids a poll-tax on all non-Muslims. The *zakat*, which at first was a communal obligation to support the religion, under the Umaiyads had become organized and was collected from all Muslims by state tax collectors. Again the amounts and collections in different areas took different forms, from two and a half per cent of total property upwards. The taxes became confused for, among various reasons, under the ʿAbbasids all funds went into the central treasury in Baghdad. Later (in the fifth century AH) the *zakat* was moved from the public to the private domain and it was no longer collected by the state but became a religious obligation such as the Christian tithing. Many other taxes such as market and produce taxes, and customs duties existed, and ʿAbbasid officials were as ingenious in devising new taxes as modern states. The religious leaders at times opposed new taxes as being contrary to Islam, and revolts against the imposition of new taxes were not uncommon. Not only taxes, but also land holdings and water rights, have from time immemorial been the cause of much strife in Iran and this was also true during the 'Abbasid caliphate. Although several traditions attribute the origin of the Islamic *waqf* or (religious) endowment to the caliph 'Umar I who gave such revenues to the poor, it is more likely that the Arabs borrowed this practice primarily from the Christians in the Near East and from the Zoroastrians in Iran, both of whom had such endowments in pre-Islamic times, the Christians frequently with monasteries and the Zoroastrians with their fire temples. The finances and taxation of the 'Abbasid caliphate must be studied in detailed monographs on coinage, monetary policy and technical matters which cannot be discussed here.

To turn to the 'Abbasid administration, it is not easy to distinguish between innovations and legacies from the past. It is a mistake, however, to assume that the 'Abbasids changed most of the institutions of the Umaiyads, for there was a continuity, especially from the time of caliph Hisham whose reforms laid the basis for the 'Abbasid administration. The Umaiyads had built up the *barid*, which was more of an information than a postal service, and the 'Abbasids greatly expanded it. At the end of Umaiyad rule the *'amil* or 'tax collector' responsible to the caliph is found, and in 'Abbasid times he becomes very important. The 'Abbasids seem to have created the departments of government, or the *diwans* with their head the vizier. In effect, under the 'Abbasids this was the financial-administrative division of the government parallel to the military division and the religious establishment. The word *diwan*, which seems to be Persian in origin, having passed into Armenian and Syriac from Middle Persian, was probably used at first for the financial records, and the widening of the term for all administration is later. It came to mean simply a bureau rather than a ministry. The widespread belief that the Arabs could not write Arabic at the time of the conquests, and therefore had to rely on the subject peoples to write *everything* for them in Greek or in Pahlavi, is of course nonsense. The Arabs allowed local bureaucracy to continue as previously, but any records for the army, or for purely Arab affairs, were written in Arabic. In a sense, from the beginning there was a double bureaucracy, one for the Arabs and another for the conquered peoples, though both were under Muslim direction. The *diwan* came into prominence only in Islamic times although the word may have been used for a government bureau even in Sasanian times. Unfortunately we have no record of its existence, as far as I know, in pre-Islamic times. We have spoken of 'Umar's *diwan* for his troops earlier, and this surely provided the *Islamic* content for the later 'Abbasid *diwans*, but, to repeat, only under the 'Abbasids does the system of *diwans* flourish and expand.

As mentioned, the prototype of the vizier (*wazir*) was probably the *vuzurg framadar* of Sasanian times as stated in Islamic sources. The chief viziers under the early 'Abbasids were non-Arabs (*mawali*), but they were all subject to the whims of the caliph. The vizier was the head of the bureaucracy, the class of *katibs* (pl. *kuttab*) which grew enormously in the Samarra period of the caliphate.[3] The vizier, however, really became influential only under the Barmecids in the time of Harun al-Rashid. It was Khalid b. Barmak who organized the *diwans* of the army (*jund*) and of taxes (*kharaj*). In theory the vizier was by no means the second in power after the caliph. His main function, especially during later 'Abbasid times, was to raise money.

The revenues went into the central treasury, which from time to time pretended a distinction between the public treasury where the *kharaj* went, and the private treasury of the caliph where money from caliphal estates and from the *jizya* went, for expenses such as the pilgrimage to Mecca and the *jihad* or 'holy war' on the frontiers. The bulk of the revenue went to the army and afterwards in priority to the court and the *diwans*, with but little left for religious courts and public utilities. The caliphal court in Baghdad, and for a time in Samarra, required enormous sums of money, and confiscation of funds, both private and those designated for specific public purposes, unfortunately became a well-known feature of the caliphal court.

Local administration was modelled after the caliphal government in Baghdad, which continued earlier practices. Over a province stood an *amir* appointed by the caliph; there was in addition an *'amil* or tax collector responsible to the caliph and appointed by Baghdad. The postmaster, head of the *barid*, was also independent of the provincial government. It must be strongly emphasized that changes in meanings of words, such as *amir* or *'amil*, paralleled the shifts in individuals to different offices while still retaining old titles, thus making a consistent reconstruction of posts in the 'Abbasid bureaucracy very difficult throughout time and space, the variations in different provinces of the Iranian plateau alone being most confusing. Usually the titles over a period of time depreciated in status. What is presented here is only a general picture with many exceptions and differences, especially as time passed.

It is not our task here to analyse the 'Abbasid court and government, for this has been done by others, but the relationship of the Iranians in Persia and in central Asia to the Arabs and to Islam remains our focus. Therefore the provincial government should be examined in more detail than Baghdad. It should be remembered that when the Arabs settled down in Iranian lands in many areas they settled in cantonments, as the British in India, or in parts of towns, quartered on the natives. Since they mostly settled in the strategic cities on the trade routes, such as Raiy, Merv and Bukhara, these cities naturally became the centres of reaction between Muslims and the native people. As was to be expected, villages maintained their old customs and beliefs long after the cities became Muslim. Islam often has been described as a culture based on urban life, and by dominating the cities it was inevitable that the surrounding countryside would in time follow the lead of the urban centres. Traditional Iranian towns are described as having a citadel (Arabic *qal'a* or *hisar*, Persian *kuhandiz* or *diz*), with sometimes an inner fortified residence of the ruler (Ar. *qasr*, Pers. *arg*), the city proper (Ar. *madina* or more rarely *qasaba*, Pers. *shahristan*), and the suburbs (Ar. *rabad*, which has no Persian equivalent, though sometimes the word *rusta* is found for 'suburbs'). Sometimes the city with suburbs, in the modern sense, is called *balad* in Arabic and *shahr* in Persian. This did not apply, however, to all cities in Iran, for there were other forms in some cities; for example Gurgan and Isfahan were twin or double cities, a form well known in Hungary (Budapest), on the Volga (Khazar capital of Itil) and elsewhere. Whether the double city arose originally in the time of the Arab conquests when, like the British conquests in India, garrison towns or cantonments were created next to the old cities, is likely but not certain since double cities did exist in antiquity. In any case, the origin of the typology of double cities, mentioned above, was probably Iranian. Ishfahan, Kazerun, Nishapur and Qazvin, on the other hand, were conglomerations of villages–what one might call compound cities.[4] The administrative area outside a city, sometimes the suburbs plus villages, was a *nahiyya* in Arabic (*rustaq* in Persian), and as we have noted in Iran the *rustaq* administratively was divided into *tassuj*. Some provinces were divided into *kuras* (*ostans* in Persian). Again there was no uniformity because of geography and different traditions of different areas from Sasanian times. On the Iranian plateau and in central Asia geography and the lack of water have always determined the sites of settlement, and the salient characteristic of settlement is the oasis, even though it might be a large oasis like Isfahan or Bukhara. The sites of cities such as Nishapur may have changed throughout history because of the water supply or other reasons, or the site may have been surprisingly stable throughout the centuries, like Hamadan.[5]

By the 'Abbasid period many cities, such as Merv or Nishapur, had become overwhelmingly Muslim, while others not on the strategic road to the east, such as Isfahan or Kirman, although with a Muslim government, still had large numbers of Zoroastrians, Jews and others. Since the administration or rule was everywhere in Muslim hands, except in the Caspian Sea provinces, the Muslim character of provincial organization everywhere became similar. On the whole four officers were to be found in almost every city or town which was not a provincial capital where, quite naturally, the provincial bureaucracy was much larger than in other towns. The first officer was a *wali*, or local governor of the entire *rustaq*, appointed usually by the governor of the province, and more rarely directly from Baghdad. Thus the governor of Khurasan would appoint the sub-governors of the many districts under his jurisdiction. The local tax collector or *ʿamil* was also a provincial appointment, although he too, like the other two officers, the *sahib al-barid* or postmaster and the *qadi* or judge, might receive appointment directly from Baghdad. The caliphal court in Baghdad was constantly thronged with seekers after provincial and local offices. Lobbies and factions from all over the caliphate, of course, existed in the capital city. Needless to say practices varied, but almost all local governments were characterized by corruption, the existence of groups or cliques struggling against each other, and loyalty or responsibility only to the ruler not to the public. Gradually as time passed in some towns the various quarters had their own chiefs or *shaikh*, and a *ra'is* or mayor, would be the chief officer in a town. Also two separate administrations grew up in Islamic cities, what one might call the central government establishment, staffed by soldiers, clerks and higher officials of the financial and military branches, many of whom were outsiders sent to the town, and the urban establishment. The last was the organization of the permanent inhabitants of the city, the *ra'is*, the *shaikhs*, who were also in charge of education in their quarters, the *qadis*, other mosque officials and members of important families. One might call this group of urban officials also the 'religious' establishment, for as the caliphate declined, the influence of local religious leaders increased in the towns. As Islam became stronger and the various 'schools of law' developed, factions in the large cities such as Nishapur, Raiy and Merv became more powerful. For example, in the fourth century of the *Hijra* Raiy and Bukhara were dominated by the Hanafi faction, while Merv, Qazvin, Shiraz, Ardebil and other cities were Shafiʿi, and in Isfahan and Samarqand the two factions were about equally divided. Very little is heard about the Zoroastrian population except in Fars province, and we should turn briefly to them.

The Zoroastrian books of the ninth century, and the 'intellectual renaissance' in Fars province, and elsewhere in western Iran, has been studied by De Menasce and others.[6] It is impossible here to discuss the interesting details of legal problems between Zoroastrians and Muslims as contained in the Zoroastrian books. The ghettos of minorities which probably existed in the Sasanian empire continued into Islam, with the difference that now the Zoroastrians were subject to others, the Muslims. Unfortunately information about the Zoroastrians in Iran is very scant, for the most part brief notices in Arabic geographies, and books on religion which here and there give a sentence to Zoroastrians. Usually the former simply mention the existence of fire temples, while the latter books talk about heresies or about unimportant details. As a result we are obliged to interpolate and guess at the position of the Zoroastrian religion in various parts of Iran during ʿAbbasid times. From the sources it is clear that the centres of Zoroastrianism, other than the isolated Caspian provinces, were Fars with Kirman and a few areas of Azerbaijan. Certain districts elsewhere, for example, in Raiy and Isfahan, had fire temples and worshippers, but with the lack of support from the state the number of Mazdeans grew less and less.[7] A statistical survey of fire temples, both active and abandoned, in the Arabic sources would only confirm the pattern mentioned above. Conflicts between Muslims and Zoroastrians, which in the early days of Islam were frequent, became rarer as regulations between the communities were fixed, and the Zoroastrians withdrew into their ghettos. Ibn al-Athir (vol. VIII, 522) reports a violent fight between Muslims and Zoroastrians in Shiraz in 369/979, which was stopped by the government. Such clashes, however, are rarely reported in the sources and they cannot have been of frequent occurrence after the eleventh century.

Let us survey the provinces of Iran and central Asia to determine the local situation at the end of the ninth century when the religious revolts, to be discussed in the next chapter, were over and Islam seemed dominant everywhere. Fars province remained divided into five districts, but change had occured in the demography of the province with new settlements. For example, the seaport of Siraf on the Gulf had brought the interior into contact with Africa and the Far East.[8] At the beginning of the Islamic conquest there had been many revolts in Fars, especially in the capital Istakhr, but after the severe suppression of these revolts many people became Muslims and Islam grew, with the result that the Zoroastrians became reconciled to their masters and thereafter we hear of very few revolts.[9] After Shiraz became the chief city of the province, replacing Istakhr probably in the ninth century, Zoroastrians still existed there, but even more in Kazerun, which had replaced Sabur or Bishapur as the principal city of that district.[10] An indication of the problems of the Zoroastrians under Muslim rule is given by the story that Shaikh Abu Ishaq al-Kazeruni, founder of a dervish order, molested the fire temples of the district and was such a thorn in the side of the Zoroastrians that they wished to migrate. Since the local governor was also a Zoroastrian, they protested to him and he in turn went to Shiraz to complain to Fakhr al-mulk, the Boyid prince.[11] The shaikh, according to the complaint, had gathered around him ruffians (*aubash*) and fought the Zoroastrians, who, however, in turn had caused troubles for the shaikh. The Boyid ruler tried to make peace but was not too successful. On the whole, however, the people of Fars were noted for their obedience to the government, and their easy-going ways have been manifested throughout history.[12]

Arabic geographies mention the gypsum fort (*qalʿa jiss*) in Arrajan province where Zoroastrians lived and kept their books, including histories of pre-Islamic Iran.[13] This was probably one of a very few places in Iran in the tenth century where Zoroastrian writings were preserved and copied. One wonders how much of the Middle Persian inscriptions the *mobad* Marasfand from Kazerun could read at Persepolis for the Boyid ruler ʿAdud al-daula in AD 955.[14]

If Zoroastrianism was declining in Fars, it was even weaker elsewhere. Khuzistan, according to Muqaddasi (p. 414), had few Christians and fewer Jews and Zoroastrians. At the time of the Arab conquest Christianity was the dominant religion in Khuzistan, and most of the Christians became Muslims. Since Arabs were apparently settled in Khuzistan even in pre-Islamic times, the transition to Islam must have been faster here than on the plateau. In history one great area has been neglected, namely the tribal groups in the foothills of Khuzistan and in much of Fars province. Tribes always have been a feature of Persian history, but the sources are extremely scant in reference to them since they did not 'make' history. The general designation 'Kurd' is found in many Arabic sources, as well as in a Pahlavi book on the deeds of Ardashir the first Sasanian ruler, for all nomads no matter whether they were linguistically connected to the Kurds of today or not. The population of Luristan, for example, was considered to be Kurdish, as were tribes in Kuhistan and Baluchis in Kirman.[15] One may suppose that Iranian-speaking nomadic tribes, such as the Bakhtiyaris of today, roamed much the same winter quarters and summer quarters in the past as at present. There undoubtedly was a rise and fall in the power and influence of the tribes in ancient as in more recent times. Likewise tribes were mostly self-governing, sometimes paying taxes or tribute to a settled government, but mostly not. If the sources only contained more information we might gain a better insight into tribal-village relationships, which, in any case, have hardly changed over the centuries.

It should be mentioned that the rich linguistic diversity of Iran, especially in the Zagros mountain chain, was even greater in the past than today. The rugged geography of western Iran probably contributed to the conservatism of Fars and al-Jibal in holding to both Arabic and local dialects as their 'tool' languages, whereas in the east New Persian became the *lingua franca*. This will be discussed later, when speaking of the Tahirids and Samanids.

Kirman was considered almost as an extension of Fars province, but it was independently governed under the ʿAbbasids. The province was divided into five *kuras*, called after their capitals: Bardashir or Bardasir (from Veh Ardashir) modern Kirman, Sirjan, Bam, Narmashir (Nev Hormizd Ardashir) and Jiruft. All exist today save Narmashir, the ruins of which are found to the east of Bam. Sirjan was the early capital but in the tenth century AD Bardashir or present-day Kirman became the capital. The province of Kirman was known until recently as a centre of Zoroastrians, but this is primarily because the religion died out elsewhere while in Kirman province it remained as a relic in an out-of-the-way area. On the other hand it seems that larger segments of the population became Muslim here earlier than in Fars. The inhabitants of the Bariz mountains in southern Kirman were converted to Islam at the beginning of the ʿAbbasid period, but they remained independent of government control until they were partially conquered in the time of the Saffarids.[16] Although the language of Kirman was Persian, the inhabitants of the Bariz area, the wild Qufs, probably spoke a special Iranian tongue as did, of course, the Balus or Baluchis. Kirman was always isolated and the population was smaller than elsewhere.

Media never had the unity, geographical or otherwise, which Fars had, and it is difficult to reconstruct the administrative, and even the purely geographical, divisions of this large area. From Arabic sources it seems that the name al-Jibal was applied primarily to the plateau area with the three main cities of Hamadan, Isfahan and Raiy, all ancient centres. Kurdistan was frequently included in al-Jibal, but Azerbaijan was not. It is interesting that we do not know the administrative divisions of al-Jibal (*kuras*) as we do in Fars and Kirman. Changes were too frequent and the political situation not as stable as in the south. Zoroastrians existed in al-Jibal as well as in Fars, and for a time under the ʿAbbasids the chief *mobad* of al-Jibal was the head of all Zoroastrians in Iran.[17] According to one source, Jews were found in the towns of al-Jibal more than Christians.[18] In al-Jibal the Kurds were perhaps more extended in the ninth and tenth centuries than at the present and it is clear that they were quite active in local politics. One may presume little change in the life of the population of Kurdistan from that time to almost the present. Numerous references in the Arabic sources tell us that the Kurds were prone to attack caravans and towns, retreating thereafter to their mountain abodes. As already mentioned, 'Kurd' seems to have been a generic term for nomads all over Iran, except for Arab tribes, which though few and small were to be found, especially in Khurasan. The linguistic situation, not only in central Iran but probably almost everywhere in al-Jibal, was well described by a geographer of the end of the ninth century AD, who said of the town of Saimara in Luristan that the inhabitants were a mixture of Arabs,

Kurds and Persians, but that they spoke Persian.[19] Likewise Qazvin, Nihavand and Dinawar were cities with both Arabs and Persians, while in Raiy there were very few Arabs.[20] Even more interesting regarding the common language of central Iran is the statement of Ibn Hauqal that all the population of the city of Qum was Shi'ite and the majority of them were Arabs but their language was Persian.[21] This in a nutshell tells what happened to the Arabs in Iran. They had to learn Persian.

As mentioned above, pockets of Zoroastrians still existed in the central part of Iran, especially in villages along the desert from Raiy to Qum, Kashan, Nayin and Yazd.[22] Zoroastrians were not confined to a ghetto, however, and some Zoroastrians were very active in public life. For example, Abu Dulaf mentions a Zoroastrian he met in Raiy in 333/944, who was not only wealthy and supplied the army of Khurasan (the Samanid army?) with their food and necessities, but was also famous for his generosity.[23] In short, central Iran, al-Jibal, was comparable to, and only a little later than, Khurasan in the process of fusion of Arabs and Iranians to form an international Islamic culture.

Azerbaijan was like Fars somewhat out of the way of the main course of events and the population was very diverse with many dialects spoken. Not only did the people there speak Persian, but there apparently was another Iranian tongue called Azeri, for it is mentioned in several sources as being understood only by people from that province.[24] In addition to this old Iranian language of Azerbaijan, which has attracted the attention of linguists (who, to find it, have sought out various Iranian dialects in villages of modern Azerbaijan), both Persian and Arabic were used. Ibn Hauqal (p. 348) says that most people in Azerbaijan, as well as in Armenia, spoke Persian but also knew Arabic, especially the merchants and those working in the government bureaucracy. In the sources one comes across a few brief notes on the settlement of Arabs in the province but it seems clear that neither the weather nor the rough topography appealed to the Arab conquerors. Ibn Hauqal (p. 337) tells of an important Arab family called the Banu Rudaini which gave its name to the district of Ushnuya, south-east of Lake Urmiya, near Tabriz, but the family was finally absorbed by the surrounding population. The two cities of Azerbaijan which are mentioned in the sources as capitals, either concurrently, or as capitals of eastern and western Azerbaijan, were Ardebil and Maragha. The latter was the capital of the whole province in the time of Harun al-Rashid and al-Ma'mun.[25] This name was given by the Arabs to the Iranian town perhaps called originally Afrazarud or Apzaharud. In passing it should be noted that Arabs settled in Iran not only during the conquests but also later under the 'Abbasids. For example, in Azerbaijan Hamdanid Arab tribesmen settled in 'Abbasid times. South Arabs were settled down near Tabriz by the caliph al-Mansur.[26] In fact it seems that al-Mansur settled many Arabs in various places in Iran. It is a mistake to assume that there was no movement or settlement of people after the Arab conquests, although large numbers, of course, were not involved.

Ardebil, the second capital of Azerbaijan, was known as Abadan Piruz or Shahram Peroz in Sasanian times, and at the time of the Arab conquest was apparently the only capital of the province, and many Arabs consequently settled there. In the villages around Ardebil, according to Ibn Hauqal (p. 347), the people spoke a dialect unlike Azeri or Persian. Since there were many Armenians, Kurds and Georgians in Azerbaijan the Zoroastrians relatively were not as numerous as in the south. In the Mughan steppe on the River Aras, however, were many villages with Zoroastrian inhabitants during the ʿAbbasid period.[27] Also one of the great fire temples of Sasanian Iran, that called *atur gushnasp*, continued to function at Shiz, today called Takht-i Sulaiman, south of Lake Urmiya. We cannot say how long the fire continued in service beyond the tenth century, for it seems to have died out gradually and not through any act of repression by the Muslims. Azerbaijan just as Transoxiana was a frontier area, a place of refuge for rebels and heretics.

Armenians, Georgians and Albanians (Arabic: Arran) were to be found in the cities of northern Azerbaijan, but much of the population had converted to Islam at an early date, certainly earlier than Fars or even parts of al-Jibal.[28] Although the Hanbalite school of the Sunnis was strong, heretics were plentiful, including, it seems, remnants of the pre-Islamic Mazdakites who will be discussed in the next chapter.

The areas surrounding Azerbaijan to the north-west, north and north-east, were tributary or dependent on Azerbaijan. The rulers of Georgia, Armenia and Sharvan usually paid tribute to the caliphate, but after the revolt of Babak was crushed many Armenian and Albanian princes were deported to Iraq and the way was open for new Islamic dynasties to take their places. Iranian colonies existed in the Caucasus, especially at the famous military barrier the wall of Derbend, and it was only natural that the Arabs should continue their conquests to the old Sasanian boundaries in the north. The town of Bardaʿa (Iranian: Partav) became the military centre of the Arabs in the Transcaucasian area, and Derbend submitted to them in 25/645. During the wars against the Khazars under the Umaiyads many Arabs were settled in Derbend. Tiflis was also occupied by Muslim forces, although the surrounding areas were ruled by Georgian princes, while Muhammad b. Khalid b. Yazid b. Mazyad, governor of Ganja, from 245/859 held sway as an independent ruler, and from 255/869 the Hashimid family ruled Derbend as an independent appanage. Both houses were of Arab origin. Just as in Transoxiana, so on the Caucasus

Metalwork: The Continuity of Imperial Motifs

1 Bronze censer from Nakitcheran, Armenia. Date unknown, Sasanian style.

2 *Below left* Late Sasanian or early Islamic silver plate showing bear hunt.

3 *Below right* Stone plate from Transcaucasia, Islamic period, copying Sasanian motifs.

4 *Above* Hephthalite silver bowl from Chilek near Samarqand, sixth century.

5 *Above* Musician depicted on late Sasanian silver bowl. The same motifs appear on early Islamic objects.

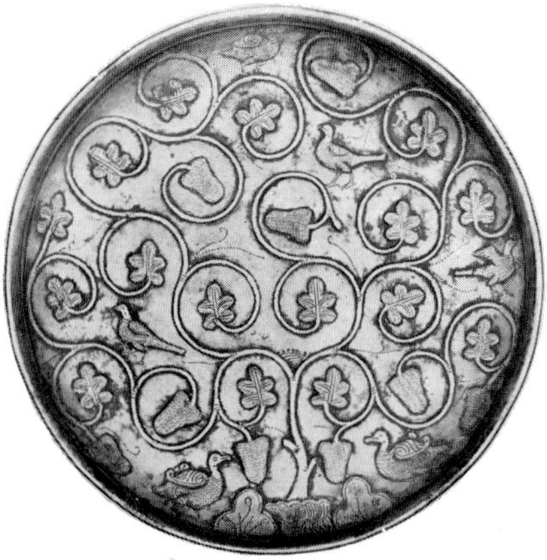

6 *Above left* Sasanian silver bowl with traditional motifs.

7 *Above right* Silver bowl of the Islamic period with Sasanian motifs.

8 Boyid gold medal in archaizing pre-Islamic style, motif of the ruler hunting.

Popular Arts and Crafts

9 *Left* Folk art decoration on West Persian manganese painted white ware. Probably ninth century, continuing a Sasanian tradition.

10 Recent pottery from Istalif, Afghanistan, with classical Islamic motifs.

11 Brass candleholder inlaid with silver, dated 1225, in ornate style of the Seljük period. Decoration combined with utility.

12 *Above* Qajar tile work from Isfahan showing the ancient tradition of the hunt.

13 Remains of a shield from Panjikant showing a Sogdian warrior from the time of the Arab conquests.

14 Head from wall painting in Lashgari Bazaar, Bust, Afghanistan, from the time of Sultan Mas'ud.

15 *Above left* Sasanian textile from a tomb in the Caucasus.

16 *Above right* Caftan in silk with motif of the simurgh bird in a circle of pearls. From the tomb of an Alan prince in the north Caucasus; dated *c.* eighth century AD.

17 Sasanian motif in Islamic, textile made in Khurasan for a Turkish general, Abu Mansur Bukhtigin (d. AD 961).

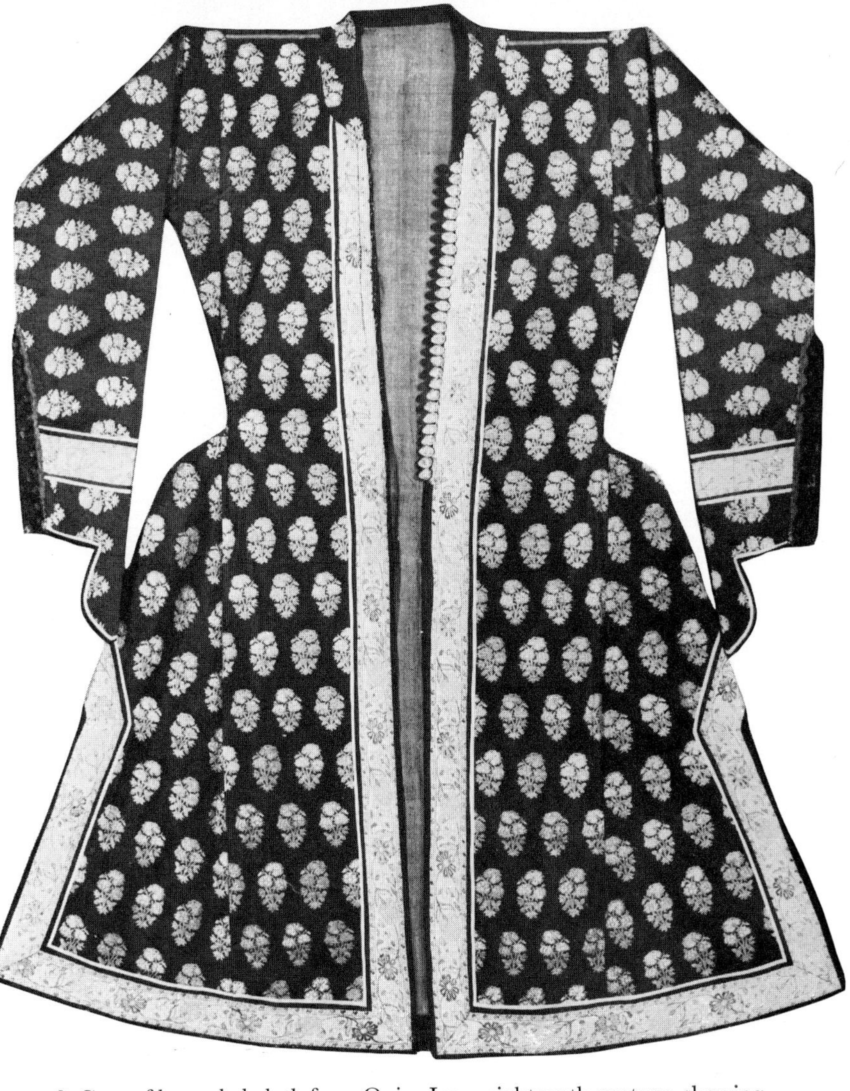

18 Coat of brocaded cloth from Qajar Iran, eighteenth century, showing persistence of old motifs.

19 Cloth covering of a tomb in the shrine of Imam Reza in Mashhad, sixteenth century. The angel reflects ancient traditions.

Architecture

20 *Above* Imamzadeh Ja'far in Arrajan near Behbehan; style of architecture peculiar to south-west Persia.

21 *Left* Sanctuary known as Daniel's tomb in the mosque courtyard of Susa, south-west Persian style.

22 *Opposite above* Ribat-i Safid, around thirty miles south of Mashhad. Typical ruins of a *chahar taq*, date unknown, probably third century AD.

23 *Left* Tomb tower of Lajim in Mazandaran built AD 1022 for an Ispabadh Abu'l-Fawaris Shahriyar.

24 *Right* Tomb tower of East Radkan (north-west of Mashhad) from the end of the thirteenth century. One of the many such towers in northern Iran.

25 *Left* Ruins of *madrasa* at Chisht, Afghanistan, from the end of the twelfth century.
26 *Right* Ruins of mosque at Chisht, built by Sultan Ghiyath al-Din Ghuri b. Sam at the end of the twelfth century.

27 The 'Khuda-khana' in the central courtyard of the main mosque of Shiraz, from the Saffarid period, showing old traditions of building.

28 The city walls of Yazd, now destroyed. Typical of medieval cities in Iran.

29 Sasanian bridge at Shustar, perhaps built by Roman captives.

30 Safavid bridge of Ali Verdi Khan at Isfahan.

31 *Left* Sasanian column base, Kermanshah, tagh-e-Bostan.

32 *Left* Islamic stucco in Sasanian tradition; a vine leaf.

33 *Right* Islamic stucco revetment of a building in Sasanian style, from Damghan.

34 *Left* Islamic *mihrab* with old Iranian motifs in the decoration.

35 *Below* Timurid shrine of Gazurgah near Herat showing Far Eastern motifs in the decoration.

The Art of Calligraphy and Illumination

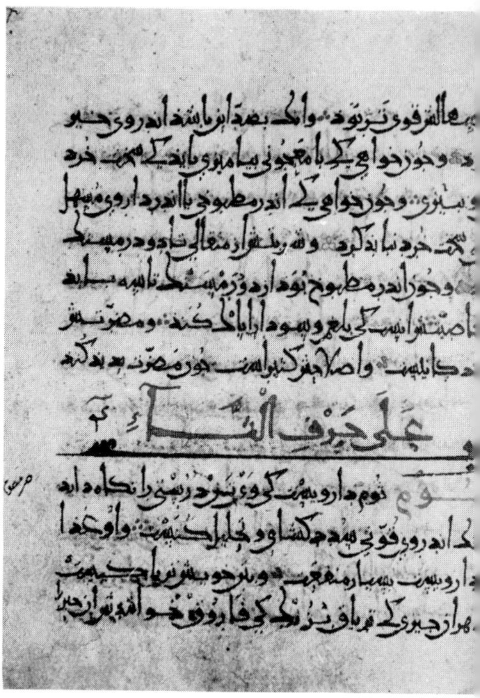

36 *Above left* Qur'an, copied in Iran and dated 1050, showing Persian style of writing in Arabic.

37 *Above right* The oldest manuscript in Persian.

39 *Right* Page from *Shahname*, dated *1482. Ancient heroes in later garb.

38 *Opposite below* Miniature showing Rustam and his horse slaying a dragon. Story in the *Shahname*, fourteenth century.

40 *Left* Miniature showing philosopher with a book, angel above, based on earlier motifs.

41 Qajar miniature, calligraphic picture showing traditional motifs in depicting ‘Ali. Nineteenth century.

frontier of the caliphate, Muslim *ghazis* were active against the infidels. The political history of Arran, with its capital at Ganja, and of Derbend has been summarized by Minorsky, and need not be repeated here.[29] The boundaries of Islam on the north varied from time to time and as the power of the caliphate declined not only did Muslim governors obtain independence but Armenian and Georgian rulers extended their domains. Since Albania or Arran was an area subject to the raids of the Khazars from the north, some of whom settled there, and of *ghazis* from the south, it became very mixed in population. The language of Arran, ancient Albanian, although spoken in Bardaʿa (Ibn Hauqal, p. 349), and elsewhere in the land, was hard pressed by Armenian and Persian. It probably went out of general use even before the Turks consolidated their rule over the whole area. Unfortunately we know less about the Caucasus area than about Iran, and much work is necessary before an adequate survey of the cultural and social history of this area can be reconstructed.[30]

The most important historical event in the history of Azerbaijan and the Transcaucasian areas during the rule of the ʿAbbasids, and before the rise of local dynasties, was the revolt of Babak, about which fortunately we have much information in the sources.[31] His revolt occurred in the period of a spate of revolts which followed the civil war between the two sons of Harun al-Rashid, al-Ma'mun and al-Amin. The former was victorious, but he remained in Merv for over five years, even after his victorious general Tahir had entered Baghdad in 198/814. The immediate background of Babak's revolt was the revolt of al-Ma'mun's governor of Azerbaijan, Hatim b. Harthama, whose father had been one of the two generals of the caliph, the other being Tahir. Harthama was imprisoned and executed by the caliph, probably at the instigation of the chief minister Fadl b. Sahl, so his son revolted.

Among the people Hatim sought to persuade to join his revolt were the adherents of a Zoroastrian sect called the Khurramdin (Arabic: Khurramiyya). The governor died, however, while the headship of the sect in Azerbaijan was assumed by Babak who himself revolted in 201/816, and through many battles with ʿAbbasid troops maintained his position until 838 when an Iranian general of al-Ma'mun, al-Afshin from Ustrushana, defeated him and then captured him and sent him to Samarra where he was executed.

It is clear that the significant 'Iranian' revolts against the caliphate or against Islam took place on the borders of the caliphate, in Azerbaijan, in the Caspian provinces and in Transoxiana rather than in Fars, Kirman or al-Jibal. The success of Babak in Azerbaijan apparently did, however, inspire his partisans in Isfahan and al-Jibal to revolt in 218/833 but they were quickly suppressed. In those provinces instead we hear of Islamic heresies, the Kharijites, who were strong in southern Iraq (and also in Seistan), or Shiʿites and not Zoroastrians or Zoroastrian sectarians. It is significant that these southern areas were also the centres of Zoroastrian orthodoxy as evidenced in the Zoroastrian books of the ninth century which were written in the south. This division is, I believe, significant for the story of the rise of the New Persian language and literature which will be discussed later. Let us turn to the Caspian provinces.

The Caspian provinces could be entered easily by an army only from the east, and so the early Arab raids took place from Gurgan. The early raids under the first Umaiyads secured tribute but no real submission. Indeed several times, in the caliphate of Muʿawiya, Muslim armies were destroyed in the passes leading into Tabaristan.[32] The earlier name of present Mazandaran was Tabaristan, land of the Tapuri, ancient inhabitants of the area. In the time of Yazid b. al-Muhallab, when he was governor of Khurasan under the caliph Sulaiman about 716, the Muslims raided Gurgan and Tabaristan and after much fighting secured the submission of the former but only a truce with the latter.[33] The people of the plains were more vulnerable than those in the mountains, but the isolation of all of them from the plateau made any pretence of ruling them unreal. Not until the time of the ʿAbbasids did either caliphal rule or Islam make any inroads in the Caspian provinces even though the Ispahbad or ruler of Tabaristan paid tribute from time to time. The caliph al-Mansur sent a large army against the Ispahbad about the year 141/758–9 and the principal city of Sari was captured while Amul and other towns of the lowlands were also occupied. Amul became the ʿAbbasid capital of the province which was divided into eight districts according to Baladhuri or fourteen according to Ibn Rusta.[34] The Ispahbads who lived in Sari had issued their own coins with a portrait similar to Chosroes II and with Pahlavi writing on them, dated according to an era of Tabaristan, from 11 June 652, following the death of Yazdegird III. After the conquest of Tabaristan and the installation of a Muslim governor, the old coins continued to be minted until as late as 175/791.[35] In 780 a revolt of the local population occurred in Tabaristan when instead of tribute, the ʿAbbasid governor ʿAbd al-Hamid Madrub tried to impose new taxes. The leader of the revolt, Windad Hurmizd b. Qarin, was able to maintain his forces in the mountains in spite of several attempts to subdue him. The government in Baghdad realized it could not control Tabaristan so peace was made and it was agreed that the Ispahbads ruled the highlands and the ʿAbbasid governors the lowlands.

Unfortunately the small princes of the mountains could rarely unite, and thus their strength was spent on local wars. The Ispahbad fought several times with the ruler of the area north of Mount Demavand (Dunbawand) called the Masmoghan (literally, chief of the Magians).

Khalid b. Barmak was governor of Tabaristan for a time (767–71) and after initial fighting made peace with the local rulers, but the calm did not last.

All was changed with the fascinating career and revolt of Mazyar (Iranian: Mahyazdyar) b. Qarin, who has been the subject of novels and poems in Persian. Mazyar was an ambitious and cruel ruler, who killed his uncle to seize his domain, and continued his conquests until he saw that his own acceptance of Islam would further his career. He took the name Muhammad and was rewarded by the caliph al-Ma'mun by being given the office of Ispahbad of Tabaristan, and, as he had killed the ruler of the principality of Sharvin, he also took the title Padashkhwargar shah (perhaps: king of the mountains where the sun is) the mountain area around Demavand. The members of the displaced dynasty called Bavend were killed or dispersed, but after the fall of Mazyar one of them regained his old title and patrimony. Meanwhile Mazyar's power and influence was growing until he accused the caliphal governor Muhammad b. Musa of Shiʿite heresy and besieged Amul, the latter's capital, captured it and imprisoned the governor. Consequently, according to some sources, he felt strong enough to abjure Islam, and about 836 or 7, in the reign of the caliph al-Muʿtasim, he openly revolted. He came into conflict with ʿAbdallah b. Tahir, governor of Khurasan, who persuaded the caliph of the danger of the revolt. Several armies were sent against Mazyar, and in the face of desertions from his own ranks, the rebel surrendered. He was sent to Samarra where he was executed in 224/838 after serving as a witness in the famous trial of the general Afshin.[36]

After the death of Mazyar, the uncle of ʿAbdallah b. Tahir was made governor of Tabaristan and was followed by Tahir, son of ʿAbdallah, and then by other relatives, so that Tabaristan in effect became subordinate to Nishapur rather than to Baghdad. After Mazyar the new Ispahbad Qarin b. Shahriyar, a member of the Bavend family, accepted Islam in 240/854. Then a change came with the invasion of the eastern part of the Caspian provinces from the west, the expansion of Zaidi Shiʿites. We must turn to Dailam and Gilan, which were more isolated than Tabaristan, to explain the new era which was inaugurated in all the Caspian provinces by the spread of Zaidi Shiʿism.

The western part of the Caspian provinces, comprising both high and lowlands, as in the east, was isolated from the east by high mountains coming down to the sea, along the coast near present-day Chalus. The mountaineers of Dailam were a particularly aggressive people known for their martial qualities by Islamic times.[37] A survey of the history of the Caspian provinces indicates that throughout the Umaiyad caliphate there occurred almost yearly raids by the Dailamites against Qazvin, which was a fortified centre of caliphal military activity against the mountaineers. After the advent of the ʿAbbasids the raids continued, and in 143/760 Mansur issued a call for volunteers to fight a holy war against the Dailamites, but obviously it was not successful since succeeding years brought new and futile attempts to subdue and convert the Dailamites. Islam, however, was to penetrate and to be spread by the activities of Shiʿite missionaries, who as early as 175/791 fled into the mountains to escape caliphal vengeance. The form of Shiʿism called Zaidi, after the grandson of Husain b. ʿAli who was martyred in 122/740, was spread throughout Dailam. The first ruler of the Zaidis was al-Hasan b. Zaid, who set himself up as an independent ruler shortly before 250/864. Many local petty dynasties existed in the western part of the Caspian provinces, but in Dailam the family was called after its founder Jastan, and these princes nominally ruled, although the Zaidi *imams* led the people in their expansion.[38] In 250/865 the Ispahbad of the east Qarin b. Shahriyar, together with Sulaiman b. ʿAbdallah b. Tahir and his army of Khurasan, was defeated by al-Hasan b. Zaid and Qarin was forced to swear homage to him in 252/866. The successor and brother of al-Hasan b. Zaid (d. 270/884) Muhammad took the surname al-Daʿi 'the missionary' and expanded Zaidi power into Gurgan. Here he came into conflict with the Samanids who had been granted the governorship of Tabaristan together with Khurasan by the caliph. The Samanid general Muhammad b. Harun al-Sarakhsi defeated and killed Muhammad b. Zaid in a battle near Gurgan in October 900. His son was taken to the Samanid capital Bukhara and a general persecution of the Shiʿites in the Caspian provinces followed. This ended the period of the expansion of Zaidi Shiʿism and set the stage for the rise of local dynasties, for the caliphate no longer had any power or influence in Iran.

Thus, throughout the ʿAbbasid caliphate until the time of the Saffarids, Samanids and Boyids, the Caspian provinces had maintained their independence with only a nominal submission to Baghdad. Sunni Islam had penetrated Gurgan and the lowlands of Tabaristan, but had made no headway in the west, in Dailam or Gilan. In Dailam it was left for refugees from the caliph's domain, Zaidi Shiʿites, to spread the religion of Islam in the mountains. In Gilan, west of the Safid Rud (river) many people were converted to Sunni, Hanbali Islam at the end of the ninth and beginning of the tenth century AD. What was the religion and general culture of those not converted to Islam before the tenth century?

The damp climate and the use of wood in building in the Caspian provinces have combined to destroy ancient remains of fire temples or other buildings from the pre-Islamic period. The persistence of Zoroastrianism, however, is attested not only in the sources but by the continuation of ancient customs and practices late into Islamic times.[39]

Furthermore the existence of at least two towers with Arabic and Pahlavi inscriptions, both highly stylized, gives us the latest surviving Pahlavi historical inscriptions in Iran. These are the tower of Mil-i Radkan in western Gurgan and the tower of Lajim in eastern Tabaristan. The two towers were built at about the same time, Radkan being finished 411/1020 and Lajim in 413/1022, and both erected by members of the local Bavend dynasty ruling in the mountains.[40] These towers with their Pahlavi inscriptions bear witness to the persistence of the ancient religion and language in the Caspian provinces long after Pahlavi had retreated on the plateau to the fire temples as the special province of *mobads*. Once Islam spread over the Caspian area, however, many soon converted to the new faith. As usual with new converts, however, the conversion to Islam produced many fanatics in the Caspian provinces who did not care to maintain ancient relics or practices. Later when Shiʿite zeal was combined with the martial qualities of the Dailamites the result was the conquest of the plateau.

Because of the relative isolation of Seistan, it became an area of refuge for rebels and heretics, and the Kharijite movements of the Umaiyad period did not cease with a change to the ʿAbbasid dynasty. The famous Karkuya fire temple, located on the road between Zaranj the capital and Juwain, and mentioned in many sources, was apparently in service as late as the tenth century but probably not much later. The province was a centre of the Kharijites from early Umaiyad times, and one of the leaders in the propagation of Kharijite doctrines in Seistan was an Arab called Qatari b. al-Fuja'a, who even issued coins in Fars, Kirman and in Zaranj between the years 689–97, with a legend in Pahlavi giving his name and the caliphal title 'amir of the faithful'.[41] Even after the famous Umaiyad governor Hajjaj b. Yusuf had crushed the Kharijites, they continued to exist in out of the way areas of Seistan and Kuhistan.

With the advent of the ʿAbbasids the revolts of the Kharijites did not cease. Several serious revolts are mentioned for the years 757–8 and 791–3, but the most serious uprising took place in 796.[42] At first the leader Hamza b. Adhrak, a pure Iranian, subdued other Kharijite groups, for this heresy had many factions which fought among themselves. Hamza terrorized the countrysides of Herat, Nishapur and Zaranj. Finally the caliph himself, Harun al-Rashid, moved against Hamza but the caliph died near Tus in 193/809. After this time, however, Kharijite activities declined and Hamza, who had lived a kind of bandit life, died in 828. The fighting among the various factions of the Kharijites in Seistan made any lasting Kharijite rule of the province impossible. Likewise the *ghazis* on the eastern frontiers of Seistan gave the province an element of instability. The town of Bust was the centre of the *ghazis* in the south-east of the caliphate, as Bardaʿa was for the

Caucasus area and Shash for Transoxiana. Since much less is known of the warriors for the faith in the area of present-day Afghanistan than in the Caucasus, on the Byzantine frontier or in central Asia, we should devote some space to them and to their enemies.

From Umaiyad times expeditions were continuously launched from Seistan and Herat against the mountainous area of central Afghanistan. As a result forts and *ribats* were built surrounding the mountain massif, and from these *ghazis* raided into Ghur, Zamindawar, Ghazna and even to Kabul. The local inhabitants retaliated and the frontier between the *dar al-harb* and the *dar al-Islam* was the scene of much fighting. The Arabs had conquered Sind in Umaiyad times, but we do not know how far their rule extended to the north or how long it lasted in many areas. Baladhuri (p. 445) lists the governors of Sind under the ʿAbbasids and tells us how they conquered Multan and even Kashmir, although the latter is mere fantasy for Kashmir was not conquered until many centuries later. The Muslims did raid to the north, however, and established their hegemony for short periods over various areas in the western Punjab. In any case, Islam expanded northwards from Sind and north-east from Seistan. In the area of Ghazna and present-day Qandahar we have already encountered the *zunbil*, but the lack of sources, especially of any coins with this title on them, unfortunately limits our knowledge. By the time of the ʿAbbasids Islam had begun to make inroads into the centre of Afghanistan and the leading non-Muslim power was that of the Turki Shahis of Kabul, who had been established first in Kapisa, modern Begram in the Koh-i Daman valley north of Kabul, but who *c.* 750–70 expanded and conquered Kabul and Gandhara or the lowlands to the east.[43] We do have coins of these Turkish princes of Kapisa, and the Shahi Tigin of the coins may be the conqueror of the areas mentioned above.[44] It seems that one Turkish prince, called Barhatigin in the sources, after the conquest of Kabul, moved his capital there and took the ancient title of the Kabul rulers – Khingila or Khimgila, which title is recorded in Arabic sources, such as the historian Yaʿqubi (vol. II, p. 479).

In the year 178/794 Ibrahim b. Jibril, governor of Seistan in the caliphate of Harun al-Rashid, raided Kabul and brought from there enormous booty.[45] Although the ruler of Kabul was not apparently converted to Islam at that time, in 199/815 we hear of the gift of a crown and in 200/816 the gift of a throne to the Kabʿa at Mecca from the Kabul Shah, newly converted to Islam. This conversion may have been the result of the activities of al-Fadl b. Sahl, vizier of Ma'mun.[46] Although the conversion of the ruler is mentioned at this time there is no evidence that many of his subjects followed suit. More conversions probably followed Yaʿqub b. Laith's capture of the city and environs in 870. The occupation must have lasted a few years for we have silver coins from Panjhir (today Panjshir) north of Kabul from 256/870 to 278/891–2, near silver mines in the mountains. About 890, however, a change occurred and the Turki Shahi dynasty was overthrown by the Brahmin Hindu vizier of the last Turkish ruler. The new ruler, called Lalliya Shahi, represented the resurgence of Hinduism in eastern Afghanistan, for it had been growing steadily at the expense of Buddhism since at least the seventh century. Lalliya may have become a vassal of another Hindu ruler, Mihira Boja, to the east, but we cannot follow events in India. It should be mentioned in passing, however, that the southern part of the Hindu kingdom of Udabhanda, the present-day Bannu area, had come under Muslim rule early, probably from Sind in the south, but in this period the Hindus recovered lost ground.[47] Thus by the end of Yaʿqub b. Laith's life, Kabul and much of the mountainous area of Afghanistan was under Hindu rule. When Alptigin, the ex-governor of Khurasan for the Samanids, came to Ghazna in 962 he dislodged a Hindu governor, probably called Lawik, and then the Islamic advance was resumed by the re-conquest of the city of Gardez in 364/974, the late date indicative of the tenacity with which the inhabitants of eastern Afghanistan held to their freedom. In the central part of the country, in Ghur and the upper Hari Rud valley also, Islam made little progress before the rise of the Ghaznavids. Even the vicinity of Herat was not safe from pagan raiders from the mountains to the east, and in 953 they almost reached the walls of the city. So the mountains of Afghanistan were the last large bastion of non-Islamic settlements within the domain of eastern Islam.

We should turn now to the problem of the *Shuʿubiya* and the interaction of the two languages, Arabic and Persian, as well as Islam and the ancient culture of Iran. In the brief survey of the provinces of the plateau of Iran, plus Seistan and present-day Afghanistan in the east, which we have covered, we have concentrated for the most part on survivals of the past in the Islamic period. The rapid summary indicated that the people of the plateau of Iran had become crystallized into the ruling Islamic society and the minorities who lived a life unto themselves. The minority communities steadily continued to decline by conversions, and only the Zoroastrians at the end of the ninth century stirred themselves to produce an apologetic literature which was an attempt to record and codify Zoroastrian practices and beliefs before they vanished with the tide of conversions to Islam. The Zoroastrian priests tried to rescue the ancient religion, as Firdosi and some of his colleagues tried to preserve the ancient literature and mores, before they too were swept away by the tide of Arab Islam. The brains of Iran, however, went into the new Islamic culture which was being forged primarily in Iran, among all the lands of the ʿAbbasid caliphate. To examine briefly the movement called the *Shuʿubiya*, we must return to the capital Baghdad, where 'the Islamic action was'.

There are ample writings on the *Shuʿubiya* which need not be summarized here.[48] The movement was a literary and scholarly one of the end of the second and the third century of the *Hijra*; it did not penetrate to the masses but was mostly limited to literary circles in Baghdad. In effect, taking the word from the Qur'an, the followers of the *Shuʿubiya* proclaimed the equality of the non-Arab with the Arab in Islam. Some Persians, however, went further and proclaimed the superiority of the Persians over the Arabs. The impossibility of making clear divisions between Arabs and Persians during the 'Abbasid caliphate, however, is illustrated by an Arab poet praising the Persians, while Zamakhshari, the famous non-Arab philologist (d. 538/1144), as the last voice in the controversy bitterly attacked the *Shuʿubiya*.[49] Al-Biruni, the great scholar of the Ghaznavid period, was proud of Iranian antiquities, but he praised the Arabic language. The Tahirids were Persian governors of Khurasan who were the first to rule independently of the caliphs, yet they were great patrons of Arabic. Nasir-i Khusrau, a Persian poet and traveller said, in Persian, that the Arabs excelled the Persians in glory![50] The list of pro- and anti-Arabs is remarkable in that it includes Arabs and Iranians on both sides, and it is primarily because of this that I believe the importance of the movement was greatly exaggerated by H. A. R. Gibb when he wrote,

> the issue at stake was no superficial matter of literary modes and fashions, but the whole cultural orientation of the new Islamic society – whether it was to become a re-embodiment of the old Perso-Aramaean culture into which the Arabic and Islamic elements would be absorbed, or a culture in which the Perso-Aramaean contributions would be subordinated to the Arab tradition and the Islamic values.[51]

What Gibb does is to over-emphasize the importance of a battle between two schools of Arabic letters, roughly that of the secretaries or scribes (pro-Persian) and the scholars or philologians of Basra and Kufa (pro-Arab). He further discounts the attribution of *Shuʿubiya* tendencies to Abu ʿUbaida, a great scholar in Arabic, as claimed by Ibn Qutaiba, but this would not have been unusual. Certainly it would be possible for one to love Arabic but not the Arabs, as we have seen. Also the elevation of literary diatribes to an almost cosmic conflict between two different cultures or approaches seems to me to be exaggerated. This is not to say that there were not conflicts, but if the stakes had been so great the cleavage would have dominated the religious controversies of the Muʿtazilites and others, plus the political and social life of the caliphate, which it certainly did not. From the very beginning of the conquests, or even before Islam, Arabs and Persians had quarrelled and attacked each other in verse. Undoubtedly there were some Arabs who equated Arab mores and customs with Islam, but the majority of Arabs must have realized that many of the practices of the Arab bedouin, or even his attitudes, were almost contrary to Islam. If the religion, the culture and society of Islam were to survive, it was also clear to many that the universal aspects of each would have to prevail. Thus, to my mind, the development of Islam is to be explained as a natural and inevitable process rather than a conflict or a victory of Arabs over non-Arabs or vice versa. The exegesis of the Qur'an provided much room for controversy but no Muslim, Arab or non-Arab, questioned the Holy Book, and in spite of disputes Islamic learning was forged on the basis of the Qur'an, plus all the learning of the Greeks, Persians and others which was needed to build a civilization.

As is frequently the case with new converts, who become more royalist than the king, Iranians of all kinds devoted themselves to Islamic learning. Al-Jahiz (died *c.* 255/869), a prominent literary figure under the ʿAbbasids, and himself probably a north African, tells how a Persian in his own day used to read the Qur'an and explain it to the Arabs on his right in Arabic and to Persians in Persian on his left.[52] In the early days, after the conquests, the Arabs taught their children Arabic and the Qur'an first in primary schools (*kuttab*) under a teacher or *muʿallim*. Then the students went to a mosque or to a particular scholar (*ʿalim*) to continue their education. In the mosques one could find specialists in various branches of Islamic learning, popular preachers (*qussas*), reciters of the Qur'an (*qurra'*), specialists on the traditions of the Prophet (*hadith*), and the like. More and more non-Arabs taught and studied in the mosque schools and excelled even the Arabs in their own language. It must be remembered, however, when the early ʿAbbasid sources speak of a man from Khurasan, they do not mean necessarily an Iranian, but usually a person of mixed parentage. Jahiz could tell a Khurasani by his pronunciation of Arabic. In Iran under the ʿAbbasids the process of fusion had gone so far that in effect only poets and literary men concerned themselves with Arab or Iranian genealogies, or rather with the superiority of one over the other.

When one turns to the field of literature and learning the universal Islamic dominance as opposed to local or 'national' traditions is obvious. Persian authors in all fields of learning who wrote in the Arabic language are entirely too many to mention here. Even in Arabic poetry Persians such as Abu Nuwas and Bashshar b. Burd excelled. It would not be too much to say that such Persians were chiefly responsible for transforming Arabic poetry from bedouin songs in Arabic to a series of world poetries by different peoples but in the Arabic language. Naturally the heads of the scribes in the ʿAbbasid bureaucracy, such as al-Fadl b. Sahl, vizier of al-Ma'mun, and his predecessors the

Barmecids, although Iranians, were masters of Arabic prose. They saw no conflict in appreciating ancient Iranian traditions and at the same time upholding Islam with its superb vehicle, the Arabic language. The caliph al-Ma'mun's high regard for Persians, and dislike of Arabs who were always quarrelling (Tabari, series III, p. 1142), was a personal feeling, undoubtedly shared by many, but by that time Islam was well on the road to becoming an international culture. Jahiz tells us much of defects in Arabic speech, not only among Iranians but also with Arabs raised among Iranians. But some non-Arabs, for example Abu Muslim, were famous for their eloquence in the Arabic language. One must not forget, as Fück has shown, that the Arabs who settled down in cities all over the caliphate developed local jargons.[53] To be sure, Jahiz decries the entry of Persian words into Arabic. He tells of an Arab poet al-ʿUmmani who composed a poem in praise of the caliph Harun al-Rashid in which all of the words in the rhyme were Persian, which the caliph obviously understood.[54] Jahiz follows this remark with an Arabic poem by Aswad b. Karima which contains forty-seven words of which thirteen are Persian. The process of fusion is admirably illustrated by the importance of people from Khurasan in the early ʿAbbasid caliphate. After all, the dynasty was brought to power by the Khurasani Muslims, hence it is no wonder that the eastern province should be so influential. Furthermore, it was an enormous and rich province, and we shall examine the role of Khurasan in the caliphate in the next chapter.

If one turns to the field of literature it is clear that under the ʿAbbasids Arabic literature changed greatly from what it had been under the Umaiyads. The literature in Arabic under the Umaiyads was primarily under the influence of the bedouins and had nomadic features, warlike and rough and still attached to the desert from whence the Arabs had come. Later Arab or non-Arab poets writing in Arabic were far from bedouin life and not particularly enamoured of it. This was an almost inevitable development in Islamic life. The new Arabic poetry was extremely varied, technically polished, and with many ideas relating to philosophy, human destiny and the like. At the same time the perfection of Arabic poetry by the tenth century AD had become almost artificial. The creator of a special genre of prose literature, the *maqamat*, al-Hamadani, could translate Persian verses into Arabic verse on the spur of the moment, and verses could be composed which would read the same forwards and backwards.[55] Arabic literature had become very sophisticated but had lost its natural quality and its spontaneous character. It seems as though the Iranians, having utilized all the resources of the Arabic language in poetry and in other genres of literature, turned to Persian as a new vehicle of expressing their feelings, not because they were anti-Arabic, but because they were looking for new fields and new possibilities of expression, as well as, of course, for popular audiences.

We must turn to religious revolts and the role of Khurasan and central Asia in the ʿAbbasid caliphate, for it was the great eastern province which not only brought the ʿAbbasids to power, but also from which the Iranian dynasties, and then the Turks, brought the caliphate down. The caliphate might fall but the Islamic religion and culture would not only survive but expand under new masters. The Arab tribal background of Islam was completely transformed under the ʿAbbasids into a universal religion and culture, and one important ingredient in the mixture, Khurasan, was the scene of many revolts under the early ʿAbbasids. Here Islam was forged and the New Persian renaissance began, so one must look to the east to examine the ground from which these developments arose.

CHAPTER 7

HERESIES AND THE OECUMENE OF ISLAM

Jahiz said that the ʿAbbasids were a Persian, Khurasani dynasty (*daula ʿajamiyya khurasaniyya*) as opposed to the Umaiyads who had been an Arab bedouin caliphate with a Syrian army. He says further that the deeds of the Umaiyads are better known because of poets and tribal historians, whereas the early ʿAbbasids did not have this advantage.[1] This was seen from the time of Jahiz, for later one may say that the ʿAbbasids dominated the pages of history, and in one domain the heretical movements during the ʿAbbasid caliphate were both more numerous and more complicated than in Umaiyad times. The Iranian character of most of them is striking and testifies to the syncretic tendencies prevalent on the Iranian plateau at that time. It is sometimes difficult in the sources to distinguish between Muslim and non-Muslim heretical sects, for political revolts against the central government were frequently clothed in religious protest, and it is hard to know where to draw the line. We may, however, first speak of what seem to be non-Muslim uprisings, and then turn to those which were more clearly Islamic heretical movements.

As has been mentioned, the progress of Islam was faster in eastern Iran than in western Iran for various reasons. The settlement of Arab warriors and their families and followers was greater in such centres as Nishapur, Merv, Bukhara and Balkh than in the cities of western Iran since the need for Arab garrisons was much greater along the road to central Asia than in western Iran. Furthermore, the influence of the Zoroastrian church was weaker in the east, and especially in Transoxiana and Afghanistan, where the Sasanians did not rule, than in Fars, Isfahan or Kirman. Finally, the variety of religions in the east, plus syncretism as a result of the existence of Zoroastrianism, Manichaeism, Buddhism, Christianity, and other religions in the east, probably prepared the way for the series of religious revolts in early ʿAbbasid times. Perhaps we do not hear of such movements during the Umaiyad caliphate because the impact of Islam and the Islamic government was less overwhelming than it later became, and furthermore the historians were more concerned with Arab than with local affairs. The change from the Umaiyads to the ʿAbbasids, however, provided an opportunity for many to protest, and it released passions which led to a series of revolts.

The process of conversion to Islam was probably different in western Iran from that in eastern Iran and central Asia, primarily because the political and social conditions were different in the two areas. From the sources it would seem that the aristocracy in the Sasanian empire either fled to the east or, for the most part, became Muslim soon after the conquests. The *dihqans* of the east, in the Umaiyad period, seem to have maintained their religion and their ancient traditions longer than in the west. The Sasanian scribal class, on the other hand, went over to the conquerors quickly, but they did not need to become Muslims, and many did not. In the east the scribal class was insignificant and in its place were merchants who became Muslims only when it was to their economic advantage to convert. The common people in western Iran, especially those on the land, were converted to Islam primarily in the ʿAbbasid period and later by missionaries from the cities, including Kharijites, Shiʿites and other sectarian missionaries. Since eastern Iran and central Asia were both more city-oasis oriented than western Iran with its many villages, the process of islamicization proceeded much faster among the common folk there than in the west. Finally, the Zoroastrian priestly class of Sasanian Iran did maintain itself, even though the top echelons were lost with the fall of the empire. In the east we do not hear of a strong class of priests continuing into late ʿAbbasid times and it would seem that the local priesthoods of the east soon vanished after the conquest. Many, like the Barmecids of Balkh who in this case were probably Buddhists, went over to Islam. These general remarks, I feel, would be substantiated by detailed studies and monographs on particular areas under Umaiyad and ʿAbbasid caliphs. Let us turn to the ʿAbbasid period and the religious uprisings.

After the success of the ʿAbbasid revolt in Merv, Abu Muslim had to conquer those Muslims, both Arabs and *mawali*, who refused to accept his authority in such cities as Bukhara, Balkh and elsewhere. This was accomplished by his lieutenants, and the fame and influence of Abu Muslim, leader of the ʿAbbasid revolt in Khurasan, spread throughout the countryside. It was small wonder that after his murder in the month of Shaʿban 137/January 755, a number of uprisings occurred in protest. To be sure, there had been revolts during the last years of the Umaiyads, but we do not know whether the designations Khurramdiniyya, applied to one rebel Khidash in Khurasan, or Rawandiyya, perhaps given to extremist Shiʿites, are really contemporary names or simply names given by later authors to these movements, nor do we know just what they signified.[2] I believe that one could find a continuity of such rebel movements from the end of Umaiyad into ʿAbbasid times. Whether the continuity was doctrinal, theological, or socio-political is difficult to say in many cases, but it is striking that all these early revolts seem to have had lower-class support, whereas later in the tenth century intellectual and theological elements predominate in uprisings. But then the very nature of Islam itself and its position *vis-à-vis* other religions changes from the beginning of the ʿAbbasid caliphate to the tenth century. In the beginning, of course, disorders prevailed because of the fall of one government and the installation of another. The times were such that even in the Zoroastrian church there were troubles.

The uprising of Bihafrid, beginning in 129/746–7, seems to have been a Zoroastrian heretical movement by a priest in Nishapur who proclaimed himself a prophet. We do not know his doctrines or his relation to Mazdean orthodoxy; perhaps he sought some rapprochement with Islam although this is unclear in the sources.[3] According to them, the orthodox Zoroastrian priests asked Abu Muslim to rid them of the heretic which he obligingly did in 131/749 after he had occupied Nishapur. The tradition that Bihafrid adopted Islam and then apostatized, thus earning death, is probably unreliable.

Another Magian called Sunpad (or Sinbad) raised a revolt after the death of Abu Muslim in the same area of Nishapur.[4] He was able to move to Raiy, but an army sent by the caliph in 137/755 defeated him and he fled to Tabaristan where he was put to death by order of the Ispahbad of Tabaristan. From the few and contradictory sources about Sunpad one may infer several points. First, Sunpad was close to Abu Muslim and revolted after he heard of the death of Abu Muslim. Secondly, because of his connections with Abu Muslim, various persons and groups discontented with the ʿAbbasids joined him. Although his following seems to have been primarily Mazdeans and not Muslims, various heretics including Muslims probably became his partisans.[5] It should be noted that the Shiʿite belief in a saviour or *mahdi* and the Zoroastrian expectation of the return of a messiah called Vahram-i Varjavand from a mythical 'copper city', in the early ʿAbbasid period, at times seemed to coincide. Such similarities in Iran between Islam and Zoroastrianism make it difficult to disentangle some of the religious movements in this period to decide what doctrines were professed. For example, both religions believed in the doctrine of the mean (MP: *patman*, Arabic: *wasat*); both believed in angels and demons, and we know of many Zoroastrian shrines which later became Muslim places of pilgrimage, a not uncommon feature in the history of religions. It is not our intent to go into detail into the history of each religious revolt under the ʿAbbasids, which has been done elsewhere, but rather to try to discern a pattern in them. Let us examine briefly the others.

The revolt of Ishaq the Turk in Transoxiana, which lasted from about 137/755 until 140/757, was similar to that of Sunpad, in that the name of the dead Abu Muslim figured prominently in the propaganda, but in this case as a hidden messiah sent by Zoroaster to restore to power the ancient religion of the Persians, according to the sources. Just how far one can believe the Muslim Arabic sources obviously hostile to all of these strange religious revolts, is naturally difficult to determine. It would appear that Ishaq, whose name indicates that he was a convert to Islam (and then an apostate?), was more a proponent of Abu Muslim as a hidden messiah than a follower of Zoroaster. Perhaps with Ishaq one may see the fusion of extremist Shi'ite with Zoroastrian beliefs possibly to win support from different people. Whatever the religious beliefs or doctrines of these two rebels, however, we see the emergence of what one might call a syncretic sect or movement of Muslims and Zoroastrians in the name of Abu Muslim. The doctrine of metempsychosis (*tanasukh*) was used by many orthodox Islamic writers as a general term of abuse against those who may or may not have believed in the transmigration of souls, so it is extremely difficult to determine the truth of the accusations. Likewise, those who believed that Abu Muslim would return to lead them obviously had various motives, political as well as religious, and in the sources the Abu Muslimiyya are so shadowy that we can only say that such people existed and little more.

More significant than the revolts mentioned above was that of Ostadh Sis or 'master Sis', whose centre of activity was in Badghis, north-east of Herat. He seems to have been a follower of the teachings of Bihafrid, whatever they were, but he too claimed to revolt in revenge for the death of Abu Muslim. Several armies sent against him were unsuccessful until finally in 150 or 151/767–8 he was captured and executed. The circumstances of his capture and death are predictably unclear, and we can only say that in this case his followers did not vanish from the pages of history but are mentioned later in the sources as causing trouble for caliphal officers. Again we must be on guard against the tendency of our sources to apply known later labels for want of better nomenclature to describe these early heretical revolts. From the sources, however, it seems clear that the leaders of these uprisings did proclaim various mixtures of Islamic and Zoroastrian beliefs as the religious basis for opposition to the 'Abbasid caliphs. Undoubtedly both Zoroastrians and Muslims were led to syncretic beliefs by these religious rebels, an indication of the interaction of two religions, both of them in a process of change.

The continuity of these revolts is surprising. After the revolt of Ostadh Sis was quelled still another broke out, this time in Seistan and followed by partisans of the same movement in Transoxiana. The leader of this uprising was a certain Yusuf b. Ibrahim, also called al-Barm, who had an initial success in Fushanj near Herat about 160/776, but was defeated by troops of the caliph Mahdi and fled to Bukhara. Whereas Yusuf had first espoused the Kharijite cause, in Bukhara he seems to have become a proponent of those who were called followers of the Khurramdin (in Persian literally the 'happy religion'), which was a half Muslim, half Zoroastrian syncretic movement. The many names which are applied in the sources to the syncretic movements of the eighth century AD confuse the scene, because we cannot tell whether the designations Khurramite, Khurramdin, Muhammira, 'red flags', and 'white garments', are identical or to be differentiated from each other. We also cannot determine whether Yusuf al-Barm, for example, was acting as an extreme Kharijite or as an anti-Muslim syncretist. The governor of Seistan was sent against Yusuf, who had returned from Transoxiana, and in 161/778 captured him and many of his followers, whom he sent to Baghdad where the caliph Mahdi had them executed.[6]

The revolt of Yusuf was followed by the more serious and longer one of al-Muqanna', 'the veiled prophet of Khurasan'. The sources describe the leader of this uprising as one who believed in metempsychosis and claimed to be an incarnation of Abu Muslim and previous prophets. Many stories are told about al-Muqanna', and how he deceived his followers with various tricks and ruses. He began his movement in Merv but soon went to Nakhshab and Kish in Transoxiana where he assembled a large following who wore white garments which could be interpreted as a sign of opposition to the 'Abbasids who used the colour black extensively. Muqanna' invited Turkish nomads to help him, and his activities were directed against Muslims. From 159/775 to 166/783 it would seem that Muqanna' was very active in Transoxiana, and according to several traditions at the end he committed suicide rather than fall into the hands of the caliph's troops. The fact that his followers continued to exist after his death is an indication that his movement was primarily a religious uprising and not political or rather not predominantly political.[7] The revolt of Yusuf al-Barm, on the contrary, had political as well as religious motives. Likewise, the movement of Babak was perhaps more social or possibly political than religious although this is not easy to determine from the sources.

The uprising of Babak lasted longer than the others, at least from 201/816, if not earlier, until 223/838 when Babak was executed by the caliph al-Mu'tasim in his capital of Samarra. Although the sources are more plentiful, the movement is more difficult to judge than those in the eastern part of the caliphate, primarily because there were no antecedents in Azerbaijan where Babak flourished, and parallels to, or connections of, the movement are not apparent. The general opinion that this revolt was a Zoroastrian, or even a special Zoroastrian, namely a socialist Mazdakite, uprising is hardly acceptable.[8] Again one must not forget that we know about Babak from his enemies, and the sources cannot be trusted to give an accurate picture of his beliefs. Furthermore, many of the sources, such as Shahristani, Baghdadi, Ibn Hazm and others, who write about sects and religions, like to make neat divisions and put those rebellions, which basically had an anti-ʿAbbasid bias, into the most pernicious category – one which would be an anti-Islamic movement with the prime aim of overthrowing Islam and re-establishing the religion of Zoroaster as the ruling religion. Yet after the establishment of the ʿAbbasid caliphate, can anyone have believed seriously that the Zoroastrianism of the Sasanian state could be restored as the ruling religion in the eastern part of the caliphate? The great difficulty, I believe, in studying the religious situation in the early ʿAbbasid period is the tendency to regard both Islam and especially Zoroastrianism as essentially monolithic. Surely the existence into the present of such religions, or groups, as the Mandaeans, the Yazidis, Ali-Ilahis, Ismaʿilis, and others, should indicate the even greater complexity of the religious milieu of the ʿAbbasid period when even Sunni orthodoxy had not yet been formulated. Before we further discuss the above mentioned, and other revolts, we should examine those uprisings which are given an Islamic base by the sources, or which are distinguished from the above by the designation of Islamic heresy. By comparing the two groups we will be in a better position to determine their natures.

It must be remembered that the concept of orthodoxy and heresy in Islam is nothing like that in Christianity. Indeed, one may ask whether such concepts make sense in Islam, for who was to determine what orthodoxy or heresy was? The ʿAbbasid caliph turned more and more from the traditions of rule of the first four caliphs to assume the imperial role of the heritage of the ancient Near East, the equal of the Byzantine emperor and the heir of the Sasanian king of kings. Until the fourth century of the *Hijra*, when al-Ashʿari laid the basis of the Sunni profession of faith in order to protect the faith one first had to know what the faith was, and in the confusion of the first two centuries of Islam, followed by the varied intellectual freedom of the third century with Muʿtazilites and others disputing questions of philosophy and religion in Baghdad, who could pass judgement on the beliefs of Muslims? It is clear that a revolt against ʿAbbasid rule in which the rebels were primarily Arabs, or especially led by Arabs, could be called a heretical Islamic movement, such as the Kharijites or the Shiʿites, whereas an Iranian-led revolt would be called a Zoroastrian revolt against Islam. Actually, the aims of all the rebels were much the same, opposition to the ʿAbbasids, and the results were the same, defeat and execution by the caliph's troops. This is perhaps an overly simplified, and even cynical, view of the revolts during the early ʿAbbasid period, but when one compares the revolt of the Kharijite al-Shaibani, killed in 138/755, al-ʿIjli in Raiy, the uprising of Shiʿites in Merv in 140/757–8, and others, with the 'Zoroastrian' revolts, the various names of the leaders of the revolts provide the only real differences. Further, when one compares the beliefs of the extremist Shiʿites (*ghulat*), with their ideas of the reincarnation of an *imam* in his successor, with similar beliefs of the 'Zoroastrian' rebels, there is little to choose between them. This is not to suggest that all rebels held the same or even very similar beliefs. On the contrary, one may assume that there was great diversity and the spectrum of beliefs was wide, but the certainty with which many of our sources classify the revolts of the early ʿAbbasid period does not inspire confidence in the capability or knowledge of the authors who, in any case, are writing much later than the events. When one finds the Khurramdiniyya, described by many sources as a sect of the Zoroastrians,[9] and by Muqaddasi, in his geography, as one of the Islamic sects found in rural districts, then one may well suspect the reliability of the sources.[10] On the other hand, since some sources claim that the Khurramiyya disguised themselves as Muslims, then the problem is to determine whether the former considered themselves as secret Zoroastrians who proclaimed themselves as Muslims, or as Muslims who held (aberrant) beliefs similar to the Zoroastrians.[11] This would be very hard to determine but the latter suggestion is more likely.

As mentioned, theological Islamic orthodoxy was long in the formation, but this did not prevent theologians from condemning some groups, such as the extreme Shiʿites, for exaggerating greatly (*ghuluw*) in their profession of Islam, hence to be excluded from Islam. Whether this, or the similar charge of *bidʿa* 'innovation' in Islam, really meant more than a verbal condemnation by most theologians in this early period is difficult to determine. We do not hear of any of the Kharijites, for example, accused of one or the other 'heresy' in our sources. Kharijites were not executed for *bidʿa*, but rather for revolting against the state. There is another term, however, which was much more serious, *zandaqa* or being a *zindiq*, for which people could be arrested by the government and executed. Such was the fate of Jaʿd b. Dirham, who was accused of being a *zindiq* and executed in 125/742 by the Umaiyad government. The significance of *zindiq*, however, had changed from Sasanian times, where we first find it in the inscriptions of Kartir, the famous Zoroastrian priest of Shapur I, and his successors. In the latter part of the third century the term seems to mean Manichaean, and this sense persisted into Islamic times. Jaʿd, however, espoused what later came to be Muʿtazilite doctrines, and surely he was not a Manichaean. It would seem that in Islamic times the term *zindiq* was given to anyone (other than a Zoroastrian) who held dualist beliefs, or, by extension, any beliefs contrary to the basic tenets of Islam rather than different interpretations of the Qur'an and Islam. The accusation of *zandaqa* was brought against poets or writers such as Bashshar b. Burd, Salih b. ʿAbd al-Quddus or Ibn al-Muqaffaʿ, all of whom may have held heterodox ideas but were hardly active followers of the Manichaean religion. They, and others, were put to death by order of the caliph. This is not to say that there were no Manichaeans in Iraq, or elsewhere in the caliphate. Furthermore, Manichaeism may have had a great influence on one or another new Muslim convert, but to equate scepticism, free thinking, or plain unbelief with Manichaeism is, of course, nonsense. History, on the other hand, is full of nonsense, and if the caliph wished to dispose of an opponent or someone who annoyed him, what better way was there than to accuse him of being a *zindiq*?

The reader may object to the placing of Bashshar b. Burd and Ibn al-Muqaffaʿ together, since the former could be accused of one deviation and the latter of another or others, but my intention is not to discuss fine points of personal beliefs, but rather to indicate the uncertainty and vacillation of our sources in discussing heretics and those who did not conform to proper conduct, usually as set by the government. For example, the Qadarites, or Muslim philosophers or theologians who believed in free will as opposed to predestination, were called the Zoroastrians of Islam in some sources, and this was used against them. It is clear that the religious situation under the early ʿAbbasids was quite fluid, with gnostic ideas entering Shiʿite beliefs, with dualism, early mysticism and a host of other tendencies in the air, rather than sects or well-defined groups.

The entire question of Manichaeism in the early ʿAbbasid caliphate is not clear, for we are unsure of the extent of Manichaean activities, not to speak of a 'Manichaean church' in Iraq. All indications point to a retreat of the Manichaeans from the west to Samarqand and the east in late Sasanian times, which was reversed after the establishment of the Umaiyad caliphate. It would be natural for Manichaeans to attempt to rebuild their 'church' in Mesopotamia, homeland of Mani, after the fall of the Sasanian empire. Perhaps the Manichaeans hoped to establish some detente with the new religion Islam, which had eluded them with the bitterly hostile Zoroastrianism or Christianity.[12] They were unsuccessful either in re-establishing themselves or in coming to terms with Islam. The persecution of Manichaeans lasted from 163 to 170/779–86 through the caliphates of Mahdi and al-Hadi, but the Manichaeans who were attacked were not found in Iran. The caliph Mahdi on his way to Aleppo began the inquisition in northern Mesopotamia, for adherents of this religion were found there, or in Basra or Kufa, rather than in Iran.[13] According to the sources, the last surviving Manichaeans left Iraq for Samarqand under caliph Muqtadir (908–32), and nothing more was heard of them in the caliphate although people were accused of *zandaqa* even later. Vajda has shown that only one of the large number of personal names given by Ibn al-Nadim in his *Fihrist* actually could be considered a true Manichaean while others were extreme Shiʿites or followers of other sects. It is clear from the sources that the Manichaeans, or their ideas, were primarily active in Mesopotamia, not in Iran, and their influence was concentrated in learned and literary circles. Accusations against individuals, however, clouded the picture of the history of this religion, or heresy, under Islam.

The reader will naturally ask whether the Zoroastrians possessed any heretical sects as the Muslims did. Since the religion of the Sasanians obviously had been well established at the beginning of Islam, there must have been deviations from its norm. In the case of Zoroastrianism, perhaps to a greater extent than with Islam or Christianity, orthopraxy was a better word to use than orthodoxy. For the religion of the Mazda worshippers had become a legalistic faith of rites of purification, of the recitation of many litanies, and the like. There was a word for heresy in Middle Persian, *ahrmokih*, which meant disbelief in Ahura Mazda (MP: Ohrmazd) and refusal to perform the rites and rituals which went with the worship of Ahura Mazda. Obviously, as in any religion, there were backsliders, and others who were called heretics. In the history of Sasanian Zoroastrianism the most prominent heretic was Mazdak who was put to death by Chosroes I when he was still crown prince in about AD 528. The emphasis of the Mazdakite movement, it would seem, was social rather than religious, although it is difficult to separate the two. The Mazdakite uprising made such an impression on contemporaries, as well as on later authors, that the fame of the Mazdakites persisted into Islamic times. The question one must ask is whether or not a social revolt in Islamic Iran, supported by Zoroastrians, was a revival of the Mazdakite movement simply because the lower classes participated in it for aims of social change. Nizam al-Mulk, in his book the *Siyasat name*, asserts that the Khurramdin rebels in Islamic times were simply Mazdakites, including Sunpad, although he says that Sunpad told his followers, who were of the Khurramdin persuasion, that Mazdak was a pre-Shiʿite and that they should make common cause with the Shiʿites.[14] The author of the *Siyasat name*, however, wrote long after the events he is describing when the word Mazdakite had only a general and uncertain connotation of a social rather than a religious rebel.

To return to the religious revolts of Bihafrid, Sunpad, Muqannaʿ and Babak, is it possible to determine what each was and whether the term Zoroastrian, Mazdakite or some other name should be applied to any or all of these movements? At the present state of our knowledge it would be foolhardy to put a definite label on any of them, but I believe, even though this is speculative, one may discern the trend from the beginning to accommodate the Islamic religion in various ways. In other words, most if not all of the religious movements seem to have been syncretistic, as well as with a social protest since they were all supported primarily by common folk. On the other hand, Molé was probably right in calling Mazdak the *zindiq par excellence*, since he sought an unorthodox interpretation of the Zoroastrian religion whereas Mani started a new faith.[15] But as mentioned, the word *zindiq* was applied early in Islam to various beliefs and it is frequently very difficult to determine what it really means. If al-Hallaj, the famous mystic, could be called a *zindiq*, then the word could be used of any free thinker or deviator from the norm, whatever that might have been in the eyes of those in power.

To sum up, one would suggest that the religious rebellions in Iran were on the whole social or even political uprisings of common folk against the ʿAbbasid caliphate, while from the religious point of view the leaders tried to reconcile ancient beliefs with Islam, slightly at first, but to a greater degree as time passed.[16] For Islam would clearly not only remain in Iran but it would supplant all religions which existed there. The revolts were, on the whole, of a local, revolutionary character against injustices in tax collecting or the distribution of revenues, and they could easily assume an anti-Sunni character in the eyes of the government, since the state was a Sunni government. From the religious point of view, the 'heretical' movements described above were, I believe, mostly attempts to join ancient Iranian to Islamic beliefs, Shiʿite for the most part. The possible influences of Zoroastrianism on Shiʿism in Iran will be discussed in the next chapter. None of the revolts succeeded in separating any appreciable territory from the caliphate for anything but a short period of time. Successful separatist movements came later under the Tahirids, Saffarids and Turks, and they were all Islamic. There was a legal problem involved with the Zoroastrians who, after much dispute, seem to have obtained consideration as *ahl al-kitab* or 'people of the book', entitled to the protection of the government on paying the *jizya*. For a long time, however, it was uncertain whether the inhabitants of an area were entitled to this status or not. This was usually determined by the local *dihqans* who, in the early days of the ʿAbbasids, were for the most part tax collectors for the government. The determination of who was an accepted Muslim or who was to be placed in another category was obviously of importance to the tax collectors. Further, a Shiʿite who refused to pay any taxes to a government which was unlawful in his eyes was clearly more dangerous to the caliph in Baghdad than a Zoroastrian dissident, who, in any case, would be disciplined by his own community. Only if he became a threat to the government need more severe measures be taken by the government. Clearly the Shiʿites, and other definitely Islamic rebels, were potentially the most dangerous opponents of the caliphs, and much energy had to be devoted to the suppression of these dissidents.

The Shiʿite movements were complex, but all were directed against a Sunni institution in the process of solidifying. The Sunni establishment, for many Muslims, was simply an arm of the state and too rigid in its outlook. The Shiʿite uprisings were at first primarily political, but later, under the Qarmatians, Fatimids and others, social protests loomed large, while the third feature of Shiʿism, its dogmatic ideas, played a leading role primarily with extreme Shiʿites, those who believed in the divinity or near divinity of ʿAli, or in reincarnation or similar doctrines. The domination of Shiʿites in Gilan and Tabaristan was more of a threat to the ʿAbbasids than the rule of local Zoroastrian princes ever had been, and it is no wonder that the Shiʿites and Kharijites worried the ʿAbbasids more than other dissidents. The ʿAbbasids were not noted for their religious tolerance, and the Shiʿites were persecuted and some executed during early ʿAbbasid rule, especially under Harun al-Rashid. The change in policy under his son al-Ma'mun (813–33) was an exception. The strange development, which led to a declaration by the caliph in Merv in 816 that his successor was to be ʿAli b. Musa b. Jaʿfar al-Rida, the Shiʿite *imam*, cannot be discussed here for it is an involved and unclear story.[17] The murder of the chief minister of Ma'mun al-Fadl b. Sahl and the following events are all part of the history of the ʿAbbasid court and also of the Shiʿite episode of al-Ma'mun. Furthermore, by the end of al-Ma'mun's reign, the question of the claims of the Shiʿites to the caliphate had become academic, while the general tolerance of the caliph was a welcome change from the rigidity of his predecessors.

One might say that the intolerance of the ʿAbbasid government was an important factor in the many revolts which took place under the early caliphs. Although it is not part of our subject, the migration from lands under Muslim rule to Byzantine rule by a large number of Armenians in the time of Harun al-Rashid can be attributed to the spirit of intolerance in the caliphate. One symbol of this spirit was the *mihna*, an inquisition, which term is generally used for the results of the controversy, mainly in Baghdad, between the Muʿtazilites and their opponents who upheld doctrines of predestination against free will, as well as other doctrines. We have seen that another inquisition existed under the caliph Mahdi, so the term could have many ramifications. Under al-Ma'mun the Muʿtazilites imposed their views on others, whereas under Mutawakkil (847–61) the tables were turned and the Muʿtazilites were persecuted. At the same time, Mutawakkil persecuted the Shiʿites and destroyed their shrine at Kerbela. In his time many Christians and Jews were removed from public offices and were made to wear certain signs on their clothes. The Christians and Jews, however, were never as important in Iran as they were in Mesopotamia or the western part of the caliphate. As minorities they kept very much to themselves and we know little about their activities or about any schisms which appeared among them. None the less it is clear that heresies also existed among them and we should consider them very briefly.

Christians were especially strong in northern Mesopotamia, as we may surmise because of the many monasteries and cloisters there, whereas in Iran monasticism did not have much success. After the Islamic conquest Christians found themselves isolated from their western centres and many conversions to Islam followed. By the time of the Umaiyads the Nestorian church had suffered internal political strife, which Hajjaj the governor of Iraq used to weaken further the position of the church by permitting the joint occupation of bishoprics and other offices of the church by rival parties, to the overall detriment of Nestorian Christianity. The catholicos Timotheos I, who occupied the top post of the church from 780 to 823, was able to secure from the caliphs the supreme jurisdiction over all Christians in the caliphate, which gave the Nestorian church a great advantage over the other churches. Although more and more Christians converted to Islam, the church continued to exist and even flourish after Timotheos, except, as noted, during the reigns of Harun al-Rashid and Mutawakkil who both began persecutions for personal reasons. Otherwise there was no force to compel conversion; but taxes and social stigmas, such as signs on clothing, restrictions on riding horses and the like, provided reasons for conversion to Islam. The interesting activities of Christians in medicine and in translating Syriac and even Pahlavi texts into Arabic cannot be discussed here for it would require a separate book. Likewise the competition between the Jacobites in northern Mesopotamia and the Nestorians in the south cannot be described, but one may say that on the Iranian plateau, and especially in eastern Iran and central Asia, the Nestorians remained the only Christians who were successful not only in maintaining themselves but in expanding. Although it is impossible to determine the influence of Christian converts to Islam on the development of Islamic theology and philosophy, it would seem that they played a larger role than, for example, the newly converted Zoroastrians, whereas the Persians were certainly more active in the history of mysticism or Sufism in Islam.

It was under Islam that the Nestorian missions spread to the east, and for a time, although ultimately unsuccessful, into Yemen and south Arabia. Before the time of Timotheos I, Christianity had been spread in central Asia by merchants, but in the ninth century a regular missionary activity to the Turks and to China began. It was paralleled by a much smaller Jacobite and even orthodox Christian effort to convert in competition with the Nestorians. In the end the Nestorians were victorious and some entire tribes in Mongolia were converted. Ruins of Christian cloisters in Turfan and elsewhere in Chinese Turkistan have been found and Syriac inscriptions on tombstones in Semirechiye (in Russian Turkistan) testify to the success of the Christian mission as late as Mongol times. Christianity in central Asia, however, did not survive the break-up of the great Mongol empire, which is beyond the scope of this book.

The Jews on the whole fared better under Muslim rule than under the preceding empires, but they too were subject to heresy and dissent. The most famous of the sectarians of Judaism in this period was 'Anan b. David, who flourished in the time of caliph Mansur (754–75) and was the first recorded leader of the Qaraite movement in Judaism. Like many later Christian sects which proclaimed a return to the Bible, so did the Qara'im 'text reader' oppose the supporters of the Rabbinate by returning to the Old Testament. What was not to be found in the Old Testament was to be rejected as being later and corrupt practices. The sect reportedly arose in the time of the Umaiyad caliph 'Abd al-Malik, but this is difficult to determine since the Qaraites claimed a chain of teachers or rabbis going back to the first century, and the origins are consequently unclear. We hear later of Jews from Iran who were leaders in this sect, Benjamin from Nihavand, Daniel b. Moses from Qumis, and perhaps Musa al-Nikrisi from Gurgan, the informant of al-Biruni. The history of eastern Judaism is very little known and much work is needed before one can even begin to reconstruct the history of Jews in Iran. We know the names of Jewish scholars of heretical bent from the east, such as Abu 'Isa from Isfahan, Yudghan of Hamadan, Mushki from Qum, and, the most famous of all, Hivi from Balkh, but whether they were Qaraites or not we cannot tell. One hears of strife between the exilarch in Iraq, the Resh Galutha, and the Rabbinic academy of Pumbadita in Iraq regarding jurisdiction over a Jewish colony in Khurasan, which really only tells us of the existence of colonies in the east. How ancient and what sizes they were and when they flourished we do not know. The discovery of tombstones with Hebrew inscriptions from the centre of Afghanistan in the mountains of Ghur dating from the twelfth century, as well as an earlier inscription from Tang-i Azao written in Jewish Persian, are indications of the activity of Jewish communities in areas where one would hardly expect them.[18] The Jews did, however, participate in the Iranian culture of the time, and usually wrote in Arabic as most learned people of the time did.[19]

After the middle of the ninth century the religious picture in the caliphate changes, for the possibility of a change from an Islamic back to a Zoroastrian or Christian society was gone, and the threat of non-Muslim uprisings gives way to Islamic heretical movements which threaten the stability of the ʿAbbasid caliphate. Rebels are no longer branded as threats to an Arab or Islamic culture, for this now dominates the whole caliphate. In the earlier period the four Sunni law schools founded by Abu Hanifa (died 767), Malik b. Anas (d. 795), Shafiʿi (d. 820), and Ibn Hanbal (d. 855) were being formed. Sunni theology was a parallel development yet was integrated with the legal schools by Abu 'l-Hasan ʿAli al-Ashʿari, who died in 935 in Baghdad. The period after 850 was to see the rise of mysticism and new sects different from the earlier movements. There also seems to be a difference in the nature of the progress of Islam in the period before the 850s and after. In the earlier period, especially under the Umaiyads, there is a lack of enthusiasm at making converts to Islam since this reduced the tax income and endangered the privileged position of the ruling Muslims. As conversions none the less continued the attitude of what had been at first a minority ruling elite, now become a majority, changed. A desire to convert all the people in the caliphate to Islam comes to the fore on the part of some new missionaries. New sects like the Karramiyya, discussed below, were concerned with proselytizing, and the acquisition of new dialectical weapons by the Muslims probably gave a great impetus not only to the development of theology and philosophy, but also to the maturing of Islam in all spheres. This maturing went hand in hand with a rapid growth of conversions to Islam, and, incidentally, at the same time the migration of Zoroastrians to India. Before we turn to these matters, however, we should recapitulate the religious history of the early ʿAbbasid caliphate.

By the time of the ʿAbbasid revolution Islam had not only gone beyond the ancient frontiers of the Sasanian empire, but it had successfully withstood attacks of internal and external enemies, such as the Turks in central Asia. The imperial idea of a state reaching from the Mediterranean (and beyond to north Africa) to the Indus had been re-established, so the ʿAbbasids did not have to re-fight the battles of their predecessors, but they had new struggles against internal foes who sought legitimacy in place of the ʿAbbasids, whom they considered as usurpers in the caliphate. This does not mean that there were no *local* revolts, especially in Iran, which had as their aim the founding of a non-Islamic local state independently of the caliphate. It hardly can have been in the minds of the supporters of rebels like Sunpad, Muqannaʿ or Babak that they would replace the caliphate with their own government and religion. Babak probably thought he could maintain his own small state in Azerbaijan apart from the caliphate, while the trial of the Afshin Haidar b. Kaus was a personal affair, not to be confused with the religious revolts of the time. The Zoroastrian princes of Gilan and Mazandaran are another matter, since their relations with the caliphate were of a treaty, or even a kind of vassal or tributary, relationship, but we cannot exclude the possibility that one or another rebel on the plateau thought that he might obtain support from the non-Islamic rulers of the mountains or the seashore. After the ʿAbbasid Caliphate was firmly established, however, that possibility became remote, and only later with the expansion of the Dailamites on to the plateau in the tenth century did such nostalgic but improbable themes as a return to Zoroastrianism or, more to the point, the restoration of a Persian monarchy, gain currency among some Persians, who were usually Muslims themselves.

In addition, by the time of the consolidation of ʿAbbasid power the relations between Muslims, Zoroastrians, Jews and Christians had become well established and the orthodox Zoroastrians were as dismayed at heretical or syncretic 'Zoroastrian' revolts as were the Muslim authorities. This would help explain why Sunpad, Muqannaʿ and others did not receive widespread support from the Zoroastrian communities. Furthermore, to repeat, these revolts were more in the nature of social or economic protests than religious uprisings, and perhaps only the movement of Bihafrid could be called a 'Zoroastrian' revolt, although even that is dubious since Zoroastrian *mobads* did not support him. One always must be on guard not to confuse popular folk beliefs with organized religious dogmas. Thus it seems apparent that the ancient Iranian celebrations, such as the new year *noruz*, the Mihragan ceremonies and others were accepted by Islam in Iran as not harmful to the Muslim faith. Many rationalizations or accommodations were obviously made to bridge the gap between Iranian folk beliefs and Islamic practices. Naturally the Zoroastrians did not have grave-shrines, since the bodies of the dead were exposed to vultures and not put in the earth. But the Zoroastrians of Iran did have shrines to various angels or deities (*yazatas*) and it was relatively easy to convert some of these to Muslim, or more especially Shiʿite, *imamzades*, reputed burial places of the children of Shiʿite *imams*. The name *pir* or 'old man, saint', was applied to these shrines by Zoroastrians, possibly to protect them from Muslim desecration, and this only made easier the transfer from a Zoroastrian to a Muslim shrine. The change of the famous Zoroastrian shrine Bibi Shahrbanu near Tehran to a Muslim shrine was made with the help of the Shiʿite tradition that the daughter of Yazdegird III, the last Sasanian ruler, had married Husain, son of the caliph ʿAli, and was the mother of the fourth *imam* Zain al-ʿAbidain. The probable story of the transformation of the shrine, which seems to have occurred in the tenth century, has been told by M. Boyce, and can be paralleled by similar cases elsewhere in Iran.[20]

Many other beliefs or practices, in addition to shrines and festivals, entered Islam in Iran or at least influenced Muslim practices. The legal system of the Muslim courts was naturally influenced by local customs, but wide diversities existed. Cases of conflicts between Muslims and non-Muslims must have been numerous, and we hear echoes of them in the Zoroastrian books of the ninth century as well as in Arabic sources. Abandoned fire altars continued to be used as symbols by Iranians who did not give up their fascination for fire with their conversion to Islam, as witness the use of an ancient fire altar as a fire container even today in the village of Aghda north-west of Yazd.[21] One may readily imagine that the rapid Islamic conquests led to many marriages and concubinage in Iran, such that many Iranian mothers passed on local lore and local customs to their Muslim sons and daughters. As we have noted previously, many practices or customs of the Zoroastrians fitted in well with Islam, for example, the institution of the *waqf*, which existed in pre-Islamic Iran. Suffice it to say that the points of similarity and of easy conversion from Zoroastrianism to Islam were many and the process by which Iran became a Muslim land is not wrapped in mystery.

The middle of the ninth century saw the rise of new movements and sects, as well as a great expansion of the activities of Muslim missionaries. It also saw the rise of Islamic mysticism in Iran, in a special form with Abu Yazid (Bayazid) of Bistam, the first of the 'intoxicated' Sufis, who died in 261/875. The striking personalities of many Sufis and missionaries caused a large number of Iranians in the countryside to convert to Islam. Prior to the ninth century Islam was dominant only in the towns and cities, while the countryside was predominantly non-Muslim, but through the efforts of the Muslim missionaries even the countryside was made Islamic, predominantly Shiʿite, or at least not orthodox Sunni, in persuasion. Thus throughout the Umaiyad and early ʿAbbasid caliphates Islam was predominant in the cities of Iran, and, in some cities along the highway from Baghdad to Samarqand, Muslims were possibly in the majority. The countryside, however, for the most part was devoid of Muslims. In the hundred years from 850 to 950 the countryside is converted, to such an extent that Firdosi and other Iranian literary men or intellectuals tried to save something of their ancient legends and culture which had almost become extinct. Probably the increased missionary activity of the Muslims, which went parallel with the flowering of Islamic science, theology and philosophy, helped to inspire the Nestorian expansion and the Zoroastrian literary activity in the ninth century, as well as the migration of many Zoroastrians to India. Before turning to the Zoroastrians, however, let us investigate briefly the new Muslim impetus to convert others.

As many conferences and publications on the Islamic city have shown, the Islamic religion favoured urban society whereas Zoroastrianism extolled the virtues of farming and herding. Villages enjoyed a great degree of autonomy under Islam which meant that the government left them alone as long as taxes came regularly into the cities. But with the foundation of new cities and the expansion of the old the contacts between the urban and rural population increased. The old feudal system of the *dihqans*, who controlled the countryside, broke down as Islamic egalitarianism began to play an important role in shaking the authority of the *dihqans*. A growing internal proletariat also presented a danger to the stability of the old system as a new society of merchants, bureaucrats and artisans grew in influence. It is interesting that the Islamic geographers, describing the lands of Islam in the ninth or tenth centuries, speak of Arabs, or even Arab tribes, as inhabiting various cities of Khurasan, but not the countryside.[22]

Since life on the Iranian plateau depends so much on water, it was inevitable that rich city dwellers should extend their influence to the countryside in controlling water distribution. Frequent conflicts between peasants and landlords have been an endemic feature in the entire history of Iran, and with changes in land ownership taking place in this period disputes naturally arose. Under the 'Abbasid caliphs crown lands increased in size and number all over the lands of the caliphate.[23] Although we do not have specific data, it would seem that at the same time the number of small landlords decreased, while the sharecroppers and the landless agricultural workers, practically serfs, increased in number. The institution of *iqta'*, or land grants to military leaders for services rendered to the state, comes into prominence at the end of the tenth century and later, and will be discussed below. Here we cannot discuss the involved problems of land tenure and taxes except to note the general trends. Generally one might say that under the Umaiyads and early 'Abbasids cities and towns were more under and dependent on central governmental supervision, whereas the villages and countryside were left under old landowners and old systems. With the breakdown of caliphal authority and the spread of Islam to the countryside together with the rise of military land grants to Muslim generals, usually Turks or Dailamis, the cities became more independent and self-sufficient, frequently out of necessity, whereas the villages sought the protection of local Muslim military leaders in exchange for services which put them more and more in bondage to the military landowner. As the central government became ever more ineffectual, the cities were obliged to fend for themselves, and the *ra'is* or 'mayor' of a city became an important official. Our sources are full of stories of the activities of the citizens of various cities organizing their own defence, and acting in effect as independent city-states, especially in the eleventh and twelfth centuries when Turkish nomads over-ran the eastern caliphate.

To return to the Islamic movements or sects which arose in the ninth century, their religious bias is apparent when compared, for example, with the Kharijites who were politically motivated to change the existing government. Although they remained active and strong in Seistan until the time of Ya'qub b. Laith the Saffarid, the last large dangerous uprising was by Hamza b. 'Abdallah al-Shari Adhrak who first appears in 179/795, or possibly a few years earlier, and was finally killed in 213/828 when al-Ma'mun sent his chief general Tahir against him.[24] In a sense the place of the Kharijites in Khurasan and the east was taken by the Karramiyya. This movement was founded by Abu 'Abdallah M. b. Karram from Seistan, but who was of Arab descent. His main base of operations, however, came to be the city of Nishapur. He was a Muslim evangelist and made many converts in the mountains of western Afghanistan mainly among the lowest classes. He was especially noted for his piety and his ascetic life, together with his rejection of both Sunni formalism and Shi'ite excesses. Centres (*khanagah*) of the sect were established in many towns of Khurasan, much like later dervish meeting houses. The Sunni establishment did not take kindly to the sect and Muhammad b. Tahir, governor of Khurasan from 248–59/862–73 held the founder of the sect in custody for eight years. He died in 255/869 but his followers spread his sect to Syria, Egypt and the Hijaz. The leader of the Karramiyya, who played an important role in the inner city politics of Nishapur in the tenth century, was a certain Abu Ya'qub Ishaq b. Mahmashadh (d. 383/993) who was reputed to have converted more than five thousand Zoroastrians, Christians, and Jews, men and women, to Islam in the city of Nishapur alone.[25]

It should be mentioned in passing that in western Iran and in Iraq at the end of the ninth century the sect established by a certain Hamdan Qarmat became popular. The Qarmatians then shifted to Syria and northern Arabia, where in 930 they captured Mecca and for a time removed the black stone in the Ka'ba. We cannot discuss the Qarmatians here or their relations to the Isma'ilis and the Fatimids, for both are outside the scope of this book. This indicates, however, that Iran was not alone as a fertile ground for sects and movements to separate from 'Abbasid rule.

Related to the Qarmatians were the Isma'ilis who later, as the infamous 'Assassins', played an important role in the history of Iran. About the middle of the ninth century Isma'ili missionaries began to appear all over the Islamic world to propagate their beliefs. This Shi'ite sect followed one son of Ja'far al-Sadiq, the sixth *imam* of the Shi'ites descended from 'Ali, rather than the line of succession of another son Musa al-Kazim, which is the line followed by the 'twelver' Shi'ites, the state religion of Iran today.[26] In the cities of Kashan, Raiy and especially Qum 'twelver' Shi'ism was well established. We cannot discuss here the rise of the Isma'ilis, especially their successes in Yemen, north Africa and finally in Egypt where their Fatimid caliphate became a great Islamic cultural centre. Shi'ism was popular in many areas of Iran, and we have already mentioned the establishment of the Zaidi *imams* in Gilan and Tabaristan, where al-Hasan b. Zaid held sway from 250–70/864–84. The Zaidis were the mildest of the Shi'ites for they would recognize any descendant of Hasan or Husain if he could obtain the office of *imam* by his perseverence and by his personal qualities, and they further believed that there might be several *imams* in the world at the same time or none at all. A certain Isma'ili missionary called Khalaf came to Raiy in the second part of the ninth century and secretly began religious propaganda for the sect.[27] Several important persons were converted to the sect in the tenth century, including rulers of the Musafirid dynasty of the Caspian Sea provinces such as al-Marzuban b. Muhammad, who ruled from 330/941 to 346/957. Likewise some persons at the court of the Samanid Nasr b. Ahmad and possibly even the *amir* himself, were converted. The fascinating story of the rise of Isma'ili influences at the court of Bukhara and the counterattack of the Sunnis under Nuh the son of Nasr gives an indication of the extent of Islamic domination of the entire society, but this was an Islam which is much more heterodox than that of the early 'Abbasid period. The intellectual background for the flowering of Islamic thought will be discussed briefly in the next chapter. This Islamic intellectual outpouring completely overshadows or swamps the efforts of Zoroastrians or Christians either to save their communities from conversion to Islam by an expenditure of intellectual effort, or just to oppose the Muslims. The masses of Khurasan and eastern Iran, who became overwhelmingly Muslim in the tenth century, provided the broad base and a reservoir of manpower for the 'renaissance' of New Persian which flowered in the tenth and eleventh centuries. We do hear of large conversions to Islam in the eleventh century, but these were 'mopping up' operations in the countryside, and are usually mentioned in the sources to show the accomplishments of some religious leader or scholar. For example, Ahmad al-Jami, known as Zhindapil, who was born in 1048 and who is buried in the Turbat-i Shaikh Jam in Khurasan, is said to have converted 60,000 people to Islam, but this information may be apocryphal. In any case Islam was almost universal in eastern Iran by the end of the tenth century. Without this islamification of the Iranians in the east the cultural flowering, of course, could not have taken place. Western Iran remained less touched by Islam not only because of rough terrain but also because of local conditions.

It is instructive to read the Islamic geographers of the tenth and eleventh centuries on the existence of Zoroastrians and fire temples in various towns and villages of Iran. The infrequent mention of fire temples in eastern Iran contrasts strongly with the abundance of them in the west, especially in Fars province, the centre of Zoroastrianism. Elsewhere in western Iran we meet with information such as the following: near the town of Idhaj in Khuzistan, in the mountains, there was a fire temple until the time of Harun al-Rashid.[28] Or in the town of Farahan, on the road from Qum to Hamadan, was an important fire temple destroyed by a Turkish governor of Qum in 282/895.[29] This is indicative of the steady decline of Zoroastrianism in the central part of the land, although here and in Azerbaijan isolated settlements of Zoroastrians continued to exist even after the tenth century. Fars, Yazd and Kirman were more isolated from the highways of trade and conquest, from the plains of Mesopotamia to the east, and Zoroastrianism was better able to exist in these areas than in the north or east. Even there the Islamic missionary expansion of the tenth century was felt, although seemingly later than elsewhere. In 369/979 the Muslims in Shiraz attacked the Zoroastrians and rioting occurred.[30] Under Boyid rule in Fars the position of the Zoroastrians probably was better than it had been previously, for the Boyid rulers were not averse to using Zoroastrians as their lieutenants in governing the province. Furthermore, as we shall see later, the Boyids were partial to representatives of the ancient culture of Iran, even though this partiality seemed to have an antiquarian flavour. There exists an account of how the children of a famous *mobad* of Fars, Adhurbad b. Marasfand, sought exemption from paying the *jizya* or capitation tax on the *dhimmi* or 'people of the book' on the grounds that the caliph 'Ali had granted them this right. The ruler of Fars, Samsam al-Daula (380–8/990–8), sent a letter to this group of Zoroastrians in 995 accepting their claim, which was obviously unhistorical.[31] In spite of these few favours shown to the Zoroastrians their ranks steadily decreased in Fars, as elsewhere on the Iranian plateau. This was also the time of the great missionary activity of the founder of a Sufi order, Abu Ishaq al-Kazeruni, who died in 426/1034, but of whom we have a biography with much information about clashes between Muslims and Zoroastrians in various towns of Fars.[32] Through the efforts of such people as Abu Ishaq the number of Muslims in Fars greatly increased and the Zoroastrians lost much ground. The end of the tenth century was probably a period of increased immigration of the Zoroastrians to India, although the stories of the migration of the Parsis to the western coasts of India do not give us definite dates on the migrations, and surely these were more than one or two. The history of the Parsis in India is beyond the scope of this volume but controversies on the dates of migration and the establishment of fire temples should not obscure the fact of a migration in this period.[33] Other Zoroastrians from other parts of the country fled to the east even as far as China, where in

1955 a Middle Persian and Chinese bilingual inscription on a tombstone in Shansi province was found. The inscription is dated in 872 and records the death of the daughter of a deceased general in the Chinese army, who was also a Persian noble of the Suren feudal family.[34] This corroborates literary evidence for the existence of Zoroastrian fire temples in China.

The religious picture in recapitulation does not seem to present any great problems from the beginning of Islam to the end of the tenth century. Under the first four caliphs the Arabs were engaged in conquest and consolidation of their military gains by the settlement of Arab garrisons, together with their non-Arab *mawali*, in the cities of Iran, primarily along the great trade route to the east. Sometimes the soldiers were quartered in the towns, and as part of the peace treaty some of the local inhabitants had to turn over their houses to, or had to share their homes with, the conquerors. At other times (as at Baruqan near Balkh) the Arabs simply built camps near cities where they settled and lived much as the British in India in their cantonments. One can reconstruct the settlement of Arabs from notices in the Islamic geographers: for example, that Isfahan had few Arabs in it whereas Nishapur, Merv and other towns on the east–west trade route had many. The large number of concubinages as well as marriages early produced many children who were half-Arab and half-Iranian, but overwhelmingly Muslim in religion. As the need for more support for the conquests in central Asia and on the borders of India brought more Iranians into the armies, Islam also increased among the local people and the armies began to lose their Arab nature and become more mixed while still Muslim in character.

Under the Umaiyads the Arabs sought to maintain their dominance in government, in the armies and elsewhere, but it was a losing struggle, and furthermore not consistent with the precepts of the faith. Economic considerations determined many policies, including attempts to limit conversions to Islam. The Arabs were no longer merely garrison troops in Iran, but they entered into trading partnerships with the local population and became identified more and more with local interests rather than with those of far-off Damascus. There were few religious clashes or uprisings since Umaiyad policy, on the whole, was to keep the religions separated; this included legal matters and tax collection, so that there was not much cause for the revolt of local people against the government in Damascus. The Kharijites, Shi'ites and other Arab movements sought aid in their primarily political opposition to the Umaiyads from the Iranians, and a few, including Zoroastrians, joined the ranks of the rebels. The overwhelming majority of Iranians who joined a movement against Damascus were Muslim Iranians who felt much the same sentiments of resentment against the Umaiyads as their fellow Arab rebels. Islam by the end of the Umaiyad caliphate was too firmly established in the principal cities on the Iranian plateau to be in danger of anything but a local anti-Muslim uprising, rather than a universal movement to restore the Sasanians. This does not mean that the Muslims were a majority in all Iranian cities at the time of the victory of the ʿAbbasids. But they were in control of the government and the army, and, with the change in the written language of the bureaucracy from Pahlavi to Arabic, the powerful class of scribes and officials had long since adjusted to the new administration and were loath to consider any return to the past. Economically too the caliphate had brought new opportunities for trade and a great expansion of markets. For example, the trade of the oasis of Bukhara with Merv, Khwarazm and farther afield soared after the coming of Islam in comparison with the past, since before Islam all three cities had been in different states.[35] Muslims, both Arabs and Iranians, were able to take advantage of their privileges to make a better profit in the trade than non-Muslims. Within the heart of the former Sasanian empire, in western Iran, however, the advantages of being a member of a huge caliphate were not so apparent as in eastern Iran or in central Asia. Furthermore the number of Arabs settled in western Iran was proportionately much less than in the east, hence the reasons for conversion of the local people to Islam were fewer.

By the end of the Umaiyad caliphate enough Iranian Muslims had become interested in affairs in Damascus to take sides with the Arabs among them in supporting or denouncing the Umaiyads. Most were anti-Umaiyad, but not necessarily pro-ʿAbbasid. The murder of Abu Muslim, who had secured a large and devoted following on his road to victory for the ʿAbbasids, caused much trouble for the new caliphate, since at least the way he was murdered turned some Iranians against the ʿAbbasids. Most Iranians, however, and especially the upper classes, the bureaucracy and those concerned with trade, accepted the ʿAbbasids and sought to maintain the *status quo*. It is significant, I think, that each of the series of 'religious' revolts which took place at the beginning of the ʿAbbasid caliphate was supported by the lower classes, and had primarily a rural base. The disorders of the change in caliphates had cost much money, upheaval, and a certain amount of damage to the economy, if only by drawing people from productive to economically non-productive activities. Taxes had to be increased and unrest naturally followed. The 'heretical' revolts were supported by farmers, who with their local folk beliefs and practices were probably on the whole poor Zoroastrians, as well as poor Muslims, if any of the latter did join the movements. One may guess that some did, and the results, religiously speaking, were attempts to join Islam with ancient beliefs into a new sect, or set of beliefs, which would appeal to the masses. Only the movement of Babak, however, had any prolonged and widespread success. The social and even communistic practices of some of the rebels were more prominent than their religious beliefs. All the revolts were suppressed with severity but partisans of Babak, and in central Asia of Muqanna', continued to exist and to excite the curiosity of their neighbours. Once the threat to the unity of the caliphate had been averted, small groups of heretics, especially if they were quiet, did not alarm the government. This indicates that the threat had been political or social rather than religious, at least in the eyes of the government.

By the end of the eighth century the 'Abbasid caliphate is firmly established and in its golden prime. The intellectual and literary flowering of Islam is under way and a spirit of enquiry and tolerance prevailed. This was to change under the caliph al-Mutawakkil, but the progress of science, literature and general culture under the banner of Islam continued. Many intellectuals converted to Islam bringing new ideas, such as those of free will versus predestination, into the body of Islamic thought. Although this atmosphere stimulated the Zoroastrians, Christians and Jews, they in the end withdrew into their ghettos and Islamic culture reigned triumphant. Henceforth all protest, religious or otherwise, would be Islamic, but of different directions and hues. The protests too became more idealistic or religious than political, in contrast to earlier times. The new sects, the new insurgents, were sectarian rebels, for they were now more interested in changing the minds of the masses than in organizing a rebellion to overthrow the government in Baghdad. The new struggles were not to control the caliphate, but to win men's minds. Energies were now turned in the direction of missionary activities, to convert non-Muslims as well as 'orthodox' Muslims to a new sect, or a revised set of beliefs, such as that held by the Karramites or Isma'ilis. In this new surge of missionary zeal the countryside, which had remained mostly passive in the past, was penetrated by Muslim sectarian evangelists. As greater numbers of peasants were converted, they brought their ancient beliefs and practices, some Zoroastrian but mostly just local and ancient, into Islam which began to change correspondingly. Thus the Isma'ilism of north Africa began to look different from that of rural Iran because of the inclusion of local practices and beliefs into the Isma'ili dogma in both areas.

The second half of the ninth century and the tenth century saw this great change in the thrust and direction of Islam. In the wake of this upsurge of Islamic piety and evangelism, the frontiers of Islam in central Asia expanded. Although we shall return to this in a later chapter, the attraction of the frontiers of Islam was a great one to those newly converted, or to those seeking to express their devotion to the religion of the Prophet in a more active and tangible way. This is the period of the *ghazis* or *muttawwiʿa* 'volunteers', or 'warriors for the faith', when large numbers of Muslims went to the frontier against the Byzantines in Anatolia, or to central Asia against the Turks to fulfil Islamic obligations of *jihad* or 'holy war' against the infidels, or simply for adventure which was, however, approved of or even sanctified by Islam.

Together with this outburst of energy on the part of Islam went a change in the nature of Islam which will be discussed in the next chapter. It was, briefly, the change in Islam from a restricted religion of Arab background with bedouin mores, to a world religion of universal dimensions and with a new hellenistic-Arab-Iranian synthesis. All the developments in the second half of the ninth century, the intellectual as well as the religious, social and even regional, pointed in the same direction, and they all played a role in creating the new oecumene of Islam.

CHAPTER 8

IRANIAN CONTRIBUTIONS TO ISLAMIC CULTURE

The famous philosopher of history, Ibn Khaldun, living in the fourteenth century in north Africa, wrote the following:[1]

It is a remarkable fact that, with few exceptions, most Muslim scholars both in the religious and intellectual sciences have been non-Arabs . . . Thus the founders of grammar were Sibawaih and, after him, al-Farisi and az-Zajjaj. All of them were of Persian descent. They were brought up in the Arabic language and acquired knowledge of it through their upbringing and through contact with Arabs. They invented the rules [of grammar] and made it into a discipline for later generations. Most of the *hadith* scholars, who preserved traditions of the Prophet for the Muslims also were Persians, or Persian in language and breeding because the discipline was widely cultivated in Iraq and regions beyond. Furthermore, all the great jurists were Persians, as is well known. The same applies to speculative theologians and to most of the Qur'an commentators. Only the Persians engaged in the task of preserving knowledge and writing systematic scholarly works. Thus the truth of the statement of the Prophet becomes apparent, 'If learning were suspended at the highest parts of heaven the Persians would attain it.' . . . The intellectual sciences were also the preserve of the Persians, left alone by the Arabs, who did not cultivate them. They were cultivated by arabicized Persians, as was the case with all the crafts, as we stated at the beginning. This situation continued in the cities as long as the Persians and Persian countries, Iraq, Khurasan and Transoxiana, retained their sedentary culture. But when those cities fell into ruins, sedentary culture, which God has devised for the attainment of the sciences and crafts, disappeared from them.

The remarks of Ibn Khaldun are not in dispute but the extent of Iranian influences on Islam, the Arabs and the Arabic language needs to be examined and classified. I propose to discuss these influences under the following rubrics: administration and government, religion and philosophy, science and medicine, commerce and crafts, the fine arts and finally literature and language, where the rise of the New Persian language and poetry will be treated.

ADMINISTRATION AND GOVERNMENT

In general terms the debt of Islam to Iran in the area of government and bureaucracy was enormous, especially in the formation of the ʿAbbasid court. The Arabs had conquered not only provinces of the Byzantine empire, but they had also conquered the entire Sasanian empire. Only in Iran did they find the complete blueprint of an imperial establishment, and no matter how much the ʿAbbasid caliphs might hearken back to the first four caliphs, the new caliphate was an empire with imperial needs and manifestations. The Sasanian bureaucracy was taken over by the Arabs *in toto*, certainly modified, but basically a continuation of the pre-Islamic past.

From the early days of the Islamic conquest two *diwans* or bureaucracies existed in Kufa and Basra, one in Arabic to handle Arab affairs, and another in Pahlavi for matters relating to Iran.[2] We know that in 78/697 Arabic replaced Pahlavi in Iraq, and more slowly over the eastern caliphate, so by the end of the Umaiyad caliphate Arabic had replaced Pahlavi everywhere. We know that the scribes were primarily Iranians; as Jahshiyari says, 'most of the scribes in Khurasan were Magians and the books were kept in Persian'.[3] We also know that the Iranians learned Arabic and continued in their jobs as the majority of the scribes. Less known are the Arabs who learned Persian, although there were many of them in high positions in the bureaucracy, such as Ziyad b. Abihi, and, as the caliphate developed from a personal kingdom under the Umaiyads to a bureaucratic empire under the ʿAbbasids, all kinds of people joined the bureaucracy.[4] It is clear, however, that Iranians not only dominated the bureaucracy (the *kuttab*), but all branches of the government. Many times in the sources we find statements that the Persians were famous for their ability to manage a state.[5] Furthermore the Sasanian empire was considered a model state for its good organization.

We have discussed the word *wazir* above.[6] Although Abu Salama, the banker of Kufa who helped finance the first ʿAbbasids, was the first person to whom the title vizier was given, there was no office of vizier at that time. The title as an office first appears under the caliph al-Ma'mun, but the office really remained one of personal service to the caliph until the fourth century AH (tenth century AD), in the time of the caliphate of al-Qahir (320–2/932–4), when it becomes a regular office of government under the rules (*rusum*) of the ʿAbbasid establishment. This parallels a growth in power of the military group which not only made and unmade caliphs, but selected the vizier. The office of the vizier had gained in power and importance in the period of the preceding caliph al-Muqtadir (296–320/908–32) when, after a struggle with the theologians, primarily Muʿtazilites, the *kuttab* had triumphed.

This meant that the administrative organ of the state, the bureaucracy, had gained over the legal, represented by theologians, including judges (*qadi*). The viziers, of course, had to show considerable financial as well as administrative talents to retain office. Since the *kuttab* maintained a close union or guild organization their chief the vizier was of necessity almost invariably from their ranks; further we have the *aulad al-kuttab*, or 'children of scribes', almost in a nepotistic order of father to son. Even the viziers at times seemed to form a dynasty of *aulad al-wuzara* 'children of viziers'. One does not need to discuss the Iranian viziers such as the Barmecids from Balkh, the Banu'l-Jarrah from Khurasan, Ibn al-Zaiyat from Gilan, Ibn Yazdad from Merv or al-Fadl b. Sahl, who had been a Zoroastrian before he was converted to Islam. The vizierate has been discussed ably by D. Sourdel, and he mentions that they remained faithful to their ancient Iranian culture while at the same time accepting the Islamic society which was evolving, and, of course, the Arabic language.[7] It is true that these men perhaps at times introduced old Sasanian practices into the government, such as al-Fadl b. Sahl, who is said to have introduced Sasanian ceremonial practices into the caliphal court when Ma'mun was in Merv.[8] These practices, however, only show that the bureaucracy was being forged into a primarily Arab-Iranian synthesis, which is not at all unexpected.

Until the fourth century AH the *kuttab* were the dominant institution of the government, but their influence was waning and was being replaced not only by soldiers but also by the other two classes or groups of Islamic society, the *udaba'* or 'literary people', and the *'ulama'* or the religious leaders. In the fourth century the literary elements reached a peak of importance, perhaps partly because the *'ulama'* were quarrelling and divided into schools. Later, however, the religious institution was to dominate Islamic society. Conflicts between members of these groups of society, primarily in Baghdad, lie beyond the scope of this book, but the general trend of Islamic society had to be mentioned.

An influence of Iran on the government and administration of the caliphate can be seen in some titles and offices. For example, the *jahbadh*, or the expert on money, the intermediary between the taxpayers and the *'amil* or tax collector in the *diwan*, was an important local personage in the provinces.[9] Just how the word, which was probably of Iranian origin, came into Arabic, is unknown, while the etymology itself is uncertain.[10] Other Iranian words which entered the 'Abbasid government can be found. For example, the caliph al-Mutawakkil instituted a *diwan al-jund wa'l-shakiriyya* in place of the previous simple *jund*, and all words in this are Iranian, *diwan* from old Iranian **dipi-pana*, *jund* from Middle Persian *gund*, attested in Parthian *gwnd*, perhaps ultimately of ancient Near Eastern origin, and *shakiriyya* from MP *čakir* 'slave, servant', possibly of central Asian origin. To add to the list of Iranian words relating to the administration found in Arabic sources only shows an expected influx of Iranian influences into the bureaucracy of Islam.[11] Perhaps one might ask instead why the borrowing of Iranian words was none the less, comparatively speaking, small. The answer, I believe, is to be found in the attempts to islamicize, which in the early ʿAbbasid period meant also to arabicize, the institutions of government which had been borrowed or adapted, for the new Islamic culture and society was theoretically to be independent of external influences in nomenclature if not in fact. Iranians contributed greatly to the creation of new terms in Arabic to fit all needs, making of Arabic an international language of high precision and culture.

It is not so much in the actual offices or forms of government and administration that the influence of Iran is evident as in the theories of government and administration which were the bases on which the details were realized. If one reads the early works in Arabic on statecraft and government, the great reliance on examples from the Sasanian empire is striking. Ibn Qutaiba (*c.* 213–75/828–89) in the first book of his *ʿUyun al-akhbar*, 'sources of information', on kingship, constantly gives us information from Sasanian times. Here and elsewhere the Persian dictum that state and religion are brothers or twins and that one cannot exist without the other is propounded. Even in far-away Spain where Ibn ʿAbd Rabbih (d. 329/940) compiled his literary encyclopedia *al-ʿIqd al-farid*, the first book of the work dedicated to the manners of kings, is almost a Persian 'mirror of princes'. This position of duality, of course, was paradoxical since the Sasanian king of kings had been an autocrat practising the divine right of kings. Likewise Islamic theory supported a theocratic form of government in which the political and religious institutions were united. The Islamic caliphate, just as the Sasanian empire, however, had to compromise between ideals and reality, and the declining power of the caliph at the end of the third century AH brought a recognition that the caliph henceforth could only hope to be a religious leader, for the army generals took over the temporal authority. Later even the ʿAbbasid caliph's religious supremacy was challenged by a rival Shiʿite caliph in Fatimid Egypt.

The impetus to speculate and write about Islamic theories of government was begun by translations from Pahlavi into Arabic by ʿAbd al-Hamid (d. 132/750) and especially by Ibn al-Muqaffaʿ (d. 139/757), whose name before conversion to Islam was Rozbih. Much has been written about Ibn al-Muqaffaʿ who was the 'founder' of Arabic prose, for his style had a great effect upon his successors. He was accused of being a *zindiq* or Manichaean, and was executed, but he was not alone in bringing ancient Persian wisdom to the notice of Muslims. We have preserved not only in Persian but also in Arabic admonitions of the ancient Persian kings to their sons or to their people, and theories of the state, of classes of society and the like are presented in many Arabic writings. It is not possible to discuss these writings, but one may note that they present a pre-Islamic approval, as it were, of the state of affairs in the 'Abbasid caliphate, in the relations of the caliph with his subjects and with the organs of government and classes of society. This *andarz* 'advice' literature or 'mirrors for princes' had been especially widespread in the Sasanian empire but also to a lesser extent in the Byzantine empire. The Arabic translations of the Sasanian *andarz* literature which have survived have been islamicized, of course, and favourable references to the Zoroastrian religion have been deleted.[12] Praise of the class system of Sasanian Iran, however, is either left intact, or possibly even added by the translator or later scribes. The rules of conduct and etiquette of the Sasanian court and aristocracy were also a favourite theme of translators into Arabic; these were found in the *ayin* books of the ancient Persians. The translators were not secretly imposing this genre of literature on the Islamic society of their time, but were responding to the wishes of an Islamic society which had become sophisticated. The ideals of the *dihqan* class were not only preserved from Sasanian times into the Islamic period by the Persians; they were also passed to the Arab aristocracy, which fused with Persians and others into an Islamic aristocracy. Since the 'mirror for princes' literature existed both in Arabic and later in Persian we may suppose that the ancient Iranian maxims and explanations of how to run a government were widespread in the Islamic world. We know of a Sicilian, Ibn Zafar, who wrote such a book in Arabic containing much Persian lore, and of Ibn Abi Randaqa of Tortosa, Spain, also in the sixth century AH, who wrote a book on advice to kings.[13] Titles of books relating to the administration and government of the Sasanians, translated from Pahlavi into Arabic, are given by Ibn al-Nadim but very few have survived and those only in fragments in other books.[14] Although an enormous amount of Sasanian political beliefs and practices came into Muslim culture they were assimilated and given an Islamic colouring. Later writings in Persian on the subject of kingship are fully Islamic even though they too contain much Sasanian lore.

If we follow the development of the caliphal bureaucracy it is clear that Sasanian practices continued into Islamic times, and the 'Abbasids simply added to the Umaiyad organization of government.[15] The practice of having an office of the 'seal' (*diwan al-khatam*), for example, was introduced by Ziyad b. Abihi in the time of Mu'awiya, and was copied from the Sasanian administration.[16] The 'Abbasid administration, however, soon far exceeded any previous bureaucracy, and it is difficult to follow the rise and fall in importance of the various *diwans*. It is not the intention here to discuss the *diwans*, which in any case has been described competently elsewhere.[17] One may surely say that Iranians played a dominant role in the development of the ʿAbbasid bureaucracy, as well as in the creation of a universal Islamic culture.

RELIGION AND PHILOSOPHY

'Truly man is distinguished only by religion, and piety cannot be abandoned on account of racial reasons. Islam exalted the Persian Salman, polytheism humiliated the noble Abu Lahab.'[18] So wrote an unknown Persian poet in the Arabic language. Although we have seen an Iranian Buddhism which flourished in Bactria under the Kushans, an 'Iranian' Islam did not develop. The Persians contributed much to the formation of oecumenical Islam, but they did not seek to put Islam into a narrow national or racial framework. Zoroastrianism was limited to Iranians but Islam was universal in the eyes of the Persians. We have mentioned possible influences of Zoroastrianism on Islam, but those were active before or at the time of the Prophet, if at all, and any direct influences later are subject to much dispute and uncertainty. Indirect influences in the realm of thought and philosophy are even more difficult to determine, but if they were borrowed by Islam it was not as a conscious borrowing from another religion, but on the plane of universal questions and problems common to most if not all religions. Iranian words in the Qur'an do not give us much information, but certain ideas have been singled out as Iranian borrowings.[19] The angels Harut and Marut, of course, are clearly borrowed from Iran and one might theorize on such borrowings with little concrete result. When one turns to general religious ideas the picture is different. In the domain of religion the learned men of Iran who contributed to Islam are legion and their many achievements cannot be examined here.

Before the systematization of Islamic Sunni orthodoxy between al-Ashʿari (d. 935) and al-Ghazali (d. 1111) there were constant polemics between various groups of Muslims seeking to establish the supremacy of their beliefs over those of their fellow men. In eastern Iran Sunni Islam became dominant, particularly the law schools of the Hanafites and the Shafiʿites. In western Iran, especially in Tabaristan, Raiy, Qum and other centres, the Shiʿites were strong and active, although Sunnis, of course, were in the majority. The geographer al-Maqdisi (or Muqaddasi) said that in eastern Iran the theologians ('*ulama*') were highly esteemed, and had a great tradition of studies whereas in western Iran the scribes were honoured.[20] We should explain that eastern Iran became the centre of Islamic thought, whereas western Iran produced far fewer Islamic scholars.

Cities such as Bukhara and Nishapur became great centres of Islamic learning, and the two greatest collectors of *hadiths* 'traditions' of the

Prophet: Muhammad b. Isma'il al-Bukhari (d. *c.* 870) a Shafi'ite author of the famous *Sahih*, and Muslim b. al-Hajjaj al-Qushairi (d. 875), came from Bukhara and Nishapur respectively. Neither they nor the hordes of scholars who left Khurasan to go to Baghdad felt themselves other than Muslims writing in Arabic. We know next to nothing of the intellectual life of Khurasan in pre-Islamic times, but the material culture, as revealed by archaeology, was high and even luxurious. Furthermore, as we read in the sources, some of the companions of the Prophet accompanied the early armies of the Arabs in the conquest, and they settled in the east. They were followed by other Arabs who were interested in their own religion and propagated it. So the east became a breeding ground for theologians and Islamic scholars. Also the army which brought the 'Abbasids to power, and which enabled al-Ma'mun to defeat his brother al-Amin and secure the caliphate, was a Khurasani army. So the 'Abbasids had special connections with eastern Iran and they favoured the easterners. It is noteworthy that the Arabic spoken later by the learned men in the east was said to be close to Qur'anic Arabic, and erudite Khurasani scholars took great pains to learn correct Arabic.[21] The east was rich and able to pay for a scholar class because trade and industry provided wealth for such pursuits. In western Iran, however, hardly any of the above factors applied, for few Arabs had been settled there. Zoroastrianism was more firmly entrenched than in the east, and a development comparable to that of the east did not occur.

Some readers may be surprised to learn that Iran, and especially the eastern part, was a great centre of Sunni orthodoxy, for Iran has been considered by many as the home of heterodoxy and Shi'ism. Actually, if one surveys the early Shi'ite revolts, it is clear that Iraq, and particularly the city of Kufa, was the birthplace and centre of most of the Shi'ite movements. It is true that Iraq was part of the Sasanian empire, the capital was even located there, and the lowlands were always connected with the Iranian plateau. None the less early Shi'ism was predominantly Arab, and the various religions of Iraq, such as Mandaeism, provided ample sources for heterodox ideas. One should not forget the religious movements in Khurasan and Azerbaijan, which have been mentioned in the previous chapter, but on the whole they had little to do with the Shi'ites. Italian scholars have analysed the early Shi'ite uprisings and have come to the following convincing conclusions:[22] first, the early Shi'ite movements cannot be classified as moderate, intermediate or extreme, since there was no fixed theology in the early 'Abbasid caliphate and political considerations were foremost. Secondly, religious enthusiasm of the early period frequently embodied itself in a person, usually the *imam* in the case of the Shi'ites, whom the people who followed this line of thought at times even deified. For example, in the time of the caliph al-Mansur a group called *Rawandiyya* insisted on worshipping the caliph as the incarnation of divinity, although they also expected the coming of the *mahdi* or saviour, but they were suppressed. Some, though not all, believed in metempsychosis. The most important belief of the Shi'ites, however, was the allegorical interpretation of the precepts of the Qur'an and of Islam. The esoteric and allegoric exegesis of the Qur'an was to become the hallmark of later Shi'ism, especially the Isma'ili sect, and through this channel many gnostic ideas entered Islam. It is difficult to assign this or that idea or tendency to Iranians, because Islam had become supra-national, and any attempt to disentangle origins and influences is almost impossible with the sources we have.

If one nevertheless were to seek, one could possibly find some elements of ancient Iran which survived in the thought of Islam. This is different from possible direct influences on practices and popular beliefs; the reading, for instance, of the Qur'an after the death of a member of the family which was similar to Zoroastrian practice, or the significance in both religions of the number 33, or prayer five times a day.[23] If one were to guess at possible Zoroastrian or even plain Iranian influences on the thought of Islam, perhaps the outstanding feature of religious thought would be dualism. Zoroastrian dualism was primarily an ethical dualism and not, like platonic or gnostic dualism, one of spirit versus matter. Zoroastrian dualism does not equate matter with evil, and matter is not opposed to spirit. On the contrary, only in matter can the struggle for good against evil be fought and won. In a sense in Zoroastrianism matter is the highest aspect of spirit, which in this way is active in this world. Zoroaster is supposed to have smashed the bodies or the bodily forms of the demons, thus rendering them less dangerous. Perhaps the dualism of Zoroastrianism could be described as cosmic as well as ethical, for the earth or matter is important in the struggle against evil. This carries over into the Zoroastrian conception of destiny and free will, for destiny or predestination rules the world of matter, whereas in the realm of spirit there is free will. Destiny in this world is the visible aspect of a transcendental spiritual prototype in the world of spirit, and this prototype is free. But the spirit which is free cannot act save though incarnation in this world in the struggle against evil, and in this world one finds that destiny holds sway. One problem in understanding Zoroastrian thought is that it is expressed so often in myths or in mythical language, and ideas are personified as spirits, or angels. The doctrine of angels in Zoroastrianism is very important – even time is personified as an angel.

Such Zoroastrian ideas surely influenced Islamic thinkers, especially those Iranians who were converted to Islam. It has been said many times that the Mu'tazilites were greatly indebted to Zoroastrian ideas, which may be true, but not one of the early Muʿtazilites was an Iranian. In my opinion some of their ideas may have been engendered by discussions with Zoroastrians, but the Muʿtazilites were a good example of the development of Islamic thought as catalysed by Greek, Mesopotamian and Iranian ideas. The Muʿtazilites, the 'seceders', called themselves the 'people of unity and justice', for they denied the separation of divine attributes from God, insisting upon His unity, and they claimed that God punishes sinners and rewards the good. Thus deeds were just as important, if not more so, than faith. The main doctrines of the Muʿtazilites, for which they were noted, were those pertaining to free will, or man's freedom to choose between good and evil. This of course is similar to the orthodox Zoroastrian position, but no borrowing can be shown. The Muʿtazilites also believed in a metaphorical interpretation of such matters as the bridge (*sirat*), recording angels after death, and the like. In this too they resemble the Zoroastrians, but again no real connection can be established. The question of the created Qur'an, which played such an important role in the disputes at the caliph's court, was actually more of a symbol or catchword than a significant or integral part of Muʿtazilite thought. In the end we are left with general resemblances which cannot be used to prove borrowing. Only the use of the same words, or proper nouns, by both parties would provide substantial evidence of borrowing. Undoubtedly points of contact existed and the possibility of influences or borrowing is plausible, but we cannot go further.

The same uncertainty about influences and borrowings exists in the question of early Sufism or mysticism. The example of Christian monks and monasteries in the western part of the caliphate may well have impressed early Muslim Sufis, but this could hardly be true of Iran where we find no evidence of early Sufism in the west. The east again seems to be the birthplace of a special kind of Sufism, exemplified by Bayazid of Bistam (d. 261/875). He was not the first of the Iranian Sufis, however, and we must examine them before speaking of Abu Yazid (Bayazid). The life story of Ibrahim b. Adham of Balkh (d. 160/777) is so much like that of Buddha that one wonders whether the biography of Ibrahim was fitted into the pattern of Buddha. Indeed all that we know of Ibrahim and his disciple Shaqiq (d. 194/810), also of Balkh, indicates a strong Buddhist rather than Zoroastrian background to the asceticism preached and practised by these two. Although our sources are discouragingly scanty for these early Sufis, we may suggest that Sufism in Iran received an initial impulse from Buddhist monks, perhaps from the famous Naubahar Buddhist monastery or *vihara* in Balkh. Shihab al-Din Suhrawardi I (d. 632/1234), founder of a Sufi order, mentioned a group of people in Khurasan called Shaguftiyya, who lived ascetic lives in caves far from towns and settlements.[24] The sources do not inform us about Buddhist influences on the development of Islamic mysticism in Iran, and I am not competent to discuss problems of mystical thought, but we know that Buddhists did exist in Khurasan at the time of the Arab conquests. So historically contacts were not only possible but probable. Whether one should go as far as Horten in postulating many particular Indian influences on Sufism I am unable to say.[25] As archaeology reveals more of the culture of eastern Iran and central Asia, however, it is clear that an important cultural area existed which must have contributed much to the general Islamic civilization which evolved under the ʿAbbasids. One might say in a general way that Iran contributed a practical rather than a theoretical base to early Islamic Sufism. This changed later with the great theoreticians and of course with the famous poets and their remarkable language.

If the practices of Ibrahim b. Adham and his followers in the east much resemble Buddhist monasticism, then the ideas or utterances of Bayazid of Bistam are more convincing about Indian influences on early Islamic mysticism. Whereas we know next to nothing of the doctrines of the earlier Balkh school of mysticism, Bayazid is better known. This is not the place to analyse the sayings of this Sufi, but it is interesting to note that Jami, in his biographies of Sufis, says that Bayazid learned about the doctrine of the annihilation of the self in God (*fana'*) from a mystic of Sind called Abu ʿAli, while ʿAttar in his *Memoirs of the Saints* says that Bayazid became acquainted with the Indian practice of holding one's breath, which became a religious exercise on the path to God.[26] Bayazid was the first Muslim Sufi to expound the doctrine of the annihilation of the self in God, and his description of the path he followed provided a model for later Sufis. Historically we may propose that Bayazid was a creative representative of an eastern school of Sufism, which owed much to the east Iranian milieu in which it arose; whether ultimately all or most of the impulses for the development of this school came from India is difficult to determine, but influences certainly existed. Suffice it to say that this stream of Sufism entered Islamic civilization and influenced its religion and philosophy. The experiences of Hallaj and other mystics are beyond the scope of this book, which is to indicate only the part that Iran played in the unfolding of Islam. The Khurasani school, however, was far from the only influence on Islamic mysticism. Later the great poets of Iran had a profound impact on Sufism, but they belong to a later period and later problems which we cannot discuss here.

To turn to philosophy one might, of course, consider Sufism as a branch of Islamic philosophy, but it would be better, in my opinion, to limit ourselves to that branch of Sufism which was codified by Ibn al-ʿArabi (d. 638/1240) as a subject in the ranks of philosophy. He founded a school which may be characterized as concentrating on gnosis (*ʿirfan*) almost as a philosophical system. Of course it is very difficult to draw boundaries between Sufism and the gnostic movements in philosophy, especially when the language of both later become mixed, and *ta'wil*, or the symbolic esoteric interpretation of texts applies to both. This symbolic exegesis, of course, is not to be confused with the use of allegory as in Avicenna. It is far beyond the competence of the author to analyse the many currents in both Sufism and philosophy in Islam, especially after the eleventh century and after al-Ghazali united the two in relation to the orthodox Sunni religion. On the other hand one of the areas of philosophy to which Persians certainly contributed was just that of *ʿirfan*, founded by Ibn al-ʿArabi. Indeed the master seems to have found more of an acceptance among the Persian poets, such as Shabistari and Jami, than among his fellow Arabs.

The two schools of philosophy which are considered as classical are those of scholastic philosophy or theology (*kalam*) and the opposite peripatetic school (*masha'i*), derived from Aristotle, which contended that knowledge, or rather reason (*ʿaql*), was alone important to find the truth. Scholastic philosophy needs no comment since it was in the mainstream of the Islamic faith, and was given its real start by al-Ashʿari, mentioned above. With successors of al-Ashʿari, such as Abu Bakr al-Baqillani (d. 403/1013), *kalam* became the orthodox Sunni philosophy supported by the state, especially under the Seljüks. The peripatetic school, on the other hand, was distinctly a heritage from the ancient Greeks. The first of the peripatetic philosophers was said to have been a Persian called Iranshahri, but nothing is known about him save his name.[27] The first of these philosophers whose works have survived was Abu Yaʿqub al-Kindi (d. 252/866). The peripatetic school, if one may thus call this large area of Islamic philosophy, flourished during the prime of the ʿAbbasid caliphate, and such philosophers as al-Farabi and Muhammad Zakariyya al-Razi continued the tradition until Abu ʿAli Sina or Avicenna (d. 428/1037) summed up much of the philosophy of his time. He was born near Bukhara and died in Hamadan, and his entire life was spent in the Iranian cultural area. The peripatetic school suffered a decline under attacks by al-Ghazali, and Avicenna was criticized by the philosophers in Spain, especially Ibn Rushd or Averroes. In the Arab world the influence of this school declined considerably whereas in Iran there was a revival of Avicenna's teachings led by Nasir al-Din Tusi (d. 1274), which had proponents in the eastern Islamic world almost down to the present day. Such fascinating figures as Mir Damad and Mulla Sadra in the Safavid period, took their origins from Avicenna. So the peripatetics have been very well represented in the Islamic history of Iran.

Just as neoplatonism took its name and origin from the master, although its doctrines went in a different direction, so the peculiarly Persian school of philosophy called *Ishraqi* or 'illuminationist' took its departure from the peripatetics. In brief, Shihab al-Din Suhrawardi II (d. 587/1191) believed that reason and intuition (*dhauq*) or *sapentia* should be combined. Suhrawardi reconciled the differences of the rationalists and the mystics, but he drew on many and varied traditions of the past to accomplish this. Of interest to us is his use of the wisdom of the ancient sages of Iran, including the symbolism of light and darkness, good and evil, of Zoroastrianism. Apparently Suhrawardi believed that all ancient wisdom was universal and should be united in a new philosophy. It is fascinating to find an Islamic philosopher who, even though relatively late in time and a Persian, traced the origins of his thought in two lines back to Plato and to Zoroaster. One may well speak of the symbols or myths of ancient Iran interpreted in a novel way by Suhrawardi, but I fail to see any real historical continuity or connection between the thought of ancient Iran and the philosophy of Ishraq.[28] This philosophy asserts that the universe is composed of light and the absence of light, and bodies are the darkness through which light does not penetrate. The soul comes from heaven (the east: *sharq*) and it seeks to return to heaven from its 'occidental exile'. The great amount of symbolism in Suhrawardi's writings strikes the reader, and it is possible that he borrowed some ideas as well as symbols from Zoroastrianism, especially in his doctrine of angels and his use of illumination or 'vision'. Further discussion of Suhrawardi's philosophy is far beyond the scope of this book, but it had to be mentioned because of the great influence which the Ishraqi school of philosophy had in the later history of Iran, and because of supposed ancient Iranian elements in the philosophy of Suhrawardi. Even though continuity is difficult to prove it is significant that a thinker of the twelfth century should revive symbols of ancient Iran to promulgate a teaching which incidentally cost him his life in a prison in Aleppo.

The reader may object to the speed with which important schools of learning and thought are passed over without attempts to analyse them in detail. We are concerned, however, only with the history of Iran under the caliphate through the rise of Iranian local dynasties and down to the coming of the Seljüks, seeking to understand the process whereby Iran, east and west, became Muslim. Of necessity much has to be omitted and perhaps more time and space should be devoted to one subject rather than to another, but the main purpose of our inquiry should not be forgotten even though some details seem more productive of insight than others. When we turn to science and medicine we find a picture similar to that in philosophy.

The contributions of Iranians to Islamic mathematics is overwhelming. Undoubtedly Iran acted as a middleman for the transmission of a good deal of mathematical knowledge from India, and it is not easy to determine the source of many ideas, but Iranians were active and did contribute much. The centre of scientific activity was, as expected, Baghdad. The caliph al-Ma'mun collected a great number of mathematicians and astronomers at his court, almost all of them from eastern Iran. Perhaps the most famous of the mathematicians was Muhammad b. Musa al-Khwarazmi (d. *c.* 850) who wrote on algebra, and it is possible that this word comes from his book *al-Jabr* just as the word algorism, the decimal system of computation, most probably comes from his own name. To record even the names of the scientists of Iranian origin who flourished in the time of al-Ma'mun would occupy much space, and their contributions to learning and science were extensive. The Banu Musa, three brothers, were instrumental in translating Greek and Pahlavi manuscripts on scientific subjects into Arabic under al-Ma'mun. Abu Ma'shar of Balkh was more an astrologer than a mathematician but many of his works were translated into Latin and were well known in Europe where he was called Albumasar. The mathematical tradition was continued in Iran by Abu 'Abdallah Muhammad al-Mahani (d. *c.* 884) from the famous shrine town near Kirman, and Abu'l-'Abbas al-Nairizi (d. *c.* 922) from the town near Persepolis. More famous than these two was Abu'l-Wafa' al-Buzjani (d. 997), from a town in Kuhistan, eastern Iran, who made significant contributions to trigonometry, especially in studies on the tangent. The list could be extended to include many lesser lights such as al-Khujandi from Transoxiana who died *c.* 1000, and the famous 'Umar Khaiyam (d. 515/1122) who is better known in the west as a poet. He was, however, a great mathematician and also an astronomer. He reformed the old Persian solar calendar which had continued in use in Iran beside the Muslim lunar calendar. This new calendar, called the Jalili, was more accurate than the Gregorian calendar. It was formally inaugurated on 16 March 1079. The name of Abu Raihan al-Biruni (d. 1048), from Khwarazm, must be mentioned since he was one of the greatest scientists in world history. His encyclopedic knowledge is evident from his many and varied writings which have survived. His works include treatises on geography, geology, mathematics, astronomy and history, which include a great deal of information on philosophy and religion. To describe the contributions of al-Biruni and other Iranians to the body of mathematical knowledge in the Muslim world would far exceed the scope of the present volume.

Astronomy and astrology were difficult to separate in the Middle Ages both in Europe and in the orient. In Sasanian times astronomy must have been popular since we know of many translations from Pahlavi books on this subject into Arabic, as well as the existence of official astronomical tables in the Sasanian court. The astronomers from Iran who contributed to Islamic astronomy are also many. At the beginning of the ʿAbbasid caliphate we find a family which, from father to sons, contributed much to the intellectual and scientific life of the new capital. This was the famous Naubakht family, the founder of which helped to lay out the future city of Baghdad.[29] The capital was not the only place where astronomical observations were conducted, for at the famous medical and scientific school at Jundisabur in Khuzistan a certain Ahmad al-Nihavandi was making observations in about the year 800. The first astrolabe was constructed, according to tradition, by Muhammad b. Ibrahim al-Fazari about the year 777, and the Musa brothers, mentioned above, were also active in astronomy in Baghdad. Likewise in the capital making observations was Habash al-Hasib al-Marwazi from Merv and al-Mahani, cited above. Although the ʿAbbasid capital completely dominated the intellectual and scientific scene, provincial cities in Iran were also sites of activity. In Balkh, for example, an astronomer called Sulaiman b. ʿIsmat al-Samarqandi was active in astronomical observations in the year 257/871. Later in Shiraz, when that city had become the capital of the Boyid ruler ʿAdud al-daula, an astronomer called ʿAbd al-Rahman al-Sufi from Raiy invented a meridian ring to determine the length of the seasons. We will speak of the Boyids in the following chapter, but here their patronage of learning should be mentioned. Several astronomers were active under their rule in Raiy; one was Abu'l-Fadl al-Harawi from Herat who was observing in 348/959, and another was Abu Mahmud al-Khujandi who constructed a huge sextant in 384/994. To continue with names such as Abu'l-ʿAbbas Ahmad b. Muhammad al-Farghani, known in Europe as Alfraganus, who flourished under al-Ma'mun and who measured the diameter of the earth, or al-Biruni again, or others would only fatigue the reader. The tradition of astronomy was continued after the fall of the ʿAbbasid caliphate to the Mongols in 1258. In Maragha Azerbaijan a large observatory was built for the savant Nasir al-Din Tusi who wrote about the astrolabe and many other astronomical subjects. Thus in astronomy, as in mathematics, Iranian scholars were leading contributors to the advancement of knowledge. It must be again emphasized, however, that these savants did not think of themselves as Iranians or as Arabs, but only as servants of the Islamic oecumene.

In medicine the name of Burzoe, chief physician to Chosroes I has survived from the Sasanian period, as well as the activities of the school of Jundisabur, which became a great medical centre after the destruction of the city of Edessa, also a medical centre, by the Byzantines in AD 489. Apparently there was a substantial medical literature in Syriac which has not survived. The medical traditions of Jundisabur continued into Islamic times, for we find the Bukhtishuʿ family, Nestorian

Christians, who came from there and who served several ʿAbbasid caliphs as their personal physicians. In the domain of medicine the Iranians were at first less prominent than in other fields, for the outstanding early physicians were from Mesopotamia, such as Yuhanna b. Masawaih (d. 857), Hunain b. Ishaq (d. 877), who translated many Greek works on medicine into Arabic, as well as many other works on various subjects, Thabit b. Qurra (d. 901), a Sabian from Harran, and others. The organization of Islamic hospitals, or the hospital system, seems to have been built on the Sasanian model of Jundisabur, later copied in Baghdad, Shiraz and elsewhere.[30] The first Persian Muslim, who replaced the Persian Christian physicians (Bukhtishuʿ and Masawaih or Masuya), was Ahmad b. al-Taiyib al-Sarakhsi (d. 900). There was also a Persian physician at Jundisabur at the time of the others, called Sabur (Shapur) b. Sahl (d. 869), who wrote one of the first books on antidotes in medicines called *Aqrabadhin*, which had many successors. As time continued in the field of medicine, too, Iranians dominated the field. Perhaps the most important later figures in medicine were ʿAli b. Rabban al-Tabari, a Muslim convert and son of a Persian Jew, who flourished under the caliph al-Mutawakkil, and who wrote on medicine, Muhammad b. Zakariyya al-Razi (d. 924) mentioned above, ʿAli b. al-ʿAbbas al-Majusi (the Magian, d. 994) and Avicenna. All of them were practising physicians, as well as scholars in other areas, and all wrote books on medicine. There were, of course, many others such as al-Jurjani and al-Qamari, but the four names above were far more significant in the history of medicine. Razi was head of a hospital in Raiy for a period until he went to Baghdad to direct a hospital in the capital. He is said to have been the greatest clinical physician in Islam, and his works were translated into Latin. Al-Majusi came from Ahwaz and his work is characterized by greater organization and order than that of Razi whom indeed he criticized for his disorder.

Avicenna is known in medicine for his great work the *Qanun* or *Canon*, which had a great influence in medieval Europe. His observations were remarkable for his time and he combined these with the learning of the past to make the *Canon* an encyclopedia of medical knowledge which had as important a place for a long time among physicians in the Near East as in Europe. It is interesting that after Avicenna medical knowledge does not progress and since medicine is of great concern to the common people, later books on medicine in Iran were written in Persian rather than in Arabic. Later productions, however, add little to the masterly work of Avicenna.

In addition to mathematics, astronomy and medicine there were other sciences which flourished under the ʿAbbasid caliphate. Alchemy, of course, was popular but not without its opponents, Hunain b. Ishaq and al-Kindi being the two most prominent adversaries of the alchemists. In the realm of the technical or applied sciences there was less progress than in other fields, but some branches of knowledge, such as the book on optics by the Arab al-Kindi, provided Europe with a basis on which to build for future discoveries in the west. Naturally problems of irrigation, water supply and canal building, were a special concern for the Iranian peoples, who lived, for the most part, in dry, arid lands. Even a governor of Khurasan, ʿAbdallah b. Tahir, wrote a book on irrigation canals, *Kitab al-quniy*, which has not survived. Many books on mineralogy, on the other hand, have survived, perhaps the most famous of them by al-Biruni. One could continue in the fields of botany, zoology and general science to list the Iranians who studied and wrote, contributing to the general store of knowledge in Islamic civilization, but this would do no more than further emphasize the immense contribution of the Iranian peoples to the culture of Islam, so much that one might be entitled to designate the Islam which came into being in the tenth and eleventh centuries as Iranian Islam using the Arabic language.

Our purpose in the rapid survey above was to confirm the picture of a similar development of Islamic learning in all fields in the eastern caliphate. This was the overwhelming dominance of Baghdad and Mesopotamia as the place of activity, but almost all the scholars who produced this activity came from *eastern* Iran where a secondary provincial centre of intellectual ferment existed. Thus we seem to have a Baghdad-Khurasan axis, not only in the army which put the ʿAbbasids in power and set al-Ma'mun on the throne in his struggle for power, but also in learning and other activities. It seems clear that the manpower, or brainpower, for the ʿAbbasid flowering came from Khurasan, and not from western Iran, Arabia, Syria or elsewhere. I have deliberately omitted Mesopotamia or Iraq, because this was the site of the capital, the former heartland of the Sasanian empire, and consequently in a different position from the other provinces of the caliphate. Furthermore, as we have seen from the family names, the savants of Jundisabur were primarily Persians. One can suggest, simply by the use of statistics, that the Baghdad-Khurasan axis really existed, because of the reservoir of learned men of Buddhism, Manichaeism, Nestorianism, plus the economic well-being of an area grown rich by the utilization of the great opportunities for trade and commerce offered by an enormous caliphate. Industry flourished and Khurasan prospered to a greater degree than other provinces of the caliphate because Khurasan took more advantage of being a part of the caliphate than did other provinces. In effect, Khurasan took over the ʿAbbasid caliphate. We need not spend further time and space on the expansion of savants and learning from the east, but let us turn to the economic and then to the artistic sides of this central Asian expansion, before we consider literature and language.

COMMERCE AND CRAFTS

It is, unfortunately, very difficult to obtain information about commercial activities in the caliphate since our sources are overwhelmingly concerned with religious or political affairs and economic matters are usually limited to the type of produce of one area or another, as found in geographies. We have mentioned how the Azd tribe in Merv and elsewhere in central Asia under the Umaiyads joined the local weavers in joint commercial enterprises. We have also mentioned the results of archaeological work in central Asia at Panjikant and elsewhere, which have revealed a high level of culture, one might say a 'luxury civilization' in central Asia especially in the century before the Arab conquests. If we turn to the Arabic sources the importance of such cities as Nishapur, Merv, Bukhara and Samarqand for the textile industry is undeniable. We know, for example, that the cloth called Zandaniji was manufactured in the oasis of Bukhara, where the town of Zandana is located, and the cloth, or garments made from it, were sent all over the caliphate.[31] We could accumulate more information to show the great importance of the weaving industry in Khurasan and Transoxiana, but would it indicate a predominance of these provinces in the eastern part of the caliphate over the west? Tabaristan was also an important textile centre, but the cities in western Iran were less so at this time. The sources clearly indicate that textiles were exported from the east, but there is no evidence of any imports into the east except from China, which would only enhance the economy of the transit area of central Asia to the Near East. In other words there is much evidence that Khurasan and Transoxiana were great exporters of textiles to other parts of the caliphate in the 'Abbasid period, and the commercial activity in textiles in these provinces was greater than in other provinces. The important point to remember is that the caliphal capital of Baghdad provided a great market for luxury goods, including textiles and silks, and Khurasan and Transoxiana supplied many of the luxuries. It was a grand epoch requiring luxuries, and upon them the wealth of the east was built.

Textiles, of course, were not the only materials for clothing in the Near East, although cotton was widely used and silk was popular among the wealthy. Even though the climate was warm in Mesopotamia and Syria, on the Iranian plateau winters could be cold. It is of significance to note that 'furs were widely used in the costume of 'Abbasid times, and the survey [by Sergeant] hardly shows how generally they were employed by the wealthy and men of fashion'.[32] Khwarazm was the great centre of the fur trade from east Russia and Siberia, and undoubtedly one of the principal reasons for the many hoards of coins from the eastern caliphate found in Russia and Scandinavia was the fur trade. Another item of trade from the north was honey, the sweetener of antiquity, while amber, which supposedly had medicinal qualities as well as decorative, walrus ivory, wax, hides and even dried fish were important. That trade was brisk between central Asia and the Volga region is attested in the Arabic geographers. Mas'udi tells us that the (local) rulers of the Persians, among others, loved to wear furs, but the trade in furs extended all over Europe and to the Far East, and it was an important part of the economy.[33] From Ibn Fadlan's account of his trip from Baghdad to the Bulghars on the River Volga (AD 921) through Bukhara and Khwarazm, one can discern the importance of Transoxiana in the caliphate, even later in the time of the Samanids. We learn that Ibn Furat, one time vizier of caliphs, owned land in Khwarazm, an indication of the economic centralization of the caliphate in Baghdad and far-flung connections.[34] Later, trade relations between India and the Volga over Merv were not uncommon. One index of the great expansion of trade and commerce is the town of Panjikant, which, according to the archaeologists, in the fourth and fifth centuries AD had a few small houses, but in the seventh and eighth centuries had many large houses, richly adorned with wall paintings. This picture is fully in accord with Arabic sources which tell of the great commercial activity of the Sogdians in the early Islamic era.

One of the important items of trade which Iran and central Asia both sent to the north was silver, either in coins or in decorated plates, cups and bowls. It is clear that many of these, which have been found in north Russia, came from central Asia rather than from Persia, and many objects in 'Sasanian' style are really central Asian in origin and from the Islamic period, but again this is a vast area of study which cannot be entered here. The problem of the disappearance of silver from the Islamic east in the eleventh century has not been answered satisfactorily and we cannot explain why the great influx of silver coins into eastern Europe during the Samanid kingdom suddenly ceases. It seems that the Qarakhanid conquest of the Samanid state at the turn of the millennium stopped the trade with eastern Europe, but a reduction, which was hardly a cessation, of the trade would not explain the silver famine. We will return to this question below when dealing with the Turkish ascendancy. Here we simply wish to point out briefly the economic factors which provided a basis on which the intellectual and cultural flowering of Khurasan and central Asia was built. This by no means implies that the rest of the caliphate was left out of the general economic prosperity of the times, but only that Khurasan and Transoxiana were the first provinces to utilize the advantages in trade and industry which the ʿAbbasid caliphate offered. To document fully this point of view would require many articles on a host of subjects, which is not in the purview of a book such as this. Enough indications of the validity of the thesis of a Baghdad-eastern Iranian connection have been given above to permit one to seek ramifications in its history. There is no mystery or traces of a conspiracy between Baghdad and the Khurasanis to raise the contention of an Iranian uprising against Arabs or Arabism. Rather, quite naturally, Khurasan and Transoxiana were the theatres of the process of amalgamation between Arabs and Iranians, a process which began under the Umaiyads and which brought splendid fruit in the ʿAbbasid period. It is significant that the amalgamation was with the eastern Iranians rather than with the Persians, the western Iranians. This will be explored further when discussing the rise of the New Persian language in Khurasan and central Asia rather than in western Iran.

LITERATURE AND LANGUAGE

English is a language rich in vocabulary because it has a double source for words, Latin (and French), and a Germanic base. The New Persian language is similar, for it draws on Arabic as well as its own Iranian base. It is doubtful whether Persian poetry could have flourished the way it did if there had been no rich Arabic vocabulary, and the rules of Arabic poetry to stimulate creativity within those ample rules. For, if one compares New with Middle Persian literature, the contrast is striking. Much of Middle Persian literature has not survived, but what little we know of is so poor in comparison with the outpouring of New Persian literature that one is driven to the conclusion that Arabic provided the catalyst to make a world literature in New Persian. Poets and troubadours certainly existed in Sasanian Iran but they were also in pre-Islamic Arabia, and whereas the Persians gave their energies to many facets of culture, the Arabs concentrated on the spoken word. Even in the limited surroundings of sand, camels and fellow men Arabic poetry shows great imagery and skill in the use of words. This was the one thing the bedouins of the desert could teach their sophisticated subjects, and the Persians learned well.

It was only natural that Iranians would have to learn Arabic and begin to study it. We hear of *mawali* in Medina who worked on Arabic grammar in the first century of the *Hijra*, but it would be a mistake to assume that Arabic grammar was first studied by Persians. It was first studied by Arabs who taught Persians and fellow Arabs. The tradition, probably reliable, is that a certain Arab called Abu'l-Aswad al-Du'ali (d. 69/688) was the first grammarian of the Arabic language.[35] In the two garrison cities of Basra and Kufa more Persian was at first spoken than Arabic, so bilingualism grew apace. Many stories are told about the defective Arabic of some of the heroes of early Islam, such as ʿUbaidallah b. Ziyad, who grew up in a Persian-speaking milieu in Basra.[36] Sibawaih or Sibuye (d. *c.* 793) was the greatest of the early Arabic grammarians, but his teacher was al-Khalil b. Ahmad, an Arab from Oman. So Persians and Arabs both contributed to the study of Arabic grammar and, of course, also to Arabic poetry. Bilingualism was a feature of the courts of Harun al-Rashid and al-Mahdi, and even Persian sobriquets were given to Arab poets, as ʿAli b. Khalid, who was called al-Bardakht, from Persian *pardakht* 'the polished one'.[37] Many stories are told about Persians who mispronounced Arabic but even Arabs were criticized for faults in pronunciation, which is not surprising after the natural decline of Qur'anic Arabic. We should remember that not only did Arab colonies exist in Iran, but we learn from the geographers that Persian colonies were settled in Arabia and Syria and bilingualism was common. In the bilingualism of the time we hear of teachers who used both languages in the same lesson. Thus Musa b. Saiyar al-Uswari taught the Qur'an, explaining in Arabic to the students on one side and in Persian to those on the other.[38]

We have mentioned Ibn al-Muqaffaʿ and ʿAbd al-Hamid, both Persians, as the founders of Arabic prose, but if one goes through the names of poets composing both in Arabic and in Persian in the fourth volume (on Khurasan) of al-Thaʿalibi's *Yatimat al-dahr*, an anthology of poets, one finds both Iranians and Arabs. For example, a certain Abu'l-Taiyib al-Musʿabi ibn Hatim, who was an accomplished poet in both Arabic and Persian, was an Arab.[39] In short, both Persians and Arabs participated in Arabic poetry, but also both composed verses in Persian in the eastern part of the caliphate. The participation of Arabs in Persian was, of course, much more modest than the reverse, and from them nothing but Persian words in Arabic verses have survived, but the participation of Arabs in Persian poetry should not be surprising since many Arabs lived in a Persian-speaking milieu as Persians did in Arabic-speaking surroundings. Likewise in the literary movement of the *Shuʿubiyya* Persians attacked Arabs in the Arabic language, and Persians defended Arabic in the Arabic language. There were even Arabs who did not equate Islam and Arab, and one Umaiyad poet, at the time of Qutaiba b. Muslim, said that his father was Islam and not Tamim or Qais as other Arabs claimed.[40] This position was rarer than finding Persians defending Arabic. Later when Arabic was on the decline in the east, al-Biruni hotly defended it and Zamakhshari (d. 538/1144) violently attacked those who were enemies of the Arabic language. The situation was such that Tahir b. Husain (d. 207/822), governor of Khurasan, was renowned for his epistolary style in Arabic yet claimed to be a descendant of Rustam and was proud of his Iranian origin. As late as the Boyids the famous vizier of Fakhr al-daula, the Persian Sahib b. ʿAbbad, defended the Arabs against the Persians.[41] Some Persians were proud that they had become arabicized, while others lamented the fact and recalled ancient glories, and from both one can only gather that all kinds of people lived in Iran, but Islam dominated all.[42]

From the beginning of the conquests both Arab Muslims and Persian Muslims went to schools where the Qur'an was taught, and gradually other ancillary disciplines such as grammar and rhetoric were added to the curriculum. As already noted, even Persian teachers taught Arab children the Qur'an, as did Salman al-Farisi from the early days of Islam. The Qur'an was not easy to understand, for the Prophet himself had to explain verses from the Book to his listeners. We do not know whether other schools, for scribes and bureaucrats, were established after the conquests, but such a development would not have been unusual. In any case the Arabic that was taught everywhere was Qur'anic Arabic and the Arabic dialects soon began to widen the gap between themselves and Qur'anic Arabic. Iranians, however, maintained their tradition of Qur'anic Arabic since it was the only kind of Arabic taught to them. It is clear that even Zoroastrian Iranians like the Barmecids and the family of al-Fadl b. Sahl (converted to Islam in 190/806) had mastered Arabic before they were converted to Islam. Just how they learned Arabic is unclear. Yet if we look at the life of ʿAbd al-Hamid (d. 132/750), mentioned above, who was secretary to the Umaiyad caliph Marwan II and perhaps the first great grammarian and stylist in prose, we may postulate a flourishing scribal tradition in teaching Arabic parallel to the Qur'anic schools. This was perhaps the main way through which many Persian expressions and customs entered Arabic and, of course, vice versa. Some of the scribal families such as the Barmecids and Sahlids have been mentioned, but there were many others such as the Naubakht family mentioned above who were active in translating from Pahlavi to Arabic, including the Banu Jarrah and other families.

We have noted that Arabic dialects began to diverge from each other more and more as Arabs settled in areas from India to Spain. The Umaiyad caliphs began to send their children to the desert to acquire proper pronunciation and style in Arabic, since there was an ever-changing *koiné* used by the army in its far-flung conquests, which itself diverged because of the different regions in which Arabs settled. By the tenth century the inflections of words in Arabic had vanished and to use them was considered pedantic.[43] Many of the Arabs who settled in Khurasan were outstanding teachers or even companions of the Prophet, such as Qutham b. ʿAbbas who died in Samarqand, as did al-Hudain b. al-Mundhir, Dahhak b. Muzahim al-Khurasani who died in Balkh, and many others. The first Arabic dictionary is said to have been written in Khurasan by al-Khalil b. Ahmad (d. 175/791), teacher of Sibawaih, mentioned above. So Khurasan became a centre of Islamic learning *both* because of the Arabs who settled there and the Iranians. According to the geographer al-Muqaddasi (d. 390/1000) the purest Arabic in his time was spoken in Khurasan, because the Iranian Muslim scholars made great efforts to learn correct Arabic.[44] The Arab geographer was, of course, speaking of the learned men of Khurasan, not the common people. It was inevitable that the same kind of people should participate in the creation of the New Persian language and literature, to which subject we should now turn.

Jahiz tells us that the first Persian couplet recorded in literature was composed by the Arab poet Yazid b. Muffarigh (d. 69/689), who lived in Khurasan but died in Kirman.[45] It is important, I believe, to note this information even though it cannot be authenticated, for just as the Islamic conquests brought the Persian language to central Asia, so the Arabs are credited with 'starting' Persian poetry. If this information is true, what does it mean? Does it mean that Ibn Muffarigh was the first to write Persian poetry in the Arabic alphabet, or the first to apply Arabic canons of poetry to the Persian language? It is generally accepted that the process of the entry of Arabic into Persian began with the conquests, but the converse is not so apparent: that Arabs also learned Persian, and that Persian words entered the Arabic language brought to Khurasan and central Asia by Arabs as well as Persians. According to the *Fihrist* (p. 129) the first book we know of on the Persian language was written by an Arab, Abu'l-Qasim Ibn al-Jarrah (d. 391/1000). It would be interesting if one might suggest that the Persians were the first to interest themselves in Arabic grammar, and, conversely, the Arabs in Persian. Arabs were definitely interested in Persian, contrary to general belief. At the court of Harun al-Rashid an Arab poet called al-'Ummani recited a poem of which the rhyming words were all in Persian.[46] Therefore the rise of New Persian poetry could conceivably be assigned to poets of Arab origin. Rather, since the Iranians were so active in Arabic poetry under the 'Abbasids, we can well imagine some of them experimenting with Persian poetry. Since Persian poetry appears from the beginning with a great richness of verse forms and techniques, obviously either a long development predated the first Persian poetry which has not survived or, more likely, bilingual poets simply applied Arabic genres and rules of poetry to Persian.

There are several problems in discussing the rise of New Persian poetry. First, what constitutes New Persian poetry as opposed to Middle Persian, or even local folk poetry? Secondly, can we rely only on what has survived, or what was written down, as a necessary criterion of poetry when the nature of poetry in those days was primarily oral for recitation? The results of study on the first point are not unequivocal. What little remains of Middle Persian poetry indicates that it was primarily accentual, but in any case unlike New Persian classical poetry based on quantities of syllables as in Arabic poetry. Folk poetry, which did not adhere to scholastic canons, existed in all periods. If we define early New Persian poetry as that which adheres to the classical rules of later Persian poetry, then we could not include many fragments (such as those of Yazid b. Muffarigh) as part of New Persian poetry, but could merely say that they were Persian utterances neither in prose nor in poetry, which is not very satisfactory. Enough work has been done on the origins of New Persian poetry to summarize the conclusions of scholars.[47] Persian rustic poetry existed and exists; it was always a source of themes and influence on formal Persian poetry. It was always an element present in the development of New Persian poetry. Since this poetry was oral, and rarely written, we have few traces of it in history, though under the Parthians it seems to have flourished when the minstrels (*gosan*) were such a prominent feature of Parthian society.[48] The rustic poetry of Iran in many dialects continued to exist in provincial centres and in the countryside after the Islamic conquest, and even the *dihqans*, the local feudal lords, encouraged such poetry. But, as more and more people converted to Islam, Arabic poetry became the proper and sophisticated medium by which poets should sing praises of their patrons, or even, in Arabic, extol the glories of the Iranian past.

It may be coincidental, but it is noteworthy that new Persian literature rose as Arabic had passed its apogee in literary development and had become somewhat decadent in its exaggerations of style and figures of speech. As mentioned, it almost seems that the Iranians, having exhausted the possibilities of writing Arabic forwards and backwards, now turned to a new challenge, the Persian language as a vehicle of poetry and *belles lettres*, although Arabic remained as an instrument of science and learning. This subject, the decline of literary or Qur'anic Arabic, or rather the decline in knowledge of the language except among savants, and its relation to the rise of New Persian has not been studied thoroughly, although the indications of a relationship are present. It is significant that the earliest Persian prose writings were translations from Arabic. The common people were too lazy to learn Arabic, as some sources have it, so translations had to be made into Persian. In the poetry ancient or Zoroastrian elements may have been the mode, but New Persian was thoroughly Islamic in its origins. The entire question of the use of Arabic and Persian in Iran in the tenth century AD might be seen as a parallel to the British in India. From the site of Varamin near Raiy archaeologists have found some ostraca engraved with Arabic and some with Pahlavi dating from the ninth and tenth centuries, which indicates that Arabic was used by local officials, or scribes, as was Pahlavi. This was in western Iran, for in eastern Iran one would only find Arabic at this period since Pahlavi never had been entrenched as in the west, and eastern Iran, furthermore, was more islamicized than western Iran. Let us return to the rise of New Persian literature.

Persian was basically a dialect of Fars raised to an imperial language by the Sasanian government. It absorbed many Median, Parthian and other words, and it was the official spoken language of the Sasanian empire when the Arab conquests began. Under the Arabs this language spread in central Asia and to the River Indus as the *lingua franca* of the eastern caliphate, and was used by Arabs as well as by the local populations. Arabic replaced Pahlavi as the written language, but it did not replace Persian as the universal spoken language. Obviously some Iranians experimented with writing Persian in the Arabic alphabet long before the time of the Samanids. Jews wrote Persian in Hebrew characters and Christians in Chinese Turkistan wrote Persian in the Syriac script.[49] Poetry seems to be the first literature we find in most languages and this was true of New Persian, for prose came later. The history of Seistan claims that a certain Muhammad b. Wasif was the first to compose a poem in Persian in AD 867 because his patron Ya'qub b. Laith complained that he could not understand some of the Arabic verses composed in his honour.[50] The poem was not folk poetry, but composed in an Arabic style, and we may accept this account as substantially true, for this might well have occurred in minor courts of the east, where a person such as Ya'qub would prefer Persian to Arabic poetry, and would also prefer a high style of Persian as befitting his station rather than a rustic poetry understood possibly even by the peasants. So New Persian poetry probably began as a court poetry and developed as an Islamic language copying Arabic metres and verse forms. As I have stated elsewhere, New Persian poetry began in the east because the population was more mixed with Arabs, and more Islamic than in western Iran. Furthermore, there was not the sharp division between Iranians as Zoroastrians and Arabs as Muslims, the former with Pahlavi as their written language, and the latter with Arabic, as there was, for example, in Fars province. Likewise there was probably a larger class of arabicized *'ulama'*, and *udaba'* 'literary men' in the east, whereas the *kuttab* 'scribes' were more prominent in the west. Persian, or Dari, the court language of the Sasanians, was, of course, spoken both in east and west, but in the east it had to compete with Sogdian, Khwarazmian, Bactrian and Parthian which it came to replace. In western Iran, on the other hand, many Persian dialects existed in many villages, which were more difficult to replace, and we know that poetry was composed in many dialects. In the Caspian provinces Tabari and other Caspian dialects attained a written, literary status in the eleventh and twelfth centuries. We know that Khwarazmian was written in Arabic characters and there must have been other experiments at writing Iranian languages or dialects in the Arabic script, but Persian triumphed. Perhaps the final reason why Persian triumphed is the patronage it received at the courts of the Saffarids and Samanids. Literature in dialect could not compete with Persian and was relegated to folklore.

I have not here the intention to expand on the development of different metres of Persian or types of poetry, such as the *ruba'i* made famous in the west by 'Umar Khaiyam, or the *mathnavi*, both of which are probably new creations of Persian poets and not borrowed from Arabic. It is possible that the former is derived from an older non-quantitative verse form found in pre-Islamic Iran, and that several quantitative metres are derived from similar accentuated verse.[51] If this is so, then both Arabic poetry and old Iranian poetry must have contributed to the rise of New Persian poetry, which seems most likely. The contributions would not only be in content but in verse forms. The epic, of course, was peculiarly Iranian, and the work of Firdosi was consciously an attempt to save or resurrect the past so that it would not be forgotten; for Arabic had so much entered the warp and woof of Persian that literary figures such as Firdosi feared that the Persian language and all the heritage of the pre-Islamic age would vanish. An attempt to make a scientific language out of Persian later failed, for just as the more recent attempt of Reza Shah to purge the modern Persian language of Arabic failed, so did the attempt in the tenth and eleventh centuries to replace Arabic by Persian. The archaic Iranian words which were then uncovered by some savants were completely unintelligible to Muslim Iranians who had been reared on Arabic as the language of science and learning. It was too late to turn back the clock, for the new Islamic culture in the east was at harmony with both Arabic and Persian as twin stars in the Islamic firmament.

CHAPTER 9

ARTS AND CRAFTS

The arts and crafts of Iran are world famous, as every tourist to that land today knows. This is a vast and at times elusive field of inquiry and one which cannot be covered adequately, even in general terms, in one short chapter. Therefore, of necessity, only comprehensive questions dealing with cultural history and with the transformation of Iranian art into an Islamic art can be sketched here. Obviously one would like to survey the whole gamut of the visual arts before assessing their significance in the cultural history of Iran and in the wider Islamic world, but this is not possible and only the briefest mention will be made of individual monuments or art objects.

The western approach which distinguishes between the fine arts and the crafts makes little sense in an Iranian context, for here the cultural distinction between the craftsman who makes something for use and the artist who creates objects for aesthetic contemplation has no validity. Certainly the Iranian potter knew and felt the difference between a crude unpainted clay pot and superb glazed lustreware, but there was no sharp division in his mind between utility and beauty.[1] Further, the distinction between the craftsman who repeated and embellished old traditions and the artist who created original material would never arise in the east. Europe before the Renaissance provides the only western parallel to this art which is unattached to personality. But the use of such parallels outside the Iranian cultural area does not really throw much light on the question of artistic creation and craftsmanship within Iran. A comparison of attitudes in the other arts found in Iranian society might prove more instructive, and poetry comes at once to mind. Just as in Persian poetry, where innovation did occur, but only in the perfection of established norms rather than in complete departure from the rules of prosody, so also in the visual arts the artist repeated and perfected old forms and motifs. But just as in poetry where the rules permitted an almost infinite variety of possibilities, so in the visual arts the artist enjoyed freedom within a structure, deploying his materials in a great variety of ways while conforming to canons which at times stretched far back into antiquity.

This is not to say that there have been very few changes in three thousand years of art history in Iran, but rather that one is impressed more by constancy and continuity than by change. We may say that the Arabic adage that culture (*al-adab*) belongs to the Iranians remained true of the peoples of Iran throughout history – the inhabitants of Iran were conspicuous from the earliest times for their artistic abilities. Again, variety existed even in antiquity, for the almost surrealistic forms of the pottery of the Caspian Sea regions from Marlik, Kaluraz and other sites, more than three millennia ago, are breathtaking in their affinity with some modern art.

When it was suggested that one should not distinguish between the crafts and arts in Iran, this was not to say that everything was made just for utility. Decoration and ornament have always characterized the arts in Iran, and both of these features were considered necessary even for utilitarian objects. Perhaps it would be more meaningful to distinguish between the arts (and crafts) which were produced under the patronage of the ruler or the aristocracy, and popular art, which, on the whole, was an art of the city rather than the countryside or the village. We shall speak later of urbanization in the world of Islam in the tenth and eleventh centuries, which produced the great flowering of Islamic art in the later Seljük period. That was the period when the art of Sasanian Iran, greatly modified, of course, changed from an art of the aristocracy to one of the middle class, a true Islamic art. But that is a later story and we must go back to the Arab conquest.

What sort of art did the Arabs find when they overran the Sasanian empire? There is no evidence of a Zoroastrian art comparable to Christian or Buddhist art. At least there is no iconographic material in the Zoroastrian religion similar to the cross or the figure of the Buddha, and this fact immediately suggests that it was easier for the Muslim Arabs to borrow artistic forms and ideas from the Persians than from Christians in Syria and Egypt and even in Iraq, for the Christians not only had an art full of iconographic motifs, but also this art was related to the Christian art of the unconquered Byzantine enemies of Islam. Furthermore, it would seem that the Sasanian art of the seventh century was not characterized by great use of human and animal forms, as were the arts of the Christians to the west and of Buddhists or Hindus to the east. Sasanian art, as preserved in architectural decorations and fragments of textiles and the like, shows a taste for geometric designs or vegetal motifs, usually floral patterns, or abstractions from architecture such as frames, doors or arcades. Human and animal figures seem to have been much more prominent in Christian art and in the wall paintings of pre-Islamic central Asia than in western Iran. Art for the

Sasanians on the whole appears to have been secular and their religion might be considered almost as austere as Islam itself.

Thus Sasanian art, of the court or even of the city, is to be understood more in a social or individual context rather than in a spiritual one. Yet if there was no religious art properly speaking in Iran, there certainly was an imperial art, conscious of a great past, and monumental in many respects. The traditions which had surrounded the king of kings made the imperial art more than just luxurious and impressive, but also a reflection of the almost mystical power which the concept of kingship held for most of the inhabitants of the empire. The symbolism of Sasanian art is then royal rather than religious, and as such it was easy for the caliphs of Islam to accept. The forms and the meanings of Sasanian imperial art could be taken over by Islam without any clash with Muslim religious sentiments. And even the tales or stories connected with this art could be accepted into an Islamic repertoire without conflict. This, in my opinion, is an all important reason why Sasanian art was one of the prime movers in the creation of an Islamic art throughout the ʿAbbasid caliphate, of course more so in the east than in the west.

City art under the Sasanians, if one may speak of such an entity, could have been little more than a pale copy of imperial art, since the court dominated the life of Sasanian Iran, with its hierarchy of classes. Furthermore, Zoroastrianism, unlike Islam, was pastoral and agriculturally oriented rather than commercially or city oriented, and one may suspect that non-imperial art was produced more in the town villas of the nobility than in the bazaars of towns. Undoubtedly folk art existed as well, but here we simply do not have the data or the remains to study such influences. The very nature of Islam as a popular movement would have encouraged a contribution from non-aristocratic people in the creation of an art as well as a culture. Documentation of this influence, however, is extremely difficult to find, especially when we use such a vast category as Islamic art, which could be compared to 'western art' in its extent. Can one even speak of a unity of Islamic art?

In the beginning of Islam there could have been very little concern with the arts since in Arabia we do not find remains, either of architecture or objects, which would indicate any great creative activity. This is not unexpected, but when the Arabs expanded over the Fertile Crescent and into Africa and Iran of necessity this attitude changed, for Muslims were then confronted with artistic cultures and had to come to terms with them. From the beginning a puritanical streak existed in Islam, and even though there is no express prohibition against the representation of living beings in the Qur'an, the prejudice against such representations must have been strong. There must obviously have been a reaction against the Byzantine world, where art was in the service of the church. There was apparently no cult of the image in Sasanian Iran as in the Roman empire, and later in the image of Christ in the Byzantine empire. Hence there could hardly be a continuity of the Iranian 'image' into Islam, even if Islam accepted images, which it did not. The depiction of human forms brought up ideas of image or idol worship, and it was better to reject such representations completely rather than to try to differentiate good images from bad. The crystallization of this attitude into a policy, at first not theologically grounded, took place in the eighth century, almost a hundred years after the Prophet's *Higra*. We see it first and most clearly in the reform of coinage under the Umaiyad caliph ʿAbd al-Malik mentioned above. This was followed by the decree of the caliph Yazid II in 721, ordering all religious images to be destroyed, especially those in churches.[2] Even though this decree was probably directed against the Byzantines, it surely reflected a growing Islamic sentiment against the representation of living beings in any form. Decoration, which did not represent any belief, iconography or the like, came to replace the specific symbolism which was a hallmark of Byzantine Christian art, and even of some of the Sasanian forms. Calligraphy became a new Islamic art, and even this new imagery of writing lacked the specific meaning of much of pre-Islamic art. Decorative Islamic writing is frequently difficult to interpret and ambiguous in content: perhaps ambiguity itself is a characteristic of early Islamic art.

In any case the imperial art of the Sasanian court adopted and adapted by the caliphs was not an art bound to any religion or to local custom; rather it was an international culture, intelligible to Byzantine, as well as Sasanian, princes or to the caliphal court. What was this art, other than royal architecture, as at Ctesiphon or Firuzabad? Gold work, and to a lesser extent anything made of precious metals or jewels, as well as splendid textiles, were obvious media in which imperial or aristocratic art forms would find expression. The Sasanian government more or less controlled such art objects and the caliphal court of Baghdad had no compunction in accepting such art forms *en masse*. Imperial motifs suggesting the 'glory of the king of kings' could be accepted easily by the caliphs who were the heirs of the Sasanian monarchs, and Islamic art in Iran until the tenth century, on the whole, is modified Sasanian court art. Of course other influences entered this amalgam, especially from Iraq and Syria, but with this large subject we cannot be concerned. To the north-east, however, was another, lesser known, cultural area to which we should turn.

In central Asia the Arabs encountered another cultural world, also primarily Iranian but different from western Iran. In the domain of art the Arabs seemed to have borrowed less from eastern Iran than from the west. One reason for this, of course, was the inability of a small court in central Asia to compete in richness and splendour with the court of the king of kings of Sasanian Iran. Patronage, especially by the ruler, was necessary for the arts to develop and flourish, and Sasanian Iran was second to none in the brilliance of its court. However, at the end of the Sasanian empire constant foreign wars and internal strife probably did not encourage the growth of the arts; in central Asia on the other hand the rise of rich, trading city-states promoted them. These mercantile city-states would have been easily comprehensible to Arabs who followed the religion of Muhammad, who had been a merchant living in the commercially oriented towns of the Hijaz. Too little is known about the central Asian cities at present, however, to discern whether they had any influence outside central Asia. But future archaeological excavations, both in Iran and in central Asia, may revise our views of cultural influences.

It must be confessed that our knowledge of the arts of the Umaiyad and early ʿAbbasid periods in Iran is almost nil. There have been no extensive excavations of sites from this time-period, and until the results of such excavations as Siraf on the Persian Gulf and the Islamic strata at Bishapur are published in full we shall not even know about pottery, the most ubiquitous source of information for the archaeologist. Likewise, information from Sasanian sites is scanty and, apart from preliminary work at Ctesiphon and Bishapur, this period of transition to an Islamic culture in Iran is virtually a blank. Art objects from this time, of course, have survived to be tentatively dated by museums, but they are few and too uncertain to be very helpful in establishing the process by which Sasanian art became Islamic art in Iran. It is true that as soon as an Arabic inscription occurs we have an object of Islamic art, but such inscriptions, unfortunately, are rare and late. We must remember that art probably closely followed the general cultural development of the Islamic world already sketched, and the time of the formation of an Islamic art would vary from area to area. A flowering which began in Iraq and Syria in the eighth and ninth centuries, spread in the east under the Samanids in central Asia at the end of the ninth and the beginning of the tenth century. This corresponds with the rise of New Persian poetry and the creation of a general Islamic Iranian culture. In western Iran the process seems to be a century later, as in literature.

This is not the place to discuss the philosophy of Muslim art – a discussion of Islamic symbols and their meanings would require a book.[3] Similarly, any comprehensive discussion of the rise of Islamic art would have to explain the development of such institutions as the mosque, on which various decorative arts were employed. This is beyond the scope of the present book and the competence of the author. Suffice it to say that just as the Islamic scientist used the knowledge of the Greeks and others to form new combinations which one can designate Islamic science, so the Islamic artist used ancient motifs and forms in new ways to form an Islamic art. On the other hand some features were new, such as the use of calligraphy mentioned above, and there are examples of novelties in the art of ceramics. Naturally the very size and unity of the Islamic world, especially under the ʿAbbasid caliphs, brought a great exchange of forms from east to west, and, to a lesser extent, in the reverse direction, engendering a great variety of forms of art. We should briefly examine the various genres of Islamic art in Iran to see if they present a unified picture. Commerce and the crafts have been mentioned in the preceding chapter, and here we view the arts primarily in a cultural and social setting.

Progress in our knowledge of art objects in gold or silver has been encouraging, in spite of many problems such as modern forgeries. Since even Arabic poetry uses Persian words, for which there are no Arabic equivalents, in describing silver and gold plates, goblets and bowls, we may presume that the prime influence on Islamic objects of this genre came from Iran rather than from Syria, Egypt or elsewhere.[4] In the pre-Islamic period such objects were once all designated 'Sasanian silver', but now we can classify them into eastern and western Iranian, and pre-Islamic and Islamic silver. The eastern Iranian objects may be subdivided further into Sogdian, Khwarazmian and Bactrian, although sometimes it is very difficult to determine to which area an object belongs. Obviously the same artists and craftsmen continued to work after the fall of the Sasanian dynasty, but presumably patronage was not as munificent, for a small Iranian prince of the Caspian area could not vie with the king of kings in support of the arts. None the less in metalwork one can see the continuation of Sasanian motifs, even though these are usually not understood by the craftsman, in the eastern Islamic world through the Boyid and Samanid periods to the Seljük flowering of a universal Islamic art of the bourgeoisie, when mass production, to use modern terms, spread objects everywhere and not just to the castles of the nobility. The old Sasanian motifs of hunting, drinking or holding court in a garden, the crescent and star, and others, continued to be used, but now in an Islamic and more egalitarian context rather than the old courtly association. Calligraphy, arabesques and other new designs came into use on metalwork as in other genres.

Turning to painting, we are seriously handicapped by lack of examples from Iran before the twelfth century. We do not have any 'ancient' miniatures except those from Chinese Turkistan, primarily on pages from Manichaean books. These we may compare with Armenian or Byzantine miniatures since nothing has survived from the Iranian plateau or Iraq from the pre-Islamic period, but such comparison with external evidence is fraught with pitfalls, for one never knows how relations, if any, occurred. It is always best to seek internal evidence. From literary sources we learn of the existence of books with illustrations or portraits of the Sasanian rulers, but no miniature paintings have been preserved. Pre-Islamic wall paintings have been found in central Asia, however: in Panjikant to the east of Samarkand, at Varakhsha in the oasis of Bukhara, in several sites of Khwarazm, in Balalyk tepe north of Termez, and in other sites.[5] On the Iranian plateau, fragments of pre-Islamic wall paintings have been found at Kuh-i Khwaja in Seistan and at Bishapur. At the Ghaznavid centre of Lashgari Bazar near Bust in southern Afghanistan, and at Nishapur, Islamic wall paintings in poor condition have been discovered.[6] Finally there are fragments of wall paintings from Samarra, the short-lived caliphal capital north of Baghdad, but from these fragments it is very difficult to reconstruct a view of painting in the early Islamic period. The Samarra paintings, it would seem, are ultimately of Sasanian inspiration, highly decorative, perhaps somewhat sedate or solemn but certainly Persian in character. This is not unexpected since Sasanian influence was widespread, even to wall paintings of ruined Umaiyad palaces in the Syrian desert to the west.[7] This style has been designated by some as the Mesopotamian school of an early expressionist style, and it continued from Umaiyad times through Samarra into twelfth-century miniatures from Mosul and northern Iraq.

The pre-Mongol period of the history of painting in Iran might be described as an interregnum between the Sasanian 'heraldic' style, and the glorious new world of Persian miniature painting which developed as a result of contact with Chinese art. Just as Arabic brought an enormous richness and a new direction to the Persian language, so did China act as a similar catalyst for Persian painting. One might, on the other hand, view this period in painting as simply a continuation of a modified Sasanian tradition in art, which has been described as the 'expressionist' style in Iranian art.[8] The story of the remarkable schools of Herat, with the master painter Behzad, and the later schools of Shiraz and Tabriz, followed by the perfection of miniature painting at the Safavid court in Isfahan, is beyond the scope of this book, but the background was prepared in the earlier period when Islamic culture became oecumenical. Later Persian painting must be distinguished from productions in the Arab world or in Turkey; for the present-day Near East goes back to the split in the Sunni and Shiʿite worlds, the Ottoman and Safavid empires. But this too belongs to another story.

The influence of Chinese art on Iran was operative in another sphere, seemingly earlier than in painting, and this was in ceramics. At first glance we would think that pottery was one product which could not have travelled far, but this is apparently not true, for potsherds of the Chinese T'ang dynasty have been found in Samarra, Nishapur and Siraf. The superb wares of Iran, only surpassed by China in the skill and creativeness of her potters, probably began with attempts to copy metalwork. The end result was lustre ware, specimens of which, however, hardly date before the eleventh century of our era. Because of the comparatively large number of specimens of pottery and sherds which have been found, one is able to assign certain pottery techniques and designs to certain areas. Distinctions can be made between pottery from Iraq and western Iran and pottery from eastern Iran and central Asia, although certain types were apparently made in western as well as eastern Iran. But the sheer quantity of potsherds makes classification and study difficult, because of problems in the handling and comparison of great quantities of varied pottery. Differences in the two areas can be found; for example, the imitation lustre vessels made in the east in the ninth and tenth centuries are not found in western Iran. The two main sites or sources for this pottery were Nishapur and old Samarqand Afrasiyab.[9] Writing, animals, especially stylized birds, floral designs, and finally a few human representations, riding horses, seated or in other poses, are the most prominent features of this eastern pottery. The great amount of sherds found indicates that the pottery was not made just for local nobles, but rather for a wider spectrum of society, primarily for merchants and middle-class city dwellers. This would account for the vast majority of pots decorated with writing, birds and designs more congenial than older aristocratic motifs to a Muslim middle class.

The division between western and eastern Iran which one can observe in pottery, as well as in literature and other aspects of culture, could be studied further. For example, even in the east it has been possible to distinguish between wares made in Nishapur and those made in Afrasiyab, and further refinements in classifications could be proposed.[10] Just as in other arts, so in ceramics the beginning of an Islamic culture in eastern Iran in the tenth century moved westward in the eleventh and twelfth centuries. Kashan, in western Iran, became the outstanding centre for the production of pottery and glazed tiles, so much so that the term *kashi* came to be the common word for tile in Iran. One may predict that pottery will serve as the basis for further developments in the entire field of early Islamic art, since it alone can provide the quantity of material on which to base overall theories and judgements.

It is no less complicated to determine the origins and influences of Iranian architecture, for the same difficulty of lack of remains or sources plagues this study. There is a gap between the Sasanian and Seljük periods in Iran which must be filled, on the whole, by informed conjecture. Since the main edifice of Islam was the mosque, this is the one kind of building on which we have information and much has been written about the early Islamic mosque. It is not possible to discuss here the different types of mosque structures in Iran since this would involve an investigation of the various mosques in Arabia, Iraq and Syria as a preliminary study before turning to the Iranian plateau. The early, simple square or rectangular courtyard with a flat roof supported by columns at the end facing Mecca, primarily found in western Iran, such as at Nayin and Demavand, was not generally employed all over Iran. Perhaps it was felt to be unsuitable for the plateau after the Arabs had introduced it from the west. Since Islam did not require any imposing places to worship, and prayers could be held anywhere, there were at the outset no architectural requirements for the mosque building. It would seem that the Muslims had little compunction about converting a church or even a fire temple (perhaps as at Yazd-i Khwast south of Isfahan) into a mosque. It has been suggested that in western Iran the Zoroastrian fire temple, the *chahar taq*, or dome on four pillars with arches between, was the prototype of the later *kushk* or kiosque mosque with its vaults and domes. The question of origins is not only difficult but many conflicting theories about the first mosque types exist.

Another mosque type was the building with a large façade called an *aiwan*, which seems to have been especially popular in eastern Iran. It is interesting to note that a Buddhist monastery from Adjina tepe, south of Dushanbe, Tajikistan, dating from the seventh or eighth century of our era may be one of the oldest prototypes of the four-*aivan* mosque enclosing a courtyard, later widespread all over the eastern Muslim world. This is not to say that in Buddhism we can find the source of that mosque style which became so characteristic of the Iranian world, but the style seems to have grown to fruition in the east.[11] The *aiwan* mosque was joined to the domed kiosque to produce the world-famous masterpieces of Iranian architecture, such as the Safavid mosques of Isfahan. In retrospect it may be said that early architecture in Iran seems prosaic and lacks the ethereal quality of later buildings which have a variety of forms for mausolea, dervish centres and other purposes. A new Islamic symbolism permeates the buildings which reflect the later culture of Islamic Iran, so devoted, as it seems, to mysticism.

In illustration of the difference between the utilitarian early architecture and the later, mystical symbolism of some of the architecture in Iran, one could compare the tomb and shrine of Nimatallah Vali in Mahan near Kirman city from the fifteenth century with the tomb of a Samanid prince in Bukhara from the tenth century. It is not merely the difference between the simple brick structure of the latter, where the only decoration is also in brick, and the lovely tiles of Mahan. The mausoleum of the Samanid looks like a kiosque used as a burial site, whereas the later shrine is not just an individual tomb, but is dedicated to a belief, or a series of mystical symbols exalted by the Nimatallah order of dervishes. Each is lovely in its own, but different, way and the messages they convey are different.

Not even to mention Persian carpets in any discussion of arts and crafts would be an inexcusable omission. On the other hand, the vast subject of Persian rugs could not receive justice in a few paragraphs, so here only their role in the life of the people can be briefly sketched – for carpets have been the prime mark of concern and respect for the arts in the lives of ordinary Persians over centuries. Much more than the preoccupation of a modern American with his automobile, a rug for every Persian is his symbol of hearth and home, frequently the only object of value in an otherwise barren mud house. Furthermore, the rug is not new in Persia or surrounding lands, for beautiful piled knotted woollen carpets from the Near East have been found frozen in tombs in Siberia, dating from the sixth or fifth century BC. The techniques used and the quality of workmanship on these ancient rugs provoke a feeling of awe in the viewer. The same traditions of excellent work and high quality, characteristic of modern Persian rugs, are found two and one half millennia ago, revealing the continuity not only of artistic motifs but of techniques in rug weaving.[12]

Persian rugs were highly prized by all the conquerors of the Iranian plateau, from Alexander the Great and the Greeks, through the Arabs, Turks and Mongols. Not only woven woollen rugs but masterpieces in silk, as well as more plebian felt carpets, decorate the homes of Persians today, and a rug accompanies a Persian from the cradle to the grave, as a prayer mat, a bed, or an adornment hanging on the wall. Just as poetry represented the highest expression of the mind and tongue of the Persian, so the rug was the parallel masterpiece created by his hands. Rugs were frequently discussed and assessed in homes and in the bazaar with as much interest as football is followed in Britain. Carpets were never merely objects of export for tourists but represented a fundamental part of the life of the people. In no other art or craft is the genius of a people so well represented as in the art of rug making for a Persian.

Superb textiles, the glyptic art of seals and precious stone cutting, bookbinding and other arts have not been discussed because of the special problems each presents and the lack of space. Enough has been said, however, to indicate several general themes. First, the separation of eastern and western Iran is evident, and throughout Iran's history the western part of the land has been frequently more closely connected with the lowlands of Mesopotamia than with the rest of the plateau to the east of the central deserts. At times eastern Iran has had more connections with India and further central Asia than with western neighbours. None the less, paradoxical as it may seem, as with the eastern and western arms of the Fertile Crescent of Iraq and Syria, throughout history eastern and western Iran have been united for long periods. The inhabitants of both were, after all, Iranians. This vacillation between separation and connection is seen throughout the cultural history of Iran, but the period with which we are primarily concerned, the first four centuries of Islam, was one of an ever-growing unity of eastern and western Iran under the banner of an oecumenical culture of Islam.

Secondly, the change in art from the first four centuries of Islam to the artistic explosion of the Seljük period, the highpoint of which lasted from 1150–1225, was a change primarily from a continuation of Sasanian motifs and forms to a new oecumenical Islamic culture.[13] There were many reasons for this phenomenon, including the great urbanization of the east with the growth of a bourgeoisie, the long rule of the Seljüks, and the enormous expansion of commercial activities; the developments in art reflected all of these. But ancient values continued to dominate the new culture even though the chivalric class of lower nobility, the *dihqans*, lost its power and influence. The bourgeoisie exalted the old ideal, learned over the centuries, that those with the capacity to serve, if done with style, and even the ability to suffer, if endured with grace, are the true aristocrats of life. Thus were the Iranians able to absorb Islam and transform it in the cultural sphere.

CHAPTER 10

THE IRANIAN DYNASTIES

The rise of native Iranian dynasties in the eastern part of the ʿAbbasid caliphate has been described by some scholars as the political manifestation of the *Shuʿubiyya* movement in literature, or as the rise of anti-Islamic Iranian nationalism. Actually the coming to power of the Tahirids, Saffarids or Samanids had nothing to do with the *Shuʿubiyya*, unless some of the partisans of the latter happened in their writings to extol one of those rulers as his ideal of a *Shuʿubite* prince. Likewise none of the dynasties mentioned were anti-Islamic. On the contrary they were strong supporters of Sunni Islam, except possibly for one Samanid monarch, and they all strove to strengthen or extend Islam in their domains. The Shiʿite Boyids in western Iran were somewhat different, but even they had no intention of abandoning a religion which had become firmly installed all over the Iranian plateau. The Iranian dynasties were rather the instruments of the internationalization of Islam, pointing the way for the spread of Islam anywhere in the world, without the native people giving up their language or culture for Arabic. In north Africa and even in Spain the words Arab and Islam remained synonyms, whereas in Iran they were separated and the Arabic language was recognized only as the primary, but not the exclusive, vehicle of Islam in all its facets. Those who accepted Islam and learned Arabic did not thereby become Arabs. Such was one contribution of Iranians to the building of Islamic culture.

How did the Tahirids come to power? It was perhaps inevitable that the provinces of the caliphate should become more independent as the central power of Baghdad weakened. The court, the central bureaucracy and the army in the capital required an enormous collection of taxes from the provinces to support them, and as Baghdad grew to be a megalopolis more revenues were needed. The basic source for more revenue was land and the ʿAbbasid caliphs farmed out lands to obtain more returns more quickly, rather than pursuing a long-term policy of developing and protecting the source of major income. We know from Arabic books that the revenue from the land in Iraq declined, and the provinces, naturally, did not relish being milked to support the capital. As the governors grew more independent they usurped the local tax collections and the control of the revenues which formerly had been in the hands of tax collectors appointed by Baghdad. One of the principles of 'Abbasid administration had been a separation in the provinces between the financial administration, which was accountable to the capital, and the civil governors and military leaders. The centralization of control over expenditures was maintained for a long time in the civil bureaucracy of Baghdad under the caliph. As mentioned, as the caliph sought more revenue, he sold governorships to individuals who, in effect, paid tribute to the caliph instead of taxes. The financial and the military position of the caliph was thereby weakened. As early as the year 800 Harun al-Rashid granted Ibrahim b. al-Aghlab a hereditary fief over Tunisia in return for a yearly tribute of 40,000 dinars. Thus arose the Aghlabid dynasty. In 872 the caliph placed the head of finances in Egypt under the military governor a Turk called Ahmad b. Tulun, which resulted in the founding of the independent Tulunid dynasty.

Perhaps the caliph had little or no alternative, since Tunisia and Egypt were far from Baghdad and difficult to control from the capital. It may have been expedient for the caliph to give such outlying provinces to strong men as fiefs, so that money could be expected from them without any expenditure of effort on the part of the caliph. Not only did the caliphs need more money in the court but such crises as the Zanj revolt and the Kharijite threats demanded a great concentration of resources at home. These troubles in Iraq persuaded al-Muwaffaq to grant Ibn Tulun control over the finances of Egypt in return for gifts and money payments in lieu of taxes.

The situation in Baghdad itself, the over-expansion of the bureaucracy and its division into feuding factions, the development of parties, almost dynasties of civil and military officials, brought the caliph's power to its lowest ebb. The granting of state domains to the officials and their greed in expanding their personal estates contributed greatly to the weakening of the 'Abbasid caliphate. The Tahirids in Khurasan were a much better investment from the caliph's point of view than were the Tulunids, since the former placed a high value on their investiture by the caliph, sent regular tribute, and were staunch defenders of the central government against heretics and anyone who might dispute the *de jure* authority of the 'Abbasid caliphate in the east. There was no question of any Iranian nationalism in Khurasan since the Tahirids ruled in the caliph's name, and almost as foreign overlords with a mercenary army over the populace. The only local support would come from the governor's ability to maintain peace and order, rather than any separatist sentiments. Later the Saffarids, and to a certain extent the Boyids, were different for they wrested power from the caliphal representatives as rebels or adventurers who looked to local support, but in the end even they sought to obtain official recognition from the caliph for their usurpation of power, perhaps more than anything else in an effort to placate any local, orthodox Islamic opinion which continued to support the caliphal rights. The hereditary governorships thus were an expected development of the calpih's loss of authority.

THE TAHIRIDS

The Tahirids claimed descent from a certain Ruzaiq, who had been a client of Talha al-Khuza'i, a governor of Seistan in the heyday of Umaiyad power.[1] His son Mus'ab b. Ruzaiq had joined the 'Abbasid movement at an early date and had even served as a secretary to one of the 'Abbasid missionaries. As a result after the victory of the 'Abbasids Mus'ab obtained the governorship of Herat. In 160/776 he was driven from the town of Fushanj or Pushang on the Hari Rud by the rebel Yusuf al-Barm, but soon recovered it and his son Husain succeeded him there. In 190/806 Rafi' b. Laith, grandson of Nasr b. Saiyar, last Umaiyad governor of Khurasan, revolted against 'Ali b. 'Isa b. Mahan, the 'Abbasid governor of Khurasan. Rafi' had been a protégé of the Barmecids, and by them had been given the governorship of Transoxiana, under the governor of Khurasan, but after the fall of the Barmecids he decided to revolt. Harun al-Rashid sent a general called Harthama b. A'yan with his son Ma'mun against the rebel and Tahir b. al-Husain joined the 'Abbasid army. The death of Harun changed the picture, and al-Ma'mun, who held the eastern part of the caliphate, made peace with Rafi' to concentrate on the struggle with his brother in Baghdad. In 195/810 Ma'mun at the advice of his chief councillor al-Fadl b. Sahl, appointed Tahir to command the army he was sending against that of his brother which was led by 'Ali b. 'Isa.

Tahir captured the city of Raiy before 'Ali could move from his camping ground at Hamadan. He did finally advance and the two armies met in battle near Raiy. Tahir was victorious and 'Ali was killed. Tahir was nicknamed *Dhu'l-yaminain*, 'the man with two right hands', because of his personal agility and bravery in this battle. After this victory the way to Baghdad was open but Tahir had to fight several battles with armies sent against him by Amin, one of which he besieged in Hamadan for two months until it capitulated. Finally Baghdad itself was besieged and captured, and Tahir put Amin to death in 198/813, so Ma'mun became ruler of the entire caliphate. Tahir took over the governorship of Iraq and the capital while Ma'mun remained in Merv. The killing of Amin seems to have displeased al-Fadl b. Sahl, Ma'mun's vizier and patron of Tahir, so in place of Tahir the vizier's brother Hasan was made governor of Iraq and western Persia. Tahir, however, was ordered to combat several anti-Ma'mun Arab chiefs in the west, and he made his headquarters at the city of Raqqa on the River Euphrates. Hasan had trouble in maintaining order in Baghdad and urged the caliph to come to his capital, but in 202/817 his brother al-Fadl was assassinated, which ended opposition to Tahir. The latter consolidated his position in Raqqa, and Ma'mun finally entered Baghdad in 204/819, later confirming Tahir in his post, which included not only a military command but also leadership of the local police and the post of tax-collector in northern Iraq.[2] In 205/820 Tahir's son 'Abdallah succeeded his father at Raqqa while Tahir himself became governor of Khurasan. The sources report a growing coolness between the caliph and Tahir, because the caliph could not forget that Tahir had put to death his brother Amin. It is possible that harem intrigues had poisoned the mind of Ma'mun against Tahir, but in any case Tahir thought it wise to remove himself as far as possible from Baghdad and through intrigue he was able to secure appointment to the governorship of the east.

The attitude and actions of Tahir in Khurasan have been discussed by many scholars. Coins of his exist from the year 206/821–2 which omit the name of the caliph, usually a sign of revolt against him. Also some sources report that he omitted the name of the caliph from the Friday prayers, which was also a sign of rebellion. He died, however, in 207/822 before anything developed and again the sources disagree as to whether he was poisoned by an agent of the caliph, or died naturally.[3] At his death his son Talha succeeded him, while another son 'Abdallah continued to hold office in Raqqa where he was engaged in fighting an Arab rebel in northern Iraq called Nasr b. Shabath. We may assume that the caliph was unable or unwilling to dispense with the services of the Tahirids, who had consolidated their positions in Iraq and Khurasan. We must remember that this was also the time of the rebellion of Babak in Azerbaijan and of Kharijites in Seistan, so it was not a propitious moment to try to remove the sons of Tahir who had many supporters. Furthermore the caliph was flirting with the Shi'ites and the Mu'tazilites, and orthodox Sunni leaders were not supporting these policies. Therefore it is probable that Ma'mun really had little choice, although more likely his vizier, Ahmad b. Abi Khalid, was probably bribed by Talha to support him at the caliphal court. For Ahmad led a large army into Khurasan less than a year after Tahir's death, and Talha supported him on his expedition against Ustrushana whose king had stopped sending tribute.[4] This expedition was successful and the king, father of Haidar Afshin, conqueror of Babak, accepted Islam and renewed his allegiance to the caliph. If Ahmad had wished he could have removed Talha at that time, but this did not happen and the Tahirid remained a loyal governor until his death in 213/828.

Talha was succeeded by his brother 'Abdallah who had had a distinguished career in the west, not only in Iraq but also in Egypt, where in 210/825–6 he had successfully ended an occupation of the port of Alexandria by pirates from Spain, and had put down an internal revolt.[5] Another brother 'Ali maintained Tahirid rule in Khurasan at the death of Talha until 'Abdallah was able to assume the post of governor in 215/820. It is clear that the caliph favoured the Tahirids, for if they had rebelled and Ma'mun had wished to remove them he could have done so. With the accession of al-Mu'tasim in 218/833, however, the atmosphere cooled considerably, but the new caliph was now unable to remove the powerful governor, so he confirmed him in his office. Although relations between the caliph and the governor were strained they were correct. 'Abdallah continued to own land in Iraq from which he obtained a large revenue, and he still nominally held several official positions in Iraq such as chief of police in Baghdad. This was during the Samarra period of the 'Abbasid caliphate. The Tahirid governor 'Abdallah was in effect ruler of the eastern caliphate. As such he sent expeditions against the Turks in central Asia and into the mountains of Afghanistan to extend his authority. In the Tahirid domains were many vassals or sub-rulers such as the Samanids, who shortly will be mentioned. We have already noted 'Abdallah's interest in irrigation, indicated by the book he wrote on the subject, but he also engaged in several irrigation projects in Transoxiana; furthermore he secured the financial aid of the caliph in building a large canal in the province of Shash, in the vicinity of modern Tashkent, a precursor of the modern great Ferghana canal.[6] The province of Khurasan flourished under Tahirid rule, but this only incited the envy of others.

It is not certain whether Haidar the Afshin of Ustrushana, who finally defeated and captured Babak, wanted to obtain the governorship of Khurasan, but it seems he did intrigue with the Ispahbad of Tabaristan Mazyar, who was a vassal of the Tahirids, or at least had to send tribute to the caliphal court through the Tahirids. 'Abdallah's army, which invaded Tabaristan, was successful and Mazyar was captured and sent to the caliph who executed him. 'Abdallah continued to rule and to embellish his capital at Nishapur until his death in 230/845. The new caliph al-Wathiq may have tried to put another Tahirid in the governorship of Khurasan instead of 'Abdallah's son, according to several sources, but he then confirmed Tahir b. 'Abdallah as the governor, who ruled as successfully as his father until his death in 248/862. There were other members of the now large Tahirid family and we hear of one Muhammad b. Ibrahim who was appointed governor of Fars by the caliph in 232/846, while other Tahirids served as sub-governors of various provinces, or as local officials in Iraq. One might characterize the few decades of the middle of the ninth century as the era of the Tahirids. As a result of inter-family strife in 237/851 Tahir b. ʿAbdallah sent his brother Muhammad to Baghdad as chief of police as well as governor of Iraq and Fars provinces. As long as he lived (till 253/867) order was maintained in the now prolific family. At the death of Tahir b. ʿAbdallah, the caliph al-Mustaʿin tried to rid himself of Muhammad b. ʿAbdallah by sending him to Khurasan as successor of Tahir, but Muhammad refused and instead Tahir's son, also called Muhammad, was confirmed as his father's successor while Muhammad b. ʿAbdallah was not only continued in his posts, but these were increased to include the governorship of the Hijaz.

The reader will recall the second half of the ninth century not only as a period of cultural change but also of new Islamic heretical movements. The Zaidi *imams* of the Caspian Sea provinces came to power and, of course, this area was lost to caliphal and to Tahirid control. The Tahirids were now closely attached to the ʿAbbasids and the stars of both rose and then fell together. The Shiʿites of the north caused much trouble for the Tahirids, and we hear in the sources of Shiʿite uprisings in the cities of Qazvin and Raiy, as well as other towns in the Tahirid domain.[7] Armies sent from Baghdad had to help Muhammad b. Tahir to suppress these revolts, an indication of the weakened power of the governor. The final blow to Tahirid rule in Iran came from the province of Seistan, however, where a coppersmith called Yaʿqub b. Laith had succeeded in making himself ruler in a revolt against Tahirid rule, which we will discuss later.

If one surveys the half century of Tahirid rule, not only in Iran but also in Iraq, it seems clear that the Tahirids were not a separate dynasty, but merely the hereditary governors of Khurasan, always as servants of the commander of the faithful in Baghdad. All the coins struck by the Tahirids, except at the end of the life of the first governor Tahir b. al-Husain, gave the caliph's name and were no different from other ʿAbbasid coins struck during this period. The governorship of Khurasan was only one of the offices held by the Tahirid family, and, as we have seen, some of them held several offices simultaneously in various parts of the caliphate. Although in general histories of the caliphate the Tahirids are considered the first of several independent Iranian dynasties, it would be more accurate to regard them rather as an intermediate step between governors appointed by Baghdad and independent rulers. Of course the hereditary succession gives one the impression of an independent state. The Tahirids provided a capable and stable rule for the eastern part of the caliphate for a long time, and they always upheld the rights of the caliph, so that one might regard them as dependent on the legal authority of the caliph in exercising their rule. After the end of the Tahirid governorship in Khurasan in 259/873, the date of the capture of Nishapur by Ya'qub b. Laith, Muhammad b. Tahir was made governor of the area of Baghdad in 270/883, after retaining the nominal title of governor of Khurasan for more than ten years. After his death in about 297/910 other Tahirids continued to hold posts in the capital for many years. So the Tahirids should be regarded as successful officials of the 'Abbasid caliphate, who held power for a long period and in a hereditary fashion, because of the weakness of the central authority.

The fame of the Tahirids rests in their cultural patronage, and even personal achievements in this domain, rather than in their governorships. It would be too involved to discuss all the literary figures who were supported by the Tahirids, but it is important to remember that they were writing in Arabic. The letter of Tahir b. Husain to his son 'Abdallah when the latter took over his post at Raqqa became famous not only for its content but also for its excellent Arabic style.[8] Tahir was also known for his aphorisms and his ability to give good advice, and all the Tahirids were well educated and capable aristocrats. Books and poems written by various members of the Tahirid family are mentioned in the sources although none have survived. Even though such literary figures as Ibn al-Rumi and 'Ali b. Jahm were supported by the Tahirids, the question of the feelings of the Tahirids towards Iranian culture has raised controversy among scholars. There are a number of passages in various sources claiming that the Tahirids, as good Muslims, were indeed hostile towards anything Iranian, and that they ordered Pahlavi books to be thrown in the water or burned since the reading of the Qur'an and *hadiths* sufficed for everyone.[9] This story may be apocryphal, but it also may well represent the snobbish attitude of those, either Persians or Arabs, who considered Arabic the only proper language for recording anything worthwhile, from poetry to science. Certainly rustic Persian poetry existed and flourished, but this kind of poetry was hardly to be supported by Islamic governors or aristocrats, even Persians. This does not mean that the Tahirids were hostile to the Persian language or even to pre-Islamic culture, but they had become true sons of Islam who would listen to Persian songs, but who believed that the rules of Arabic versification, with long and short syllables, provided the only criteria for proper poetry. It is possible that under the Tahirids attempts were made to write Persian verse with Arabic metrical rules, for some sources report that Hanzala of Badghis, who lived in Nishapur about 840, was one of the first New Persian poets. By this is meant Persian poetry scanned in quantity like Arabic verse and not like Middle Persian verse. The Tahirids, however, were too well versed in Arabic to need praises in New Persian verse befitting great rulers. In all probability the question of the Iranian feelings of the Tahirids never came to the fore, because Persian Islam had not then been forged, and Pahlavi was finished as a literary vehicle. At home, drinking wine, members of the Tahirid family probably enjoyed stories or songs about pre-Islamic Iranian heroes recited in Persian, but for more formal courtly pursuits, Arabic was supreme and Islam provided a sufficient cultural framework. As aristocrats the Tahirids can hardly have failed to appreciate the pre-Islamic Iranian past, for even the Arab aristocracy preferred interesting tales of the Sasanians, recited in Arabic, rather than stories of the camels in the desert of the *Jahiliyya*, or pre-Islamic Arabia. When rich Arabs or Persians tried to collect antiquities, or ancient works of art, they perforce had to acquire Iranian art objects rather than stones from ancient Arabia. In other words the Tahirids must have shared the viewpoint which saw the continuing fusion of Arab and Iranian society into an Islamic society. This process of fusion was the crown and glory of Islam, for it replaced the narrow provincialism of the Arab tribe or of the Persian provincial estate or town. Later, of course, this oecumenical culture was again to disintegrate, and local nationalisms were to reassert their influences on the society and on the state.

The Tahirids then, in my opinion, should not be viewed as the first local dynasty to champion Iranian nationalism. The sole criterion for this charge seems to be the hereditary succession to the governorship in the family, which admittedly was an innovation. If, however, the principle of heredity had now replaced the arbitrary appointment of governors and other officials to various posts, then the Tahirids should be viewed not as radical innovators but rather as a family in step with the changing times. When we look at the growth of cities in this period we see the same tendency of fixing offices as hereditary charges in one family. For example, in the city of Qum, one Arab family had hereditary charge of the bureau of the water supply, while custodianship of the mint was in the hands of another family.[10] One might argue that Qum was an exceptional city, since the Arabs who settled there did not mix with the local population as readily as they did in Merv and Nishapur. Later the people of Qum are reported to have had their own individual system of weights and measures, and they followed a calendar or timetable of tax collections and other events differing from that of their neighbours. But as far as hereditary rights to offices are concerned, Qum was in the same position as Raiy, Qazvin, Nishapur and other cities where we find a growth of local city authority as the central caliphal authority declined. The rise of the office of *ra'is*, 'chief' or 'mayor', in the cities is traceable back to this period of the middle tenth century. Under the Samanid and Boyid successors of the Tahirids, the power of the towns grew apace. If one is to speak of a growth of 'national' feeling in this period, the term local patriotism would be more to the point.

THE SAFFARIDS

The epitome of this local patriotism was the Saffarid family of Seistan which represented the people of that province rather than any aristocracy. This was probably the main reason why the Saffarids continued to rule in part, if not the whole, of Seistan down into the fifteenth century, one of the longest-lived dynasties in Islamic history. The Saffarids rather than the Tahirids might be termed the first Iranian dynasty to break away from the caliphate, or rather they were the first in the east to challenge successfully the claim of the ʿAbbasids to rule the whole of Islam as one political community. The Saffarids rose to power not as rebellious governors, but as bandits who by force of arms seized power from the Tahirid sub-governors. The sources, on the whole, are hostile to the Saffarids who were upstarts of low birth, for the written sources were usually commissioned by governors, the caliphs or aristocrats, and the Saffarids represented none of the ruling establishment in the eastern caliphate. They arose from the common folk of Seistan, which had been a centre of the Kharijites, although by the middle of the ninth century the movement had lost much of its extremism and violence. But memory of the Kharijite anti-caliph Hamza b. Adhrak who ruled Seistan in defiance of the ʿAbbasid caliphs from 179/795 to 213/828, was still fresh in the minds of many people of Seistan, and the province remained a centre of opposition to the ʿAbbasids, especially in the rural districts. The Tahirids sent sub-governors to Seistan, usually with troops, but effective rule hardly existed beyond a few towns, including the capital Zaranj. Taxes could not be collected on a regular basis and security in the province was precarious. In such a situation that part of the local population which remained true to the rule of the Tahirids had to organize groups of local militia to fight the Kharijites and others. These warriors were recruited under the banner of Sunni orthodoxy to combat heresy (the Kharijites) and infidels (to the east of Seistan). They were the counterpart of the *ghazis* or *muttawwiʿa* or 'soldiers for the faith' on the central Asian frontiers of the caliphate, but they frequently developed into bandits and are called in some of the sources *ʿaiyar*. The word *ʿaiyar* properly means 'rascal' or 'scoundrel', and it was probably applied to many whose motives did not deserve such an opprobrious appellation. The word was also sometimes used as a synonym for bands of Sufis or dervishes or, as noted, for volunteers for the holy war of Islam.

This is one of the first notices about an institution, or movement, in

Islam which later became widespread and very significant in social history. The concept of *javanmardi* or 'chivalry', became a code similar to the code of knighthood in medieval western Europe. This is a fascinating subject, and one might trace its origins back to Sasanian or even Parthian times, but in eastern Islam it appears first among the warriors for the faith. This is not the place to enter the controversy about the origins or nature of the later *futuwwa*, or chivalric order of feudalism, to use general western terms, which is tied to the Crusades and the conduct of Christian knights and their Muslim counterparts in the Levant. We may say that Iranians certainly played an important role in the formation of this institution, or way of life, both in the ancient traditions of the aristocracy, and in the rise of Sufism and dervish orders in the eastern caliphate. This does not mean that bedouin Arab ideals of the *fata* or of the *fityan* were unimportant. On the contrary, the frontier against the Byzantines was the main frontier of Islam where the holy war was waged, and the society which developed on both sides in Cilicia and north Syria provided the most significant background for the later development. Stories of frontier heroes, similar to those about the Diogenis Akritas on the Byzantine side or the Cid in Spain, also existed on the Muslim side. There was a parallel in Seistan and in central Asia, but in the east the opposition to Islam collapsed in the tenth century, turning attention to the west.

In returning to the Saffarids, however, we shall start with Ya'qub who was one of the warriors for the faith in Seistan. He had been a coppersmith, whence the name *saffar*.[11] About 238/852 he and his three brothers joined a band of warriors for the faith in the town of Bust strategically located at the juncture of the Arghandab and Hilmand rivers. From this frontier town of Islam against the east the band, with its chief called Salih, marched against the capital Zaranj where they laid waste the countryside. The following year they expelled the Tahirid governor from the capital. In 244/858 Salih lost the rule to another leader called Dirham b. Nasr. A few years later Ya'qub felt himself strong enough to challenge Dirham and in 247/861 he overthrew him and became ruler of Seistan. The Tahirid governor, who still maintained himself in the province, sought aid from the pagan ruler, the *zunbil*, of the mountainous area of Afghanistan against Ya'qub, but in 251/865 Ya'qub defeated and killed both the allies. In the same year Ya'qub was able to crush the Kharijites, many of whom fled to the Herat district while others submitted to and joined Ya'qub. The latter treated his defeated enemies well and gave them high posts in his army according to their ability. His reconciliation of the Kharijites caused him to be called by some sources a follower of their beliefs, but all indications point to a lack of interest in religions on Ya'qub's part, or rather his use of religion for political aims. In 253/867 he had consolidated his power sufficiently in Seistan to be able to expand into the area of Herat. He was successful here and in Badghis, and again the Kharijites in the latter district joined the Saffarid army after their defeat. About the same time, or perhaps a few years earlier, Ya'qub was active in campaigns in the pagan lands of mountainous Afghanistan. The details are unclear and contradictory, but we may conclude that Ya'qub made an extensive raid against Ghazna, Kabul, Gardez and perhaps Bamiyan, but in none of those places did he maintain his rule, for after his departure the Turkish dynasty ruling Kabul was replaced by a dynasty of Hindushahis.[12] Ya'qub fought against Muslim as well as pagan rulers, for Gardez was at that time ruled by a Muslim Abu Mansur Aflah who paid tribute to Ya'qub. For several years, however, Ya'qub must have maintained control of the silver mines of the River Panjshir north of Kabul since he struck coins there which have survived.[13] Much booty was secured, and contrary to expectations Ya'qub was careful to send some of it to Baghdad to show his fealty to Islam and to the caliph. The idols of gold and silver sent by Ya'qub aroused considerable interest which was reflected in the literature of the time. Although neither the caliph nor the Tahirids could approve of Ya'qub's seizure of power in Seistan, his further campaigns in the east could be tolerated, especially when some of the booty arrived in Baghdad. Undoubtedly Ya'qub's activities in Afghanistan fostered the spread of Islam in those parts.

When Ya'qub's ambition turned to the west, however, he was bound to clash with caliphal authority. The last Tahirid governor of Khurasan was young and weak, with many problems in the Caspian provinces and elsewhere, so Ya'qub quite naturally moved against the weakest province of the Tahirid state, Kirman, in the year 255/869, which was during his campaigns in the east. He was met by the governor of Fars, 'Ali b. al-Husain (Hasan in some sources) b. Quraish, but Ya'qub defeated and captured him. Some sources say that the caliph had granted both Ya'qub and 'Ali the rule over Kirman so that they would fight among themselves and destroy each other. The victory of Ya'qub, however, was a blow to the caliphate for Ya'qub appropriated the revenues of both Fars and Kirman although again he sent rich presents to conciliate the caliph. At this time Ya'qub was not able to control Fars, however, and it was threatened with disorder until the caliph al-Mu'tamid appointed his brother as governor of the province in 257/871 and sent him with an army and with the 'Abbasid tax collectors back into Fars. None the less 'Abbasid rule was short, for in 261/875 a rebel Muhammad b. Wasil killed the 'Abbasid governor, who had replaced the caliph's brother, and seized power. After consolidation of his eastern territories Ya'qub in 261/875 again invaded Fars where he rid the province of the rebel and established order in it. This did not satisfy Ya'qub's ambitions, however, and he made ready to invade the lowlands of Khuzistan and Iraq.

The relations between Ya'qub and the 'Abbasid house are not clear, but he had been given *de jure* recognition of his conquests in the east at various periods, and he ruled Seistan, Kirman, Herat and the domains of Islam to India in the name of the caliph. It is possible that the caliph simply followed the lead of the governor of Khurasan, Muhammad b. Tahir, when the latter had given Ya'qub the governorship of all the east after Ya'qub had seized Herat and defeated the Tahirid army at Fushanj in 867 (which army incidentally was commanded by Ibrahim b. Ilyas, one of the Samanid brothers). An uneasy peace had remained between Muhammad b. Tahir and Ya'qub until the latter found an excuse to attack his weak rival, nominally his overlord. In 259/873 Ya'qub captured the last Tahirid in his capital of Nishapur and kept him with him on his campaigns in the west. With the fall of the Tahirids Ya'qub inherited their legacy, and he at once invaded Tabaristan where an opponent of his from Seistan had taken refuge with the Shi'ite ruler there, al-Hasan b. Zaid. In 260/874 Ya'qub won a victory but before he could reap its fruits he had to retreat in the face of disease and sickness among his troops who were unaccustomed to the jungles of the Caspian Sea coast. The caliph was shocked at the capture of the last Tahirid governor and condemned Ya'qub's seizure of power in Khurasan. Not long afterwards, however, Ya'qub invaded Iraq, as we have mentioned above, and the caliph in alarm hurriedly granted Ya'qub rule over all of Khurasan, Tabaristan, Fars and part of al-Jibal with the capital at Raiy. He was also given the office of chief of police of Baghdad which had been almost a hereditary grant to the Tahirids, and furthermore Friday prayers were to be said in his name, as well as that of the reigning caliph. Ya'qub may have thought that he could himself have taken all that and more, for he continued his march into Iraq. Almost a miracle occurred, however, for the army of al-Muwaffaq defeated Ya'qub in 262/876 not far south of the capital and the Saffarid was forced to retreat. After some negotiation the caliph again recognized Ya'qub's rule over the Iranian plateau. Ya'qub died at Jundisabur in 265/879 and was succeeded by his brother 'Amr, who obtained from the caliph a patent of authority over the east.

Even before Ya'qub's death, several rivals to the Saffarids had appeared in Khurasan and 'Amr had much fighting before he could consolidate his position. A former Tahirid general called Khujistani had seized Nishapur after Ya'qub had gone to Fars and while 'Amr was in Herat. In 266/880, after Ya'qub's death, Khujistani had even raided into Seistan but could not secure support in that province so he had had to return to Nishapur. In 268/882 Khujistani was killed and was succeeded by Rafi' b. Harthama, also a former Tahirid supporter;

and now Muhammad b. Tahir the former governor of Khurasan, who had fled from Yaʿqub's captivity to Baghdad, persuaded the caliph al-Muwaffaq to appoint Rafiʿ as his representative in Khurasan with himself again as *de jure* governor in 271/884. The caliph did this and disowned ʿAmr. The latter had been active in Fars successfully suppressing several revolts, but with the changed attitude of the caliph ʿAmr was put on the defensive. In 273/886 caliphal troops defeated ʿAmr and drove him from the province of Fars and an attempt to regain power in Fars from Kirman was stopped by the caliph al-Muwaffaq himself in 274/887. It seemed as though the caliph's power would be restored but threats in the west from Egypt and from the Byzantines induced the caliph to make peace with ʿAmr and restore him as governor of Fars, as well as Khurasan and the east. In 276/889 the caliph yet again deposed ʿAmr, but ʿAmr defeated the ʿAbbasid army sent against him, and peace was again restored with the patent to rule the east as before the fighting.

Meanwhile, as we have seen, ʿAmr's position in Khurasan had deteriorated and Rafiʿ b. Harthama ruled from Raiy to Herat, but a new caliph al-Muʿtadid succeeded al-Muwaffaq in 279/892, and he decreed that ʿAmr should become governor of Khurasan in place of Harthama. The latter, looking for allies, denounced the ʿAbbasid caliph and gave his allegiance to the Shiʿites of the Caspian, in return for assistance. ʿAmr now had the support of the orthodox Sunnis against Rafiʿ, and he was able to defeat him and drive him from Khurasan. Rafiʿ fled to Khwarazm where he was killed in 283/896. ʿAmr quickly re-established Saffarid rule in Khurasan, to which Raiy was added by decree of the caliph. ʿAmr, like his brother, however, was not satisfied but felt himself threatened by the Samanids to the north of the River Oxus, so he requested and obtained from the caliph investiture with rule over Transoxiana in place of the Samanids who had ruled there in the name of the Tahirids. It is possible that a quarrel with Ismaʿil b. Ahmad Samani, whose capital was in the city of Bukhara, over jurisdiction in Khwarazm was the real cause of the outbreak of hostilities but we do not know. Fighting was severe, but finally in an engagement near Balkh ʿAmr was captured in 287/900 and delivered to Ismaʿil who sent him as a prisoner to Baghdad where the caliph put him to death. Saffarid rule over Khurasan vanished, replaced by the Samanids who became heirs of ʿAmr's eastern territories. The Saffarid family, however, continued to rule at times in Fars until about 298/911 when direct ʿAbbasid rule was re-established in the province. Seistan, however, remained the stronghold of the family, to which the people had become devotedly attached, for many centuries, although allegiance at times was legally given to Samanid rulers, Ghaznavids and others later. It is impossible to follow the fortunes of the later Saffarids in Seistan, Kirman or even Fars, where rule changed hands frequently. It is interesting to note that when the Samanids conquered Seistan in the time of Ahmad b. Isma'il, the Samanid governor so overtaxed the people that they revolted. In order to secure popular support, however, the rebels felt they had to have a Saffarid at their head. So they found a ten-year-old descendant of Ya'qub and 'Amr who served as a figurehead in the successful revolt, at least until the Samanids suppressed it. Later a new Saffarid ruler Ahmad was successful and ruled the province from 923 to 963. Saffarid rule remained local, yet it continued even when for periods its authority seemed to have vanished. It was a tribute to the Saffarid family that the people of Seistan again and again rallied to its support when its cause seemed hopeless. Certainly the policy of Ya'qub and 'Amr of welcoming anyone into the ranks of the army and of promoting the capable ones gained them considerable support. There was a body of personal guards or *ghulams* attached to the courts of Ya'qub and 'Amr, and undoubtedly much of Ya'qub's military success came from the personal devotion of his soldiers to him as well as their training.

The Saffarids were more of an Iranian national dynasty than the Tahirids, for not only did they rise from the people, but the inability of Ya'qub to understand Arabic is cited as the reason for the development of Persian poetry in Seistan. The *Tarikh-i Sistan* must be regarded as overly partial to the local dynasty, but it is reasonable to suppose that Ya'qub did encourage Persian poets, who may have been among the first to put Persian into Arabic verse forms.[14] The Saffarids probably deserve as much credit as the Samanids for providing a favourable climate for the development of New Persian literature but, in as much as Ya'qub and 'Amr were continually in the field, there was not much time or leisure to promote culture. Under the Saffarids the same tendency to growing independence by cities and towns appears both in eastern and in western Iran. We hear in the sources of the consolidation of city factions behind various law schools of Sunni Islam, although this feature of city life becomes very important only in the tenth and eleventh centuries. In the *Tarikh-i Sistan* (p. 275) we hear of the conflict between two groups, the Sadaqi and the Samaki, which was said to go back originally to conflicts between the Arab tribes of Tamim and Bakr who settled in Seistan. This enmity, whatever its origin, developed in Zaranj, as in Nishapur and in other cities of the east, into Hanafi–Shafi'i factions which frequently came to blows with each other. The factional conflicts in the Iranian cities at times seemed to be little more than conflicts over personal interests, like the destructive quarrels of the factions of scribes in Baghdad in the ninth century, such as the Banu'l-Jarrah versus the Banu Furat, which dissipated the resources of the central government, and nullified the efforts of the caliphs al-Mu'tamid (really his brother al-Muwaffaq who ran affairs) and al-Mu'tadid (d. 289/902) to restore the authority of the caliphs by control over the army. In the end the scribes so antagonized the army that the military finally took charge and triumphed over the bureaucracy, but then the Boyids appeared on the scene, as will be discussed later.

THE SAMANIDS

We now turn to the Samanids, the aristocratic Iranian dynasty under which the New Persian flowering of literature and culture occurred.[15] The Samanids grew strong under Tahirid protection, but they were active in the east even before the Tahirids. Saman, the ancestor of the family, was supposedly descended from the Sasanian general Bahram Chobin, a noble of the ancient Mihran feudal family, who played an important role on the stage of history of the later Sasanians. Saman accepted Islam in the Umaiyad period, and his son Asad served the early 'Abbasids, while his four sons were rewarded for their support of Ma'mun against the rebel Rafi' b. Laith by appointment over four places: Nuh over Samarqand, Ahmad over Ferghana, Yahya over Shash and Ilyas over Herat. This was about the year 204/819. Ibrahim, the son of Ilyas, was the commander of the Tahirid army which was defeated near Fushanj by Ya'qub b. Laith, and he later surrendered to Ya'qub. Only the descendants of Ahmad in Ferghana prospered, for Nasr b. Ahmad soon took over Samarqand, the main city of Transoxiana and consolidated his power with one brother Ya'qub in Shash and another Isma'il in Bukhara. With the breakdown of Tahirid rule in Khurasan, Nasr found himself the virtually independent ruler of most of Transoxiana although he was still officially ruling for the Tahirids and, of course, for Baghdad; for in 261/875 the caliph al-Mu'tamid sent the investiture for all of Transoxiana to Nasr which he kept until his death in 279/892. The real founder of Samanid power, however, was Isma'il his brother, who, after a quarrel and armed conflict with Nasr over the taxes, defeated him and became the real power although Nasr still ruled in name.

After the victory over 'Amr b. Laith Ism'ail received authority for rule over all Khurasan from the caliph. Although these investitures did not mean any actual increase in territory, for that had to be won by the sword, none the less a patent from the caliph loomed large in the eyes of many of the people of the eastern caliphate, for legitimacy was a powerful political instrument for securing and maintaining authority. Isma'il expanded the Samanid state to the north by a raid to Talas or Taraz in 280/893, and another in 291/903 both of which made secure the northern frontiers of the state against raids of the Turks and enabled

Muslim missionaries to penetrate into the steppes of central Asia. It seems that in 893 he ended the local dynasty of Ustrushana, placing it under a Samanid governor, while other local potentates became vassals of the Samanids. In southern Khwarazm, the ancient local dynasty submitted to Isma'il and remained in power as Samanid vassals, while in the northern part of the country a Samanid governor was installed. This situation remained until 995 when the governor defeated the *shah* in the south and united the entire country under one rule.

To the west Tabaristan was conquered by a Samanid general who then revolted, and Isma'il himself in 288/901 had to lead an army to the west to re-establish Samanid rule, which he did. Not only Tabaristan, but also Raiy submitted to Isma'il, but the rest of al-Jibal and Seistan remained outside his rule. After his conquest of Tabaristan Isma'il returned the lands, which had been seized and redistributed by the 'Alid rulers, to their original owners, and his policies in Raiy and Qazvin show a great concern for the old aristocratic families. Throughout Samanid rule relations with the caliphate were correct, and each *amir* of the house of Saman sent gifts to Baghdad in return for a patent of investiture, until the capture of Baghdad by the Boyids temporarily changed the picture. Isma'il died in 907 and was succeeded by his son Ahmad, who was granted by the caliph the additional province of Seistan, which he then proceeded to annex. The turbulent Caspian Sea area broke away from Samanid rule, to submit to a Zaidi Shi'ite leader called Nasr al-Kabir in the sources. Before Ahmad b. Isma'il could move against the rebellious province he was assassinated by some of his slaves in January 914.

Nasr b. Ahmad was only eight years old at the death of his father, and the early years of his reign were beset with many troubles, not the least of which were internal revolts by members of his own family. After much conflict, reconciliation and new uprisings Nasr was able to secure the allegiance of the rebels and re-establish his authority. He also reconquered Raiy and Tabaristan, but his authority in that province was constantly challenged. Nasr became friendly with Isma'ili missionaries and in some sources he is said to have been converted himself to the Isma'ili sect. The army leaders, in any case, were discontented and plotted to overthrow Nasr, but the latter's son Nuh uncovered the plot and made a compromise whereby his father abdicated and he succeeded him. This occurred in 943 and a bloodbath of the Isma'ilis followed which ended any chance of the propagation of Isma'ili beliefs in Khurasan.

The reign of Nasr was the high point of Samanid rule, for under him a galaxy of learned and literary men flourished through his patronage. Not the least of these were his viziers Jaihani, chief minister from 914 to 922 and from 938 to 941, and Abu'l-Fadl al-Bal'ami, who was vizier from 922 to 938. The former was a prolific author, and his geography was apparently the basis of much of the knowledge of later geographers about the eastern Islamic world, China and Russia. Bal'ami's son was the author of a Persian translation of the great history of Tabari. Another author Abu Dulaf lived at the court of Nasr, and he went on an embassy of Nasr to China, which provided him with material for a book of travels.[16] The names of the scholars and poets who flourished under the Samanids would make a very long list. In the fourth volume of the *Yatimat al-dahr* of Tha'alibi we find recorded the names of poets who composed in Arabic at the Samanid court, and many of them were also poets in Persian. The Samanid age differed from that of the Tahirids where Arabic had been supreme. Under the Saffarids Persian poetry had been tolerated by educated people, but under the Samanids it flowered with such poets as Rudaki (d. 940), Daqiqi (d. *c.* 978), Shahid al-Balkhi and others. Whereas earlier Persian poetry might have been considered frivolous or entertaining, it had expanded by the time of the Samanids to encompass a variety of serious as well as light themes, panegyric and satire. It is clear that the Samanid court was the nourisher of New Persian literature. In the Samanid state we can see the classical division of the three classes of literate people: the scribes (*katib* or *dipir*), the learned men of religion (*'ulama'*), and the literary class (*adib*, pl. *udaba'*). Sometimes two, rarely three, functions were combined in one person, as in 'Ali b. 'Isa (d. 334/945), the 'Abbasid vizier, but in Khurasan the three groups were increasingly differentiated, and frequently in conflict, especially the scribes and the men of religion. In very general terms one could say that the scribes still maintained their status and influence during Samanid rule, but after the coming of the Turks the *'ulama'* definitely gained the upper hand, especially after orthodox Sunni Islam was codified, and the *madrasa* system of schools and learning, which probably began under the Samanids, came to dominate higher education.

The bureaucracy and the organization of the Samanid court was copied from the 'Abbasid centralized system, although the Samanid state was never as completely centralized as the 'Abbasid in its heyday. The tenth century was too replete with local lords and city factions to return to the past, and the Samanids had to be content with many vassal rulers who were local dynasts ready to break the tenuous connections with Bukhara at any provocation. Actually, when we examine the sources, we may infer that the 'Abbasid caliphate did not directly control as much territory as one may suppose from the lists of governors and sub-governors. Local dynasts existed earlier too, but they do not play a role in history until they become integrated into the Islamic oecumene, which now, in the tenth century, had raised the spoken *lingua franca*, Persian, to a literary language. In my opinion the rise of

New Persian literature had great political and social as well as cultural consequences. For now outlying areas, such as Chaganiyan in central Asia, could contribute to Islamic culture through a medium more open and more suited to larger groups of the population. Persian was the language of the Samanid bureaucracy, fostered by the scribal class which could and, of course, did also use Arabic. But the *'ulama'*, who at first were champions only of Arabic, soon saw the value of Persian in reaching the masses. The learned men of religion, however, still considered Arabic the only proper language in which to write scholarly books. It was at the court of the *amir* of Chaganiyan that the poets Daqiqi and Munjik received support and encouragement, and the local courts of Khwarazm and Juzjan north-east of Herat gave similar support.

The Samanid state was really divided into two parts, Transoxiana and Khurasan, south of the River Oxus. The latter was under the rule of the commander of the principal army of the Samanids, who was also governor of the province with his capital at Nishapur. Bukhara, however, remained the capital of the dynasty until its end. In Bukhara there were two organs of control, the royal court and the bureaucracy headed by the vizier. In a way the court, under the *hajib*, with its guard of Turkish slaves, was balanced by the bureaucracy and the army, although the latter was theoretically directly under the court. In the first half of the century of Samanid rule, the bureaucracy was paramount primarily because of a succession of capable viziers. Later, however, just as in Baghdad, the Turkish slave institution gained power and dominated the court, while the governor of Khurasan, as commander of the army, also grew in power, and the result was a clash, usually between different Turkish factions, since the Turks came to dominate all military establishments. The palace school for court slaves, usually Turkish youths, was a remarkable institution for training officers for the army and officials for the court, both of which naturally came to be dominated by Turks. This system of training at the Samanid court is described in detail by Nizam al-Mulk, the vizier of the Seljüks, in his *Siyasat name*, and it is clear that the Samanid state organization was a model for the Seljüks and later dynasties.

Under the Samanids many Turkish tribes in central Asia accepted Islam, for we read of missionaries on the frontier as well as warriors for the faith. One missionary called Abu'l-Hasan Kalimati is supposed to have converted a whole Turkish people in about 960.[17] By the end of the tenth century Islam had made significant gains in Chinese Turkistan, where the process of conversion to Islam paralleled the growing Turkish influence. The motives of the Samanids in extending their frontiers to the north and east were economic as well as political or even religious, for there was a constant need for slaves and the Turks provided the best source. The slave trade was an important source of revenue for the Samanid state, for the latter taxed the transit of slaves through Samanid territory to Baghdad where Turkish slaves fetched high prices. The turkification of Transoxiana also continued to grow under the later Samanids, while externally the later Samanid state was involved with a struggle with Shiʿite dynasties to the west.

Under Nuh b. Nasr (d. 343/954) the central Samanid government was able to control various parts of its domains, but after the death of Nuh his son ʿAbd al-Malik became a puppet in the hands of the generals in Bukhara, especially of Alptigin who made himself governor of Khurasan. At the death of ʿAbd al-Malik in 961 the Turks quarrelled among themselves, and Alptigin lost; he left his capital of Nishapur and went to Ghazna, where he laid the basis for the future Ghaznavid empire. The power in Bukhara, however, remained with the Turkish military establishment, and the new *amir* Abu Salih Mansur b. Nuh (d. 365/976) devoted his energies to the patronage of musicians, poets and scholars. Much of the military effort of the state was directed against the Boyids, sometimes in support of a Caspian dynasty, the Ziyarids, who were usually allied with the Samanids against the Boyids. The Boyids were Shiʿites and the Samanids were staunch Sunnis of the Hanafite law school, so the struggle between the two had religious as well as political significance. It seems that the Samanid *amirs* especially favoured the *ʿulama'* during the last half of the tenth century in order both to secure popular support for the dynasty, and to combat heretical tendencies. The Samanids encouraged the translation of Arabic religious works into Persian so that more people could rally to the defence of orthodoxy against heresy. At the end, however, when the Turkish invaders were at the gates of Bukhara the *ʿulama'* abandoned the dynasty, for the Turks too were staunch Sunni Muslims. On the other hand the dynasty's survival until 999 was only owing to the loyalty of the people to the Samanid family in spite of poor rulers and the usurpation of power by officials. Lands in the west, such as Kirman, Tabaristan and Gurgan which had belonged to the Samanids, were lost to the energetic Boyid ruler ʿAdud al-daula.

The story of the end of the Samanid state is a complicated one of plots and counterplots among the viziers and the army officers. Three names in disputing power during the last twenty years of the Samanid state are prominent: Tash, a Turkish slave, who was made governor of Khurasan in 982 by the amir Nuh II b. Mansur; Abu'l-Hasan Simjuri, a feudal lord from Kuhistan south of Herat, who disputed the governorship of Khurasan with Tash; and the chamberlain at the court, a Turk called Fa'iq. Tash was defeated by the other two in 987 and fled to the west, and Abu'l-Hasan was succeeded as governor of Khurasan by his son Abu ʿAli, who defeated Fa'iq in 990. Meanwhile the Turkish Qarakhanid dynasty had risen to prominence in the lands to the east of the Samanid domains, and soon began to take advantage of the weakness of their neighbours. In 976 they seized silver mines belonging to the Samanids on the upper Zarafshan valley and in 980 the town of Isfijab surrendered to them. Turkish vassals of the Samanids, many of whom had secured minor principalities as rewards for service to the Samanid amirs, now submitted to the Qarakhanids as vassals of the rising power from the east. The chief Qarakhanid ruler, Bughra Khan, advanced into Samanid territory in 991 and defeated a Samanid army sent against him. The following year he entered Bukhara after Nuh b. Mansur fled from his capital. When Bughra Khan fell sick and died, however, Nuh returned to Bukhara and re-established his authority. Fa'iq, who had assisted the Qarakhanids, now joined forces with Abu 'Ali, governor of Khurasan, to put an end to Samanid rule, but Nuh turned to Ghazna for help where a Turkish ruler called Sebüktigin had succeeded Alptigin. In 994 Fa'iq and Abu 'Ali were defeated and fled to the west while Mahmud son of Sebüktigin was made governor of Khurasan by Nuh. In spite of new attempts to gain power by Fa'iq and Abu 'Ali, Nuh remained the ruler of a small Samanid state on the lower Zarafshan, primarily Bukhara and Samarqand, while the Ghaznavids inherited Khurasan. The successor of Nuh, Mansur, did not fare well, for he was deposed and blinded in 999 by a Turkish general, Bektuzun, and by Fa'iq who had succeeded in regaining power. The final result was that Mahmud of Ghazna marched against Bektuzun and Fa'iq and defeated them, securing all the lands south of the River Oxus as his domains while the Qarakhanid ruler Nasr moved against Bukhara north of the river. The last Samanid *amir* 'Abd al-Malik, who had been raised to the throne by the Turkish general and chamberlain, tried to rouse the populace to his support, but the '*ulama*' counselled the people not to fight against the Muslim Qarakhanids. So in 999 the Qarakhanids entered Bukhara and the Samanid state fell. Turks now replaced Iranians as rulers in the eastern Islamic world.

A Samanid prince tried to regain power in several daring but futile attempts to seize Bukhara, but he had to flee and was killed in 1005. Other members of the Samanid family continued to live in Bukhara but, although highly regarded by the local population, they did not play any role in subsequent history. In summarizing the achievements of the Samanids, it is clear that under them central Asia became Muslim, and a model of society and government was forged which was taken over by the Seljük Turks and spread to Anatolia and Syria, as well as over the eastern Islamic world. Before the Samanids the oases as well as the cities of Transoxiana had been surrounded by walls for protection against Turkish pagan nomads who raided the lands of Islam. Under the strong rule of the early Samanids the walls became unnecessary and fell into decay, while the Turks were converted to Islam. The consequences of allowing the walls to fall into decay were ecological rather than political, for the sands of the desert were not slow to encroach on the cultivated lands of the oases. The danger from the Turks subsided but that from the onslaughts of nature did not.

The Samanids were teachers of the Turks. From the vast number of Samanid coins found in eastern Europe and in Scandinavia we may infer that the Samanids were interested in far-flung trade relations, and in truth our sources tell of a continuous export of textiles and articles of arts and crafts from the Samanid domains. Silver and other metals were exploited and in general one may say that the economy flourished under the early Samanids. The silver crisis and decline in the economy came later. Local currencies existed parallel to the official ʿAbbasid silver coinage which remained high in quality throughout Samanid rule. Local coinage, such as the Ghidrifis, Musaiyabis and Muhammadis which were current in different cities of Transoxiana, on the other hand, depreciated greatly in good metal content and in buying power.[18] Before about the year 273/886 the Samanids did not have the right to strike silver *dirhems* but only copper *fals*. Unfortunately we know little about the local history of Transoxiana, and the economic and social developments need to be reconstructed from stray sentences buried in the sources plus an intensive study of the coins.

The Samanids are justly famous for their patronage of the arts and literature, but a distinction must be made between rustic poetry in the Persian language, classical poetry according to the length of syllables in Persian, and the use of written Persian in the Arabic alphabet. We have already discussed the first two, for rustic Persian poetry was always recited or sung but not recorded, and classical poetry probably made its first start under Yaʿqub b. Laith. The Tahirids earlier may have seen such poetry, but they did not foster it as the Samanids certainly did side by side with Arabic poetry. Under the Samanids, however, we have evidence of the use of Persian written in Arabic characters in the bureaucracy, which is not unexpected but still significant. Persian poetry in the classical Arabic manner was ideal for the court, but it did not promote the use of Persian among the common folk. In my opinion the use of Persian by the bureaucracy was a prime factor in the rise of New Persian literature under the Samanids, for it was the bureaucrats who taught Persian, which in the Qur'anic schools would either not be taught or only as an aside, after the lessons in Arabic and Qur'anic subjects. We have no direct evidence as to exactly how written Persian was taught, but the scribes would be the only group interested in teaching written Persian in the Arabic alphabet. Sogdian had long ago lost its importance and in the Samanid period it was only of antiquarian interest, as was Pahlavi. The process by which Persian became the common tongue of central Asia has been explained above. It was the *lingua franca* of the Sasanian empire and was called Dari, whereas the Arabic language in Khurasan and central Asia was called Tazik or Tajik. It was the language of Muslims, as was the form of Persian mixed with Arabic words which developed from the mixture of Iranians and Arabs. It was primarily the Turks, it seems, who then used the term Tajik to refer to the settled Muslims who spoke Persian mixed with Arabic, hence the origin of present Tajiki. So the development of New Persian is no mystery. The Samanids were its patrons, and they needed it for the subjects of their dominions. It was otherwise in western Iran as we shall discuss later.

It is very difficult to discuss the art of the Samanids since so many objects which may come from central Asia during the Samanid period are either undated or uncertain as to place of origin. From the few architectural monuments which have remained from this period, such as the mausoleum of the Samanids (formerly thought to be of Isma'il) in Bukhara and another in the village of Tim, all show a characteristic use of light-coloured baked brick for ornamental designs, a legacy from the past of Transoxiana, and different from structures in western Iran. All have low cupolas on (sometimes massive) pillars. Another characteristic of the Samanid domains were the *ribats* or fortified caravansarais, the descendants of which still may be seen in Afghanistan and central Asia. Soviet excavations in Varakhsha, old Samarqand and elsewhere have revealed the continuity of architecture with the past, and have also shown that different schools existed. For example, in Tajikistan, as in the Hindu-Kush mountains to the south, high carved wooden columns, carved doors and an artistic use of wood are features of the local architecture. It is impossible here to discuss details of carvings in alabaster and stucco and other media on which central Asian styles of decoration are found. Suffice it to say that the material culture of the Samanids paralleled in brilliance the poetry and learning at the court.[19]

MINOR DYNASTIES OF THE WEST

Before we turn to the Boyids in the west who were a parallel to the Samanids, we must very briefly survey the dynasties which arose in the outlying areas of western Iran as a result of the weakness of the caliphate. These dynasties developed from local 'Abbasid governors before the expansion of the Dailamites on to the Iranian plateau at the beginning of the tenth century AD. Azerbaijan and the south Caucasus area were natural regions where independent dynasties would develop, and Khalid, the son of Yazid b. Mazyad al-Shaibani, who had been appointed governor of Armenia by Harun al-Rashid, was the first governor to establish an hereditary succession.[20] His son Muhammad was installed as governor by the caliph in 230/844 but he faced many revolts and the ʿAbbasid general Bugha had to aid him so that only in 242/856 was Muhammad able to exercise control not only over Armenia but also over Azerbaijan and Arran. Muhammad gave up the rule of the first two and secured the consent of the caliph that his descendants should inherit the town and district about Ganja. His brother Haitham ruled in Sharvan and the centre of the dynasty remained there rather than in Arran. To the north in Derbend another Arab general established an independent dynasty in 255/869, and conflicts between the rulers of Derbend and Sharvan to the south were frequent. For a short time, 901–28, a central Asian, Yusuf b. Divdad Abu Saj, whose father came from Ustrushana, ruled much of Azerbaijan up to and at times including the domains of the two above-mentioned dynasts. He had been appointed governor of both Azerbaijan and Armenia, from the town of Zanjan on the south to Derbend in the north, and the Caspian Sea on the east. It was during his rule that the Rus made their daring expedition across the Caspian and occupied the town of Bardaʿa for a short time. From 299/912 Yusuf Abu Saj stopped paying the regular tribute or taxes to Baghdad, and a few years later he took advantage of a Samanid retreat from Qazvin and Raiy to occupy those cities. In 305/917 he defeated an army sent against him by the caliph. Attempts to bring peace failed and after several battles in July 919 Yusuf was defeated, captured and sent to Baghdad. ʿAli b. Wahsudan was made governor of the Raiy-Qazvin area, while an Arab Ahmad b. ʿAli Saʿluk was made governor of Isfahan, Qum and al-Jibal. A slave of Yusuf called Subuk took over affairs for his imprisoned master in Azerbaijan, so that the caliph was forced to come to an agreement with Yusuf, restoring him to the governorship of Azerbaijan and Armenia, to which were added Raiy and Qazvin, for a promise to pay 500,000 *dinars* tribute yearly.[21] Yusuf had to reconquer Raiy from Ahmad b. ʿAli who had seized it, but this he did in 924, killing Ahmad. Yusuf was then ordered by the caliph to attack the Qarmatians in southern Iraq which he did but was defeated, captured and put to death in 315/928. The power of the Sajids was ended, although for a few years several members of the family ruled over parts of Azerbaijan, as did several of their slaves. The stage was set for the expansion of the Dailamites.

THE BOYIDS

The Dailamites were hardy mountaineers from the area north of Qazvin, and they had raided cities on the plateau since Sasanian times. Although many of them were new converts to Zaidi Shiʿism, others remained Zoroastrians, and the two groups were united only in their military ability and desire for plunder. Sometimes the Dailamites apostatized after ostensibly accepting Islam, but in any case unlike many new converts they were tolerant of other faiths. After the rise to power of the Boyids, we find them protecting Zoroastrians in Fars against zealous Muslim neighbours, and in Baghdad they not only retained the Sunni caliphs, but on the whole were tolerant towards heretics. An atmosphere similar to the old free discussions under Ma'mun and the beginning of the Mu'tazilites prevailed in Baghdad after the Boyid occupation. At the same time they were not libertines, for we hear that Rukn al-daula forced the Shi'ites of Qum to attend the mosque and that shaikh Mahmud b. 'Uthman al-Kazeruni attributed the military success of the Dailamites to their Islamic piety.[22] The desire of the Dailamite rulers to appear cultured and to patronize literature and the arts was stronger than any fanaticism which some may have held. The political history of the Boyids is well known since many scholars have worked on it, but we must summarize some of the basic information.

'Ali b. Boya, later known as 'Imad al-daula, was a mercenary soldier like many of his compatriots from Dailam. At first he served the Samanid ruler Nasr b. Ahmad and then later a prince of Gilan called Makan b. Kaki who became governor of Gurgan for the Samanids in 924, and then in 928 'Ali was appointed governor of Raiy. Makan revolted against the Samanids and even occupied Nishapur for a brief period, but he was defeated by another ruler from the Caspian called Mardawij of the house of the Ziyarids. 'Ali and his two brothers who had joined him, took service with Mardawij. 'Ali rose in the army of Mardawij, who appointed him governor of a town called Karaj, south-east of Hamadan.[23] 'Ali consolidated his position here, and after some fighting with the governor of Isfahan appointed by Mardawij, he turned to Fars and in 934 he took Shiraz. He secured recognition as ruler of Shiraz from the caliph, but Mardawij had become his enemy, and began to threaten him until Mardawij was murdered in Isfahan. 'Ali sent his brother Hasan, better known as Rukn al-daula, against Isfahan which he captured but soon had to abandon in the face of superior forces led by Wushmgir, son of Mardawij. Another brother Ahmad (Mu'izz al-daula) campaigned in Kirman where the local ruler recognized Boyid authority. Then Mu'izz al-daula annexed the realm of the Baridis in Khuzistan and in 945 entered Baghdad where the caliph bestowed on the brothers their honorary titles.

Rukn al-daula meanwhile re-took Isfahan, and defeated Wushmgir, but only after several setbacks was he able in 335/946 to oust the Ziyarids from Raiy. Thus was created a new form of political organization: branches of one family ruled three parts of the Boyid domains, Raiy, Shiraz and Baghdad. The eldest of the family was to hold the title of *amir al-umara'* 'ruler of rulers' or senior amir. 'Imad al-daula was nominally holder of this position until he died in December 949 in Shiraz, after he had named his nephew 'Adud al-daula, son of Rukn al-daula, as his successor. Rukn al-daula became the senior *amir*, and his hands were full in northern Iran fighting the Samanids to whom in the end he had to pay tribute. He was successful in securing the submission of Tabaristan and Gurgan, but soon afterwards in 976 he died leaving the position of senior *amir* to his son 'Adud al-daula. The latter, who had previously helped his cousin, 'Izz al-daula, to retain his throne in Baghdad, now, however, resolved to put an end to this incompetent ruler. In 978 'Adud al-daula defeated his cousin and had him put to death, after which he conquered most of Iraq which had been rebellious against Boyid rule. His brother in Raiy, Fakhr al-daula, had sided with 'Izz al-daula, and now he fled from his province and 'Adud al-daula installed another brother, Mu'aiyad al-daula, as a loyal ruler. Thus 'Adud al-daula united in his hands rule over an empire including all Iraq and western Iran, Kirman and Oman, while the Saffarid dynasty of Seistan became his vassals. 'Adud al-daula ruled competently until his death in 983 and his reign was the highpoint of the Boyid era. Much has been made of the old Iranian titulary *shahanshah* 'king of kings', given to 'Adud al-daula by the poet Mutannabi in an Arabic panegyric to that ruler. This title later became common among the Boyids, and it was even used briefly by the Samanids. The significance of it, however, has been exaggerated, for it had no legal significance, but only a sentimental attachment to the past. It was a sign of opulence and splendour. We may consider the Boyid state at the time of 'Adud al-daula as a period of flowering and development, but how did western Iran at this time differ from the east?

To speak first of religion, one must remember that the Boyids came from the Caspian Sea provinces where old Iranian practices were still preserved. From the eleventh century we have the towers of the Mil-i Radkan and Lajim with bilingual Arabic and Pahlavi inscriptions on them, showing that even at this late time people existed in the Caspian area who could read Pahlavi. It is noteworthy that the inscriptions are not in New Persian in the Arabic alphabet but are written in Pahlavi. 'Ali's father had been converted to Islam while his grandfather was still a Zoroastrian. Mardawij was well known for his love of ancient Iranian customs, for he celebrated noruz, New Year's Day, and other old holidays, while his court was copied from what was known of the Sasanian court ceremonies. Many of these customs and celebrations were continued by the Boyids. There is no doubt that the expansion of the Dailamites, most of whom had been either recently converted to Zaidi Shi'ism or were still Zoroastrians, brought about a greater interest in the past of Iran and this is clearly seen in the art production of this period. The famous 'Boyid' silks found in Islamic tombs near Raiy are so completely Sasanian in inspiration, with their old Iranian motifs, such as a bird with pearls in its beak, that it is possible to believe that they are actual Sasanian art objects.[24] The medals struck by the Boyids also reveal old Iranian styles and subjects, and they have both Arabic and Pahlavi legends on them.[25] Muʿizz al-daula, when he captured Baghdad, could not speak Arabic, but later Boyids were cultured and some even composed poetry in Arabic. At the Boyid courts in Iran there was later a *katib al-farisiyya* 'scribe of the Persian language', whose function was possibly correspondence with the Samanids and others, rather than a scribe for Pahlavi to handle local affairs in western Iran, although conceivably he could have been employed to correspond with officials in the Caspian provinces. So the Boyids patronized Arabic, but more from necessity than from any great conviction. It is clear that the Boyids were moved by sentiments similar to the Samanids in the east but with at least one important difference. The Samanids, like the Boyids, turned to the past, but the past of Bukhara and Samarqand was different from the past of imperial Sasanian Iran. Yet the Samanids also felt themselves heirs of the Sasanians and at the same time they were staunch Muslims. They found a satisfactory compromise in the New Persian language, which was written in Arabic characters but which had adapted the old culture into contemporary Islamic norms. This was the superb creation of a Persian Islamic culture which had reconciled and absorbed the western Iranian Sasanian past with the central Asian and eastern Iranian past, mixed into an Arabic-Islamic crucible, with a resulting genius which opened a new vista in the history of Islam, and which soon spread to western Iran to replace the efforts of the Boyids and others to revive the past and raise it to a level with Arabic and Islam, but with little mixing of old and new. This is the fundamental difference between the Boyids and the Samanids. The former revived the past as it existed in the Caspian provinces, frozen and little changed from Sasanian times, hence ultimately doomed to failure. The old Iranian traditions might be reconciled with Islam, but they could not be fused; at least this seems to be the dominant mentality of western Iran in the tenth century. It was only natural that this should be so, for Zoroastrians still existed in considerable numbers in western Iran, especially in the Caspian provinces and in southern Iran. They were representatives and custodians of the past, and were different from the Muslims. One might imagine the religiously rather lax Boyids thinking that Zaidi Islam could be a conciliator between orthodox Sunni Islam, to which form of Islam the majority of Muslims in western Iran and in Iraq adhered, and the Zoroastrians, who represented the ideals which the Boyids tried to realize in their courts and in their culture. But it was not possible to mix the two communities, and they remained apart. 'Adud al-daula punished Muslims in Shiraz and Kazerun who caused disorders by attacking Zoroastrians, and some Zoroastrians served the Boyids as high officials. If the Zoroastrians had been capable of mounting an 'Iranian renaissance', the Boyids certainly would have supported them, but it was too late, for the Zoroastrians could only copy the past and could not create a new and dynamic culture. To sell old Iranian culture to the people it would have been necessary to do it in Arabic, which hardly would have succeeded. An attempt was made to keep Pahlavi and Arabic, Zoroastrianism and Islam on parallel lines, as we can see on the medals, in the art and on the tomb towers, but in the eleventh century this was to be swept aside by the real 'Iranian renaissance' or more properly the '*naissance*' of New Persian Islamic culture, which was a fusion of new and old but in an Islamic frame; this new culture came from the east and swept all before it. This, in my opinion, is the story of the real rise of modern Iran, and the reasons why it took place in the east rather than in the west, and why Tajikistan still exists today instead of a modern Sogdiana. The east led the way to the future whereas the west tried to save the frozen past, and the course of history was inevitable.

CHAPTER 11

TURKISH ASCENDANCY

Just as the Arab conquests brought the Persian language (Dari) from the old Sasanian domains to central Asia and India as an international language, together with Arabic and Islam, so did the Turks in the eleventh and twelfth centuries bring to western Iran, Asia Minor and the Fertile Crescent the New Persian oecumenical Islamic culture from central Asia, from the domain of their predecessors the Samanids. This may sound paradoxical, but history sometimes conceals the great movements of culture in periods when many individual deeds overshadow the development of general trends. This is the last act in the complicated drama of the transformation of Iran from pre-Islamic times finally down to the creation of an Iranian Islam which, because it was Islamic, could grow, expand and absorb other elements, and reach a level which pre-Islamic Iran could not dream of. Because Iranian Islam came into being the entire Iranian cultural area survived intact, whereas the ancient Mesopotamian, Syrian, Egyptian and north African cultures succumbed to the Arabic language and to Arab Islam, which, of course, itself underwent changes. Western Iran would have gone the same way as the lands further to the west if the process had not been stopped and reversed, not by the efforts of the Boyids to revive the past, but by the new, popular pan-Iranian Islamic culture from the east. And the political instruments or bearers of this expansion of culture were the Turks.

We have already mentioned the missionary efforts to convert the Turks in the time of the Samanids, and we know that the Volga Bulghars were converted to Islam even before the rise of the Samanids. The fascinating story of Islamic missionary activities in the steppes of south Russia and up the River Volga is beyond the scope of the present book, and furthermore it is a subject as yet little studied. Turks, of course, were no strangers to the Near East and even in pre-Islamic times both Iranians and Byzantines had relations with the Turks in the steppes. It was the slave trade and the martial qualities of the Turkish slaves which created a military preponderance of Turkish slave or mercenary armies in the Near East, and just as Arabs and Iranians mixed, so at a later period did the Turks mix with the others. Jahiz wrote a tract on the good qualities of the Turks, and after the Seljüks secured dominion, the right of Turks to the *imperium* in Islamic territories was almost uncontested. The Turks brought a new tradition into the Near East to match the Persians' pride in their pre-Islamic Sasanian kings and the Arabs' acclaim of those who descended from the family of the Prophet. The Turks, to match descent from Chosroes, or from the tribe of the Quraish, proposed descent from Oghuz Khan, eponymous ancestor of the Seljüks and of the majority of Turks who invaded the Near East. It is not our purpose to study the rise of the Turks to prominence in central Asia and their division into many tribes and coalitions of tribes. Suffice it to say that the Turks did have traditions of royal dynasties, especially the Ashina family of the Orkhon Turks, and these traditions could parallel the Iranian pride in descent from Sasanian princes.

The number of Turks increased in the Near East, either by the import of slaves or by the settlement of Turks who moved into the lands of Islam as tribes or as individuals, and we hear of sections of the cities in Transoxiana and Khurasan being predominantly occupied by them. For example, in the Persian history of Nishapur it was said of one ʿUbaidallah b. ʿAbdallah b. Abi'l-Haitham that he was the uncle of Jaʿfar al-Turk, and lived in the Turkish section of Nishapur (*dar al-Turk*) in the street of Badhan.[1] In Samarra the Turkish pages and slaves acquired by the caliphs were settled in special areas far from the markets and the centre of town. The caliph al-Muʿtasim tried to keep the Turks from marrying into Arab families by providing them with non-Arab slave girls to marry.[2]

One should also not forget that in the east there had been a dynasty of Turki Kabul shahs before they were overthrown by Hindus, and such tribal groups as the Khalaj were known in eastern Iran long before the rise of the Seljüks. Furthermore, prominent individual Turks are mentioned occasionally in the sources; for example, the family called Jamuk in Bukhara (*ahl bait al-jamukiyin*) is described as belonging to the Turkish nobility.[3] One must be somewhat wary, however, of the use of the word 'Turk' in the sources, for it may have been applied to persons from the east who were not Turks. In any event Turks were present in considerable numbers in the eastern Islamic world before the turn of the millennium, and afterwards they came in great numbers, but they were not unified as the Arabs had been. In the sources we learn of bands of nomadic Turks controlling the countryside of Khurasan and Azerbaijan in the eleventh century, for the Turks came into the Islamic world in tribes because of their conversion and the consequent collapse of the frontier for the faith in the north-east. The sources tell of *ghazis* or warriors for the faith in the tenth century leaving Transoxiana to move west against the Byzantines or south-east against the Indians. Many of these were Muslim Turks. In the middle of the tenth century we learn of bands of *ghazis* passing through the Boyid domains on their way to Armenia and Anatolia. In 355/966 a veritable army of some 20,000 asked permission from Rukn al-daula to cross his territory to fight in Armenia, but the Boyid ruler was loath to admit so many unruly warriors into his kingdom, and a conflict resulted which was won by Rukn al-daula.[4] When Mahmud of Ghazna invaded India, scores of volunteers from Khurasan and central Asia joined his army.[5]

As mentioned in the previous chapter many of these volunteers were organized bands with leaders, including religious leaders and even judges, for one may characterize the entire volunteer army as a Muslim movement parallel to that of the Crusades later in Europe. As with the Crusaders sincere religious motives were mixed with a desire for plunder and adventure, and stories and legends abounded about the holy war and its followers on the frontiers of Islam.

With the weakening of central government in the Samanid state as well as in the caliphate at the end of the tenth century, local government and city leaders come to the fore. We have already mentioned the rise in importance of hereditary offices in many cities, and certain families which occupied these offices. In the eleventh century the influence of such families grows considerably and they become significant figures on the stage of history. For example, the Mikali family in Nishapur, which claimed descent from the Sogdian ruler of Panjikant, Devashtich,[6] occupied the office of *ra'is* or 'mayor' of Nishapur for many years. Other families were also prominent and even at times contested the chief office with the Mikalis. The term *ra'is*, however, was vague, for there could be 'chiefs' of sections of towns, of guilds, or of almost any group of people, and in reading the sources one must be careful to avoid confusion.

Perhaps the towns were the real theatres where the great changes in Islamic society took place. If one were to compare the towns of the middle of ninth-century Iran with the same towns in the middle of the eleventh century, the changes could be more easily discerned. In the middle of the ninth century, as we have noted, the islamification of the entire land, countryside as well as towns, began in earnest. At that time the central government was powerful and its authority on the whole was unquestioned in the towns. The countryside, for the most part, was little different from Sasanian times, and Islam had changed it little. The towns too were not highly developed economically or otherwise, at least compared to two centuries later. The *'ulama'* were neither organized nor powerful but maintained their status more by personal influence and examples of piety than by any organized power or authority.

Two centuries later the picture was different. The *'ulama'* had become organized into different schools, and their influence over the population had grown enormously. Cities had divided into neighbourhoods, some of which were occupied by particular ethnic or religious groups. Migrants to the cities had settled in districts where others from their village or province had previously established themselves. And the cities had grown in size as peasants abandoned the unsafe countryside to take refuge behind city walls from roving bands or nomads. An oasis, or self-contained, economy flourished. As the central government declined the *'ulama'* took the place of the government officials, and organized the social and economic as well as the religious life of the towns, in co-operation with merchants and artisans. So the Muslim population was divided into various lines of allegiance within the city, with a religious leadership of guilds, markets and neighbourhoods within the city. Christians, Jews and Zoroastrians, of course, followed the Muslims in having separate communities within a city. The religious leaders of these communities were also social and political leaders who oversaw all affairs of members of their communities. There was no distinction between religious and civil functions. The shifting of power from the old landowners (*dihqans*) and from the central bureaucrats to the religious class is the main feature of change in the cities. Above the cities, of course, were the armies, more and more Turkish in composition. In the northern part of Iran in such cities as Hamadan, Raiy, Nishapur, Tus, Merv and Herat, plus Bukhara, Samarqand and Balkh, this process seems to have progressed faster than in the south, for, in reading the various local histories of Iranian cities, Shiraz, Kirman, Arrajan and other towns in the south appear to be more closely bound to the large landholdings in their surroundings and, in a word, less developed in the urban sense than cities in the north.

The plans of medieval Islamic Iranian cities were conducive to the division of the urban area into quarters with their own markets, mosques, caravansarais, and squares. Narrow winding lanes and problems of sewage and sanitation are prominently noted by our sources, but in these crowded areas poetry was composed, scholarly books were written, and masterpieces of art and crafts were made. It seems that more and more wealth in a city or district went into *waqfs* or endowments, rather than to the government, and the wealth from these endowments served as the economic base for the growing power of the *'ulama'*.

On the whole in the eleventh century the population of a city listened to and supported their religious leaders rather than the government which had become discredited. So allegiances shifted and the many examples of factional fighting within a city between religious schools of Islamic law reveal economic and political as well as religious goals. In the eleventh and twelfth centuries cities like Raiy and Nishapur were scenes of violent conflict between Sunnis and Shiʿites, and on the whole the latter were crushed between Hanafites and Shafiʿites. And villagers supported the townspeople in dividing into the same factions. Again one difference between the ninth and the eleventh centuries seems to be the closer ties in the later century between the townspeople and the peasants. One should rather say village dwellers, for some city aristocrats lived in villages, and a greater interchange between village and city developed. Unfortunately there is not enough information to elucidate further the connections, especially the religious ones, between the city and the villages. But one may say that the opposition of town and country which we find in the Umaiyad and early ʿAbbasid periods now changes to an identification of interests between groups in towns which had adherents in the countryside. This picture was not the same everywhere, of course. In some areas the city held to one religion, or law school, and the countryside to another, but the shift to identification of group interests in both urban and rural settings, was very widespread. It is clear that complications developed as loyalties crossed.

The Turkish military establishment could move into an area and, by occupying the citadel of a city, impose an order or *pax Turcica* on the conflicting elements in a district. If the armies were strong and well led, there would be quiet and order, if not then trouble would ensue.

It is fascinating to follow the histories of various cities in Iran, to see how some such as Bukhara, Qazvin, Merv and others were originally little more than groups of villages which grew together, while Raiy, Hamadan and others were ancient cities which simply expanded. Some grew up around shrines, springs, or crossroads. Villages came into existence, grew or died in a variety of patterns. The sands of the desert and a sinking water table frequently determined changing settlement patterns in Iran and central Asia. Above all the oasis nature of the majority of settlements on the Iranian plateau put limits to the development of urban and also rural complexes. For one result of recent intensive activity in the study of the Muslim city is the revelation of the complexity of patterns of settlement and growth throughout the Near East in this period.[7] The historian of architecture and the Islamic archaeologist report lovely mosques and high minarets in towns or even villages which seem today to have no other purpose than to provide a relic for the student of the fine arts. This can be misleading, for the proliferation of religious structures from the eleventh century onwards reflects the political situation in which not only provincial centres but even villages with a rich patron could erect religious monuments to vie with Baghdad or other large cities. As the Islamic religious community split into various law schools, each one felt itself permitted to transmit to posterity the cultural heritage of the once united caliphate, so Friday mosques and religious structures proliferated after the eleventh century. Thus the codification of Sunni Islam at this time in a sense did not unify the faithful. On the contrary it codified the differences. Just as Iranian Islam brought an element other than Arab into Islam, thus internationalizing it, so the same *leitmotif* of diversity under an Islamic unity was carried further in the political, social, urban and in short all realms.

THE GHAZNAVIDS

We have already mentioned the growth of minor Turkish principalities during the last part of Samanid rule.[8] Following caliphal practice the Samanid rulers gave districts to their favourites, who could sometimes become dangerous, and to officials, who during the second half of the tenth century meant Turkish army officers. The Simjurids, a Turkish family which held the governorship of Khurasan, had fiefs in Kuhistan in eastern Persia. The use of the term fief is, of course, inexact since the granting of rights to collect the taxes was not the same as the European feudal system. Such grants led almost to individual dynasties by the end of Samanid rule. For example, in the town of Bust a Turkish general called Qaratiqin maintained virtual independence from Samanid control as early as 317/929. Whether the later Turkish ruler Baituz was related to Qaratiqin is unknown, but all the rulers were products of the pages' school in Bukhara, or at least of the system of Turkish slaves or *ghulams*. The coming of Alptigin to Ghazna has been mentioned above, and he too fitted into the pattern of Turkish generals who secured virtual independence from the control of Bukhara. In the case of Alptigin and his son and successor Abu Ishaq, however, closer ties were re-established and then maintained with Bukhara than by other generals, since the frontier with the infidels was near Ghazna and the support of Bukhara was needed in the face of a strong Hindushahi dynasty in Kabul. The rulers of Bukhara were acknowledged as overlords of the Ghaznavids down to the death of Sebüktigin in 387/997, as a placing of the name of the amir of Bukhara on the coins struck in Ghazna shows. It should be mentioned that Abu Ishaq, son of Alptigin, did not rule long and was replaced by another Turkish general Bilgetigin, who in turn was followed by several other governors, until in 366/977 the last of them, Böri, was overthrown by the Turkish army in Ghazna and replaced by Sebüktigin who was the real founder of the Ghaznavid dynasty.

Sebüktigin expanded his domains, defeated Baituz and annexed Bust and surrounding areas. His conflicts with the Hindushahi dynasty are not reported in the sources, but they must have been many, and before his death Sebüktigin annexed much of the Kabul region. Mahmud did not succeed his father, probably because his mother was a local princess whereas the mother of Isma'il was a daughter of Alptigin, so the other son Isma'il succeeded his father. Mahmud, however, was much more capable and moved against Ghazna and deposed Isma'il in 388/998. A year later after severe fighting Mahmud controlled all the lands south of the River Oxus. At first Mahmud was friendly with the Qarakhanids who had replaced the Samanids north of the river but this soon changed to hostility. Mahmud was recognized as a legitimate ruler by the caliph, after the end of the Samanids, and it must have been welcome to the Sunni caliph, even though he ruled by grace of the Shi'ite Boyids, to be able to acknowledge a strong Orthodox Sunni ruler such as Mahmud.

Mahmud had married a daughter of Nasr the Qarakhanid, but this did not prevent the Qarakhanids from crossing the River Oxus when Mahmud was busy in India conquering many lands. In 396/1006 two Qarakhanid armies successfully overcame resistance and one occupied Balkh while the other took Nishapur. Mahmud quickly returned from India and in 398/1008 he defeated the Qarakhanids near Balkh and recovered Khurasan. The Qarakhanids did not again attempt to match their power south of the river against Mahmud, who then proceeded to consolidate his authority over various regions which still did not owe allegiance to the Ghaznavids. He even attempted to subdue and convert Ghur, the mountainous, central area of Afghanistan, but his efforts here only yielded a token submission by several chieftains. Seistan was conquered and taken from the local Saffarid dynasty about 1003, and Mahmud sent troops into Baluchistan and other desolate areas in the south to establish his authority. Later when the power of the Ghaznavids was curtailed by the Seljüks these outlying areas slipped away from Ghaznavid rule. Mahmud was not content, however, to restrict his rule to areas south of the Oxus. The small principalities of Khuttal and Chaganiyan in present-day Tajikistan submitted to him, and their rulers continued to serve as vassals of the Ghaznavids. Mahmud also turned his attention to Khwarazm, and provoked the Khwarazmians to such an extent that he easily found a pretext for invading the land in 1016 and putting an end to the family which had ruled the entire country since 995. Mahmud installed one of his officers, Altuntash, as governor with the old title of Khwarazmshah. Thus both in the north-east and in the north-west Mahmud secured his own flanks against any Qarakhanid danger. There was at the time in fact little need to fear Qarakhanid designs since that kingdom was divided by internal conflicts and there was little chance of aggression against such a powerful neighbour as Mahmud.

Mahmud's main fame, and perhaps even his main interest for us, came from his invasions of India; for under him not only were the Ghaznavid domains extended on to the plains of the sub-continent but the way was opened for Islam to expand to the east and south-east, although Mahmud was too busy seeking plunder to do much about the propagation of Islam. Many volunteers joined Mahmud on his expeditions and a pattern of yearly raids in the winter was evolved. The real conquests began as early as 1001, when Mahmud defeated Jaipal, the Hindushahi ruler of the strongest state in north-west India. Not until 417/1026 after many battles did Mahmud smash the Hindushahi dynasty with the death of the last ruler. It is interesting to note that Mahmud after several raids captured Multan in 401/1010 and deposed the local Isma'ili ruler, for much of Sind had been occupied by Isma'ili chieftains, who had replaced former orthodox Muslim rulers. Mahmud, as defender of Sunni orthodoxy, ordered the Isma'ilis to be killed, and wherever he went he sought to install Sunni Islam. In 417/1026 Mahmud penetrated further than any Muslim ruler before him, for he captured Somnath in the peninsula of Kathiawar on the Indian Ocean, and secured immense booty from a famous Hindu temple, as well as many slaves. Indian slaves became a glut on the market in Ghazna.

To the west of Khurasan were various small dynasties, and Mahmud secured the submission of Qabus b. Wushmgir, the Ziyarid prince of Gurgan and Tabaristan, and, after the death of Qabus in 402/1012, the dynasty continued to serve the Ghaznavids as vassals. The Ghaznavid army, however, made no move against the Boyids until the campaigns in India and elsewhere were over. In 420/1029 the Ghaznavid army captured Raiy and removed the Boyid ruler Majd al-daula from power. Mas'ud, son of Mahmud, was in charge of operations in the west, and he had had some local successes to the west of Raiy and was advancing on Isfahan when in 421/1030 he learned of his father's death and returned to Ghazna where his brother Muhammad had succeeded to the throne. Just as in the case of Mahmud's accession, so Mas'ud gained the support of the army and overthrew his brother. Mas'ud led several campaigns into India to consolidate his father's conquests and to add a few of his own. At first he was successful in establishing his own authority in southern areas such as Baluchistan, and even in securing the submission of Kirman in 424/1033, but his rule there lasted only a year. Mas'ud's ambitious plans to defeat the Boyids and rescue the caliph from reliance on them came to naught, for the Seljüks brought an end to Ghaznavid hopes of further expansion, and indeed soon restricted Ghaznavid rule to lands south of the Hindu Kush mountains.

THE QARAKHANIDS

The dynasty which put an end to Samanid rule and remained strong opponents of the Ghaznavids brought imperial Turkish traditions into the Islamic world. The Ghaznavids, although former slaves, and of course Turks, were completely iranicized and islamified, so they did not change the structure of society or culture which they found. The Qarakhanids, on the other hand, had not passed through any pages' school, and had never been slaves, but were rather a royal dynasty of pagan Turks who had been converted to Islam. It should be emphasized that in the sources this dynasty is called variously the Ilik khans, the kings of the Khaqaniyya, or the Al Afrasiyab 'family of A.', a reflection of the Iranian epic tradition. Pritsak has shown that the dynasty sprang from the ruling family of the Qarluq Turks, itself going back to the rulers of the Orkhon Turks.[9] Because of the principle of double kingship among the Turks, the Islamic sources are frequently confused about the identity of various rulers who changed their names or titles as they advanced from one post to another and higher one when the senior ruler died. The title or rather appellative of the eastern, and principal, ruler was Arslan Qara Khaqan while the co-ruler of the west was called Bughra Qara Khaqan, and these names were originally the totems (lion and camel) of the two chief tribal divisions of the Qarluq people. Under the two top rulers were four sub-rulers called by the names Arslan Ilik, Bughra Ilik, Arslan Tigin, and Bughra Tigin, and as mentioned, persons changed positions according to a special principle of seniority. The system did not always function according to plan. After conversion to Islam these rulers took Arabic names and nicknames which further complicated the picture. Again it is not our task to discuss either the Qarakhanid system of rule or the history of the many rulers and sub-rulers of the dynasty who frequently fought each other. Sometimes the family was able to unite in face of opposition, as for example in 420/1019 when the united Qarakhanid army again was defeated by Mahmud of Ghazna. Transoxiana, including Bukhara and Samarqand remained in the hands of various members of the dynasty, frequently quarrelling among themselves. The importance of the Qarakhanids, however, lies in the Turkish Islamic literature which was created in the eastern part of their domains, especially in the city of Kashgar. The 'mirror for princes' called the *Kutadgu bilik*, 'knowledge for attaining the kingly charisma', which was written about 1069, is the first Turkish Islamic literary work we have, and it pointed the way for the development of the third, Turkish, component of the literatures of the Near East, in addition to the Arabic and Persian. The Turkish steppe traditions of rule, a kind of steppe feudalism, were brought into Islam by the Qarakhanids and passed by them through the Seljüks, or rather through the Ghuzz tribesmen, to the Ottoman Turks. It is very difficult to follow the details of the Turkish conception of family rule, as opposed to primogeniture, and their idea of double kingship, which came later after the Seljüks because of the Turkish synthesis with Islamic and ancient Near Eastern traditions. The significance of a Turkish continuity can, of course, be exaggerated but it did play a role in succeeding Turkish dynasties not only in Iran but elsewhere.[10] It should be remembered that the Qarakhanids were legitimate rulers in the eyes of the Turks, descended from previous Turkish ruling families, whereas the Seljüks were merely bandits who rose to power by their own qualities and had no claim to royalty. Thus the Qarakhanids provided a basis for Turkish Islamic legitimacy whereas the Seljüks were upstarts.

Under the Qarakhanids, as well as under the later Ghaznavids, we see an interesting development in the eastern Islamic world which comes to fruition under the Seljüks. This is the rise of the power and influence of the *'ulama'* at the expense of the scribes and literary men (*udaba'*). We have heard even before this period of competition between scribes and religious leaders over better command of the Arabic language. The growing influence of the *'ulama'* is revealed in the change of the New Persian language from its Dari form to a language replete not only with Arabic words, but even with Arabic expressions. It was this change to a new language which persuaded Firdosi that the old Dari tongue and the ancient traditions of Iran should be preserved in the face of the great changes which were taking place in the Persian language of his day. Later Daulatshah, in his anthology of Persian poets, ridiculed the simplicity of the poetry of Rudaki which he said never would have won any prizes in competition with the ornate and highly arabicized language of Daulatshah's day (fifteenth century).[11]

The growth in the number of mosques and religious edifices, especially in Transoxiana, in the Qarakhanid period is indicative of the influence and power of the religious leaders. We have mentioned that the *'ulama'* did not rally the people of Bukhara to the support of the last Samanid ruler, and later it seems at times as if there were a working alliance between the military and religious leaders in the various Turkish states after the tenth century. One may imagine that the Turks, still attached to their nomadic background, mistrusted the cities of the Islamic east, hence they would be happy to find lieutenants in the towns to manage affairs for them which they little understood. Thus, in a sense, the centre of real power moved from the city court of the Samanids to the nomadic encampment of the Qarakhanids and later the Seljüks. Eventually a vacuum of power arose in the cities because of this situation, and it was filled by the religious leaders. This does not mean that the Qarakhanid rulers were always happy about the role of the orthodox Sunni *'ulama'* in Transoxiana. On the contrary, the Qarakhanids had been converted to Islam by not too rigorous missionaries, including Sufis, and at first the Qarakhanids regarded the *'ulama'* with suspicion, preferring instead to support the bureaucracy, thus favouring the scribes over the religious leaders. It was impossible to go counter to the times, however, and the religious leaders not only maintained but increased their power and influence in spite of this.

In the rule of the cities of Khurasan and Transoxiana the growth in the authority of religious leaders was exemplified in several leading families to whom they belonged, for such families occupied the important posts, sometimes in unity and harmony and sometimes in competition and conflict with each other. It is fascinating to follow the careers of such families as the Isma'ili *imams* and the Saffari *imams* in Bukhara, who are first found under the Samanids, but who flourished in the eleventh century, finally giving way to the family of *sadrs*, or chief religious authority, called the Al-i Burhan which ruled the city after the decline of the Qarakhanids in the twelfth century.[12] Again the local histories of east Iranian or central Asian cities are far beyond the scope of the present work, but the tendencies and trends in all of them are clear. In Nishapur factionalism was rampant and the important families were also clearly leaders of different legal schools which usually fought among themselves, although at times they would unite in the face of external danger. Nishapur was perhaps more typical of Iranian cities than was Bukhara, but in each city there were local differences and local problems which provided a variety of local conditions.[13]

The important point is that the history of the Iranian Islamic world changes with the coming of the Turks in the eleventh century. Not only did the populations of areas of Transoxiana and Azerbaijan become Turkish in language, but the Iranian local history changed from a pattern of cities and towns in the ninth century which were ruled by central government officials and controlled the countryside, then being islamicized, to almost independent cities and towns of the eleventh century which maintained a type of treaty relationship with Turkish nomadic rulers who dominated the countryside. The later social and cultural history of Transoxiana and Khurasan is fascinating in the changes which occurred but that is far beyond the limits of this book. Just as Persian and Arabic had existed side by side until Arabic was absorbed into the New Persian literary language, so later Turkish existed side by side with New Persian. Many people were bilingual, and, just as in the Samanid period when one Islamic literature existed in two languages, Arabic and Persian, so after the Mongol invasions we find poets able to compose in both Persian and Turkish. Mir 'Ali Shir Navoi, who lived in Timurid Herat, is a striking example of the bilingual capacities of many writers of his period. The Qarakhanids were the first Turkish Islamic dynasty to foster the bilingual literature of Turkish and Persian, and perhaps more than any other were the forerunners of the Ottoman Turks who cherished their nomadic central Asian origins as much as they did the Persian (or Arab-Iranian) Islamic culture into which they fitted. The Seljüks were vehicles of this culture, and their Turkish–central Asian background was perhaps less vaunted or promoted by them than by other Turkish dynasties.

THE SELJÜKS

Since these Turks were the heirs of both the Ghaznavids and the Boyids, as well as the spreaders of both Sunni orthodoxy and the Iranian-Islamic culture of the east to the west, a few words about them would not be out of place. For with the Seljüks our story ends, since after them the pattern of orthodox Sunni Islam is frozen and the heritage of the Samanids and the Ghaznavids is spread by the Seljüks all over the Islamic world. International Islam is not only everywhere in the Near East triumphant, but also the lines of Islamic religion, philosophy, art and general culture are laid down and matured, so the future is more a series of variations on old themes than new creations or new directions. The Seljüks represent the end of one Islamic age, of which the high point could be considered the ʿAbbasid caliphate under al-Maʾmun; the beginning of a new age, in the codification of the religion by al-Ghazali; and the justification of the sultanate in Islam. This new age of Islam ended only with the First World War, and our own day when the impact of technology and European ideas has again changed the history of the Near East.

The Seljüks were a family of the Ghuzz (or Oghuz) Turks, who wandered over central Asia from the Caspian Sea, around the Aral Sea, to the upper course of the River Jaxartes or Syr Darya. In some Islamic sources they are also called Türkmen, which at times seemed to have a connotation similar to bedouin as opposed to the settled Arabs. The Seljüks infiltrated into the Samanid domains at the very end of the dynasty and they supported the last Samanid prince, who tried to regain his throne until he was killed. Then they fought for and against various Qarakhanids until about 1025 when they received pasture lands in the oasis of Bukhara. Shortly thereafter they and their Qarakhanid patron ʿAli Tigin were defeated by Mahmud of Ghazna, and some of the Ghuzz asked Mahmud to allow them to settle in Khurasan to the south of Merv. This he did, but then thought better of his decision for the Türkmens were a restless and lawless group and the settled folk complained bitterly of their depredations. To make a long and involved story short, Mahmud attacked and scattered them, many fleeing to western Iran where they infested the roads. Masʿud tried to end Türkmen disorders in western Iran by seizing and executing many of their leaders in Raiy in 424/1033, but this only turned the nomads into bitter enemies of the Ghaznavids. The Seljük family, however, had remained in the region of Bukhara, and again they participated in the fighting between ʿAli Tigin, their Qarakhanid patron, and Mahmud's son Mas'ud. With the death of 'Ali Tigin the Seljüks moved first to Khwarazm and then fled south to Nisa after being defeated by a Turkish ally of the Ghaznavids called Shah Malik. The Seljüks were able to defeat a Ghaznavid army detachment sent against them in 1035 and soon they threatened Merv. The ease with which the Seljüks obtained the submission of Merv in 1037 and Nishapur the following year can be explained only by the desire of the local populations to end the pillaging and economic losses caused by the Turkish nomads. It was better to join them than to risk starvation by hoping for support from distant Ghazna, whose ruler seemed to be more concerned with booty from India than with protecting his possessions in Khurasan and western Iran. But finally Mas'ud realized the great danger threatening him in Khurasan and gathered an army to put an end to the Türkmen menace. At first he was successful in recapturing Nishapur and other towns, but in 1040 the Ghaznavid army was decisively defeated at the battle of Dandanaqan, the site of a *ribat*, or fortified caravansarai near Merv. This defeat marked the end of Ghaznavid rule in Khurasan for Mas'ud turned towards India and was killed by rebellious troops in 432/1041 when he was in the Punjab. Thus the powerful Ghaznavid empire in eastern Iran fell to Türkmen nomads and they lost no time in spreading over Khurasan, placing members of their family in various cities as rulers.

Meanwhile in western Iran the power of the Boyids had diminished considerably as various members of the family, following the principle of the senior *amir* which had now come to mean very little, fought with each other over the patrimonies of the different branches of the once unified family. Tabaristan and Gurgan passed into the hands of the Ziyarids while southern Azerbaijan around the city of Zanjan fell into the hands of another Dailamite family called the Musafirids. Even Isfahan was held by a Kurdish prince Ja'far 'Ala al-daula b. Kakuya, who acted independently even though he was related to the Boyids. Under him we hear of mosques, caravansarais and other buildings erected to embellish the city of Isfahan, and a flowering of culture took place. He was a patron to many poets and scholars, while Ibn Sina (Avicenna) became his vizier for a time, and wrote Persian books and poetry as well as some of his Arabic works under the Kakuyid. In his reign the east Iranian Islamic culture reaches western Iran, and afterwards in language and cultural production it is difficult, if not impossible, to distinguish between eastern and western Iran. Qabus b. Wushmgir, the Ziyarid prince of Gurgan (366–403/976–1012) was a patron of Persian as well as Arabic, and so was Majd al-daula, the Boyid ruler of Raiy (387–420/997–1029), but the latter's chief minister, the famous Isma'il b. 'Abbad was the first prominent western Iranian figure who encouraged Persian poetry as well as Arabic learning. Under his patronage the poet Mantiqi from Raiy flourished, as well as others. So the east Iranian Islamic cultural creation reached western Iran about a century after it began with Isma'il the Samanid, and henceforth western Iranians were to share laurels in this domain with their eastern brethren.

The east, however, did not remain static, for under Mahmud of Ghazna there was a brilliant assemblage of poets and scholars at his court. There were so many poets in Ghazna that Mahmud created the office of *malik al-shu'ara'* 'king of poets', and gave it to the poet 'Unsuri of Balkh. Firdosi, Farrukhi Sistani, Manuchihri of Damghan and others adorned the court, not to speak of savants such as al-Biruni. Such was the reputation of these poets that they are credited with creating the Khurasani style (*sabk*) of poetry which dominated schools of poetry everywhere, and especially the lyric, such that western Iranians tried to emulate their colleagues in the east, which also united the two in their literary creations. One might suggest that poets from western Iran, from such centres as Raiy, Hamadan and Isfahan, contributed models of Arabic rhetoric and complicated Arabisms to the more pure Persian poetry of the east, but this is very difficult to measure, and is a subjective judgement, for soon, as noted above, east and west were united. It is again beyond the scope of this book to discuss the development of various genres of Persian poetry such as the *mathnavi*, *ruba'i*, and others, as well as various metres such as the *mutaqarib* and *ramal*. Persians did not simply slavishly copy Arabic metres but made innovations themselves, and this is a fascinating but involved question. Likewise the mingling of stories from India and Greece, as well as the Arab–Iranian basis, produced a very cosmopolitan and rich Persian literature. The history of such literature, not to mention prose books and various learned productions, during and after the Ghaznavid period is much too vast a subject to be treated in this publication. For our purposes, it is enough to indicate the joining of eastern and western traditions into an all-Iranian development after the turn of the millennium.

To return to the Seljüks, we come to the end of one era and the beginning of another, for the Seljük Turks reunited the lands of Islam from the Mediterranean Sea to central Asia, spreading the new iranified Islamic culture, the new *madrasa* system of education, and a form of government sanctioned by Sunni Islam, plus the codified Sunni orthodoxy, which was reconciled with Sufism, wherever the Turks went. Tughril Beg (d. 455/1063) was the first great Seljük ruler, and his successors Alp Arslan (d. 465/1072) and Malikshah (d. 485/1092) were the architects of the new world.

It is difficult for the modern reader to picture the anarchy in the countryside of eleventh-century Iran when no government was able to protect towns and villages from the depredations of the Ghuzz Turks.

Page after page of the work of the historian Ibn al-Athir are filled with accounts of bloodshed and rapine.[14] An examination of the copious sources on the Seljüks reveals that the breakdown of central authority was not stopped by the Seljük government and the insubordination of the Turkish tribes continued throughout the entire rule of the great Seljüks and indeed for centuries afterwards. The Turkish nomads continued to infiltrate the Near East from central Asia, and together with local brigands made roads unsafe and insecurity rampant. As a result there was a serious decline in agriculture and the rural economy which was essential to the health of the entire land. As noted above, in parts of Iran the countryside was denuded of population, much of which flocked to fortified cities for protection against the nomads or bands of ruffians. Perhaps one might term the period from the Seljüks to the Safavids as one of the nomadization of Iran, in a way parallel to the *Jahiliyya* of pre-Islamic Arabia. Azerbaijan was a favourite goal of the Turkish nomads because of its good pasture lands, and the Turks were not slow to seize control of the land in this part of Iran and begin to turkify it. One reason for the unruliness of the Ghuzz and especially for their disobedience to the Seljük government was their mistrust and dislike of Seljük governmental policy. For the Seljüks had been obliged to turn to the *dihqans*, the Iranian aristocracy of Khurasan, in order to govern their new empire. The Seljüks not only had to take over the system of rule and the bureaucracy, but also they had to rely on those who really ran the country such as Nizam al-Mulk, the great vizier of Alp Arslan, and Malikshah. This alliance between the *dihqans* and the Seljüks aroused the resentment of many Turkish tribesmen, and after the capture of Baghdad by Tughril Beg in 1055, which almost had taken the form of a Sunni offensive against the Shiʿite Boyids to free the caliph, the tribesmen in effect revolted against the Seljük government, and maintained a state of revolt for many decades. The Seljük government realized that it would be unable to control the tribesmen except by placating the chiefs of tribes, so they borrowed the institution of the *iqtaʿ* from the Boyids and spread it in Khurasan and the east. One might say that just as the *iqtaʿ* system was brought from western Iran to all parts of the east by the Seljüks, so in exchange they brought the *madrasa* institution from the east to the west.

The Boyid *iqtaʿ* system of granting fiefs in lieu of wages or rewards to officers of the army was well suited to the turbulent Turkish chiefs.[15] The grants, of course, varied considerably as they did under the Boyids, for sometimes only the revenue from some locality was assigned as an *iqtaʿ* and no proprietorship of the land, while at other times huge districts, almost provinces, were given as *iqtaʿ*. Under the Boyids we find *iqtaʿs* of shops in the bazaar, of water rights, and others. But under the Seljüks the *iqtaʿ* system primarily meant large land grants both to military leaders and to tribal chiefs. The bankruptcy of the state and the need to pay for services rendered to the state caused the great growth of the *iqta'*s by the end of Boyid rule. Furthermore the rise in prices at the end of the tenth century, combined with the silver famine and the hoarding of precious metals, contributed to the increase of *iqta'*s. The price of gold soared and the government even had to borrow money from bankers. In the eastern part of the Islamic world silver *dirhems* were debased, which caused a further rise in prices. The great shortage of silver which lasted for more than two centuries in the Muslim East has been noted by many scholars, but no comprehensive study of the causes and consequences of this shortage as yet has been made. The evidence of the coins is present for all to see, but the reasons for debasement are many and complex. Certainly the Turkish expansion, which included south Russia as well as the Near East, plus the Viking raids in Russia, helped to create the silver shortage, but this is only a part of the story. From the sources we learn that the prices of land rose greatly in Khurasan and Transoxiana at the end of Samanid rule as well as prices in general. Thus inflation caused havoc with the traditional economy, and the Seljüks could not return to the past but had to live with the situation which they inherited. Together with the large number of nomads and a decline in the tillage of land went the decline of the *dihqan* class in eastern Iran, a decline of the textile industry of Transoxiana, and the shifting of the centre of culture from central Asia to western Iran. This set the pattern for the future which has lasted until recent times.

The Seljüks appeared on the scene at the right moment, for the 'Abbasid caliphate had been discredited and bankrupt both as an effective ruling power and even as a source of justice. It was mainly the latter which turned the '*ulama*' and the people away from the 'Abbasids, for the claims to legitimacy by the 'Abbasid family and their attempt to legalize these claims in religion were rejected by people who saw the corruption at court, the lack of justice and finally the assumption of power by the Boyids. The unity of Islam which had existed under the 'Abbasid caliphate had been shattered, never to be re-established, and the doctrine that might makes right held sway and was ideal for the Seljüks. The instrument of religious sanction for the holding of power by the Seljüks was the *madrasa*, which by its concentration of higher education led to or rather imposed a unity or standardization of Sunni Islam which completely changed the religious picture. Henceforth doctrines and teachings were fixed and prescribed, and this led to a consensus or a spiritual unity which more or less froze any change. It would seem that the earliest *madrasas* were found in Khurasan at the end of the Samanid period, although this is uncertain.[16] For one thing, it is very difficult to determine when we have a school and when a *madrasa*, for in both at first there was only one teacher. The main distinction was the different organization of the *madrasa* as opposed to an ordinary school. In the former there were rooms for students, and the *madrasas* came to be supported by *waqfs*. Perhaps convents or centres for Sufis provided a model for the *madrasa*, while the easterners may have borrowed ideas from the Shi'ite academies created in Fatimid Egypt. Later *madrasas* grew and had not only more than one teacher (*ustadh*) but also preceptors or tutors (*mu'id*) who oversaw the memorization of texts. A whole system of licences (*ijaza*), each one to teach one book, developed and a chain of permissions (*isnad*), similar to the chain of traditions about the Prophet, developed in the *madrasas*. The importance of this institution for the Seljüks was obvious, for it united various factions, but it eventually produced the justification for the rule of the sultan, the temporal power beside the caliph, custodian of the religion.[17] While al-Mawardi, living under the Boyids, in his book on the principles of rule had justified the sultanate beside the caliphate, it was left to al-Ghazali, a teacher in the Nizamiyya *madrasa* founded by the Seljük vizier Nizam al-Mulk, to state authoritatively the new Islamic position on the division between the temporal and religious authority, which incidentally was an old Sasanian dogma, if not exactly a reality in those times. So the Seljüks in more ways than one were the harbingers of the new order in Islam, but this story belongs to another book with different aims and scope.

In conclusion, it is obvious that the story is far more detailed and complicated than the few remarks above would indicate. The theory of the sultanate, which was evolved by the Seljüks, became the basis of the Ottoman empire; the system of higher education, especially the *madrasa*, also became the pattern for the future, and Sunni Islam and Sufism were fused into one system by al-Ghazali under the Seljüks. Finally the Iranian Islamic culture of Transoxiana and Khurasan was brought to Asia Minor and to Mesopotamia and Syria by the Turks. The bureaucracy lost to the '*ulama*' under the Seljüks, or rather they fused with the religious element in a partnership of dominance. It is true that the caliphate was strengthened by the Seljüks in comparison to Boyid times, so that after the decline of the great Seljüks (to the death of Sanjar in 1157) the caliphs for a time regained temporal power, but this was only an interlude in the process of the relegation of the office of caliph to religious matters. The art of the Seljük period too was a continuation of motifs begun under the Boyids, where ancient Iran reasserted itself. Again this art was carried by the Turks to Anatolia and Syria, and Iranian influences became current in the western Islamic world. The art was more Persian than east Iranian.

Later the rise of the Ottoman empire and the Safavid state was to polarize the Near East between a Sunni Turkish state and a Shi'ite

Turkish state, both descendants of the heritage of the Seljüks. When the Ottoman Sultan Selim wrote to his opponent Isma'il, he did so in Persian, whereas Isma'il answered in Turkish. But later the Safavids became more Persian and the Ottomans more Turkish, and each went their own ways in literature, art and culture. Persian poetry, of course, delighted the educated inhabitants of both states, as it does people of all times and climes, since it is universal in its appeal as in its messages. The Near East assumed its modern shape of division into Arabs, Turks and Persians, but the past weighed heavily on all. The heritage of the arts of the Iranians and the religion of the Arabs was common to all, and this heritage was by no means a one-way street. The universal Islamic culture, fashioned primarily by the fusion of Arab and Iranian ideals, in time divided into national cultures and led to the national states of today. Such was the course of history. In the final chapter we shall examine some of the legacy of the past, the heritage of the Arabs in Iran, as well as of the Iranians in Islam.

CHAPTER 12

THE HERITAGE OF THE ARABS

To refer to the heritage of the Arabs is comparable to speaking of the heritage of first Rome and then Italy in the western world. The Roman–Latin background of modern Europe is undeniable while the Arab basis of the Islamic world is evident. But just as the Roman past is not the only component of modern Italy, so the Islamic culture of the Arab world is not exclusively Arab. And just as the Latin component of the civilization of modern Germany is very important but far from the sole ingredient, so the Arab element in the civilization of modern Iran is prominent but not overwhelming. We tend to think in easily definable categories such as Iranian or Arab cultures, which can be misleading even at the present day. But in the period from the birth of the Prophet to the rise of the Seljüks it is especially difficult to separate the various strands in the new Islamic civilization which was being created. The process carried out by Islam as a universal religion not only accepted countless non-Arab, and even non-Islamic (as seen from the eyes of the companions of the Prophet) features into the religion, but it homogenized or islamicized everything it absorbed. If one were to object that this view robs Islam of its basic principles and its unique character, the answer would be that it survived and grew primarily because it developed both a universality and a great multiplicity of facets without compromising the basic and simple tenets of the faith. The glory of Greece, the dignity of Israel, the mysteries of India, all found a place in Islam.

For few will doubt that the Islamic civilization of the third and fourth centuries of the *Hijra* was a high point of human achievement. It was not only a golden age of the Islamic world, but of the whole world at that time. Why this culture in following centuries did not grow and continue to flourish is an involved problem which cannot be answered here. Our task has been to examine the heritage of the Arabs in Iran, but if we follow the line of thought above we cannot really do this but must perforce substitute the word 'Islamic' for 'Arab', and, of course, we must remember that the two are far from being synonyms. Furthermore, how is one to distinguish Syrian, Egyptian or Mesopotamian features of Islamic culture from Arab contributions? And what is 'Arab', and how is it different from 'bedouin'? Obviously one must somewhat arbitrarily decide certain criteria for determining differences, and in my opinion the only effective and meaningful criterion for determining a person's identity is by the language he speaks at home with his parents. If this is Arabic, he should be considered an Arab, no matter what the shape of his skull or the colour of his eyes, or his adoption of various cultural particularities such as religion or style of dress. This may be decried by many as too simplistic and unsophisticated, but I can find no other adequate measuring rod for differentiating people in an historical context. Of necessity then we are thrown back on language as a means of differentiation. That many Iranians were not just adept or masters of the classical Arabic tongue, but really enamoured of the superb tool which Arabic was, is clear from our sources. Al-Biruni said that the beauties of the Arabic language penetrated the very blood of those who learned it, even though they considered their own native language highly.[1] He continues that in his own case he had to learn both Arabic and Persian, for his native language Khwarazmian was incapable of expressing all the sciences of the world. In fact if a science were preserved in his native language, he says, it would be as strange as a camel walking on the eaves (of a house), or a giraffe in a herd of prize horses. He continues that he would rather be ridiculed in Arabic than praised in Persian, for Persian is a language fit for stories about the Sasanian kings and to be told at night. He further tells us that even though Mahmud of Ghazna hated Arabic, he was forced to acknowledge that one must learn it for the sciences and for medicine. It is fascinating to note that just as the written Middle Persian language, or Pahlavi, in a sense, was rendered easier by the use of Aramaic ideograms, so New Persian was enriched through Arabic words, and this style of New Persian is called Farsi. That style of New Persian which had few Arabic words in it was called Dari. The great Khwarazmian savant was objective, however, and he criticized the Arabic script for its ambiguous nature, since in his time it was frequently written without, or with few, points. Al-Biruni had difficulty in copying Greek names of drugs into Arabic, and in this regard he recognized the superiority of the Greek alphabet.[2]

A number of statistical studies has been made on the number of Arabic words in Persian.[3] This is extremely difficult to determine since there are pre-Islamic Iranian words borrowed by Arabic and then given back to the Persians after the Islamic conquests, words such as *jauhar* 'jewel', *jauz* 'nut', and many others. Then there are words in both languages such as *barid* 'postal service', the origin of which is uncertain. From statistical work it would seem that the greatest influx of Arabic words into Persian in medieval times corresponded to the change from a Dari or pure Persian in the tenth and eleventh centuries, to a later Farsi style of Persian, a feature in the poetry noted by Daulatshah. It must be strongly emphasized that the terms I use, 'Dari' style and 'Farsi' style, are my own suggestions to differentiate *in general* the early poetry of Rudaki from the later ornate arabicized Persian poetry. It is sometimes impossible to draw a temporal or a geographical line between the two kinds of Persian in the sources. The view that Arabic was present in Persian almost from the beginning of the Islamic era, and grew in a regular and steady manner as time progressed, is thus not tenable. Although much more statistical work needs to be done, I would venture to suggest that a historical reason which would explain the change from Dari to Farsi could be the expansion of the use of written Persian all over the Iranian plateau, into Anatolia under the Seljüks, and elsewhere. For the common denominator of all Persian dialects was the Arabic element. I believe then that the growth of Arabic vocabulary in New Persian in those days was, in some measure, the result of the use and spread of a standardized Persian with many Arabic words as a written *lingua franca* instead of Dari Persian or various local Iranian dialects. For obviously a common Islamic Arabic word would be better understood in Samarqand, Shiraz and Tabriz than a local dialect word of any of those three cities. Thus, from a certain viewpoint, the spread of Persian also increased the knowledge of Arabic, paradoxical though it may at first glance seem.

This is not to discount the influence of various fads or modes of culture, in which a predilection for Arabic words and expressions may have been prominent over a period of time, or the opposite, the last example of which we saw in the activities of the *Farhangistan-i Iran*, 'Iranian Academy', under the late Reza Shah, when many Arabic words were expunged from the Persian vocabularly. Several studies on the Arabic words in the *Shahname* of Firdosi have not been very rewarding, for they show that the Arabic words in the Persian epic deal primarily with warfare and luxuries.[4] There are, however, also a very large number of Persian words in those categories, and Firdosi's attempt to keep Arabic words at a minimum was a great feat for his time, since Firdosi probably did not know Pahlavi. Arabic had already massively penetrated Persian by the poet's time and later became even more prominent in the language. Arabic was and is too much a part and parcel of the Persian language, not to speak of aspects of culture and religion, to eliminate it from a very important role in Persian.

We have already mentioned the great influence of Arabic poetry on Persian poetry, for the metrical system of the latter was adapted from Arabic. The metres were, of course, modified and adapted to the

Persian language, while new forms were created which were completely different from the known Arabic poetry, based primarily on the *qasida*. This was recognized by Persian authors such as Daulatshah, and Nizami 'Arudi from Samarqand in his book 'Four Discourses'.[5] Much has been written about the influence of Arabic literature on Persian literature and especially poetry, but the latter became more diverse, rich and voluminous than Arabic poetry. For even the Arabs said *al-adab 'inda'l-Furs* 'literature belongs to the Persians', as religion to the Arabs.

It is not our intention to discuss later developments in the history of Iran, for the creation of the Shi'ite state of the Safavids in the sixteenth century also sharpened the antagonisms, some of them latent, between the Persians and their neighbours to the west. New relationships and exacerbations replaced the religious and cultural unity of the Arab and Iranian worlds. Certainly after this period relations and influences between the two declined. Not only did their religious paths part, but the development of culture and thought went more and more along separate ways. Again we must refrain from discussing the fascinating flowering of philosophy in Iran with such figures as Mulla Sadra of Shiraz (1571–1640), and the previous religious thinkers of Isfahan such as Shaikh Baha' al-Din 'Amili (1546–1622), and Mir Damad (d. 1631). They were the continuers of the classical tradition of Islamic thought, which after Averroes died in the Arab west. The Persian schools of thought were the true heirs of the great Islamic thinkers of the golden age of Islam, whereas in the Ottoman empire there was an intellectual stagnation, as far as the traditions of Islamic philosophy were concerned. Although much of the production of the Persian schools was in the Persian language, Arabic was not neglected; but the curtain between Iran and the Ottoman empire was as much closed as that between the Ottomans and western Europe.

Just as the Persians continued to study, promote and develop Islamic philosophy, so did they also become the continuers of Sufism. For later Sufism became identified with the great Persian poets such as Farid al-Din 'Attar, Jalal al-Din Rumi and Hafiz, and it may be said that the torch of Islamic mysticism was carried by the Persian poets more than by any others. The Arab world had less sympathy for the dervishes; in any case it considered them with some suspicion, since they came from Persia and were out of the centre of orthodox Sunni Islam, if not somewhat heretical. On the other hand, even though the Iranian and Arab worlds had become separated, influences did go both ways. Again it is not the purpose of this book to discuss such late events as the rise of Wahabism in Arabia and its influences in the east, or the movement of the Bab in nineteenth-century Iran and echoes of this movement in the west. Suffice it to say that the heritage of the extraordinarily close relationships of the Arabs and Iranians in the past did continue, albeit on a very much reduced scale, in later periods of the history of the Near East.

In conclusion, it is fascinating to find in the present-day islands of Arabs still living in the east, and the final remarks are directed to this little-known phenomenon. The villages of Arabic speakers which have been reported all exist in northern Afghanistan and Soviet central Asia. The Arabs in northern Afghanistan have not been studied and information about them and their language is lacking, for we do not even know exactly where they are, some reports claiming that they are settled in villages near Aqcha west of Balkh, while others stress their nomadism.[6] It is claimed that in the village of Zari, some hundred kilometres south of Balkh in the region of Keshen Deh, a semi-nomadic population of some five thousand people still speaks Arabic, but this needs further confirmation.[7] It seems probable that families of Arabs are to be found in many towns and villages of northern Afghanistan whereas they are only concentrated in a small number of villages in the north from Balkh to Andkhoi.[8] The history of these Arabs is unclear: they claim to be descendants of the original Arab warriors who came here under the Umaiyads, but this is not very likely. Whether they were moved here from Arab lands in the time of Timur or wandered here from Iran later is veiled in mystery. The Arabs of the Soviet Union, however, have been studied and a few more suggestions may be made about them, although their origin, according to their own traditions, is linked with the Arabs of northern Afghanistan. The Soviet Arabs are found in two areas, the oasis of Bukhara and in the Kashka Darya district of the Uzbek SSR. These latter consider themselves as immigrants from northern Afghanistan, and probably the Bukharan Arabs also came north from the same area.[9] Since Arabs are mentioned in sources of the fifteenth century, we may assume some of them were to be found in this area at least as early as the Timurid period, and possibly even earlier. Unfortunately the dialects of the two areas are so mixed with Uzbek and Tajik words and expressions that the Arabic spoken in the Bukharan and Kashka Darya regions is mutually unintelligible. Historically the indications of these dialects, sparse though they are, suggest that they are more closely related to Iraqi and to bedouin dialects than to other contemporary Arabic dialects, which is not unexpected.

It is surprising that Arabic-speaking groups should survive at all in the east, but one may suggest that both the prestige generally accorded to a knowledge of Arabic and the fact that in the past all educated people would know some Arabic would help to preserve the Arabic tongue of native speakers. Geographical and historical circumstances naturally played the major role in this preservation of Arabic, but the tenacity of the small groups of speakers of Arabic in a sea of Turkic and Persian speakers is noteworthy. The Arabs of Khuzistan and of the seaports of southern Persia are simply an extension of Arab settlements from the west and need not concern us here.

Unfortunately in the technological revolution which is now sweeping the Islamic world, such a concept as the 'Islamic world' is losing its meaning. Young Iranians* now disdain to learn Arabic, and Arabs no longer understand the role of Iran and the Persian language in the formation of Islamic culture. Perhaps they wish to forget the past, but in so doing they remove the bases of their own spiritual, moral and cultural being. It might be possible to so sterilize the people of the Near East that they willingly abandon their own heritage for 'westernization', but then they will be more like machines than men. I suggest that a rehabilitation of the ideals of Islamic culture and faith is the best way to develop all the technology, industrialization or 'westernization' one wants in the Near East. Without the heritage of the past and a healthy respect for it, for the good can be preserved and the bad discarded, there is little chance for stability and proper growth. Social, economic, political, indeed all change is, contrary to the opinions of some, part of the heritage of the Islamic past, and to condemn the entire past for mistakes made is to condemn all history. As an individual matures he learns from the past to create a better future. The future of the Arab world, I believe, is bound to that of Iran, and vice versa, and both are Islamic, but if both reject this premise then there will be mistakes and sorrows. Let us hope that their common heritage will draw them together as they once were in the time of the 'thousand and one nights'. Then the heritage of Islam of the Arabs and of Iran will all be complementary and not clashing. Of such is the progress and destiny of man.

* By Iranians today I mean Afghans, Beluchis, Kurds, Ossetes, Persians and Tajiks.

Iran in the seventh century

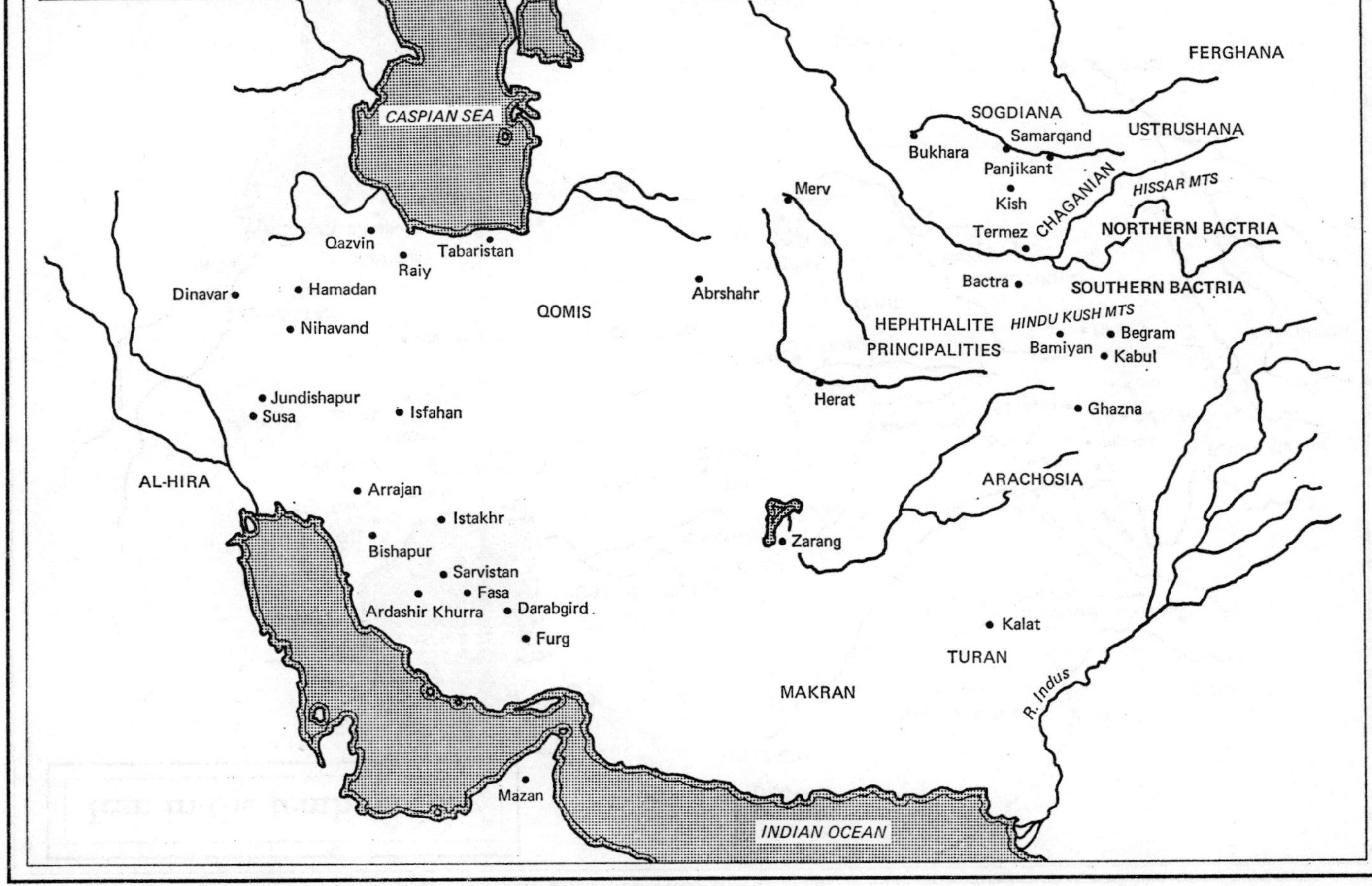

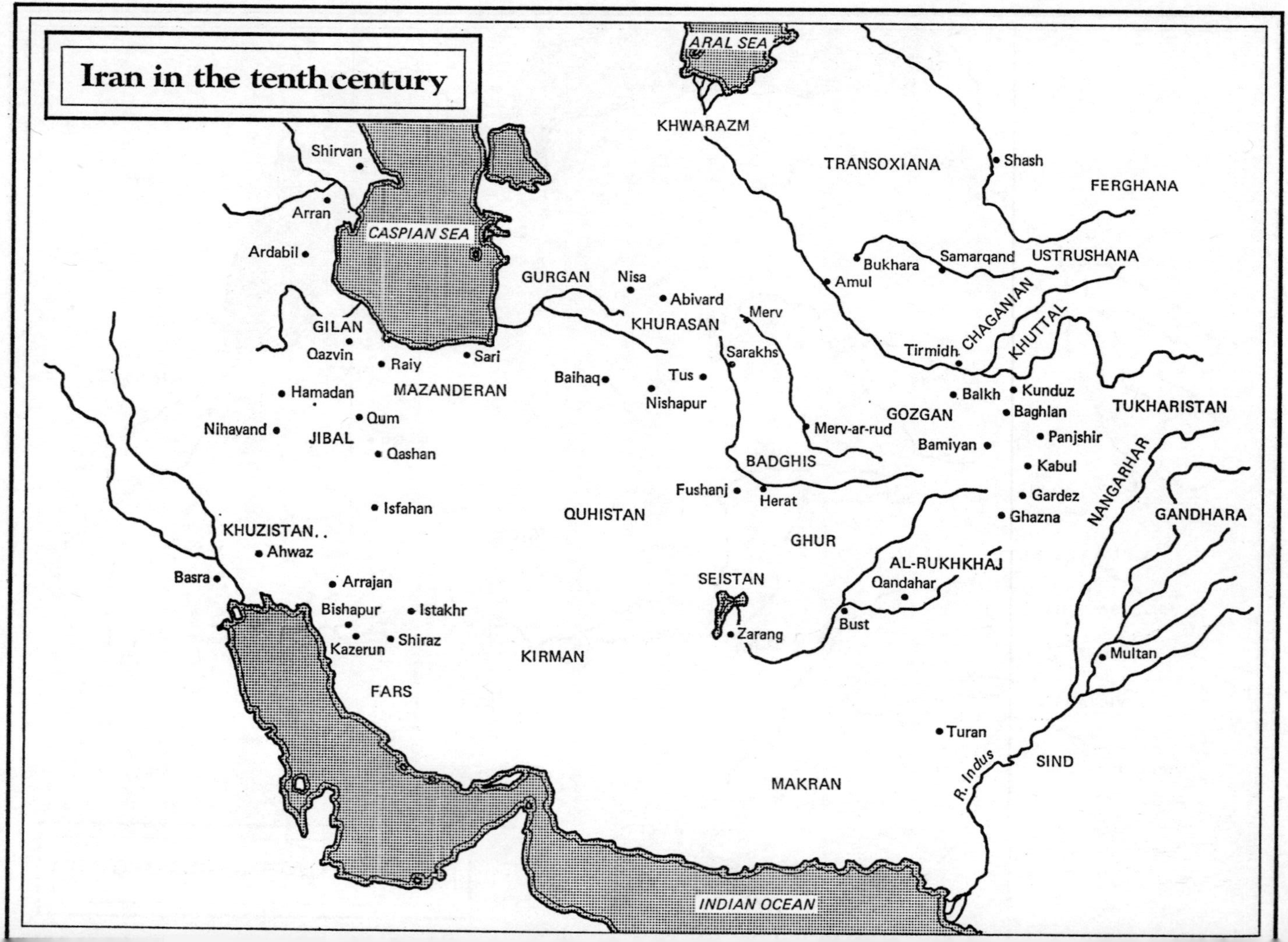

Iran in the tenth century
ARAL SEA
KHWARAZM
TRANSOXIANA
Shash
FERGHANA
Shirvan
Arran
CASPIAN SEA
Ardabil
Bukhara
Samarqand
USTRUSHANA
Amul
GURGAN
Nisa
Abivard
Merv
KHURASAN
CHAGANIAN
KHUTTAL
GILAN
Qazvin
Raiy
Sari
Sarakhs
Tirmidh
Baihaq
Tus
Nishapur
Hamadan
MAZANDERAN
Balkh
Kunduz
Baghlan
GOZGAN
TUKHARISTAN
Qum
Nihavand
JIBAL
Merv-ar-rud
Bamiyan
Panjshir
Qashan
BADGHIS
Kabul
NANGARHAR
Fushanj
Herat
Gardez
Isfahan
QUHISTAN
Ghazna
GANDHARA
KHUZISTAN
Ahwaz
GHUR
AL-RUKHKHAJ
Basra
Arrajan
SEISTAN
Qandahar
Bishapur
Istakhr
Bust
Zarang
Shiraz
Kazerun
KIRMAN
Multan
FARS
Turan
R. Indus
SIND
MAKRAN
INDIAN OCEAN

APPENDIX I

PERSIAN WORDS IN ARABIC*

Much has been written on the Persian words which have penetrated the Arabic language from pre-Islamic times down to the present.[1] The vast majority of these words are from Persian rather than from other Iranian languages, although in a few cases one may find borrowings such as Sogdian *k'γδyh* or *k'γδy'kh* which gave New Persian *kāghad* and Arabic *kāghidh*, although ultimately the origin of the word may be Chinese. The remarks below are only intended as a brief survey, since material on this subject is enormous.

One would expect the Persian words which entered Arabic to be from the realms of government, law, art, music and general culture rather than from religion or philosophy, and such are the results of study. We are not concerned with rare words such as *jāhbad* or 'tax middleman', mentioned in the text, for these were used for a brief period and then vanished.[2] Several Persian words which remain in Arabic to the present in the realm of government are *dīwān* 'court', *rank* 'coat of arms' (in Mamluke Egypt), from Persian *rang* 'colour', *furāniq* 'army leader, courier', from Persian *parvāne*, MP *prw'ng* 'leader'. The word *askadār*, also 'courier', is found in medieval Arabic texts but not at present. The word *muhraq*, from MP *mwhrk* 'seal', means a 'page, papyrus' or even a 'book' in Arabic. The Persian word for 'throne', 'platform' or 'board' *takht*, also entered Arabic in several forms. Arabic *ṣakk* from Persian *chak*, meaning a document, bill or, of course, a bank cheque, is one of the economic terms borrowed by the Arabs. The Arabic word for admiral of a fleet *nākhuda* is clearly borrowed from Persian, and the old title of the rulers of Egypt *khedive* is also taken from Iranian. Whether Arabic *dhabr* 'book, sheet of paper', *dhābir* 'learned' and *mudabbir* 'scribe' are all related to MP *dbyr* 'scribe' is uncertain, especially the forms in *dh*-. The list of Persian words from the bureaucracy or the army borrowed by Arabic could be extended, but no pattern of borrowings emerges from the lists compiled by those who have written on this subject (note 1).

In the realm of music, art and sport there are, as expected, many Persian borrowings into Arabic. We find many Persian names of musical instruments: *ribāb*, *ṣanj* 'harp' from MP *chang*; *mustaq* (*ṣīnī*) or New Persian *mushtak*(*-i chīnī*) is found in MP *mustak*, an unknown kind of instrument. The *ṭunbūr* is clearly

* See p. 272.

from Persian *tanbūr*, MP *tambūr*, while *barbaṭ* is MP *barbūt*, a kind of zither. The *nāy* 'flute', *wanj*, MP *vanjak*, a special 'reed flute', and many other names of instruments, as well as musical terms, for example *zīr* and *bamm* names of 'chords of music', *awāz* 'note', all testify to the overwhelming influence of Persian music on that of their western neighbours.

In art and architecture one would also expect considerable borrowing from Persian into Arabic. Architecture provides *qūs* and *jausaq* from MP *kushk* 'kiosque', *ṭāq* 'arch' from MP *t'g*, *junbudh* from MP *gwmbt*, NP *gunbad* 'dome', *usṭuwāna* (and other forms) 'portico, column', from MP *stūn*, *darbzīn*, *darābzūn* 'balustrade', probably a combination of NP *darb* 'door' and Arabic *zain*, 'decoration, decorated', and many other words such as 'window' and 'fountain'. The word *handāz*, *handasa* 'geometry' also means 'architecture' and 'engineering', from MP *handāčak*. As one would expect, words such as *ṭanfasa* 'small carpet', from NP *tanfasa*, and *ibrisīm* 'silk', MP *aprīshm*, *istabraq* 'silk brocade' (in the Qur'an), MP *stabr* 'thick (clothes)', *namraq* 'cushion', MP *narm*, Parthian *nmr* 'soft' (also in the Qur'an), and many other words in the category of cloth and clothes come from Iran.

In sport or games we have 'polo' *ṣaulajān* from MP **čōlegān*, probably popular pronunciation for *čōpegān*, *nard* 'backgammon' from MP *nēwartashīr*, *shaṭranj* 'chess' from Sanskrit *caturanga* by way of MP *čatrang*. There are many Persian words in Arabic dialects, especially in Iraq, but even in Oman one finds many such as *ṭasūh* 'a small coin' from MP *tasūk*, a fourth of a *dang* or one-twenty-fourth of a *dīnār*. Such dialect words cannot be discussed here.

The list could be extended indefinitely with common words such as *ustādh* 'teacher' from MP *ōstāt*, *ward* 'rose', *firdaus* 'paradise', *khandaq* 'ditch', *sirāj* 'lamp', *sarāwīl* 'trousers', and many others. It is clear that Persian words in great number and from many spheres of life entered the Arabic language.

Finally, as a brief guide to phonetic changes in the passage from Persian to Arabic the following observations on borrowings can be made (drawn from works listed in the bibliography):

Vowels: MP *ō* usually gave Arabic *ū*; MP *ē* gave Arabic *ī*; MP *ī* sometimes gave *ā* (as *bāla* 'sack', from NP *bile*); Persian *a-* frequently became *i-* (as *ibrisīm* 'silk'), while Persian *ā* sometimes gave *a* in Arabic. For the diphthong *-au-* we find frequently *-ai-* in Arabic (as *naurūz* and *nairūz*, *naubakht* and *naibakht*).

Consonants: Persian *p-* gave Arabic *f-* or *b-*; Persian *t* frequently appears as *ṭ* in Arabic, and *d* as *dh*. The Persian sound *č* is found both as *ṣ* and as *s* in Arabic, while *x* frequently appears as *ḥ* (e.g., NP *khunb* 'a water vessel', *ḥubb* in Arabic). Persian *s* usually was the same in Arabic, but sometimes gave *ṣ*, as Arabic *ṣard* 'cold', *ṣanj* 'cymbal'. Persian *sh* frequently was given by *s* in Arabic, as in the name *Sābūr*. Persian *k* also mostly gave Arabic *q* (as *kurte* 'tunic' and *qurṭaq*). Persian *g* gave Arabic *j* (as *tāj* 'crown'), while final *-āk* endings in MP usually became *-ā* in Arabic, whereas *-ak* is found as *-a*, written with a final *-h*.

APPENDIX 2
TABLES

CALIPHS

Umaiyad Caliphs	*Date of accession*	*'Abbasid Caliphs*	*Date of accession*
Mu'āwiya	41/661	Al-Saffāḥ	132/749
Yazīd I	60/680	Al-Manṣūr	136/754
Mu'āwiya II	64/683	Al-Mahdī	158/775
Marwān I	64/684	Al-Hādī	169/785
'Abd al-Malik	65/685	Hārūn al-Rashīd	170/786
Al-Walīd	86/705	Al-Amīn	193/809
Sulaimān	96/715	Al-Ma'mūn	198/813
'Umar b. 'Abd al-'Azīz	99/717	Al-Mu'taṣim	218/833
Yazīd II	101/720	Al-Wāthiq	227/842
Hishām	105/724	Al-Mutawakkil	232/847
Al-Walīd II	125/743	Al-Muntaṣir	247/861
Yazīd III	126/744	Al-Musta'īn	248/862
Ibrāhīm	126/744	Al-Mu'tazz	252/866
Marwān II	127–32/744–50	Al-Muhtadī	255/869
		Al-Mu'tamid	256/870
		Al-Mu'taḍid	279/892
		Al-Muktafī	289/902
		Al-Muqtadir	295/908
		Al-Qāhir	320/932
		Al-Rāḍī	322/934
		Al-Muttaqī	329/940
		Al-Mustakfī	333/944
		Al-Muṭī'	334/946
		Al-Ṭā''ī	363/974
		Al-Qādir	381/991
		Al-Qā'im	422/1031

MINOR IRANIAN DYNASTIES

Ṭāhirids		*Saffārids*	
Ṭāhir I	205/821	Ya'qūb	253/867
Ṭalḥa	207/822	'Amr	265/879

Ṭāhirids
ʿAbdallāh 213/828
Ṭāhir II 230/845
Muḥammad 248–59/862–73

Saffārids
Ṭāhir b. Muḥ. b. ʿAmr 288/901
Laith b. ʿAlī 296/908
Muḥ. b. ʿAlī 298/910
ʿAmr b. Yāqūb b. Muḥammad b. ʿAmr 299/912
Aḥmad b. Muḥ. b. Khalaf b. Laith 310/922
Walī al-Daula Khalaf b. Aḥmad 352/963

Sāmānids
Isma'īl b. Aḥmad 279/892
Aḥmad b. Isma'īl 295/907
Al-Amīr al-Sa'īd Naṣr I 301/914
Al-Amīr al-Ḥamīd Nūḥ II 331/943
Al-Amīr al-Mu'aiyad ʿAbd al-Malik I 343/954
Al-Amīr al-Sadīd Manṣūr I 350/961
Al-Amīr al-Riḍā Nūḥ II 365/976
Manṣūr II 387/997
ʿAbd al-Malik II 389/999
Isma'īl al-Muntaṣir 390–5/1000–5

UMAIYAD GOVERNORS OF KHURASAN
(some of the early appointments are uncertain)

Qais b. al-Haitham as-Sulamī 32/653
ʿAbdallāh b. Khāzim 33/653
Khulaid b. Qurra al-Yarbū'ī 36/656
Qais b. al-Haitham al-Sulamī 41/661
ʿAbdallāh b. Khāzim 43/663
Al-Ḥakam b. ʿAmr al-Ghifārī 44/664
ʿUmair b. Aḥmar al-Yashkurī 45/665 (only in Merv)
Anas b. Abī Unās 47/667
Al-Ḥakam b. ʿAmr al-Ghifārī 47/667
Ghālib b. Faḍāla al-Laithī 48/668
Anas b. Abī Unās 50/670
Khulaid b. ʿAbdallāh al-Ḥanafī 50/670
Al-Rabī' b. Ziyād al-Ḥārithī 51/671
ʿUbaidallāh b. Ziyād 53/673
Aslām b. Zur'a 55/675
Sa'īd b. ʿUthmān b. ʿAffān 56/676
ʿAbd al-Raḥmān b. Ziyād 59/678
Salm b. Ziyād 61/680
ʿAbdallāh b. Khāzim 64/683
Al-Muhallab b. Abī Ṣufra 65/684 (under Ibn Zubair)
ʿAbdallah b. Khāzim 71/690
Bukair b. Wishshāḥ 72/691
Umaiya b. ʿAbdallāh b. Khālid b. Asīd 74/694
Al-Muhallab b. Abī Ṣufra 78/697

Yazīd b. al-Muhallab 82/701
Al-Mufaḍḍal b. al-Muhallab 85/704
Qutaiba b. Muslim 86/705
Yazīd b. al-Muhallab 97/716
Al-Jarrāḥ b. ʿAbdallāh al-Ḥakamī 99/717
ʿAbd al-Rahmān b. Nuʿaim 100/718
Saʿid b. ʿAbd al-ʿAzīz b. al-Ḥārith b. al-Ḥakam 102/721
Saʿīd b. ʿAmr b. Aswad al-Ḥarashī 103/721
Muslim b. Saʿīd al-Kilābī 104/722
Asad b. ʿAbdallāh al-Qasrī 106/724
Ashras b. ʿAbdallāh al-Sulamī 109/727
Junaid b. ʿAbd al-Raḥmān al-Murrī 111/729
ʿĀṣim b. ʿAbdallāh b. Yazīd al-Hilālī 116/734
Khālid b. ʿAbdallāh al-Qasrī 117/735
Jaʿfar b. Ḥanzala 120/738
Naṣr b. Saiyar 120/738

ARAB TRIBAL ALIGNMENTS UNDER THE UMAIYAD CALIPHS

Northern tribes

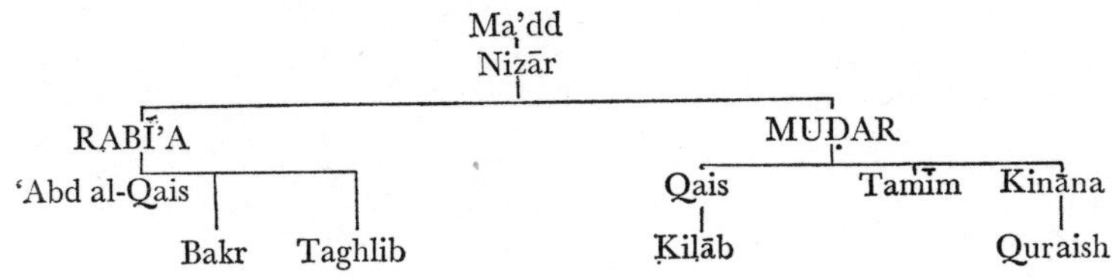

Southern tribes

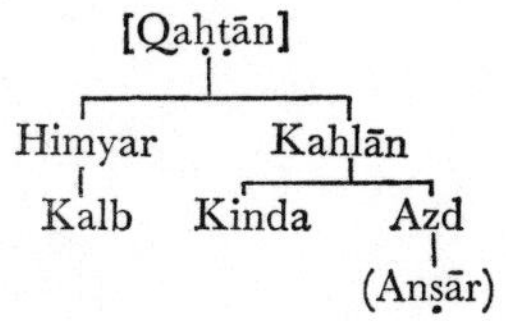

GLOSSARY OF TERMS

adab	culture, specifically literature which is *belles lettres*.
aiwān	open vaulted portal in architecture, typical of later Persian mosques with four *aiwāns* facing a courtyard.
'āmil	provincial tax collector.
amīr	leader or general, then military governor.
asawīra	Sasanian cavalry which went over to the Arabs in units.
'aṭā	the Islamic system of pensions especially for the warriors, the *muqātila*.
barīd	postal and spy system of Islam, based on pre-Islamic institution.
bitakhsh	a Middle Persian title of very high rank.
dār al-ḥarb (*Islām*)	domain of war (non-Islam), or of Islam.
dhimmī	Jews and Christians, 'people of the book', according to Muslims. Usually the Zoroastrians too were considered *dhimmīs*.
dihqān	originally Iranian landlords who were almost local potentates. Later the word meant a farmer.
dirhem	from Greek *drakhmē*, silver coin, weight 2·8 or 2·9 grams.
dīnār	from Latin *denarius*, gold coin, usually in a ten to one ratio with silver.
dīwān	the bureaucracy. At the beginning of the Arab conquests it meant the registers of the new Islamic state.
farn, farr	mystical concept of one's destiny. Also the kingly 'glory'.
farsakh	from Old Persian **parasanga*, unit of distance which varied throughout history. Today six kilometres.
fatā	plural *fityān*, a knight or one upholding ideals of chivalry. Later young men who joined orders or clubs professing ideals of honour etc.
ghāzī	a warrior for Islam, then a frontier soldier and a hero or martyr.

ghulām	a young slave, a page, then used for the Turkish court slaves.
ghulāt	Muslims, especially *Shī'ites*, who deify their *imāms* or seem to.
ḥadīth	tradition of the Prophet. Various traditions were gathered into law books to form the four Sunni law schools.
hājib	chamberlain of royal court.
hazārbad	army commander of a thousand men, i.e. Greek *khiliarkhos*.
Hijra	date of Hegira or flight of Muḥammad from Mecca to Medīna on 16 July 622. Islamic dating in lunar years begins from this date.
imām	leader of prayer and of the faithful, then religious leaders in a wider sense, or as the Shī'ite precursor of the messiah.
imāmzāde	literally 'son of an *imām*', but it came to mean Shī'ite shrines where saints were buried.
iqṭā'	system of land grants or fiefs. Later given to military officers in lieu of pay or for services.
isbāhbad	Middle Persian *spāhbed* 'army commander'. In Islamic times the title of a ruler in the Caspian provinces.
jāhbadh	Middle Persian **gāhbed*, treasurer, keeper of accounts.
jizya	first tax, then head tax on non-Muslims.
jund	Middle Persian *gund* 'army'.
kanārang	an east Iranian counterpart of *marzbān*.
kātib	Islamic scribe (pl. *kuttāb*, as a class).
khāqān	supreme ruler of Turks.
khān	Turkish title of prince or lord.
khānagāh	house or centre of Sūfīs or dervishes.
kharāj	first simply tax, then land tax.
kūra	from Greek *khōra*, subdivision of a province.
madrasa	school, but under the later 'Abbāsid caliphs a university for teaching Sunnī Islam.
majūs	Arabic form of *magus*, Zoroastrian priest, pl. *magi*.
maks, pl. *mukūs*	taxes other than *kharāj* or *jizya*.
maqāmāt	genre of prose similar to essays or discussion literature.
marzbān	warden of the marches, then governor.
maulā	clients of Arab tribes. Sometimes used in the plural *mawāli* for non-Arab Muslims.
minbār	pulpit of a mosque.
mōbad	Middle Persian *magupat* 'chief of magi' or Zoroastrian priests.
ostān	Persian 'province', also equated with Arabic *kūra*, hence subdivision of a province.

pādgospān	Middle Persian pronunciation: *pāygōs,* Arabic *al-fadhusbān,* similar to the *marzbān.*
qāḍī	Muslim judge.
rā'is	chief (of an Arab tribe), then 'mayor' of a city.
ribāṭ	fort or caravanserai in eastern Iran. A unit of distance.
rustāq	Middle Persian *rōstāg* a subdivision of a *kūra.* Sometimes equated to *ṭassūj,* sometimes larger.
ṣadr	the breast or forefront, then a title given to leaders in cities in Transoxiana after the fall of the Samanids.
sharī'a'	Islamic law based on the *Qur'ān* and the *hadīths* 'traditions', of the Prophet.
shaikh	head of an Arab tribe, then any person of importance or the head of a quarter of a town or of some organization.
shī'a	partisans of 'Alī and his descendants as the proper *imāms* of the Muslims. They follow different traditions from the Sunnīs.
sunnī	one who follows the *sunna,* or one of the traditional law schools. Opposed to Shī'a.
ṭassūj	Middle Persian *tasug* 'a quarter', subdivision of a *kūra* or sometimes even smaller, a division of a *rustāq.*
udabā'	plural of *adīb* 'literary man', the class of poets, writers and intellectuals.
'ulamā'	plural of *'ālim,* Muslim learned man, an Islamic class.
vuzurg framādār	prime minister under the Sasanians. Similiar to vizier under the 'Abbāsids.
waqf	Islamic endowment legally valid.
zakāt	Islamic tithes, in theory ten per cent of one's income, but varying. Sometimes imposed by the state as a tax.
zindīq	first a Manichaean, then anyone who held dualist beliefs and finally almost any heretic.

NOTES

CHAPTER 1: PAST, PRESENT AND FUTURE

1 Cf. R.Frye, 'The Charisma of Kingship in Ancient Iran', *Iranica Antiqua*, VI (1964), pp. 36–54.
2 Cf., for example, M.Boyce, 'Bībī-Shahrbānū and the Lady of Pārs', *BSOAS*, XXX (1967), pp. 30–44.

CHAPTER 2: SASANIAN IRAN

1 Cf. Harold W.Bailey, *Zoroastrian Problems in the Ninth-Century Books* (Oxford 1943), p. 2, and corrections by J.Duchesne-Guillemin, 'Le xvarənah', *Annali del Istituto Orientale di Napoli*, v (1963), pp. 19–31.
2 E.g. Ibn Khurdādhbih, p. 5.
3 Cf. Maximilian Streck, *Seleucia und Ktesiphon* (Leipzig 1917), p. 35. The court was called the *dar*, or *BB*' in a Semitic mask of Pahlavi, 'the gate'. Yāqūt, IV, p. 446, lists the seven towns comprising al-Madā'in but most of the names are corrupt in the text and cannot be restored with authority.
4 On the inscription see André Maricq, 'Res Gestae Divi Saporis', *Syria*, XXXV (1958), pp. 295–360. The tradition of seven great noble families was an old one in Iran.
5 Mentioned in Eghishe's *History of Vardan*, ed. E.Tēr-Minasean (Erevan 1957), p. 160, where the word is *marzpet*, with variants.
6 In Arabic books the four *marzbāns* are sometimes called the four *iṣbāhbadh* or 'army commanders'. On the other hand we find *iṣbāhbadh* confused with *padgōspān* (below), although they were two distinct titles, albeit sometimes combined in one person.
7 Ya'qūbī, *Ta'rīkh* (Beirut 1960), I, p. 177.
8 The *nahang* may have meant originally the Seleucid subdivision of a province, the eparchy.
9 In Shāpūr's inscription the Parthian word for 'city' is the Semitic mask *MḤWZ*', while the MP word is *štrdstn* or *shahristān*, the centre of government of the province. In later Islamic time the province was called a *wilāyat*.
10 The *ostān* may have been originally the royal domain but by the time of the Arab conquest the word was frequently used as a synonym of a *kūra*. The *ostāndār*, or chief of a district, is mentioned in Semitic sources; cf.

Georg Hoffmann, *Auszüge aus syrischen Akten persischer Märtyrer* (Leipzig 1880), p. 93.

11 E.g. Yāqūt, I, pp. 40–1, speaking of the province of Fārs. Ṭabarī equates the *rustāq* and the *ṭassūj*, and Noeldeke, p. 16, note 2, believes the former word was used on the plateau while *ṭassūj* was used in the lowlands of Mesopotamia.

12 Yāqūt, III, p. 676. An original Rustam Kavād is unlikely, while Rōstāk Kavād would be more plausible.

13 A discussion of the various lists may be found in Josef Marquart, *Erānšahr* (Berlin 1901), p. 145.

14 On the division into a northern part with Raiy the main city, and a southern part with Iṣfahān and Hamadhān the two main cities, see Eduard Sachau, 'Zur Ausbreitung des Christentums in Asien', *Abhandlung der preuss, Akademie der Wissenschaften* (Berlin 1919), p. 60.

15 Ibn Khurdādhbih, p. 20. Later the province of Jibāl was called 'Irāq al-'Ajamī, explained in Guy Le Strange, *The Lands of the Eastern Caliphate* (Cambridge 1930), p. 186.

16 Cf. my article, 'Sasanian Seal Inscriptions', in *Festschrift Franz Altheim, Beiträge zur alten Geschichte und deren Nachleben,* II (Berlin 1970), p. 82.

17 On Qum see the *Ta'rīkh-i Qum* by Ḥasan ibn Muḥ. ibn Ḥasan Qummī, ed. Saiyid Jalāl al-Dīn Ṭahrānī (Tehran 1935), p. 24, and the Pahlavi text *King Husrav and his Boy* by J. M. Unvala (Paris 1924), p. 11, line 1. Qum was probably separated from Isfahan by Kavad, as the *Ta'rīkh-i Qum* states. The derivation of Qum from *kumb* 'dome', by W. Eilers, 'Kyros' in *Beiträge zur Namenforschung*, XV (1964), p. 188, note 26, is unlikely.

18 On the various etymologies of Gay see Wilhelm Eilers, 'Der Name Demawend', *Archiv Orientální*, XXII (Prague 1954), p. 368, note 226.

19 The seal is of carnelian, catalogue no. A 1351.

20 In the *Dēnkart*, III, ed. Madan, p. 292, Sanjana, VII, p. 324 (no. 282) the expressions *vāspuhrakāntar* 'more noble' (this translation is preferable to 'special' for Vāspuhrākān) and *vāspuhrakāntūm* 'most noble', are used. In the inscription of Kartīr (Kerdīr) on the Ka'ba of Zardusht at Naqsh-i Rustām, we find (line 3) *w'spwtlkn* and in the corresponding passage of Naqsh-i Rustām, line 6, *w'spwxlkn* meaning 'in particular'.

21 Balādhurī, p. 303.

22 On the etymology of the name see Eilers, 'Der Name Demawend', p. 322, note 65.

23 Balādhurī, p. 318.

24 The site of Hecatompylos has probably been found by David Stronach of the British Institute of Persian Studies in Tehran, some 30 km. west of Damghan, today called Shahr-i Komis, probably the site of medieval Qumis.

25 Cf. Eilers, 'Der Name Demawend', p. 188, regarding Abrshahr, *abrēnak*, etc.

26 According to Tha'ālibī, p. 744.

27 Ibn Khurdādhbih, p. 18.

28 Contrary to Ernst Herzfeld, *Paikuli* (Berlin 1924), I, p. 230, who wrongly

sought to identify this and other places as Indian principalities tributary to the Sasanians.

29 Cf. Erich Schmidt, *Flights Over Ancient Cities of Iran* (Chicago 1940), pp. 55–7, and T.J.Arne, *Excavations at Shah-Tepé, the Sino-Swedish Expedition* (Stockholm 1945), XXVII, pp. 7–13. There is a tradition that Yazdegird II (439–57) began the wall but Chosroes finished it.

30 Yāqūt, III, p. 547; Ibn Rusta, pp. 149–50.

31 Ṭabarī, series III, p. 1275. This wall was investigated by A.D.H.Bivar, and G.Fehérvári, 'The Walls of Tammīsha', *Iran* (London 1960), IV, pp. 35–51.

32 On the *khandaq Sābūr* see Henrik S.Nyberg, 'Die sassanidsiche Westgrenze und ihre Verteidigung', *Septentrionalia et Orientalia*, Kungl. Vitterhets Historie och Antikvitet Akademien Handlingnar, Del 91 (Stockholm 1961), pp. 316–26. To the Pahlavi text discussed here should be added the references in Balādhurī, p. 298 and Yāqūt, II, p. 476.

33 Yāqūt, II, p. 476.

34 Al-Bakrī, p. 641.

35 Frye, 'Some Early Iranian Titles', *Oriens*, XV (1962), p. 352.

36 E.g. in Eghishe's *History*, ed. E.Tēr-Minasean (Erevan 1957), pp. 24, 28.

37 Khwārazmī, p. 118. The *difīra* is from Persian *dipīr* and means 'bureau', no matter what the ultimate origin of the word is; cf. Wilhelm Eilers, 'Iranisches Lehngut im Arabischen Lexikon', *IIJ*, V (1962), p. 216. The word *ruwānikān* is the plural of Persian *ruwān* 'soul', i.e. the dead.

38 Eilers, in *IIJ*, p. 212.

39 Eilers, in *IIJ*, p. 207. In the Talmudic passage Taʿanith, 20a, the term may mean an overseer of water distribution, since it follows an 'overseer of rivers'. Cf. *Aruch completum*, ed. K. Strauss, IX (New York 1955), p. 118

40 Khwārazmī, p. 64. Cf. Qudāma, p. 184. The word came to mean a 'pass' or 'document of permission' in modern Persian.

41 Whatever the origin of the word it came to Arabic through Persian; cf. Manfred Mayrhofer, *Kurzgefasztes etymologisches Wörterbuch des Altindischen* (Heidelberg 1963), II, p. 654.

42 For Arabic 'mirrors for princes', cf. Gustav Richter, *Studien zur Geschichte der älteren arabischen Fürstenspiegel* (Leipzig 1932) and the introduction to F.R.C.Bagley's translation of *Ghazālī's Book of Counsel for Kings* (London 1964).

43 Cf. the survey of Pahlavi *andarz* literature in Jehangir C.Tavadia, *Die Mittelpersische Sprache und Literatur der Zarathustrier* (Leipzig 1956), pp. 103–11.

44 *Pahlavi Texts*, ed. Jamaspji Jamaspasana (Bombay 1913), II, p. 59, *zan u frazand ī xvēštan yut az frahang bē mā hēl, ku-t tīmār u bēš ī girān bar nē rasēt, tā nē bavēh pašēmān*. The word *frahang* here might be translated 'education'.

45 Cf. Carlo A.Nallino, 'Tracce di opere greche giunte agli Arabi per trafila Pehlevica', in *A Volume of Oriental Studies presented to Edward G. Browne* (Cambridge 1922), pp. 345–63.

46 Robert M.Adams, 'Agriculture and Urban Life in Early Southwestern Iran', *Science*, 136 (1962), pp. 113–14.

47 Iṣṭakhrī, p. 124; Ibn Khurdādhbih, pp. 31, 43; Ibn Rusta, p. 153; Ya'qūbī, pp. 270–1, 273, etc.
48 Boris Litvinskii and others, *Historiography of Tajikistan* (1917–69), XIII International Congress of Historical Sciences (Moscow 1970), p. 16.
49 See Arthur U.Pope, *A Survey of Persian Art,* temporary fasicule of XV (Tokyo 1968) 'Persia and the Far East', pp. 3207–310.
50 See Roman Ghirshman, *Iran, Parthians and Sassanians* (London 1962), pp. 283–339.
51 Cf., for example, articles on Boyid silks by Ernst Kühnel and Dorothy G. Shepherd in Arthur U.Pope, *A Survey of Persian Art* (Tokyo 1967), XIV, pp. 3080–99.
52 Jean Sauvaget, 'Remarques sur l'art sassanide', *Revue des Études islamiques,* XII (1938), p. 128.
53 Cf. Werner Caskel, article 'al-'Arab', *Encyclopedia of Islam,* new edn, p. 528.
54 Cf. Vassily V.Bartold, *Tadzhiki* (Tashkent 1925), p. 98. Josef Markwart in *A Catalogue of the Provincial Capitals of Erānshahr* (Rome 1931), p. 58, disputes this derivation, claiming that the Persian designations of the Arabs as Tāčik, Tāzī, came from the verb *tāxtan* 'to make forays'. This is most unlikely.
55 Cf. Ṭabarī, series II, p. 1508, line 13.
56 Cf. Franz Altheim and Ruth Stiehl, *Die Araber in der alten Welt* (Berlin 1964), I, p. 197.
57 Al-Tha'ālibī, *Histoire,* p. 529.
58 Ṭabarī, series I, p. 845; Noeldeke, p. 67.
59 Cf. Murad Kamil, 'Persian Words in Ancient Arabic', *Bulletin of the Faculty of Arts, Cairo University,* XIX (1957), p. 66, quoting from the *Kitāb al-Aghānī* (Cairo 1345/1927), II, pp. 97–156.
60 Cf. Henrik S.Nyberg, note 32.
61 Cf. Balādhurī, pp. 78–81.
62 Ibn Rusta, p. 217, lines 6–9.
63 Cf. Arne Melvinger, *Les premières incursions des Vikings en Occident d'après les sources arabes* (Uppsala 1955), pp. 70–7. Omeljan Pritsak has prepared a large study of the history of south Russia in which, *inter alia,* he shows that the designation of the Norsemen by the Arabs of Spain as *majūs* arose from a Celtic word for merchants in southern France which was then transferred to the northerners.

CHAPTER 3: CENTRAL ASIA BEFORE THE ARAB CONQUESTS

1 On Khwarazmian see V.A.Livshits, 'The Khwarezmian Calendar and the Eras of Ancient Chorasmia', *Acta Antiqua Hungaricae* (Budapest 1968), XVI, pp. 433–46, with bibliography. For Kushan Bactrian compare J.Harmatta, 'Late Bactrian Inscriptions', *Acta Antiqua Hung.* (Budapest 1969), XVII, pp. 298–432, with H.Humbach, *Baktrische Sprachdenkmäler* 2 vols (Wiesbaden 1966–7), and V.Livshits, 'Cusano-Indica', *Ellinisticheskii Blizhnii Vostok,* Festschrift N.V. Pigulevskaya (Moscow 1967), pp. 161–71.

2 Cf. E.G.Pulleyblank, 'A Sogdian Colony in Inner Mongolia', *T'oung Pao* (Leiden 1952), XLI, pp. 317–56, and S.G.Klyashtornyi, 'Sur les colonies sogdiennes de la Haute Asie', *Ural-altaische Jahrbücher* (Wiesbaden 1961), XXXIII, pp. 95–7.
3 Narshakhī, *Tārīkh-i Bukhārā*, trans. R.N.Frye (Cambridge, Mass. 1954), pp. 17, 23.
4 Cf. R.N.Frye, 'The Significance of Greek and Kushan Archaeology in the History of Central Asia', *Journal of Asian History* (Wiesbaden 1967), I, pp. 33–44, and G.Frumkin's work on Archaeology in Soviet Central Asia in B.Spuler, *Handbuch der Orientalistik* (Leiden 1970).
5 A.Zekidi Validi, 'Über die Sprache und Kultur der alten Chwarezmier', *ZDMG*, XC (1937), *30*.
6 V.A.Livshits, in *Acta Antiqua Hungaricae*, note 1.
7 S.Tolstov, *Drevnii Khorezm* (Moscow 1948).
8 Examined on two trips, May 1952 and July 1967.
9 Cf. note 4.
10 Strabo XI.518, Herodotus IV.204; VI.9.
11 His early coins have debased Greek legends while the later series have Kushan Bactrian legends in a modified Greek alphabet.
12 H.S.Nyberg, 'The Pahlavi Documents from Avromān', *Le Monde Oriental* (Uppsala 1923), XVII, pp. 182–230.
13 *Fihrist*, p. 14.
14 Several international conferences on the date of Kanishka have been held, but no concensus of opinion has been reached. A date of *c.* AD 125–50 seems best suited for his reign.
15 Ṭabarī, series I, p. 820.
16 A.Maricq, 'Classica et Orientalia', *Syria*, XXXV (1958), p. 336.
17 G.V.Lukonin, 'Zavoevaniya Sasanidov na Vostoke', *Vestnik Drevnei Istorii*, part 2 (1969), pp. 39–44.
18 R.Göbl, *Dokumente zur Geschichte der iranischen Hunnen in Baktrien und Indien* (Wiesbaden 1967), I, pp. 29–37.
19 R.N.Frye, *Notes on the Early Coinage of Transoxiana*, Numismatic Notes and Monographs, no. 113 (New York 1949), p. 27.
20 J.Marquart, *Ērānšahr*, Abhandhungen der königl. Gesell. der Wiss. zu Göttingen (Berlin 1901), pp. 141, 157.
21 V.Minorsky, 'The Turkish Dialect of the Khalaj', *BSOS* (London 1940), X, pp. 426–9.
22 V.A.Shishkin, *Varakhsha* (Moscow 1963), p. 30.
23 A.Christensen, *L'Iran sous les sassanides* (Copenhagen 1944), p. 113. The word *dihqān* is of Persian origin and was borrowed by the east Iranians.
24 A.A.Freiman, 'Sogdiiskaya nadpis iz starogo Merva', *Zapiski Instituta Vostokovedeniya* (Moscow 1939), VII, pp. 296–302.
25 J.Labourt, *Le Christianisme dans l'Empire Perse* (Paris 1904), p. 326, and G.Messina, 'Al-Biruni sugli inizi del cristianesimo a Merv', *Al-Biruni Commemoration Volume* (Calcutta 1951), pp. 221–31.
26 See Frye, note 4.
27 Bīrūnī, *Athār al-bāqiya*, ed. E.Sachau (Leipzig 1876), pp. 288, 296.

28 *Ibid.*, p. 235.
29 *Ibid.*, p. 237.
30 G.Flügel, *Mani* (Leipzig 1862), pp. 77, 106.
31 N.V.Dyakonova, O.I.Smirnova, 'K voprosu o kulte Nany (Anakhity) v Sogde', *Sovetskaya Arkheologiya* (Moscow 1967), I, pp. 74–83.
32 T.Watters, *On Yuan Chwang's Travels in India* (London 1904), I, pp. 108, 115; W.Fuchs, 'Huei-chao's Pilgerreise durch Nordwest Indien und Zentralasien', *Sitzungsber. der Preuss. Akad. der Wiss.*, no. 30 (Berlin 1938), p. 449.
33 Marquart, *Ērānšahr*, p. 292.
34 P.Daffinà, 'Gli eretici Chi-to e la divinità di Zābul', *Rivista degli Studi Orientali* (Rome 1962), XXXVII, p. 279.
35 Bīrūnī, *Athār*, p. 35.
36 Ṭabarī, series II, p. 1237.
37 See R.N.Frye, 'Notes on the History of Transoxiana', *Harvard Journal of Asiatic Studies* (Cambridge, Mass. 1956), XIX, p. 119.
38 O.Smirnova, 'Sogdiiskie monety kak novyi istochnik dlya istorii Srednei Azii', *Sovetskoe Vostokovedenie* (Moscow 1949), VI, p. 366.
39 V.A.Livshits, *Sogdiiskie Dokumenty s Gory Mug*, part II (Moscow 1962), index.
40 Ṭabarī, series II, p. 1440.
41 Livshits, *Sogdiiskie Dokumenty* (note 39), index.
42 Ṭabarī, series II, p. 1629.
43 Livshits, *Sogiiskie Dokumenty*.
44 These are non-Turkish titles in origin; the first may be Tokharian and the second Iranian.
45 Long ago recognized as Sanskrit *pramukha* 'chief', by H.W.Bailey, 'Iranica', *BSOAS* (London 1943), XI, p. 2.
46 *Ḥudūd al-ʿālam*, trans. V.Minorsky (London 1937), p. 335.
47 One of the striking differences between Sogdiana and the Sasanian empire was the important position of the merchants in the former. In Sogdiana there were three classes of people, the aristocracy, the merchants and the common folk or workers. Cf. G.V.Livshits, *Sogiiskie Dokumenty*.

CHAPTER 4: THE ARAB CONQUESTS IN IRAN

1 See I.P.Petrushevskii, *Islam v Irane v VII–XV Vekakh* (Leningrad 1966), p. 187.
2 Tusi, *The Nasirean Ethics*, trans. G. M.Wickens (London 1964), pp. 216ff.; Niẓām al-Mulk, *The Book of Government or Rules for Kings* (*Siyāsat nāme*), trans. H.Darke (London 1960), p. 9.
3 The works of L.Caetani, *Annali dell'Islam*, 10 vols (Milan 1905–26), and B.Spuler, *Iran in frühislamischer Zeit* (Wiesbaden 1952) have been used extensively for the summary which follows.
4 Dīnāwārī, p. 117.
5 Ṭabarī, series I, p. 2184.
6 Ṭabarī, series I, pp. 2439–40.
7 *Enc. Islam*, art. Baṣra.

8 Ṭabarī, series I, p. 2569.
9 Balādhurī, p. 305.
10 Balādhurī, p. 280.
11 Balādhurī, p. 373.
12 Balādhurī, p. 265.
13 Ṭabarī, series I, pp. 2778–9.
14 Article *ʿaṭā* in *Enc. of Islam,* 2nd edn.
15 Balādhurī, p. 381.
16 A.Ben Shemesh, *Taxation in Islam* (Leiden 1967), I, p. 27.
17 *Ta'rīkh,* II, p. 234.
18 Balādhurī, p. 318.
19 Balādhurī, p. 326.
20 Sebeos, trans. F.Macler, *Histoire d'Héraclius* (Paris 1904), pp. 145–6.
21 Balādhurī, p. 329.
22 *Ibid.*, p. 388.
23 *Ibid.*, p. 374.
24 Dīnawarī, p. 73, line 3.
25 Spuler, p. 19.
26 Balādhurī, p. 405.
27 Ṭabarī, series II, p. 649.
28 Ṭabarī, series II, p. 1354.
29 Ṭabarī, series II, p. 1439–41.
30 Ṭabarī, series II, p. 902.
31 Ṭabarī, series II, p. 1543.
32 Cf. D.C.Dennett, *Conversion and the Poll Tax in Early Islam* (Cambridge, Mass. 1950), and F.Løkkegaard, *Islamic Taxation* (Copenhagen 1950).
33 Ṭabarī, series II, pp. 1111–12 and 1119–20 (year 83).
34 *Ta'rīkh,* II, p. 234.
35 On the tribulations of the *mawālī* see Goldziher, I, pp. 139–42.
36 Ṭabarī, series I, p. 3449.
37 *Ibid.*, series I, p. 2905.
38 *Fārs nāme,* ed. G.Le Strange and R.Nicholson (London 1921), p. 116.

CHAPTER 5: THE ISLAMIC CONQUEST OF CENTRAL ASIA

1 Balādhurī, p. 405.
2 Ṭabarī, series I, p. 3249; Balādhurī, p. 409.
3 In Qum the Arabs were settled in villages near the city; cf. *Ta'rīkh-i Qum*, p. 244. In Merv the Christians complained that half of their possessions were taken from them, in addition to the imposition of both *kharāj* and *jizya*. Cf. O.Braun, *Das Buch der Synhados* (Stuttgart 1900), p. 347.
4 Ṭabarī, series II, p. 17; Balādhurī, p. 409.
5 Ṭabarī, series II, p. 84; Yaʿqūbī, II, p. 264.
6 Ṭabarī, series II, p. 156, line 3; Balādhurī, p. 410. The numbers are not given by Ṭabarī and one must guard against exaggeration. According to the *Kitāb al-Futūḥ* of Aʿtham al-Kūfī, Arabic MS. Topkapisaray Ahmet III, 2956, I, fol. 167, among those sent to Khurasan were criminals

who were stationed in *ribāṭs* on the frontiers. Cf. Ibn Khallikān, IV, p. 165.

7 Ṭabarī, series II, pp. 488ff.; Balādhurī, pp. 414–16.

8 On this cf. the articles on ʿAdnān and Ḳaḥṭān in the *Encyclopaedia of Islam*. On the tribal affiliations of various Arab leaders in Khurasan see the article by Ṣāliḥ Aḥmad al-ʿAlī, 'Istīṭaq al-ʿArab fī Khurāsān', *Univ. of Baghdad Journal of Arts Faculty* (Baghdad 1958), pp. 36–83.

9 See H.A.R.Gibb, *The Arab Conquests in Central Asia* (London 1923), pp. 18–19. On the Bukharan slaves in Basra see Yāqūt, I, p. 522; Yaʿqūbī, II, p. 237; Ṭabarī, series II, p. 170.

10 Gibb, p. 20; Ibn Qutaiba, *Kitāb al-Maʿārif*, ed. Wüstenfeld, p. 101; The *Kitāb al-aghānī* and other literary works tell of Saʿid's death.

11 Balādhurī, *Ansāb al-ashraf*, v, pp. 117–19; translated by O.Pinta and G.Levi Della Vida, *Il Califfo Muʿāwiya* (Rome 1938), p. 125.

12 Ṭabarī, series II, p. 489.

13 The complicated details of the fighting have been unravelled by J.Wellhausen, *Das arabische Reich und sein Stürz* (Berlin 1902), pp. 259–62.

14 Ṭabarī, series II, p. 831.

15 Yaʿqūbī, *Taʾrīkh*, II, pp. 166, 217. Ibn al-Athīr, II, p. 366. The tradition found in later histories, such as Khwāndamīr and Firishta, that he captured Kabul and converted 12,000 to Islam is unfounded.

16 Cf. G.R.Scarcia, 'Zunbīl or Zanbīl', *Yādnāme-ye Jan Rypka* (Prague 1967), pp. 41–5, and G.Tucci, 'Oriental Notes II', *East and West*, XIV (1963), p. 163, who proposes to identify the god Zun with Śiva. Cf. C.E.Bosworth, *Sīstān under the Arabs* (Rome 1968), p. 34.

17 Balādhurī, pp. 397–8.

18 Ṭabarī, series I, p. 2705, translated and discussed by Bosworth, *Sīstān under the Arabs*, p. 20 also p. 33.

19 Cf. Bosworth, *Sīstān under the Arabs*, p. 51.

20 On the co-operation between Arabs and *dihqans* and the exploitation of the common folk in Khurasan see H.Mason, 'The Role of the Azdite Muhallabid Family in Marw's Anti-Umayyad Power Struggle', *Arabica*, XIV (1967), p. 204, where further references are given.

21 Balādhurī, p. 416.

22 Ṭabarī, series II, p. 1152, line 8. See also Mason, *Arabica*, p. 199, on al-Muhallab's policy of including *mawālī* on the *dīwān* lists of pensions, and his support of a guard of local aristocrats.

23 Ṭabarī, series II, p. 1119.

24 Ṭabarī, series II, p. 1180.

25 On Qutaiba's life see Ibn Khallikān, II, p. 415. On Iranians in Qutaiba's army Ṭabarī, series II, pp. 1244, 1256.

26 Ṭabarī, series II, pp. 1129–31.

27 Ṭabarī, series II, p. 1185; Balādhurī, p. 420; on the pearls see al-Bīrūnī, *Kitāb al-Jamāhir* (Hyderabad 1355/1936), p. 157. Miners and sappers took the town of Baikand according to Ṭabarī, series II, p. 1187; Narshakhī, p. 44.

28 Ṭabarī, series II, p. 1195; Yaʿqūbī, II, p. 287.

29 Ṭabarī, series II, p. 1199.

30 Narshakhī, p. 53.
31 Ṭabarī, series II, p. 1204, line 14.
32 Ṭabarī, series II, p. 1229; Ya'qūbī, *Ta'rīkh*, II, p. 287.
33 Ṭabarī, series II, p. 1218; Balādhurī, p. 420.
34 Ṭabarī, series II, p. 1235; Ya'qūbī, II, p. 286; Balādhurī, p. 420.
35 Ṭabarī, series II, p. 1241; Balādhurī, p. 421.
36 Bīrūnī, *Athār*, p. 36, transl. p. 42.
37 On the history of Khwārazm see the writings of S.P.Tolstov, e.g. *Po Sledam drevnexorezmiiskoi tsivilizatsii* (Moscow 1948), pp. 223–6, and the German translation of this, *Auf den Spuren der altchoresmischen Kultur* (Berlin 1953), pp. 241–4.
38 One source says Ghūrak was a Zoroastrian priest, *Kitāb al-qand fī ta'rīkh-i Samarqand* by al-Nasafī in Barthold, *Turkestan* (Russian edn), *Teksty*, p. 48. Another says he was related to the Afshīn of Ustrūshana. Cf. W.Tomaschek, 'Centralasiatische Studien', *SWAW*, LXXXVII (1877), p. 142.
39 On the conquest of Samarqand see A.N.Kurat, 'Kuteyba bin Müslim'in ve Semerkandi Zapti', *Ankara Üniversitesi Dil ve Tarih-Coğrafya Fakültesi Dergisi*, VI (1948), pp. 385–430, with an English summary.
40 Cf. especially J.Marquart, *Die Chronologie der alttürkischen Inschriften* (Leipzig 1898), and T.Houtsma's review of this book in the *Göttingische Gelehrten Anzeiger* (1899), V, esp. pp. 386–8; W.Barthold, 'Die alttürkischen Inschriften und die arabischen Quellen', in W.Radloff, *Die alttürkischen Inschriften der Mongolei* (St Petersburg 1896).
41 Ṭabarī, series II, pp. 1256–7; Balādhurī, p. 422.
42 See W.Barthold, *Turkestan Down to the Mongol Invasion* (London 1928), p. 187.
43 Balādhurī, p. 424.
44 Ṭabarī, series II, p. 1253, 1290.
45 Balādhurī, p. 438. On the conquests in Sind see F.Gabrieli, 'Muḥammad ibn Qāsim ath-Thaqafī and the Arab Conquest of Sind', *East and West* (Rome 1965), XV, pp. 281–95.
46 Balādhurī, p. 300, and for other sources see M.Sprengling, 'From Persian to Arabic', *American Journal of Semitic Languages*, LVI (1939), p. 178, cf. Jahshiyārī, p. 38.
47 See J.Walker, *A Cataloge of the Arab-Byzantine and Post-Reform Umaiyad Coins* (London 1956), introduction liii; also W.Hinz, *Islamische Masse und Gewichte* (Leiden 1955), pp. 1–2.
48 On the life of Ḥajjāj, see the article by A.Dietrich in the *Encyclopaedia of Islam* (new edn), and his biography by I.Périer, *La vie d'al-Ḥadjdjâdj Ibn Yousouf* (Paris 1904). See also Wellhausen, p. 157.
49 Tabarī, series II, p. 1054; Wellhausen, pp. 145–53; also Bosworth, pp. 55–61.
50 Ṭabarī, series II, p. 1089.
51 See the article on al-Mukhtār in the *Ency. of Islam* (new edn).
52 Balādhurī, pp. 335–8; Ṭabarī, series II, pp. 1317ff.
53 Ya'qūbī, *Ta'rīkh*, II, p. 302, and many other sources.
54 Ibn al-Jauzī, *Sīrat 'Umar ibn 'Abd al-'Azīz* (Cairo 1331/1913), pp. 88–9.

55 Wellhausen, pp. 175–94, is still the best summary of 'Umar's attempts to reform.

56 Baldāhurī, p. 426; Ṭabarī, series II, p. 1354, who says the *mawālī* in the army of Khurasan were 20,000 strong.

57 According to Ya'qūbī, *Ta'rīkh*, II, p. 306, 'Umar abolished the *norūz* and *mihrajān* gifts, which had held sway even among Muslims up till then. They were later re-introduced under Yazīd II.

58 Chavannes, pp. 164 and 204.

59 Yu. Yakubov, 'K voprosu o vremeni pravleniya Devaštiča v Sogdom', *Izvestiya Otd. Obsh. Nauk A. N. Tadzhikskoi SSR*, series I (51) (1968), pp. 77–83.

60 On these events see the chapter of Kratchkovskii in the book *Sogdiskii Sbornik* (Leningrad 1934); Ṭabarī, series II, pp. 1436ff. On the capture of Devashtich see Ṭabarī, series II, p. 1448. The Sogdian documents, and one Arabic letter written on goat skin, were found in a mound near the village of Khairabad about 120 km. east of Samarqand where the River Kum and the Zarafshan join.

61 Ṭabarī, series II, pp. 1364–5.

62 Ṭabarī, series II, p. 1472; Balādhurī, p. 428; Wellhausen, p. 283.

63 See H.A.R.Gibb, *The Arab Conquests in Central Asia* (London 1923), pp. 65–6.

64 Ṭabarī, series II, pp. 1501–3.

65 Ṭabarī, series II, p. 1508.

66 Ṭabarī, series II, p. 1518; Ibn Āthīr, V, p. 112.

67 Ṭabarī, series II, p. 1543.

68 Ṭabarī, series II, p. 1545; Balādhurī, p. 429.

69 Narshakhī, p. 59.

70 Ṭabarī, series II, p. 1490; *Faḍā'il-i Balkh*, in C.Schefer, *Chrestomathie persane* (Paris 1891), I, p. 71, or MS. Leningrad, Persian, C 753P (3088), fol. 218a.

71 Narshakhī, pp. 61–2; Ṭabarī, series II, pp. 1693–4.

72 See Ṭabarī, series II, pp. 1694–5.

73 The best account of the events in Khurasan is still to be found in Wellhausen, pp. 300–52.

74 For a survey of the Kharijite activities in Seistan with references to sources, cf. Bosworth, pp. 73–5.

75 'Biyābānak: The Oases of Central Iran', *The Central Asian Journal*, V (1960), pp. 188–9.

76 Balādhurī, p. 314.

77 Balādhurī, p. 417.

78 Ṭabarī, series II, p. 1207. A *farsakh* was probably here *c.* 6 km.

79 Ṭabarī, series II, pp. 6–8; Dīnawarī, p. 363.

80 The famous poet Bashshār b. Burd praised the people of Tokharistan, his homeland, for having more knights and greater bravery than others. The *Kitāb al-aghānī* has much on Bashshār.

81 *Ta'rīkh-i Sīstān*, p. 82; Narshakhī, p. 49. Abū Muslim called his Arab opponents 'devils', according to Ibn al-Athīr, V, p. 141.

82 *Ta'rīkh-i Qum*, pp. 254–6, 262.

83 Ṭabarī, series II, p. 1228 in Shumān.

84 Balādhurī, pp. 396 and 418.
85 Balādhurī, p. 392.
86 Ibn Isfandiyār, p. 78.
87 V.A.Livshits, *Sogdiiskie Dokumenty s gory Mug*, II, *Yuridicheskie Dokumenty i Pisma* (Moscow 1962), p. 89, *p'rsyk cp'yš*.
88 Ṭabarī, series II, p. 1518.
89 V.A.Livshits, *Sogdiiskie Dokumenty*, p. 181, A-5 lines 14–5.
90 W.Sundermann and T.Thilo, 'Zur mittelpersisch-chinesischen Grabinschrift aus Xi'an', *Mitteilungen des Instituts für Orientforschung* (Berlin 1966), XIII, p. 440.
91 E.g. Ṭabarī, series II, p. 393, for the year 680 when many Persians were brought east from Basra.
92 In Narshakhī, p. 48, for example, where 'Persian' is confused with 'Sogdian', or p. 16 where Persians are understood as west Iranians.
93 Kremer, p. 64; *Iqd*, III, p. 90.
94 Goldziher, *Muh. Studien*, I, p. 114, referring to the *'Iqd al-farīd*.
95 Ṭabarī, series II, p. 1767.
96 Ṭabarī, series II, p. 1462, 12, and 1688.
97 Ibn al-Athīr, V, p. 113.
98 Spuler, p. 249.
99 Ṭabarī, series II, p. 394, line 18.
100 *Ibid.*, p. 489, line 4.
101 Ṭabarī, series II, p. 1508; Abu Nu'aim, I, p. 9.
102 Ṭabarī, series II, p. 1636.
103 Ṭabarī, series II, p. 1022, line 9.
104 H.Masson, *Arabica*, XIV, p. 199.
105 Narshakhī, pp. 15–16, 20.
106 V.A.Livshits, *Sogdiiskie Dokumenty*, p. 37.
107 Livshits, glossary.
108 Narshakhī, p. 21 and p. 120 for further references.
109 Ṭabarī, series II, p. 1508, line 12.
110 The following books arrived after the manuscript of the present book was sent to the printers: M.A.Shaban, *The 'Abbasid Revolution* (Cambridge 1970); his *Islamic History A.D. 600–750 a New Interpretation* (Cambridge 1971); D.R.Hill, *The Termination of Hostilities in the Early Arab Conquests A.D. 634–656* (London 1971); T.Nagel, *Untersuchungen zur Entstehung des abbasidischen Kalifates* (Bonn 1972).

CHAPTER 6: THE 'ABBASIDS AND WESTERN IRAN

1 In Seistan, in the year 904 Arab tribes were fighting each other, according to the *Ta'rīkh-i Sīstān*, ed. M.Bahar (Tehran 1936), p. 276. In Juzjān an Arab tribe is found in the eleventh century according to the *Ḥudūd al-'Ālam*, trans. V.Minorsky, p. 108.
2 Ṭabarī, series II, p. 1507.
3 Cf. Dominique Sourdel, *Le vizirat 'Abbāside* (Damascus 1959), I, ch. 2. It must be emphasized that the inheritance from the Sasanians was in form and in style rather than direct and conscious borrowing.

4 Ira M.Lapidus, 'Muslim Cities and Islamic Societies', *Middle Eastern Cities* (California 1970), p. 64.
5 Lapidus, p. 64.
6 'Problèmes des mazdéens dans l'Iran musulman', *Festschrift für Wilhelm Eilers* (Wiesbaden 1967), pp. 220–30; and in his chapter on 'Zoroastrian Literature after the Muslim Conquest' in vol. IV of the *Cambridge History of Iran*. H.W.Bailey, *Zoroastrian Problems in the Ninth-Century Books* (Oxford 1943) where the problems are philological rather than historical.
7 For a good illustration of what happened in villages, compare the description of a recent closing of a fire temple in the Kirman region by M.Boyce, 'The Zoroastrian Villages of the Jūpār Range', *Festschrift für Wilhelm Eilers*, pp. 148–56.
8 The Arabic sources give us a picture of Fars at the time of the conquests, and it seems to be incomplete since, for example, the district of Qubād Khwarra, probably present-day Qīr and Karzīn is usually not mentioned. We do not know what administrative changes had been made in Fars by AD 900.
9 Ibn Balkhī, *Fārs nāme*, p. 117.
10 The *'āmil* (here just governor rather than tax-collector) of Kazerun in the time of Fakhr al-Daula was the head of the Zoroastrians there, called Khūrshīd but from Dailam in northern Iran. Cf. *Firdōs al-murshidiyya*, p. 155.
11 *Firdōs al-murshidiyya*, p. 155.
12 Muqaddasī, p. 440.
13 Ibn Ḥauqal, p. 273; Iṣṭakhrī, p. 118.
14 Recorded in an Arabic inscription in Kufic letters. Cf. Frye, *The Heritage of Persia*, p. 290, note 31.
15 Ibn Ḥauqal, pp. 257, 309, 446, and Iṣṭakhrī, p. 115.
16 Ibn Ḥauqal, p. 310.
17 Paul Schwarz, *Iran im Mittelalter*, part VII (Leipzig 1932), p. 858.
18 Muqaddasī, p. 394.
19 Schwarz, *Iran im Mittelalter*, part IV, p. 471.
20 Ya'qūbī, *Kitāb al-buldān* (BGA), pp. 272, 276–8.
21 Ibn Ḥauqal, p. 370.
22 By the end of the tenth century, however, north of Kashan Zoroastrian villages were so rare that Ibn Ḥauqal, p. 404, specifically mentions one which remained in the ancient faith.
23 *Abu Dulaf's Travels in Iran*, ed. and trans. by V.Minorsky (Cairo 1955), p. 52.
24 Yāqūt, *Irshād*, I, p. 173; also his *Mu'jam al-buldān, sub Adharbaijān*; Schwarz, *Iran im Mittelalter*, part VIII, pp. 1217–18.
25 Schwarz, part VIII, pp. 1005, 1007.
26 Schwarz, pp. 1024–5, 1056, 1183.
27 Schwarz, p. 1093.
28 Schwarz, pp. 1232–3.
29 *A History of Sharvān and Darband* (Cambridge 1958), pp. 56–65.
30 The best survey is by Ziya Buniyatov, *Azerbaidzhan v. VII–IX vv.* (Baku 1965), 380 pp. with a good bibliography.

31 The best account of Babak, with ample bibliography is by Buniyatov, *Azerbaidzhan*, pp. 223–70. See also Gholam Hossein Sadighi, *Les mouvements religieux Iraniens* (Paris 1938), pp. 229–80. The chapter by W.Madelung on minor dynasties in northern Iran in the forthcoming *Cambridge History of Iran*, IV, is a useful summary.

32 Balādhurī, p. 335.

33 Balādhurī, pp. 337–8.

34 Balādhurī, as reported in Ibn al-Faqīh, p. 303 (not in the text of Balādhurī himself), and Ibn Rusta, p. 149.

35 John Walker, *A Catalogue of the Arab-Sassanian Coins* (London 1941), intr., p. lxxv.

36 An account of the trial is given in E.G.Browne, *A Literary History of Persia* (London 1909), I, pp. 330–6.

37 Cf. Vladimir Minorsky, *La domination des Dailamites* (Paris 1932), p. 14.

38 Cf. H.L.Rabino, 'Rulers of Gilan', *JRAS* (1918), pp. 85–100, and (1920), pp. 277–96.

39 Ṣadiq Kiyā, *Vāzhe nāme-yi Ṭabarī* (Tehran 1938), p. 247.

40 E.Herzfeld, 'Postsasanidische Inschriften', *Archaeologische Mitteilungen aus Iran*, part IV (1932), p. 143 (Rādkān), and André Godard, 'Les tours de Ladjim et Resget', *Athār-é Īrān*, I (1936), p. 115.

41 John Walker, *A Catalogue of the Arab-Sassanian Coins* (London 1941), pp. 112–113. See also C.E.Bosworth, *Sīstān under the Arabs* (Rome 1968), p. 47.

42 Bosworth, p. 92.

43 Cf. G.Scarcia, 'Sulla religione di Zābul', *Annali dell'Istituto Orientale di Napoli*, XV (1965), pp. 122–4. Whether the deity Zun is related to the sun god of Multan, as proposed by Marquart, 'Das Reich Zabul', p. 262, is uncertain.

44 On the coinage see Robert Göbl, *Dokumente zur Geschichte der iranischen Hunnen* (Wiesbaden 1967), II, pp. 93–4, 322, and Helmut Humbach, *Baktrische Sprachdenkmäler* (Wiesbaden 1966), I, index. The Turks were probably Khalaj Turks.

45 Ṭabarī, series III, p. 634, and al-Jahshiyārī, *Kitāb al-wuzarā' wa'l-kuttāb* (Cairo 1938), p. 192. It is interesting to note that Kabul seems to have been the centre of the entire eastern Afghan area. Ibn Ḥauqal (p. 450) tells us that every Shahi king must come to Kabul to be crowned according to ancient rules which were still preserved in his day. See also S.Maqbul Ahmad, *India and the Neighbouring Territories in Idrisi* (Leiden 1960), p. 67.

46 Cf. *Répertoire chronologique d'épigraphie arabe* (Cairo 1931), I, nos. 100 and 116, pp. 81 and 93, and the chronicle of the city of Mecca by al-Azraqī, ed. F.Wüstenfeld (Leipzig 1858), I, pp. 158, 168.

47 Janos Harmatta, 'New Evidences for the History of Early Medieval Northwestern India', *Acta Antiqua Hungaricae*, XIV (1966), p. 461.

48 Cf. Ignace Goldziher, *Muslim Studies*, trans. S.M.Stern (London 1967), and H.A.R.Gibb, 'The Social Significance of the Shū'ūbiya', *Studia Orientalia Ioanni Pedersen dicata* (Copenhagen 1953), pp. 105–14.

49 Goldziher, *Muslim Studies*, pp. 163, 191.

50 *Dīwān*, ed. Naṣrallāh Taqawī (Tehran 1961), p. 263, line 12.

51 Gibb, 'The Social Significance of the Shū'ūbiya', p. 108.

52 Jāhiẓ, I, p. 368.
53 Johann Fück, *'Arabīya*, trans. C.Denizeau (Paris 1965), esp. pp. 44–176.
54 Jāhiẓ, I, pp. 141–4.
55 Cf. H.A.R.Gibb, *Arabic Literature* (London 1926), p. 69.

CHAPTER 7: HERESIES AND THE OECUMENE OF ISLAM

1 Jāhiẓ, *Al-Bayān wa'l-tabyīn* (Cairo 1380/1960), III, p. 366.
2 Cf. C.Cahen, 'Points de vue sur la "Révolution 'abbāside" ', *Revue Historique*, part 468 (1963), p. 324.
3 G.H.Sadighi, *Les mouvements religieux iraniens au IIe et au IIIe siècle de l'hégire* (Paris 1938), p. 131.
4 The name is difficult to explain, perhaps 'protected by the god Zun (or Sun)', rather than 'protected by a dog'.
5 G.H.Sadighi, *Les mouvements religieux*, p. 149.
6 Cf. T.K.Kadyrova, 'K izucheniyu kharaktera vosstaniya Yusufa al-Barma', *Obshchestvennye Nauki v Uzbekistane* (Tashkent 1964), I, pp. 46–50.
7 The most detailed account of Muqanna' appears in Narshakhī, pp, 65–76 and notes.
8 See B.Spuler, pp. 61 and 202.
9 See Sadighi, p. 191.
10 Muqaddasī, p. 37.
11 See Sadighi, p. 202.
12 Cf. C.Colpe, 'Der Manichäismus in der arabischen Überlieferung' (unpublished PhD dissertation, Göttingen 1954), p. 148, and G.Vajda, 'Les zindiqs en pays d'Islam au début de la période abbasside', *Rivista degli Studi Orientali* (Rome 1937), XVII, pp. 173–229.
13 Vajda, pp. 171ff., quoting Ṭabarī, series III, p. 499.
14 Trans. H.Darke (New Haven 1960), p. 213.
15 M.Molé, 'Le problème des sectes zoroastriennes dans les livres pehlevis', *Oriens*, XIII–XIV (1960–1), p. 20.
16 When one reads in the sources that a certain town or village was inhabited by Mazdakites, as Yāqūt, III, p. 569 of Darkazīn near Hamadan, it is by no means certain what is meant.
17 Cf. F.Gabrieli, *Al-Ma'mūn e gli 'Alidi* (Leipzig 1929), esp. pp. 38–50.
18 E.L.Rapp, *Die Jüdisch-Persisch-Hebräischen Inschriften aus Afghanistan* (Munich 1965), and W.B.Henning, 'The Inscriptions of Tang-i Azao', *BSOAS* (1957), pp. 335–42.
19 See the works of W.J.Fischel, such as 'Israel in Iran', in L.Finkelstein, *The Jews* (New York 1949), pp. 818–20.
20 Cf. M.Boyce, 'Bībī Shahrbānū and the Lady of Pārs', *BSOAS*, XXX (1967), pp. 21–8.
21 Personal communication of Aḥmad Iqtidārī.
22 For example Ya'qūbī, *Kitāb al-buldān*, p. 294 (Nishapur, p. 278; Herat, p. 280).
23 Cf. A.K.S.Lambton, *Landlord and Peasant in Persia* (Oxford 1953), p.25.
24 *Ta'rīkh-i Sīstān*, p. 156; Ṭabarī, series III, pp. 638, 658; Ibn al-Athīr, V, p. 143.

25 The Histories of Nishapur, ed. R.N.Frye (The Hague 1965), fol. 40a of *Kitāb aḥvāl-i Nīshāpūr.*
26 The twelfth *imām,* Muḥammad al-Mahdī, vanished in 878 in Samarra and he is the awaited messiah of the 'Twelvers', who expect his return.
27 Cf. S.M.Stern, 'The Early Isma'īlī Missionaries in North-west Persia and in Khurāsān and Transoxiana', *BSOAS,* XXIII (1960), pp. 56–90.
28 Yāqūt, I, p. 416.
29 Ibn Faqīh, pp. 246–7.
30 Ibn al-Athīr, under the year 369.
31 This story is found in an anonymous, incomplete manuscript in private possession in Baghdad, and this section is called *Nuskha manshūr kutub li-majūs* [*sic!*], for which I wish to thank Dr Donahue, formerly head of al-Hikma University.
32 Cf. F.Meier, *Die Vita des Scheich Abū Isḥāq al-Kāzarūnī* (Leipzig 1948), pp. 20–2 and *passim.*
33 Cf. J.J.Modi, *Dastur Bahman Kaikobad and the Kisseh-i Sanjan* (Bombay 1917), and S.H.Hodivala, *Studies in Parsi History* (Bombay 1920), esp. pp. 1–36.
34 W.Sundermann and T.Thilo, 'Zur mittelpersisch-chinesischen Grabinschrift aus Xi'an', *Mitteilungen des Instituts für Orientforschung,* XI (1966), p. 440.
35 See Yāqūt, I, p. 517.

CHAPTER 8: IRANIAN CONTRIBUTIONS TO ISLAMIC CULTURE

1 F.Rosenthal, trans., *Ibn Khaldûn, The Muqaddimah* (New York 1958), III, pp. 311–15; III, pp. 271–4 of Arabic edn. (A few changes in the translation have been made.)
2 See al-Jahshiyārī, *Kitāb al-wuzarā' w'al-kuttāb,* ed. Muṣṭafā al-Saqqā (Cairo 1938), p. 38.
3 Al-Jahshiyārī, p. 67.
4 For references to Arabs speaking Persian see M.Sprengling, 'From Persian to Arabic', *The American Journal of Semitic Languages and Literatures,* LVI (1939), p. 183, and LVII (1940), p. 327.
5 E.G.Jāhiz, *Fī manāqib al-Turk,* ed. G. van Vloten, *Tria opuscula* (Leiden (1903), p. 43.
6 The problem with the Arabic etymology is the paucity of word formations from a root *wzr,* and the meaning of the word would be 'helper'. The problem with the Iranian etymology is that the word has an abstract meaning of 'decision, judgement', and for an office of 'judge' or 'decider', one would expect a *-bad* or *-kār* ending in Middle Persian. Hardly from *vāze-bar* 'word bearer', according to W.Lentz, 'Die nordiranische Elemente in der neupersischen Literatursprache', *Zeitschrift für Indologie und Iranistik,* IV (1926), p. 305. As suggested above, perhaps we have a conflation of an Arabic and an Iranian word.
7 See D.Sourdel, *Le vizirat 'Abbāside,* 2 vols (Damascus 1960), esp. pp. 699–723.
8 Al-Jahshiyārī, pp. 316–17, where the scene is described.

9 Cf. Sourdel, p. 585 and *passim*.
10 W.Eilers, 'Iranisches Lehngut im arabischen Lexikon', *Indo-Iranian Journal*, v (1962), pp. 212–13.
11 Eilers, pp. 225–8, for a discussion of words such as *askadār* 'postal official', *sirdār* 'general', and others.
12 Cf. M.Grignaschi, 'Quelques spécimens de la littérature sassanide conservés dans les bibliothèques d'Istanbul', *JA* (1966), pp. 1–142.
13 See Ghazālī's *Counsel for Kings*, trans. F.R.C.Bagley (Oxford 1964), p. xii, where further references are given.
14 *Fihrist*, pp. 118, 242 *et passim*; also M.Mohammadi, *La traduction des livres pehlevis en arabe* (Beirut 1964), in Arabic.
15 G.W.Björkman, *Beiträge zur Geschichte der Staatskanzlei im islamischen Aegypten* (Hamburg 1928), p. 2.
16 Björkman, p. 4, and T.Nöldeke, *Geschichte der Perser und Araber zur Zeit der Sasaniden* (Leiden 1879), p. 354, note 2.
17 A.Mez, *Die Renaissance des Islams* (Heidelberg 1922), pp. 68–73.
18 Quoted from A.Bausani, 'Religion in the Saljuq Period', *Cambridge History of Iran* (Cambridge 1968), v, p. 285.
19 Cf. A.Bausani, *Persia Religiosa* (Milan 1959), pp. 138–47.
20 Muqaddasī, p. 440.
21 Muqaddasī, p. 32.
22 Bausani, *Persia Religiosa*, pp. 166–71, and S.Moscati, 'Per una storia dell'antica šī'a', *Rivista degli Studi Orientali* (Rome 1955), XXX, p. 251.
23 I.Goldziher, 'The Influence of Parsism on Islam', in *The Religion of the Iranian Peoples*, ed. C.P.Tiele, trans. G.K.Nariman (Bombay 1912), pp. 170–3.
24 Cf. M.M.Sharif, *A History of Muslim Philosophy* (Wiesbaden 1963), I, p. 354.
25 M.Horten, *Indische Strömungen in der islamischen Mystik*, 2 parts (Heidelberg 1927–8).
26 Abd-al-Raḥmān Jāmī, *Nafahāt al-uns*, ed. W.Nassau Lees (Calcutta 1859), *sub* Bayazid; Farīd ad-Dīn 'Aṭṭār, *Tadhkirat al-auliyā*, ed. R.A. Nicholson (London 1905), *sub* Bayazid.
27 Cf. S.H.Nasr, *Three Muslim Sages* (Cambridge, Mass. 1964), p. 9 and note 1.
28 Somewhat exaggerated in H.Corbin, *Les motifs zoroastriens dans la philosophie de Sohrawardi* (Tehran 1946).
29 Cf. 'Abbās Iqbāl, *Khānadān-i Naubakhtī* (Tehran 1933), pp. 2–3, 13, on the literary activities of the family.
30 Cf. C.Elgood, *A Medical History of Persia* (Cambridge 1951), p. 173.
31 Cf. D.G.Shepherd and W.B.Henning, 'Zandanījī Identified', *Aus der Welt der islamischen Kunst, Festschrift für E. Kühnel* (Berlin 1959), pp. 15–40, where further references are given.
32 R.B.Serjeant, 'Material for a History of Islamic Textiles up to the Mongol Conquest', *Ars Islamica* (Washington DC 1951), XV–XVI, p. 73.
33 *Kitāb al-tanbīh*, trans. B.Carra de Vaux (Paris 1896), p. 93. The text has *mulūk al-umam min al-a'ājim*, lit. 'kings of the non-Arab peoples'.
34 A.Z.Velidi Togan, *Ibn Faḍlān's Reisebericht* (Leipzig 1939), p. 110.

35 Cf. J.A.Haywood, *Arabic Lexicography* (Leiden 1960), pp. 11–19, for early grammarians.
36 Cf. J.Fück, *'Arabīya*, trans. C.Denizau (Paris 1955), p. 13.
37 Ibn Quṭaiba, *Al-Shi'r wa'l-shu'arā'*, ed. M.J. de Goeje (Leiden 1904), p. 447.
38 Jāhiẓ, *Al-bayān wa'l-tabyīn* (Cairo 1380/1960), I, p. 368.
39 *Yatīmat al-dahr* (Damascus n.d., *c.* 1880), IV, p. 15.
40 Al-Mubarrad, *al-Kāmil*, ed. Muḥ. al-Faḍl Ibrahīm (Cairo 1376/1956), III, p. 179.
41 *Yatīmat al-dahr*, III, p. 102, bottom, where a verse is given.
42 *Yatīmat al-dahr*, III, p. 129, line 17.
43 Information here taken from J.Fück, *'Arabīya*, p. 131 *passim*.
44 Muqaddasī, p. 32.
45 Jāhiẓ, *Al-bayān*, I, p. 143.
46 Jāhiẓ, pp. 141–2.
47 We follow the works of G.Lazard, such as his *Les premiers poètes persans* (Tehran-Paris 1964).
48 M.Boyce, 'The Parthian *gōsān* and Iranian Minstrel Tradition', *JRAS* (1957), pp. 10–45.
49 W.B.Henning, 'Persian poetical manuscripts from the time of Rūdakī', *A Locusts's Leg, Studies in honour of S. H. Taqizadeh* (London 1962), pp. 89–104.
50 *Ta'rīkh-i Sīstān*, ed. M.S.Bahār (Tehran 1936), p. 210.
51 G.Lazard, 'Âhu-ye kuhi . . . le chamois d'Abu Hafs de Sogdiane et les origines du robāi', *W. B. Henning Memorial Volume* (London 1970), pp. 238–44.

CHAPTER 9: ARTS AND CRAFTS

1 According to R.Ettinghausen, 'The Immanent Features of Persian Art', *The Connoisseur* (London, July 1966), pp. 2–3 (of offprint), 'The first special feature which must strike anybody who views an exhibition of Persian art, especially after having first visited the other sections of a museum containing Western art, is the recognition that basically the Iranian artist has an entirely different objective. Instead of primarily producing paintings, usually of rather large size, or statuary using the human figure, the Iranian artist through the ages has dedicated himself to the making and beautification of objects and in a majority of cases of objects for very specific uses in daily life.'
2 Various sources report the action of Yazīd. Cf. Leone Caetani, *Chronographia Islamica* (Paris 1921ff.), p. 1284.
3 A stimulating publication on these questions is O.Grabar, *The Formation of Islamic Art* (Yale University Press, New Haven 1973).
4 Cf. O.Grabar, *Sasanian Silver* (Ann Arbor 1967), pp. 35–6.
5 Cf. R.N.Frye, 'The Significance of Greek and Kushan Archaeology in the History of Central Asia', *Journal of Asian History*, I (1967), pp. 33–44.
6 As yet unpublished; see B.Gray, *Persian Painting* (London 1961), p. 15.
7 R.Ettinghausen, *Arab Painting* (London 1962), pp. 35–6.

8 D.Talbot Rice, 'The Expressionist Style in Early Iranian Art', *Ars Islamica*, v (1938), pp. 216–20.

9 C.K.Wilkinson, *Iranian Ceramics* (New York 1963), pp. 5–6.

10 C.K.Wilkinson, 'The Glazed Pottery of Nishapur and Samarkand', *Bulletin of the Metropolitan Museum of Art* (November 1961), pp. 106–10.

11 Cf. B.A.Litvinsky, *Outline History of Buddhism in Central Asia* (Moscow 1968), p. 69 and note 277.

12 See S.I.Rudenko, *Drevneishie v mire khudozhestvennye kovri i tkani* (The oldest decorated rugs and textiles in the world) Moscow 1968 (with English summary). The density of warp is 22–26 and in the woof 40–100 threads per centimetre, close to modern high standards.

13 R.Ettinghausen, 'The Flowering of Seljüq Art', *Metropolitan Museum Journal*, III (1970), pp. 113–31.

CHAPTER 10: THE IRANIAN DYNASTIES

1 I use the detailed book of Sa'īd Nafīsī, *Tarīkh-i Khānadān-i Ṭāhirī* (Tehran 1335/1957) for information about the Tahirids.

2 *Fragmenta Historicorum Abrabicorum, Kitāb al-'uyūn wa'l-hadā'iq*, ed. M.J. de Goeje (Leiden 1871), p. 363.

3 Cf. D.Sourdel, 'Les circonstances de la mort de Tahir Ier en Hurāsān', *Arabica*, v (1958), pp. 66–9.

4 Balādhurī, p. 430.

5 *Fragmenta*, p. 367; Ṭabarī, series III, pp. 1086–92.

6 V.Bartold, *K Istorii Orosheniya Turkestana* (St Petersburg 1914), p. 16; Ṭabarī, series III, p. 1326.

7 Mas'ūdī, *Murūj*, VII, p. 345.

8 Ṭabarī, series III, pp. 1046–61; Ibn al-Nadīm, *Fihrist*, p. 117.

9 E.G.Browne, ed., *The Lubabu'l-albab of Awfi* (London 1903), II, p. 2 also Browne's, *A Literary History of Persia* (London 1908), I, pp. 346–7.

10 Ḥasan b. M. Qumī, *Kitāb tārīkh Qum*, ed. Jalāl al-dīn Tehrānī (Tehran, 1313/1935), pp. 53, 39.

11 For the Saffarids see C.E.Bosworth, *Sīstān under the Arabs* (Rome 1968), T.Noeldeke, 'Yakub the Coppersmith and his Dynasty', in *Sketches from Eastern History* (London 1892), and W.Barthold, 'Zur Geschichte der Saffāriden', *Orientalische Studien zu T. Noeldeke gewidmet* (Giessen 1906), I, pp. 171–91.

12 The question of the extent of Ya'qub's conquests in Afghanistan is obscure. Cf. Bosworth, *Sīstān*, p. 120.

13 R.Vasmer, 'Über die Münzen der Saffāriden und ihrer Gegner in Fārs und Hurāsān', *Numismatische Zeitschrift*, LXIII (1930), pp. 133–4.

14 *Ta'rīkh-i Sīstān*, pp. 209–11.

15 Sources on the Samanids are few; here I follow the account of W.Barthold, *Turkestan down to the Mongol Invasion* (London 1928), pp. 222–68, and Narshakhi's *History of Bukhara*, trans. R.N.Frye (Cambridge, Mass. 1954).

16 A. von Rohr-Sauer, *Des Abû Dulaf Bericht über seine Reise nach Turkestân, China und Indien* (Stuttgart 1939), pp. 9, 40.

17 W.Barthold, *Zwölf Vorlesungen über die Geschichte der Türken Mittelasiens* (Berlin 1935), p. 79.
18 Cf. R.N.Frye, *Notes on the Early Coinage of Transoxiana* (New York 1949).
19 The best survey is to be found in *Istoriya Tadzhikskogo Naroda* (Moscow 1964), II, pp. 175–83, 210–19.
20 On Azerbaijan and the Caucasus region in this period see V.Minorsky, *A History of Sharvān and Darband* (Cambridge 1958), and Zia Bunyatov, *Azerbaidzhan v 7–9 vv.* (Baku 1965).
21 Ibn Miskawaih, I, p. 82; Ibn al-Athir, VIII, p. 99.
22 Muqaddasī, p. 395, and F.Meier, ed., *Die Vita des Scheich Abū Ishāq al-Kāzarūnī* (Leipzig 1948), p. 266.
23 On the Boyids see M.Kabir, *The Buwayhid Dynasty of Baghdad* (Calcutta 1964), and H.Busse, *Chalif und Grosskönig, die Buyiden im Iraq* (Beirut 1969), with a comprehensive bibliography.
24 G.Wiet, *Soieries persanes* (Cairo 1948).
25 Cf. G.Miles, 'A Portrait of the Buyid Prince Rukn al-Dawlah', *Museum Notes of the American Numismatic Society* (New York 1964), XI, pp. 283–93, and plates 45–7.

CHAPTER II: TURKISH ASCENDANCY

1 R.N.Frye, ed., *The Histories of Nishapur* (The Hague 1965), Persian text, fol. 12b, lines 15–16.
2 Cf. Ya'qūbī, *Buldān*, p. 259, and the translation by G.Wiet, *Les Pays* (Cairo 1937), p. 50, where further references are given.
3 Ṭabarī, series II, p. 1613, speaking of the year 119/737. Cf. R.N.Frye, 'J̌amūq, Sogdian "pearl" ', *JAOS*, LXXI (1951), 142–5.
4 Ibn Miskawaih, II, pp. 202, 222–7, trans. V, pp. 216, 234–41; Ibn al-Athīr, VIII, p. 421.
5 Gardīzī, *Kitāb zain al-akhbār*, intr. by M. Qazwini (Tehran 1937), pp. 65, 80.
6 Cf. Sam'ānī, fol. 548b. *sub* Mikālī, also in the *Tārikh-i Baihaq*, and the histories of Nishapur.
7 For symposia on cities see I.M.Lapidus, *Muslim Cities in the Later Middle Ages* (Cambridge, Mass. 1967), and various books of symposia on the Islamic city, such as I.M.Lapidus, ed., *Middle Eastern Cities* (Berkeley, California 1969).
8 On the Ghaznavids see M.Nāzim, *The Life and Times of Sultān Mahmūd of Ghazna* (Cambridge 1931), and C.E.Bosworth, *The Ghaznavids* (Edinburgh 1963).
9 On the Qarakhanids see O.Pritsak, 'Von den Karluk zu den Karachaniden', *ZDMG*, CI (1951), pp. 270–300, and his 'Die Karachaniden', XXXI, *Der Islam* (Hamburg 1954), pp. 1–68.
10 Cf. M.F.Köprülü, 'Les institutions juridiques turques au moyen-age', *II*e *Congrès Turc d'histoire* (Istanbul 1937), pp. 5–42, where other references are given.
11 E.G.Browne, ed., *The Tadhkiratu 'sh-shu'ara' of Dawlatshah* (London 1901), p. 32, *sub* Rudaki.

12 Cf. O.Pritsak, 'Āl-i Burhān', *Der Islam* (Berlin 1952), xxx, pp. 81–96.
13 On Nishapur see R.Bulliet, 'The Social History of Nishapur in the Eleventh Century', PhD thesis at Harvard University 1967, a revised study of which is now being printed by the Harvard University Press.
14 E.g. Ibn al-Athīr, IX, pp. 266–73.
15 Cf. C.Cahen, 'L'évolution de l'iqta' du IXe au XIIIe siècle', *Annales, économies, sociétés, civilisations* (Paris 1953), VIII, pp. 25–52.
16 On the origin of the *madrasa* I have drawn upon Aydin Sayili, 'The Institutions of Science and Learning in the Moslem World', unpublished PhD thesis Harvard University 1941.
17 A.K.S.Lambton, 'The Internal Structure of the Saljuq Empire', *Cambridge History of Iran*, v (1968), pp. 214–17.

CHAPTER 12: THE HERITAGE OF THE ARABS

1 In the introduction to his *Kitāb al-saidanā*, text and trans. in M. Meyerhofer, 'Das Vorwort zur Drogenkunde des Bīrūnī', in *Quellen und Studien zur Geschichte der Naturwissenschaften und Medizin* (Berlin 1932), III, pp. 157–208, Arabic text, pp. 12–13. See also F.Krenkow, 'Al-Beruni', *Islamic Culture*, IV (1932), p. 530.
2 Meyerhofer, in *Quellen und Studien*, p. 42.
3 G.Lazard, 'Les emprunts arabes dans la prose persane du Xe au XIIe sièçle: apercu statisque', *Revue de l'école nationale des langues orientales* (Paris 1965), II, pp. 53–67, where further bibliography is given.
4 P.Humbert, *Observations sur le vocabulaire du Châhnâmeh* (Neuchatel 1953), 74 pages, where further bibliography is given.
5 G.M.Daudpota, *The Influence of Arabic Poetry on the Development of Persian Poetry* (Bombay 1934), pp. 33–4.
6 On the Arabs in northern Afghanistan see H.F.Schurmann, *The Mongols of Afghanistan* (The Hague 1962), pp. 101–4.
7 'Abd al-Ghafūr Ravān Farhādī, 'Notes sur le tableau des langues actuellement parlées en Afghanistan', *Akten des 24 Internationalen Orientalisten Kongresses*, ed. H.Franke (Wiesbaden 1959), p. 446.
8 G.Jarring, *On the Distribution of Turk Tribes in Afghanistan* (Lund 1939), index, *sub* Arab.
9 G.Tsereteli, 'The Arab Dialects in Central Asia', Papers presented by the Soviet delegation at the Twenty-third International Congress of Orientalists (Moscow 1954), p. 24. Cf. I.N.Vinnikov, 'Materialy po yazyku i folkloru Bukharskikh Arabov', *Sovetskoe Vostokovedenie*, VI (1949), pp. 120–45, and his book *Yazyk i folklor Bukharskikh arabov* (Moscow 1969), 359 pages, where further references may be found.

GENERAL BIBLIOGRAPHY

(BOOKS IN EUROPEAN LANGUAGES)

Bausani, A., *The Persians* (Elek Books, London 1971).
Frye, R.N., *Persia* (Allen Unwin, London 1968).

ARTS AND CRAFTS

Erdmann, K., *Oriental Carpets*, trans. C.G.Ellis (Universe Books, New York 1963).
Godard, A., *The Art of Iran* (Allen Unwin, London 1965).
Pope, A.U., *Introducing Persian Architecture* (Oxford University Press, 1969).
Wilkinson, C., *Iranian Ceramics* (Abrams, NY 1963).
Wulff, H., *The Traditional Crafts of Persia* (MIT Press, Cambridge, Mass. 1966).
The Survey of Persian Art, ed. A.U.Pope, 6 vols (Oxford University Press, 1938).

LITERATURE

Browne, E.G., *A Literary History of Persia*, 4 vols (Cambridge University Press, 1924 and many editions).
Rypka, J., *History of Iranian Literature*, ed. K.Jahn (Reidel, Dordrecht-Holland 1968).

THE PRE-ISLAMIC BACKGROUND OF IRAN AND CENTRAL ASIA

Christensen, A., *L'Iran sous les Sassanides* (Copenhagen 1944).
Frye, R.N., *The Heritage of Persia* (Weidenfeld and Nicolson, London 1962).
Hambly, G., *Central Asia* (Delacorte Press, New York 1969).

THE ARAB CONQUESTS

Gibb, H.A.R., *The Arab Conquests in Central Asia* (The Royal Asiatic Society, London 1923).
Hill, D.R., *The Termination of Hostilities in the Early Arab Conquests A.D. 634–656* (Luzac, London 1971).

Shaban, M.A., *The ʿAbbāsid Revolution* (Cambridge University Press, 1970).
Wellhausen, J., *The Arab Kingdom and Its Fall*, trans. M.G.Muir (University of Calcutta Press, 1927).

ISLAMIC IRAN AND CENTRAL ASIA DOWN TO THE SELJÜKS

Barthold, W., *Turkestan down to the Mongol Invasion*, ed. C.Bosworth (Luzac, London 1968).
The Cambridge History of Iran, ed. R.N.Frye, vol 4 (Cambridge University Press, 1975).
Spuler, B., *Iran in früh-islamischer Zeit* (Steiner Verlag, Wiesbaden 1952).

IRAN FROM THE MONGOL INVASION TO THE PRESENT

Avery, P., *Modern Iran* (Benn, London 1967).
The Cambridge History of Iran (Cambridge University Press), vols 5, 6, and 7.
Hinz, W., *Irans Aufstieg zum Nationalstaat* (de Gruyter, Berlin 1936).
Lockhart, L., *The Fall of the Safavid Dynasty and the Afghan Occupation of Persia* (Cambridge University Press, 1958).
Spuler, B., *Die Mongolen in Iran* (Akademie Verlag, Berlin 1968).

PRIMARY SOURCES

Abu Nu'aim: *Kitāb dhikr akhbār Iṣbahān*, ed. S. Dedering (Leiden 1931).
Balādhurī: *Futūḥ al-buldān*, ed. M.J. de Goeje (Leiden 1866).
Balādhurī: *Ansāb al-ashrāf*, ed. S.D.F.Goitein and M.Schloessinger (Jerusalem 1935, 1940).
BGA: Bibliotheca Geographorum Arabicorum, ed. M.J. de Goeje (Leiden).
Bīrūnī: *Āthār al-bāqiya*, ed. E.Sachau (Leipzig 1876), trans. (London 1879).
BSO(A)S: Bulletin of the School of Oriental (and African) Studies (London).
Chavannes: *Documents sur les Tou-kine (Turcs) Occidentaux* (Paris 1946).
Dīnawarī: *Kitāb al-akhbār al-ṭiwāl*, ed. V.Guirga 55 (Leiden 1888).
Firdaus al-murshidiyya: Abū Ishāq al-Kāzarūnī, ed. F.Meier (Leipzig 1948).
Goldziher: *Muhammedanische Studien*, 2 vols (Halle 1888–9).
Ibn Khurdādhbih: *Kitāb al-masālik al-mamālik*, BGA 6 (1889).
Ibn Athīr: *Al-Kāmil fī 'l-ta'rīkh*, ed. C.J.Tornberg (Leiden 1851–76).
Ibn Balkhī: *Fārs nāme*, ed. G. Le Strange (London 1921).
Ibn al-Faqīḥ: *Kitāb al-buldān*, BGA 5 (Leiden 1885).
Ibn Ḥauqal: *Kitāb al-masālik wa'l-mamālik*, ed. I.H.Kramers (Leiden 1939).
Ibn Isfandiyār: *Ta'rīkh-i Ṭabaristān*, ed. 'Abbās 'Iqbāl (Tehran 1942).
Ibn Khallikān: *Biographical Dictionary*, trans. W.M. de Slane (London 1842–71).
Ibn Qudāma: *Kitāb al-kharāj*, BGA 6 (1889).
Ibn Rusta: *Kitāb al-a'lāq an-nafīsa*, BGA 7 (Leiden 1892).
IIJ: Indo-Iranian Journal (The Hague).
Iṣṭakhrī: *Kitāb masālik al-manālik*, BGA 1 (Leiden 1870).
JA: Journal Asiatique (Paris).
Jahshiyārī: *Kitāb al-wuzarā' wa'l-kuttāb*, ed. Mustafā al-Saqā (Cairo 1938).
JAOS: Journal of the American Oriental Society (New Haven).
Khwārazmī: *Mafātiḥ al-'ulūm*, ed. G. van Vloten (Leiden 1895).
Kremer: *Culturgeschichte des Orients*, 2 vols (Vienna 1875–7).
Marquart: 'Das Reich Zabul und der Gott Zūn vom 6.–9.Jhdt.', *Festschrift Eduard Sachau* (Berlin 1915), pp. 248–92.
Mas'ūdī: *Murūj al-dhahab*, ed. C.A.Barbier de Meynard and M.Pavet de Courteille, 9 vols (Paris 1861–77).
Muqaddasī: *Kitāb aḥsan al-taqāsīm*, BGA 3 (Leiden 1906).
Narshakhī: *History of Bukhara*, trans. R.N.Frye (Cambridge, Mass. 1954).
Sam'anī: *Kitāb al-ansāb*, ed. D.S.Margoliouth (London 1912).

Schwarz: *Iran im Mittelalter*, 9 Hefte (Stuttgart and Berlin 1896–1936).
Spuler: *Iran in früh-islamischer Zeit* (Wiesbaden 1952).
SWAW: Sitzungsberichte der Wiener Akademie der Wissenschaften, Phil-Historische Klasse (Vienna).
Ṭabarī: *Ta'rīkh al-rusul wa'l-mulūk*, ed. M.J. de Goeje, 3 sections (Leiden 1879–1901).
Ta'rīkh-i Qum: Hasan b. M. Qumī, ed. Jalāl ad-dīn Ṭehranī (Tehran 1935).
Tha'ālibī: *Histoire des rois des Perses (ghurar akhbār)*, ed. H.Zotenberg (Paris 1900).
Tha'ālibī: *Yatīmat al-dahr*, 4 vols (Damascus n.d.).
Ya'qūbī: *Ta'rīkh*, 2 vols (Beirut 1960).
Yāqūt: *Mu'jam al-buldān*, ed. F.Wüstenfeld, 6 vols (Leipzig 1866–70).
Yāqūt: *Irshād al-arīb*, ed. D.S.Margoliouth, 7 vols (Leiden 1908–27).

APPENDIX I

1 The bibliography for Appendix I is the following: A.Siddiqi, *Studien über Persischen Fremdwörter im klassischen Arabisch* (Göttingen 1919), p. 118; A.Siddiqi, 'The letter q and its importance in Persian Loan-Words in Arabic', *Fourth All-India Oriental Congress* (Allahabad 1928), pp. 224–32; M.Kamil, 'Persian Words in Ancient Arabic', *Bulletin of the Faculty of Arts*, (Cairo, May 1957), XIX, pp. 56–67; W.Eilers, 'Iranisches Lehngut im arabischen Lexikon', *IIJ* (The Hague 1962), V, pp. 203–32; M.'Alī Imām Shūshtarī, *Farhang vāzhehā-yi Fārsī dar zabān-i 'arabī* (Tehran 1347/1969). They all use sources such as *Al-Mu'arrab* of al-Jawālīqī, ed. Aḥmad M.Shākir (Cairo 1361/1942), As-Suyūṭī, *Al-Muzharfī 'ulūm al-lugha*, (Cairo 1958), Ibn Duraid, and other authors, for whom cf. the bibliographies in the above writings.

2 Eilers, *op. cit.*, pp. 212–13, discusses this title fully.

INDEX

Diacritical marks have been applied consistently only to Arabic words. The Arabic definite article al- has been omitted in initial position. Some names, such as Samarra, have not been given in their Arabic forms. Consistency has not been maintained in the text with the Arabic article al-; thus Ḥajjāj or al-Ḥajjāj.

'Ayn

'Abbāsid, 16, 18, 20, 26, 88–9, 92–5, 97, 100, 104–7, 110, 112–16, 118–119, 121–9, 131–3, 135–6, 139, 140–2, 144, 147–8, 151, 153–6, 159, 163–4, 168, 171, 176–7, 179, 180, 186–8, 191–2, 194, 197–8, 200, 202, 206, 217, 224, 228
'abd, 55, 105
'Abdallāh b. 'Āmir b. Kuraiz, 66–7, 74–5
'Abdallāh b. Khāzim al-Sulamī, 75–6, 78–9
'Abdallāh b. Mu'āwiya, 93
'Abdallāh b. Ṭāhir, 117, 165, 189, 190, 192
'Abdallāh b. Umaiya, 78
'Abd al-'Azīz, 87, *see also* Sa'īd b. 'Abd al-'Azīz al-Ḥārith
'Abd al-'Azīz b. Abdallāh b. 'Āmir, 77
'Abd al-Azīz b. al-Walīd, 82
'Abd al-Ḥamīd (al-kātib), 153, 169
'Abd al-Hamīd Maḍrūb, 116
'Abd al-Malik, 16, 77–8, 83–6, 88, 138, 178
'Abd al-Malik b. Nūḥ, 205
'Abd al-Raḥman b. Muḥammad b. al-Ash'ath, 83
'Abd al-Mu'min b. Shabath, 85
'Abd al-Qais, 25
'Abd al-Raḥman b. Muslim, 80
'Abd al-Raḥman al-Nu'aim, 87
'Abd al-Raḥman b. Samura, 45, 72, 76
'Adnān, 76
'Aḍud al-daula, 111, 163, 204, 210, 212
'ā'ila, 104
'aiyar, 194
'Alī, 71–5, 136, 140, 143, 145
'Alī b. Bōyā, 209
'Alī b. al-Ḥusain b. Quraish, 196
'Alī b. 'Isā b. Māhān, 188, 202
'Alī b. Jahm, 192
'Alī b. Khālid al-Bardākht, 169
'Alī b. Mūsā b. Ja'far al-Riḍā, 136
'Alī b. Talḥa, 190
'Alī b. Wahsudān, 208
'Alī Ilāhī, 131
'Alī Tigīn, 224
'Alid, 201
'ālim, 123
'āmil, 70, 75, 106–7, 109, 152
'Amilī, Shaikh Bahā' al-Dīn, 234
'āmma, 54
'Anan b. David, 138
'aql, 160
'Aṣim b. 'Abdallāh, 89
'Asīr, 98
'Askar Mukram, 10
'aṭā, 62, 75
'Aṭṭār, Farīd al-Dīn, 159, 234
'Ijlī, 132
'Imād al-daula ('Alī), 208–9
'Irāq, 7, 15, 26, 55, 57–9, 61, 64, 69,

70, 76, 78, 83–5, 88, 92, 114, 116, 133, 137–8, 143, 150, 165, 176, 178–179, 181–3, 185, 187–9, 190–1, 197, 208, 210
'Iraqi Arabic, 235
'irfān, 160
'Izz al-daula, 210
'Ubaidallāh b. 'Abdallāh b. Abī'l-Haitham, 214
'Ubaidallāh b. Abī Bakra, 77
'Ubaidallāh b. Ziyād, 76, 169
'ulamā', 18, 152, 155, 202, 204–5, 215–16, 222, 228–9
'Umar, 57–9, 63–6, 106
'Umar II b. 'Abd al-Azīz, 86–8, 90–1, 93, 102
'Umar Khaiyām, 162, 174
'Ummānī, 124, 171
'Unṣurī, 226
'Utba b. Ghazwān, 59
'Uthmān, 64, 66–7, 71, 73, 76, 85
'Uthmān b. Abī'l-'Āṣ, 65
'Uyūn al-akhbār, 153

Abādān Pīrūz, 114, *see also* Shahrām Pērōz
Abrshahr, 66, *see also* Nishāpūr
Abū 'Abdallāh Muḥammad b. Karrām, 143
Abū 'Alī (Hindī), 159
Abū 'Alī Sīmjūrī, 204–5
Abu'l-Aswad al-Du'alī, 168
Abū Bakr, 55–7
Abū Dulaf, 113, 202
Abū Ḥanīfa, 139
Abū 'Isā, 138
Abū Isḥāq b. Alptigīn, 218
Abū Isḥāq al-Kāzerūnī, 110, 145
Abu Lahab, 155
Abū Ma'shar (Albumasar), 162
Abū Manṣur Ajlāh, 196
Abū Mūsā, 66
Abū Muslim, 92, 101, 127–9, 147
Abū Muslimiyya, 129
Abū Nuwās, 123
Abu'l-Qāsim b. al-Jarrāḥ, 171
Abū Salama, 151
Abu'l-Ṭaiyab al-Mus'abī b. Ḥātim, 169
Abū 'Ubaīd al-Ṭhaqafī, 57
Abū 'Ubaida, 122
Abū Ya'qūb Isḥaq b. Maḥmashādh, 143
Achaemenid, 1, 3, 4, 5, 9, 13, 18, 21, 24, 25, 32–3, 34, 45, 52, 67
adab, 20, 176
Adharbāijān, *see* Azerbāijān
Adhūrbad b. Marāsfand, 145
'Adī b. Zaid, 26
Adiabēnē, 15
adīb (*udabā'*), 202
Adjina tepe, 23, 30, 183
Adonis, 18
Afghan, 4, 92
Afghānistān, 27, 31, 44–5, 72, 76, 82, 93, 104, 120–1, 126, 138, 143, 181, 190, 195–6, 219, 235
Afrāsiyāb, 28, 41–2, 52, 182
Afrāzarūd (Apzāharūd), 113
Africa(n), 1, 91, 110, 139, 144, 150, 177, 186, 213
Afrīgh, 46
afshīn, 48
Afshīn (Ḥaidar, b. Kāūs), 48, 115, 117, 139, 189, 190
Aghdā, 141
Aghlabid, 187
ahl bait al-jamūkiyīn, 214
ahl al-kitāb, 135
Aḥmad, 209, *see also* Mu'izz al-Daula
Aḥmad (Ṣaffārid), 199
Aḥmad b. Abī Khālid, 189
Aḥmad b. 'Alī Sa'lūk, 208
Aḥmad b. Asad, 200
Aḥmad b. Ism'aīl, 199, 201
Aḥmad al-Jamī Zhīndapīl, 144
Aḥmad b. Tūlūn, 187
Aḥnaf b. Qais, 65
Ahriman, 96
ahrmōkīh, 134
Ahurā Mazdā, 134
Ahwāz (Sūq al-Ahwāz), 10, 11, 16, 59, 164
Airtam, 30
aiwān, 23, 183
Aiwān-i Karkhā, 11
Aiwān Kisrā, 8
Akcha, 235
Akharūn, 79
Akhsīkath ('γsyknδh), 49
Akkadian, 18, 33
Al-i Afrāsiyāb, 221
Al-i Burhān, 223
Alan, 15, 21
Albania(n), 12, 114–15
Aleppo, 133, 161

Alexander the Great, 3, 14, 19, 32–3, 42, 71, 184
Alexandria, 190
Alfraganus, *see* Farghānī
Alkhon, 38
Alp Arslān, 226–7
Alptigīn, 121, 204, 218–19
Altai, 49
Altaic, 37–9
Altuntāsh, 219
Amīda, 10
Amīn, 115, 188–9
amīr, 70, 72, 107, 144, 205, 210, 225
amīr al-umarā, 210
Ammianus Marcellinus, 38
'Amr b. 'Adī b. Zaid, 61
'Amr b. Laith, 197–9, 200
'Amr b. Muslim, 88
Amū Daryā, 27
Amul, 46, 97, 116–17
Anatolia, 1, 2, 32, 149, 205, 215, 229, 233
andarz, 20, 154
andarzbad, 17
'ndrčpty, 17
Andkhoi, 235
Anērān, 15
Anglo-Saxon, 4
Antiochus, 30
Anūshirvān, 18, 20
'*anwatan*, 63
Aqrābādhīn, 164
'Arab, *passim*
Arabaya, 24
Arabia, 24, 54, 57, 60, 137, 143, 165, 169, 177, 183, 193, 234
Arabian, 2
Arabic, 2, 4, 5, 8, 9, 12, 15–16, 18, 19, 21, 26, 33, 49, 172–5, 177, 179, 180–1, 186, 192–3, 203, 206–7, 210–11, 221, 225–6, 232–5
Arābistān, 24
Arachosia, 45, 57
Aral Sea, 28, 224
Aramaean, 59
Aramaic, 5, 16, 18, 19, 32–5, 38, 49
Aras River, 114
Ardashīr, 2, 4, 20, 36, 111
Ardashīr Khwarra, 10
Ardebīl, 12, 71, 109, 113
arq, 108
Arghandab, 195
Aria, 13
Aribi, 25
Armenia, 9, 12, 91, 113, 207–8, 215
Armenian, 9, 12, 17–18, 38, 65, 72, 106, 114–15, 180
Arrajān, 10, 111, 216
Arrān, 12, 114–15, 208, *see also* Albania
Arslān Ilik, 221
Arslān Qarā Khāqān, 221
Arslān Tigīn, 221
Arthamukh, 46
Aryan, 44
Asad, 24
Asad b. 'Abdallāh al-Qasrī, 88–9, 90, 98
Asad b. Sāmān, 200
asārā, 95
asāwira (*suwār*), 61, 66, 94
Aṣfaḥ b. 'Abdallāh al-Shaibānī, 93
A'shā, 26
Ash'arī (Abu'l-Ḥasan 'Alī), 131, 139, 155, 160
Ash'ath, 85, *see also* 'Abd al-Rahmān b. Muḥ
Ashīna, 214
Ashras b. 'Abdallāh al-Sulamī, 88–9, 102
Asia Minor, 213, *see also* Anatolia
askadār, 239
Askajamukh b. Azkajawar, 46, 81
Assassin, 143
Assyria, 1
Assyrian, 32
Aswad b. Karīma, 124
atash hamār difīra, 17
Athens, 22
Atropatēnē, 12, *see also* Azerbāijān
Attila, 37
atūr gushnasp, 114
aubāsh, 110
auqāf, 17
Averroes (Ibn Rushd), 160, 234
Avesta, 8, 44
Avestan, 8, 16, 33
Avicenna (Ibn Sīna), 160, 164, 225
Avroman, 34
awāz, 240
āyīn, 154
Azd, 61, 76, 78, 86, 88, 92, 98–9, 101, 166
Azerbāijān, 11, 12, 15, 60, 65, 70–1, 91, 110, 112–15, 130, 145, 156, 163, 189, 207–8, 214, 223, 225, 227

Azerī, 113–14
''ztk'r, 99

Bāb, 234
Bāb al-Abwāb, 12, *see also* Derbend
Bābak, 114–15, 130, 134, 139, 148, 189, 190
Babylonian, 32
Bactra, 13, 29
Bactria, 29, 30, 33–4, 44, 50–1, 155
Bactrian, 29, 34–5, 41, 79, 95, 100, 173, 180
Badakhshān, 29, 38
Bādghīs, 13, 51, 73, 75, 80, 129, 198
Bādhān, 214
bādhusbān, 13
Bādiya, 15
Baghdād, 20, 22–3, 70, 105, 107, 109, 115, 117–18, 122, 130, 135, 139, 141, 148, 156, 162–8, 178, 181, 186–9, 190, 192, 196, 201, 203, 208–9, 210, 217
Baghdādī, 131
Baghlān, 29
Bāhila(ī), 79, 94
Baḥrain, 26, 59
Bahrām V, 38
Bahrām Chōbīn, 200
Bahrām Sīs, 97
Baikand, 47, 80, 98
Baituz, 218
Bakhtiyārī, 111
Bakr b. Wā'il, 25, 56–7, 76–8, 93, 199
balad, 10, 108
Balādhurī, 60–1, 63–7, 74, 78, 81, 87, 94, 120
Balalyk tepe, 181
Bal'amī, Abu'l-Faḍl, 201
Bal'amī, Muḥammad b. Abū 'Alī, 202
Balkh, 13, 29, 30, 43–4, 51–2, 67, 72, 75, 88, 90, 100, 126–7, 138, 146, 152, 158–9, 162–3, 198, 216, 219, 226, 235
Balūch, 111–12
Balūchistān, 14, 31, 83, 219, 220
Balūṣ, 112
Bam, 112
Bāmiyān, 29, 30, 45, 196
bamm, 240
Banū Furāt, 199
Banī Ḥanẓala, 25
Banū'l-Jarrāḥ, 152, 199
Banū Mūsā, 162–3
Banū Rudainī, 113
Bannu, 121
Bāqillānī, Abū Bakr, 160
barbaṭ, 239
Barbud, 42
Bardā'a (Partav), 114–15, 119, 208
Bardashīr (Bardasīr), 112
Barhatigīn, 120
barīd, 106–7, 232
Barīdī, 209
Bāriẓ, 112
barmak, 51, 90
Barmecid, 107, 124, 127, 152, 188
Bārūqān, 88, 90, 146
barwāna, 18
Bashshār b. Burd, 123, 133
Baṣra, 15, 16, 57, 59, 60–2, 64–6, 69, 70–2, 74, 76, 83, 89, 95, 101, 122, 133, 151, 168–9
Basurman, 28
Bāvend, 117, 119
Bāyazīd (Abū Yazīd), 141, 158–9
Begram, 31, 45, 120
Behzād, 181
Bektuzun, 205
Benjamin, 138
Besermen, 28
Bēth Arbāya, 24
Bēth Lāpaṭ, 10
Bibi Shahrbānū, 140
Bibliothèque Nationale, 11
bid'a, 132
Bihāfrīd, 128–9, 134, 140
Bilgetigīn, 218
Birāmqubād, 10
Bīrūnī, 28, 43–4, 46, 50, 81, 122, 138, 162–3, 165, 169, 226, 232
Bīshāpūr, 8, 10, 110, 179, 181
Bisṭām, 141, 158–9
bitakhsh, 9
Biyābānak, 94
Bizāmqubād, 10
borch, 98
Böri, 218
Boyce, M., 140
Bōyid, 10, 110–11, 117, 145, 163, 175, 180, 185, 188, 193, 200–1, 204, 207, 209, 210–13, 215, 219, 220, 225, 227–9
Brahmi, 33
Brahmin, 121
Brahui, 14, 31, 52

Brγ'nk MLK', 49
Brγwm'n, 48
Britain, 184
British, 107, 146, 172
Budapest, 108
Buddha, 158, 176
Buddhism, 29, 30–1, 41–2, 44–5, 100–1, 126, 155, 165
Buddhist, 23, 28–9, 30, 41, 43–4, 45, 50–1, 90, 101, 127, 158–9, 176
Bugha, 208
Bughrā Ilik, 221
Bughrā Khān, 205
Bughrā Qarā Khāqān, 221
Bughrā Tigīn, 221
Bukair b. Wishāḥ, 98
Bukhārā, 27–8, 38, 40, 46–7, 52, 76, 80, 86–7, 89, 90–1, 93, 96, 98–9, 100, 102, 108–9, 118, 126–7, 144, 147, 155–6, 160, 166–7, 181, 183, 198, 200, 203–5, 211, 214, 216–18, 221ff.
Bukhārī, Muḥammad b. Isma'il, 156
Bukhtishū', 163–4
Bulghars, 167, 213
bum, 10
Bunjikath, 48, *see also* Panjikath
Burzūnāme, 21
Būshanj, 13, *see also* Fūshang
Bust, 76, 93, 119, 181, 195, 218
Buttam, 79
Buwaib, 57
Buwaihid, 10, *see also* Bōyid
Būzjānī, Abu'l-Wafā', 162
Byzantine, 7, 8, 12, 14, 24, 38, 42, 56, 58, 65, 72, 76, 84–5, 120, 131, 136, 149, 151, 154, 163, 175, 178, 180, 195, 198, 213, 215
Byzantium, 55, 85

Caesar, 20
Cahen, Claude, 62
Canon, 164
Caspian, 12, 14, 21, 108, 115–19, 174–5, 180, 191, 196–8, 201, 204, 208–9, 210–11, 224
Caucasus, 5, 12, 14, 15, 21, 65, 71, 96, 114–15, 120, 207
Central Asia, 5, 13, 15, 22, 25, 27, 30, 31–3, 35–6, 38–9, 40, 42–3, 46, 48–9, 50, 52, 68, 74, 82, 86–7, 89, 90, 93–6, 98–9, 100–1, 107, 110, 120, 125–7, 137–8, 147–9, 159, 166–7, 173, 176, 179, 182, 184, 190, 195, 201, 203ff.
Centum, 29, 31
Chāch, 28, 36, 49, 50, *see also* Shāsh
Chagāniyān, 29, 50, 79, 203, 219
chahār ṭāq, 183
Chalôns, 37
Chālūs, 117
chiliarch, 17
China, 3, 27–8, 39, 50, 67, 87, 96, 98, 137, 145, 166, 181–2, 201–2
Chinese, 38–9, 44–5, 49, 50, 67, 146, 181–2
Chinese Turkistān, 27–9, 31, 42, 44, 49, 50, 138, 173, 180, 203
Chionite, 38
Chisht, 30
Chosroes I, 4, 8, 9, 14–15, 18, 20, 26, 39, 42, 134, 163, 214
Chosroes II, 42, 52, 116
Christ, 1, 178
Christian, 17, 28, 41–4, 55–9, 61, 72, 87, 97, 105–6, 111–12, 136–9, 140, 143–4, 148, 158, 164, 173, 176, 178, 195, 216
Christianity, 1, 2, 25, 41, 44, 100–1, 111, 126, 131, 133–4, 137–8
Cid, 195
Cilicia, 195
Cimmerian, 31
Constantinople, 20
Crusader, 215
Crusades, 195, 215
Ctesiphon, 7, 8, 23, 56, 58–9, 178–9
Cyrus, 2, 4, 32

Ḍaḥḥāk b. Muẓāhim al-Khurāsānī, 170
Da'ī, 118
Daibul, 83
Dailam, 117–18
Dailamite, 12, 71, 118–19, 140, 142, 207–9, 210
Damascus, 20, 69, 72, 88, 91, 97, 146–7
Dandanaqān, 225
dang, 240
Daniel b. Moses, 138
Daqīqī, 202–3
dār, 104
dār al-ḥarb, 93, 120
dār al-Islām, 85, 120
dār al-Turk, 214

Darāb, 10, 22, *see also* Darābjird
Darābjird, 10, 66
darbzīn, 240
Dardic, 30, 31
Darī, 16, 99, 100, 173, 207, 213, 222, 232–3
Darius, 2, 4, 18, 67
dāstān, 21
dāta, 1
Dātastān nāmak, 21
d'twbly, 17
Daulatshāh, 222, 233–4
Dauraq, 11
dbyr, 239
Demāvand (Dunbāwand), 116–17, 183
De Menase, 109
Derbend, 12, 14, 114–15, 208
Dēvashtich, 87–8, 96, 99, 215
dhabr, 239
dhauq, 161
dhimmī, 55, 68, 97, 105, 145
Dhū Qār, 55
Dhu'l-yaminain, 188
dihqān, 7, 40, 63–4, 70, 73, 87, 95, 98, 102, 127, 135, 142, 154, 172, 185, 216, 227–8
dīnār, 84
Dīnawar, 11, 64–5, 113
Diogenes Akritas, 195
dipi-pāna, 152
dipīr, 202
dipīr-i vuzurg, 17
dipīrān māhist, 17
Dirham b. Naṣr, 195
dirhem, 65–6, 83–4, 206, 228
dīwān, 59, 62, 83, 99, 106–7, 151–2, 154
dīwān al-khātam, 154
Diyāla, 22
diz, 108
dlgwš'n, 17
Dravidian, 14, 31, 52
Dura Europos, 34
Dushanbe, 23, 30, 79, 183
dzwy (*dnwy*), 47

Edessa, 163
Egypt, 1, 19, 31–2, 69, 143–4, 153, 176, 180, 187, 190, 198, 229
Egyptian, 1, 2, 32, 213, 232
Elburz, 12, 71
English, 4, 5, 168
ethnos, 9
Euphrates, 24, 34, 57, 189
Eurasian, 24
Europe, 27–8, 37, 42, 77, 162, 164–5, 167, 175, 195, 206, 215, 231

fādhusbān, 9, 12
Faḍl b. Sahl, 115, 120, 123, 136, 152, 188
Fā'iq, 204–5
Fakhr al-daula, 170, 210
Fakhr al-mulk, 110
fals, 206
fanā', 159
Far East, 4, 49, 110
Fārābī, 160
Farāhān, 145
Farghānī, Abu'l-'Abbās Aḥmad b. Muḥammad, 163
Farhangistān-i Irān, 233
Fārisī, 150
farn, 8
farr, 8
farrah, 8
Farrūkhmāhān, 26
Farrukhī Sīstānī, 226
Fārs, 8, 9, 10–11, 22, 25, 35, 44, 53, 65–6, 70–2, 78, 84, 92, 100, 109, 110–15, 119, 126, 145, 173, 191, 196, 198–9, 209
Fārs nāme, 73
farsakh, 95
Farsī, 232–3
farwāniq, 18
Faryāb, 81
Fasā, 22
fata, 195
Fāṭimid, 136, 143–4, 153, 229
fattash, 9
Fazārī, Muḥammad b. Ibrāhīm, 163
Faẓlōe, 98
Ferghāna, 28, 44, 47–9, 50, 53, 82, 87–8, 91, 96, 190, 200
Fertile Crescent, 1, 31, 61, 177, 185, 213
Fihrist, 134
Firdōsī, 21, 41, 121, 141, 174, 222, 226, 233
Fīrūz Ḥusain, 85
Fīrūzābād, 10, 23, 178
fityān, 195
Four Discourses, 234
frahang, 20

framadār, 17
French, 4, 27, 168
Fück, 124
furanīq, 239
Fūshanj, 13, 129, 188, 197, 200
futuwwa, 195

Gandhara, 120
Ganja, 114–15, 208
Gardēz, 45, 120, 196
Garshāspnāme, 21
Gava, 11, *see also* Iṣfahān
Gay, 11, *see also* Iṣfahān
Georgia(n), 9, 12, 15, 114–15
Germanic, 37, 168
Germany, 231
gezīrā, 18
gezirpat, 18
Gharchistān, 51
Ghazālī, 155, 160, 224, 229
ghāzī, 115, 120, 149, 194, 214–15
Ghazna, 31, 35, 45, 51, 76, 120–1, 196, 204, 218–19, 220
Ghaznavid, 121–2, 181, 198, 205, 218–21, 224–6
Ghiḍrifī (coins), 206
ghulām, 199, 218
ghulat (*ghulūw*), 132
Ghūr, 51, 120–1, 138, 219
Ghūrak, 80–1, 87–9
Ghuzz (Oghuz), 221, 224, 226–7
Gibb, 122
Gīlān, 117–18, 136, 140, 144, 152, 209
gittu, 18
Göbl, 37
Gōdmān, 11, *see also* Qum
Gök Turk, 49
Gōr, 10
gōsān, 172
Gōzgān, 51, *see also* Jūzjān
Greco-Bactrian, 29, 33
Greece, 24, 31, 226, 231
Greek, 1, 4, 5, 9, 10, 12–13, 19, 21–2, 30, 31–5, 38, 41–2, 71, 106, 123, 160, 162, 180, 184, 232
Gregorian calendar, 162
gunbad, 240
gund (*gwnd*), 152
Gurgān, 14, 86, 108, 116–17, 119, 138, 204, 209, 210, 220, 225
Gurgānj, 81
γw'kr, 99

gzir, 18

Habtal, 39
Hadhramaut, 68
Hādī, 133
ḥadīth, 123, 150, 155, 192
Ḥāfiẓ, 4, 234
Ḥaidar, *see* Afshīn
Haitham b. Khālid, 208
ḥaiy, 104
Ḥaiyān al-Nabaṭī, 82
ḥājib, 203
ḥajj, 54
Ḥajjāj b. Yūsuf, 70, 78–9, 80–5, 88, 119, 137
Ḥakam b. 'Amr al-Ghifārī, 75
Ḥallāj, 135, 152
Hamadān, 8, 9, 11, 60, 108, 112, 138, 145, 160, 188, 209, 215–17, 226
Hamadānī, 124
hamārkar, 18
Ḥamdān Qarmaṭ, 143
Ḥamdānid, 113
Hāmūn, 14
Ḥamza b. 'Abdallāh al-Shārī Adhrak, 119, 143, 194
Ḥanafī, 109, 155, 199, 217
Ḥanbalī(te), 114, 118
handasa, 240
handāz, 240
Ḥanẓala of Bādghīs, 192
Haraiva, 13
Harawī, Abu'l-Faḍl, 163
Harī Rūd, 30, 121, 188
Ḥārith b. Suraij al-Ṭamīmī, 89, 90–2
Ḥarrān, 24, 91, 164
Harthama, 115
Harthama b. A'yan, 188, 198
Hārūn al-Rashīd, 12, 107, 113, 115, 119, 120, 124, 136–7, 145, 167, 187–8, 207
Harūt and Marūt, 155
Ḥasan, *see* Rukn al-daula
Ḥasan (b. al-Ḥusain), 189
Ḥasan b. 'Alī, 144
Ḥasan b. Zaid, 118, 144, 197
Ḥasanōe, 98
Hāshimid, 114
Ḥātim b. Harthama, 115
hazārbad, 17
Hebrew, 138, 173
Hecatompylos, 12
Heftal, 39

Hellenistic, 24, 42
Hephthalite, 13, 37, 38–9, 51, 80
Herāt, 13, 25, 30, 35, 45, 50, 67, 73–6, 119, 120–1, 129, 163, 181, 188, 195–8, 200, 203–4, 216, 223
herbad, 66
Hermitage Museum, 47
Herodotus, 2, 3, 20, 21, 31
Ḥijāz, 26, 76, 102, 143, 179, 191
Hijra, 70, 76, 109, 122, 131, 168, 178, 231
Hilmand, 13, 14, 45, 51, 195
Hinayana, 44
Hind, 14, 100
Hindu, 121, 176, 214, 220
Hindū Kush, 13, 29, 30–1, 35, 37, 39, 44–5, 50–1, 52, 207, 220
Hindūshāhī, 45, 196, 218, 220
Hinduism, 31, 44–5, 121
Ḥīra, 15, 26, 55–8, 61
ḥisār, 108
Hishām b. ʿAbd al-Malik, 88–9, 91, 106
Hissar, 29, 37
Hivi, 43, 138
Hormizd-Ardashīr, 10
Horten, 159
Hsüan Tsang, 44
ḥubb, 240
Ḥuḍain b. al-Mundhir, 170
Ḥudhaifa b. al-Yamān, 65
Ḥudūd al-ʿālam, 51
Huei Ch'ao, 44
Ḥulwān, 58
Hun, 14, 37–8, 44
Ḥunain b. Isḥāq, 164
Hungary, 108
Hunnic, 36–8
Hurmuzān, 59, 63
Hurmizshahr, 10
Ḥusain b. ʿAlī, 76, 118, 140, 144
Ḥusain b. Muṣʿab, 188
Hyrcania, 14

Ibn ʿAbd Rabbih, 153
Ibn Abī Randaqa, 154
Ibn al-ʿArabī, 159, 160
Ibn al-Athīr, 110, 227
Ibn al-Balkhī, 73
Ibn al-Muqaffaʿ, 133, 153, 169
Ibn al-Nadīm, 34, 134, 154
Ibn al-Rūmī, 192
Ibn Bukhtīshūʿ, 22
Ibn Faḍlān, 167
Ibn Furāṭ, 167
Ibn Ḥanbal, 139
Ibn Ḥauqal, 113–15
Ibn Ḥazm, 131
Ibn Khaldūn, 150
Ibn Khurdādhbih, 11, 13, 23
Ibn Muʿāwiya, 92
Ibn Qutaiba, 122, 153
Ibn Rusta, 23, 116
Ibn Sīna, *see* Avicenna
Ibn Yazdād, 152
Ibn Ẓafār, 154
Ibn al-Zaiyāt, 152
Ibn Zubair, 76–8
Ibrāhīm b. Adham, 158–9
Ibrāhīm b. al-Aghlāb, 187
Ibrāhīm b. Ilyās, 197, 200
Ibrāhīm b. Jibrīl, 120
Ibrāhīm b. al-Walīd, 91
ibrisīm, 240
Idhaj, 11, 145
ijāza, 229
ikhshid ('γšyδ), 47, 49, 50
Ilik khān, 221
imām, 132, 136, 140, 143–4, 156
imāmzāde, 3, 140
Imra, 46
India, 5, 19, 30, 32–3, 38, 45, 52, 96, 107–8, 121, 141, 145–6, 159, 162, 167, 172, 184, 197, 213, 215, 219, 220, 225–6, 231
Indian, 30, 31, 33, 35, 44–6, 50, 215, 220
Indo-European, 29, 46, 50
Indus, 14, 31, 52, 72, 139, 173
Ionia, 32
Ionian, 32
ʿIqd al-farīd, 153
iqṭāʿ, 142, 227–8
Irān, *passim*
Irān āsān kard Kavād, 11
Irān Khwarra Shāpūr, 10, *see also* Shūsh
Irān-vinārd-Kavād, 11, *see also* Qum
Iranian, *passim*
Irānshahr, 8, 12, 13–15
Irān spāhbad, 17
Irānshahrī, 160
Iṣbahān, 11, *see also* Iṣfahān
Iṣfahān, 4, 9, 11, 12, 23, 64, 66, 94, 97, 100, 102, 108–9, 110, 112, 126,

138, 146, 181, 183, 208–9, 220, 225–6, 234
Isfijāb, 205
Isḥāq the Turk, 128–9
Ishrāq(ī), 160
Isidore of Charax, 19
Islām, *passim*
ism, 97
Isma'īl (Safavid), 2, 230
Isma'īl b. 'Abbād, 225
Isma'īl b. Aḥmad (Sāmānid), 198, 200–1, 207, 226
Isma'īl b. Sebüktigīn, 219
Isma'īlī, 131, 143–4, 148, 201, 220
Isma'īlī *imām*, 223
isnād, 229
Ispāhbad (Isbāh-), 13, 86, 116–17, 128, 190
Israel, 231
istabraq, 240
Iṣṭakhr, 8, 10, 66–7, 72–3, 110
Iṣṭakhrī, 23
Italy, 231
Itil, 108

Jabr, 162
Jacobite, 42, 137–8
Ja'd b. Dirham, 132
Ja'far 'Alā al-daula b. Kakūya, 225
Ja'far al-Ṣādiq, 143
Ja'far al-Turk, 214
jāhbadh, 18, 152
Jāhiliyya, 193, 227
Jāhiẓ, 123–4, 126, 214
Jahshiyārī, 151
Jaīhanī, 201
Jaipal, 220
Jalālābād, 45
Jalīlī, 162
Jalūlā', 58, 61–2
Jāmī, 159, 160
Jamūk, 214
Janbas kale, 29
Japanese, 23
Jarrāḥ b. 'Abdallāh al-Ḥakamī, 87
Jastān, 118
jauhar, 232
jausaq, 240
jauz, 232
javānmardī, 195
Jaxartes (Syr Daryā), 48, 224
Jew, 43, 100, 108, 111–12, 136–8, 140, 143, 148, 164, 173, 216
Jewish, 97
Jibāl, 11, 70, 92, 111–15, 197, 201, 208, *see also* Media
jihād, 54, 59, 107, 149
Jīruft, 112
jizya, 63, 69, 70, 87, 89, 94, 97, 102, 105, 107, 134, 145
Judaism, 43, 138
Junaid b. 'Abd al-Raḥman, 68, 89
junbudh, 240
jund, 107, 152
jund-i shāhānshāh, 61, 94
Jundīsābūr, 10–11, 22, 163–5, 197
Jurjān, 14, *see also* Gurgān
Jūrjānī, 164
Juwain, 119
Jūzjān, 13, 51, 104, 203

Ka'ba (at Mecca), 120, 143
Ka'ba-yi Zardusht, 9
Kābul, 30–1, 35, 45, 51, 77, 120–1, 196, 218
Kābul Shāh, 120, 214
Kāfir, 46
Kafirnigan river, 79
kāghad (*k'γδyh, kāghidh*), 239
Kakūyid, 225
kalām, 160
Kalāt, 14, 31, 52
Kalb, 76, 91
Kalimatī, Abu'l-Ḥasan, 203
Kaluraz, 176
kanārang, 9, 13
Kanishka, 34, 36
Kapisa, 120
Kara tepe, 30
Karāj, 209
Karen (Qārin), 7, 8, 73
Karīm Khān Zand, 4
Karkhā de Ledān, 11
Karkūya fire, 119
Karmānī, 92, 98
Karrāmiyya, 139, 143, 148
Kartīr, 9, 132
k'ryk'r, 99
Kash, 36
Kāshān, 64, 113, 143, 183
Kashgar, 36–7, 50, 221
kāshī, 182
Kashka Daryā, 29, 48, 235
Kashmir, 120
Kath, 81
Kathiawar, 220

kātib, 202
kātib al-fārisiyya, 211
Kavād, 10, 39
Kāzerūn, 108, 110
Kāzerūnī, Maḥmūd b. 'Uthmān, 209, *see also* Abū Isḥāq
Kerbelā, 76, 136
Keshen Deh, 235
khādim, 18
Khalaf, 144
Khalaj, 39, 214
Khālid b. 'Abdallāh al-Qasrī, 88, 91
Khālid b. Barmak, 107, 117
Khālid b. al-Walīd, 55–6
Khālil b. Aḥmad, 169, 171
Khālid b. Yazīd b. Mazyad al-Shaibānī, 207
khān, 82
khānagāh, 143
khandaq, 14–15
Khāqān, 90–1
Khāqānate, 49, 82
Khāqāniyya, 221
kharāj, 63, 69, 87, 102, 105, 107
Khārijite, 71–2, 76–8, 83–4, 92, 115, 119, 127, 130–2, 136, 143, 146, 187, 189, 194–6
Kharoshthi, 33
khāṣṣa, 54
Khātūn, 76, 81
Khazar, 15, 65, 108, 114–15
khedive, 239
Khidāsh, 127
Khingila (Khimgila), 38, 51, 120
Khirrīt b. Rāshid, 71
Khiyon, 38
Khojand, 88
khōra, 10
Khotan, 50
Khotanese Saka, 50
khudā, 47, 50–1
khudaina (*γwt'ynh*), 87
Khujandī, Abū Maḥmūd, 162–3
Khujistānī, 197
Khurāsān, 9, 10, 12–14, 26, 30, 52, 66–9, 70–1, 74–8, 84, 86, 88, 90–5, 97–9, 100–2, 104–5, 109, 112–13, 117–18, 121–6, 130, 138, 142–4, 150, 152, 156, 165, 168–9, 187–9, 190–2, 196–7, 200–1, 203, 214ff.
Khurāsānī, 226
Khurramdīn (Khurramiyya), 115, 127, 130, 132, 134
Khurzād, 47
Khusrau, 48, 89, 96
Khuttal, 29, 50
Khuttulstān (*γwttwrstn*), 51
Khūzistān, 10–11, 15, 22, 59, 60, 65, 70, 72, 111, 145, 163, 209, 236
Khwārazm, 28–9, 34–6, 40, 44, 46–8, 79, 81, 95, 147, 162, 166–7, 181, 198, 201, 203, 219, 225
Khwārazmī, Aḥmad b. Yūsuf, 17–18
Khwārazmī, Muḥammad b. Mūsā, 162
Khwārazmian, 27–8, 33–6, 41, 95, 99, 173–4, 180, 219, 232
Khwārazmshāh, 81, 219
Kidarite, 37–8
Kināna, 90
Kinda, 25, 71
Kindī, Abū Ya'qūb, 160, 165
Kirghiz, 25
Kirmān, 9, 25, 66, 70, 72, 78, 92, 108, 110–12, 115, 119, 126, 145, 162, 183, 196–9, 204, 209, 210, 216, 220
Kish, 40, 48, 78, 81, 86, 130
Kisrā, 8, 15, 20
Kitab area (Uzbek SSR), 48
Kitāb al-quniy, 165
Koh-i Daman, 31, 45, 120
Kucha, 50
Kūfa, 59, 60, 62, 64–5, 69, 70–2, 75, 83, 86, 89, 92, 95, 101, 122, 133, 151, 156, 168
Kufic, 10
Kūh-i Khwāja, 181
kuhandiz, 108
Kuhistān (Media), 11
Kuhistān (Khurāsān), 66, 73, 75, 111, 119, 162, 204
Kunduz, 29
kunyā, 97
kūra, 10–11, 108, 112
Kurd, 12, 65, 111–14, 225
Kurdistān, 112
Kushān, 9, 13, 34–5, 37, 46, 155
Kushān-Bactrian, 13, 16, 27, 34–5
Kushān-Sāsānian, 37
Kushānshahr, 36
kushk, 183
Kutadgu bilik, 221
kuttāb (*kātib*), 18, 22, 35, 107, 123, 151–2, 173

Lājīm, 119, 210
Lakhmid, 7, 15, 25–6, 55
Lālliya Shāhī, 121
Lashgarī Bazar, 181
Latin, 4, 168, 231
Lāwik, 121
Levant, 195
limes, 14–15, 26
Logar, 45
Lūristān, 111–12

Mād, 11
Madā'in, 8, 23, 58
madīna, 10, 108
Mādiyān-i Hazār Dātastān, 20
madrasa, 226–9
magūs (pl. *magī*), 17, 43–4, 116, 128, 151
Māh, 11
Māh al-Baṣra, 11, 65, *see also* Nihāvand
Māh al-Kūfa, 11, 65, *see also* Dīnawar
Mahān, 183
Mahānī, Abū 'Abdallāh Muḥammad, 162–3
Mahayana, 44
mahdī, 128
Mahdī, 130, 133, 136, 169
Maḥmūd of Ghazna, 205, 215, 218–221, 224, 226, 232
Māhōye, 74
Māḥōzē, 8
Majd al-daula, 220, 225
majūs, 26, *see also magūs*
Majūsī, 'Alī b. 'Abbās, 164
Makān b. Kākī, 209
Makrān, 14, 83, 96
maks (*mukūs*), 70
Makurān, 14
Malik b. Anas, 139
malik al-shu'arā', 226
Malikite, 43
Malikshāh, 226–7
mamlūk, 55, 105
Ma'mūn, 113, 115, 117, 120, 123–4, 136, 143, 151–2, 156, 162–3, 188–9, 190, 200, 209, 224
Manādhir, 11
Mandaean (Mandaeism), 131, 156
Mani, 41, 133–4
Manichaean, 28, 41, 43–4, 132–4, 180
Manichaeism, 42–4, 50, 100–1, 126, 153, 165
Mānshān, 51
Manṣūr, 22, 113–14, 116, 118, 138, 157
Mansūr II b. Nuḥ (Abū Ṣāliḥ), 204, 205
Manṭiqī, 226
Manūchihrī of Damghān, 226
maqāmāt, 124
Maqdisī, *see* Muqaddasī
Marāgha, 12, 113, 163
Marakanda, 47
Marāsfand, 111
Marchionite, 43
Mardānshāh b. Hurmuz, 60
Mardānshāh b. Zādānfarrūkh, 84
Mardāwīj, 209, 210
Margu, 13, 30, *see also* Merv
Marlik, 176
Marw, *see* Merv
Marw al-Rūd, 13, 81
Marwān b. Muḥammad, 91–2
Marwāzī, Ḥabash al-Ḥāsib, 163
marzbān, 9, 13–14, 46, 65, 67, 74, 97
Marzubān b. Muḥammad, 144
Māsabadān, 11, 64
Māsawaih (Masūya), 164
mashā'ī, 160
Mashhad, 67
Masmoghān, 116
Mas'ūd b. Maḥmūd (Ghaznavid), 220, 224–5
Mas'ūdī, 167
mathnavī, 174, 226
maulā (*mawālī*), 55, 61–3, 66, 68, 71, 84–9, 90–2, 95–7, 104–5, 107, 127, 146, 168
Maurya, 33, 45
Mawārdī, 229
Māy, 11
Māzandarān, 116, 140
Mazdā, 134
Mazdaism, 28, 30, 41, 43–4, 101
Mazdak, 135
Mazdakite, 114, 130, 134
Mazdean, 110, 128
Mazyār (Mahyāzdyār), 117, 190
Mecca, 5, 26, 54, 107, 143, 183
Mede, 3, 11
Media, 11, 70–1, 112, 173
Medīna, 26, 55, 59, 76
Mediterranean, 1, 139, 226

Memoirs of the Saints, 159
Merv, 13, 16, 25, 30, 35, 40, 42–3, 46, 52, 67, 70–1, 74–7, 80, 89, 90, 92, 97, 99, 100, 108–9, 115, 126–7, 132, 146–7, 152, 163, 166–7, 188, 193, 216–17, 225
Mesopotamia, 11, 22, 24, 25, 32, 33, 34, 58–9, 60, 63, 91–2, 133–4, 137, 145, 158, 164–6, 181, 184, 213, 232
Messiah, 1
Middle East, 1
Middle Persian, 8, 9, 10, 11, 12, 16, 18, 19, 24, 33, 34, 52, 96, 106, 111, 134, 146, 152, 168, 171–2, 192, 232
Mihira Boja, 121
Mihragān, 140
Mihirakula, 38
miḥna, 136
Mihr Narseh, 17
Mihran, 7, 57
Mihrijānqadaq, 11
Mikālī, 215
Minorsky, 115
Mir 'Alī Shīr Navōī, 223
Mīr Damād, 160, 234
miṣr, 59
mithqāl, 84
MLK', 34, 87
mōbad, 17–19, 111–12, 119, 140, 145
mōbadān mōbad, 17
Moghul, 45
Mohammed Reza Pahlavi, 4
Molé, 135
Mongol, 4, 13, 138, 163, 181, 184, 223
Mongolia, 28, 49
Moses of Chorene, 38
Mosul, 181
MR'y, 87
Mshatta, 91
mu'allim, 123
Mu'āwiya, 64, 69, 72, 75–6, 116, 154
Mu'āwiya b. Yazīd b. al-Muhallab, 86
Mu'aiyad al-daula, 210
Muḍar, 71, 75–8, 88, 90
Mufaḍḍal b. al-Muhallab, 79
Mugh mt., 96
Mughān, 12, 114
Muhallab b. Abī Ṣufra, 78–9
Muhallibid, 88, 92, 98
Muḥammad, 2, 26, 46, 55, 102, 104, 179
Muḥammad (Mazyār), 117
Muḥammad b. 'Abdallāh (Tahirid), 191
Muḥammad b. Hārān al-Sarakhsī, 118
Muḥammad b. Ibrāhīm, 191
Muḥammad b. Khālid al-Shaibānī, 208
Muḥammad b. Khālid b. Yazīd b. Mazyad, 114
Muḥammad b. Mūsā, 117
Muḥammad b. Maḥmūd (Ghaznavid), 220
Muḥammad b. al-Qāsim, 83
Muḥammad b. Ṭāhir, 143, 191–2, 197–8
Muḥammad b. Wāṣif, 173
Muḥammad b. Wāsil, 196
Muḥammad b. Zaid, 118
Muḥammadī (coins), 206
muhraq, 18, 239
mu'īd, 229
Mu'izz al-daula (Aḥmad), 209, 211
Mujjā'a b. Si'r, 83
mukallaf, 54, 105
Mukhallad b. Yazīd, 86
Mukhtār, 86
Mullā Ṣadrā, 160, 234
Multān, 83, 120, 220
Munjik, 203
Muqaddasī (Maqdisī), 15, 111, 132, 155
Muqanna', 130, 134, 139, 140, 148
Muqātil b. 'Alī, 97
muqātila, 59, 69, 83
Muqtadir, 133, 151
Murghāb, 13, 14
Mūsā b. 'Abdallāh b. Khāzim, 79
Mūsā al-Kāẓim, 143
Musa al-Nikrisi, 138
Mūsā b. Saiyār al-Uswārī, 169
Muṣ'ab b. Ruzaiq, 188
Musāfirid, 144, 225
Musaiyabī (coins), 206
Mushki, 138
mushtak, 239
Muslim, *passim*
Muslim b. S'aīd al-Kilābī, 88, 97
Musta'īn, 191
mustaq ṣīnī, 239
Musulman, 28
Mu'taḍid, 198, 200
Mu'tamid, 196, 200

Mutannabī, 210
mutaqārib, 226
Mu'taṣim, 117, 214
Mutawakkil, 136–7, 148, 152, 164
Mu'tazilite, 122, 131, 136, 151, 157–8, 189
Muthannā b. Hāritha al-Shaibānī, 56–7
muṭṭawwi'a, 149, 194
Muwaffaq, 187, 198, 200
mwdr(k), 18
mwγ'nc dyn, 100

Nabaṭ, 63
Nadīr Shāh, 4
Naḍr b. al-Ḥārith, 26
nahang, 9
naḥiyya, 108
Nahr Tīrā, 11
Nairizī, Abu'l-'Abbās, 162
Nakhshab, 29, 130, *see also* Nasaf
nākhuda, 239
namraq, 240
Nana (Nanai), 44
Nangarhar, 45
Naqsh-i Rustām, 9, 24, 36
Nara, 23
nard, 240
Narmashīr, 112
Narshakhī, 98
Nasaf, 29, 48, 81, 86, 130
Nāṣir-i Khusrau, 122
Naṣr b. Aḥmad (early Sāmānid), 200
Naṣr b. Aḥmad, 144, 201–2
Naṣr al-Kabīr, 201
Naṣr Qarakhanid, 205
Naṣr b. Saiyār, 84, 88–9, 90–2, 97, 99, 105, 188
Naṣr b. Shabath, 189
Naubahār, 90, 158
Naubakht, 163
nāy, 240
Nāyin, 113, 183
Near East, 1, 2, 5, 27, 33, 54, 131, 152, 164, 166, 181, 184, 214, 217, 221, 224, 228, 235–6
Nestorian(ism), 25, 28, 42, 100, 137–138, 141, 162, 165
Nev Hormizd Ārdashīr, 112
New Persian, 8, 10, 16, 21, 116, 125, 144, 150, 168, 171–4, 179, 193, 199, 200, 203, 206, 210–12, 222, 232
Nēzak, 51, 80–1
Nihāvand, 11–12, 59, 60, 62, 65–6, 73, 95, 113, 138
Nihāvandī, Aḥmad, 163
Nile, 1, 2
Nima'tāllah Vālī, 183–4
Nisa, 225
Nishāpūr, 13, 22, 66–7, 77, 92, 100, 108–9, 117, 119, 126, 128, 143, 146, 155–6, 166, 181–2, 190, 192–3, 197, 199, 204, 209, 214–16, 219, 223, 225
Nisibis, 24
Niẓām al-Mulk, 55, 134, 203, 227, 229
Niẓāmī 'Arūḍī, 234
Niẓamiyya, 229
Norman, 4
nōrūz, 2, 140, 210
nsng, 9
Nūḥ b. Asad, 200
Nūḥ II b. Mansūr, 204–5
Nūḥ b. Naṣr, 144, 201, 204
Nu'mān, 26
Nu'mān b. Muqarrin, 59–60
Numijkath, 80
Nūristān, 31

Oghuz Khān, 214
Ohrmazd, 134
Old Persian, 3, 18, 27, 28, 30, 33
Old Testament, 138
Oman, 68, 76, 78, 83, 167, 210
Orkhon, 49, 82, 214, 221
Ossete, 21
Ostādh Sīs, 129
ōstān, 10, 108
Ottoman, 181, 221, 223, 230, 234
Oxus, 27–9, 30, 46, 51, 67, 72, 76–9, 81, 89, 95, 98, 198, 203, 219

Padashkhwargar shāh, 117
pādgōspān, 9, 13
Pahlavi, 8, 10, 16, 19, 21–2, 26, 34, 38, 42, 69, 83–4, 99, 106, 111, 116, 119, 137, 147, 151, 153–4, 162, 173, 192, 206, 210–12, 233
Pāhra, 14
Pākistān, 31
Palestine, 56–7
Pamirs, 29
pand, 20
Panjhīr (Panjshīr), 121
Panjikant, 28, 40–1, 48, 52, 87–8, 96, 99, 166–7, 181, 215

Panjshīr, 196, *see also* Panjhīr
Paradēnē, 14
pardākht, 169
Paris, 3, 11
Paropanisadai, 44
Pārsa, 28
Parsi, 19, 145
Partav, *see* Bardā'a
Parthia, 34
Parthian, 9, 12–14, 19, 24, 33–5, 152, 173, 195
parvānak, 18
parvāne, 239
Pashkibur, 36
Pathan, 92
patmān, 128
pax Turcica, 217
Pērōz, 38–9, 67
Persepolis, 19, 110, 162
Persia, 57
Persian, *passim*
Persian Gulf, 65, 179
pīr, 140
Plato, 161
Pliny, 25, 31
plm't'ly, 11
Pritsak, 221
Ptolemy, 44
Pumbadita, 138
Punjab, 120, 225
Pushang, *see* Fushanj
pwrc, 98

Qābūs b. Wushmgīr, 220, 225
Qadarite, 133
qāḍī, 17, 70, 109, 152
qāḍī al-quḍāt, 17
Qādisiyya, 58–9, 61
Qāhir, 151
Qaḥṭān, 76
Qais, 71, 76–8, 88–9, 91, 169
Qais b. Haitham, 72, 75
Qājār, 4
qal'a, 108
qa'la jiṣṣ, 111
Qamarī, 164
Qandahār, 30–1, 35, 45, 51–2, 77, 120
Qānūn, 164
Qara'im, 138
Qaraite, 138
Qarākhānid, 167, 204–5, 219–24
Qarātigīn, 218
Qārin b. Shahriyār, 117, *see also* Karen
Qarlūq, 221
Qarmatian, 136, 143, 208
qaṣaba, 108
qasīda, 234
qaṣr, 108
Qaṭān b. Qutaiba, 89
Qaṭarī b. al-Fujā'a, 119
Qazvīn, 12, 71, 74, 95, 108–9, 113, 117, 191, 193, 201, 208, 217
Qizil Yilan, 14
Qūfs, 112
Qum, 11, 60, 64, 74, 96, 113, 138, 144–5, 155, 193, 208–9
Qūmis, 12, 74, 138
Qu'rān, 61, 73, 85, 122–3, 132, 150, 155, 157–8, 177, 192
Qur'ānic, 83, 156, 169, 172, 206
Quraish, 78, 214
qurrā', 123
qurṭaq, 240
qūs, 240
Qushairī, Muslim b. al-Ḥajjāj, 156
quṣṣāṣ, 123
Qutaiba b. Muslim, 46–7, 79, 80–3, 86–8, 94–5, 98–9, 169
Qutham b. 'Abbās, 170

rabaḍ, 108
Rabbinate, 138
Rabī' b. Ziyād al-Ḥārithī, 75, 77
Rabī'a, 71, 76, 78, 88, 92
Radkān (Mīl-i), 119, 210
Rāfi' b. Harthama, 197–8
Rāfi' b. Laith, 188, 200
Raga, *see* Raiy
ra'īs (*al-balad*), 9, 109, 142, 193, 215
Raiy, 11, 12, 60, 64, 79, 86, 108–9, 110, 112–13, 132, 143–4, 155, 163–4, 172, 188, 191, 193, 197, 201, 208–9, 210, 217, 220, 225–6
Rām Hormizd Ardashīr, 11
Ramaḍān, 54
ramal, 226
Rāmitīn, 47, 80
Rāmiz, 10, 11
rang, 239
Raqqa, 189, 192
Rawandiyya, 127, 157
Rāzī, Muḥammad b. Zakariyyā, 160, 164
Resh Galutha, 138

Renaissance, 175
Reẓā Shāh, 4, 174, 233
Reẓāiye (Urmiya), 11
ribāb, 239
ribāṭ, 19, 120, 207, 225
Rīshahr, 66
Roman, 1, 10, 12, 231
Roman empire, 1, 178
Rome, 24, 31, 231
rōstāk, 10
Rōzbih, 153
ruba'ī, 174, 226
Rudakī, 202, 222, 233
Rukhkhaj, 51, 77
Rukn al-daula (Ḥasan), 209, 210, 215
Rūmī, Jalāl al-Dīn, 4, 234
Rūs, 208
Russia, 4, 167, 201, 213, 228
Russian, 28, 31
Russian Turkistān, 27, 35, 40, 49, 50, 138
Rustām, 58, 169
Rustām Kavād, 10
rustāq (*rustā*), 10, 108–9
Rustaqubād, 10
rusūm, 151
ruwānikān difīra, 17
Ruzaiq, 188

Sabian, 43, 164
sabīy, 95
Sābūr, 15, 110
Sābūr b. Sahl, 164
sabk, 226
S'ad b. 'Abī Waqqāṣ, 58–9
Ṣadaqī, 199
Sa'dī, 2, 4
Sadd-i Iskandar, 14
saḍr, 223
Ṣafāvid, 2, 4, 45, 160, 181, 183, 227, 234
ṣaffār, 195
Ṣaffārī *imām*, 223
Ṣaffārid, 112, 118, 135, 143, 174, 186–7, 194–9, 202, 210, 219
Safīd Rūd, 118
Ṣaghāniyān, 29, *see also* Chaghāniyān
Ṣāhib b. 'Abbād, 170
ṣāhib al-barīd, 109
Ṣaḥīḥ, 156
Sahlid, 170
Sa'īd b. 'Abd al-'Azīz, 87
Sa'īd b. 'Amr al-Ḥarashī, 87–8
Sa'īd b. 'Uthmān b. 'Affān, 76
Ṣaimara, 112
Saivaism, 45
Sājids, 208
Saka, 13, 31, 37
ṣakk, 239
ṣalāt, 54
Ṣāliḥ (*aiyār*), 195
Ṣāliḥ b. 'Abd Quddūs, 133
Ṣāliḥ b. 'Abd al-Rahman, 84
Salm b. Ziyād (Muslim), 76, 98
Salmān al-Fārisī, 61, 155
Samakī, 199
Sāmān, 200
Sāmānid, 111, 113, 118, 121, 144, 167, 173–4, 180, 183, 186, 190, 193, 197–9, 200–7, 209, 210–11, 213, 215, 218, 220–2, 224–6, 229
Samaritan, 43
Samarqand (*sm'rknd*), 27–9, 40–1, 44, 47–8, 52, 76, 81–2, 86–9, 90, 93, 99, 100, 109, 133, 141, 166, 181–2, 200, 205, 207, 211, 216, 221, 233
Samarqandī, Sulaimān b. 'Iṣmat, 163
Samarra, 107, 115, 117, 130, 181, 190, 214
Ṣamṣām al-Daula, 145
ṣanj, 240
Sanjār, 229
Sanskrit, 22, 30, 42
Sarakhs, 90
Sarakhsī, Aḥmad b. al-Ṭaiyab, 164
sarāwil, 240
ṣard, 240
Sārī, 116
Sarmatian, 21
Sāsānian, *passim*
satrap, 9
ṣaulajān, 240
ṣaum, 54
Sawād, 15, 63
sawāfī, 63
Scandinavia, 167, 206
Scythian, 21, 31, 37
Sebeos, 65
Sebüktigīn, 218
Seistān, 13–14, 30, 45, 66–7, 70–1, 74, 77, 81–2, 85, 92–3, 95, 102, 104, 116, 119, 120–1, 130, 143, 173, 181, 188–9, 191, 194–9, 201, 210, 219
Seleucids, 12–13, 33

Selīm (Ottoman), 230
Seljūk, 160–1, 176, 182, 185, 203, 205, 214, 219, 221–9, 231, 233
Semirechiye, 28, 49, 82, 138
Semitic, 2, 8, 15–16, 25
Sergeant, 166
Shabistarī, 160
shād, 51
Shaguftiyya, 158
Shāfi'ī, 109, 139, 155–6, 199, 217
shāh, 34, 51, 81, 201
Shāh 'Abbās, 4
Shāh Malik, 225
shahāda, 54
shāhānshāh, 210
Shāhī Tigīn, 120
Shāhid al-Balkhī, 202
Shāhnāme, 21, 233
shahr, 10, 108
Shahrām Pērōz, 114, *see also* Abādān Pīrūz
Shāhijān, 13
Shahrāsiyāb, 40
shahristān, 108
Shahristānī, 131
Shaibān b. Salama, 92
Shaibānī (Khārijite), 131
shaikh, 109
shākiriyya, 152
Shansi, 146
Shāpūr I, 9, 10, 36–7, 132
Shāpūr II, 15, 25, 37
Shaqīq, 158
shār, 51
sharī'a, 54, 97
shāristān, 10
Sharvān, 114, 208
Sharvīn (Caspian), 117
Shāsh, 36–7, 49, 82, 91, 120, 190, 200
štry, 9, 10
shaṭranj, 240
shēr, 50–1
Shī'ite (Shī'ism), 2, 3, 86, 88, 113, 116–19, 127–9, 131–4, 136, 140–1, 143–4, 146, 153, 155–7, 181, 186, 189, 191, 197–8, 204, 209, 217–19, 227–9
Shīrāz, 4, 100, 102, 109, 110, 145, 163–4, 181, 209, 210, 216, 233–4
Shīz, 65, 114
Shosoin, 23
Shūmān, 51, 79
Shūsh, 10
Shustar, 10
Shu'ūbiyya, 71, 105, 121–2, 169, 186
šyšpyr, 48
Sībawaih (Sībūye), 150, 169
Siberia, 37, 167, 184
Sicilian, 154
Ṣiffīn, 71
Sijistān, 13, *see also* Seistān
Silk Road, 87
Sīmjūrī, Abu'l-Ḥasan, 204
Sīmjūrid, 218
Sind, 76, 82–3, 89, 120–1, *see also* Hind
Sīrāf, 110, 179, 182
sirāj, 240
ṣirāṭ, 158
Sīrjān, 112
Śiva, 46
Siyāsat nāme, 134, 203
Siyāvush, 28
Sogdian (*sγwδyk*), 13, 16, 28, 29, 33–6, 41–2, 44, 47–9, 50–3, 76, 80, 82, 87–9, 90–1, 95–9, 100, 167, 180, 206, 215
Sogdiana, 27–9, 34–8, 40–1, 43–4, 47–8, 49, 102, 212
Soghd, 36, *see also* Sogdiana
Somnath, 220
Sourdel, 152
Soviet, 27–9, 40, 99, 100, 207, 235
spāhbad, 8, 13
Spain, 91, 153–4, 186, 190
spx'n, 11, *see also* Iṣfahān
Srednyaya Aziya, 27
Strabo, 25, 30
stūn, 240
stupa, 45
Sebüktigīn, 205
Subuk, 208
Ṣūfī, 141, 145, 158–9, 194, 222
Ṣūfī, 'Abd al-Rahman, 163
Ṣūfism, 137, 158–9, 160, 195, 226, 229, 234
Sughdī, 98
Suguda, 27
Suhrawardī Shihāb al-Dīn, 158, 161
Sui, 49, 67
Sulaimān (Umaiyad caliph), 82–3, 86, 102, 116
Sulaimān b. 'Abdāllah b. Ṭāhir, 118
Sulaimān b. Abī'l-Sarī, 88
ṣulḥ, 63

Su-na, 45
Sunnī, 18, 114, 118, 131, 134, 136, 139, 141, 143–4, 155–6, 160, 181, 186, 189, 198–9, 202, 204, 209, 217–19, 220, 222, 226–7, 229
Sunpad (Sinbad), 128, 134, 139, 140
Sūq al-Ahwāz, 10, *see also* Ahwāz
Sūrēn, 7, 8, 14, 146
Surkh Kotal, 30
Surkhān Daryā, 29, 79
Surraq, 11
Sūs (Susa), 10, 11, *see also* Shūsh
Syr Daryā, *see* Jaxartes
Syria, 1, 57–8, 84–5, 91–2, 101, 143, 165–6, 169, 176, 178–9, 180, 183, 195, 229
Syriac, 10, 11, 18, 22, 24, 26, 106, 137–8, 163, 173, 185
Syrian, 26, 68, 83, 85, 91, 126, 181, 213, 232

Ṭabarī, 14, 36, 47, 50, 74, 79, 85, 93–4, 96, 98, 103, 124, 201
Ṭabarī, ʿAlī b. Rabbān, 164
Ṭabarī dialect, 174
Ṭabaristān, 14, 86, 96–7, 116–18, 128, 136, 144, 155, 166, 190, 197, 201, 204, 210, 220, 225
Ṭabbas, 66
Tabrīz, 113, 181, 233
Tāčik, 25
Taghlib, 25
Ṭāhīr b. Husain, 115, 143, 169, 188–189, 191–2
Ṭāhir II b. ʿAbdāllah, 117, 190–1
Ṭāhīrid, 111, 122, 134, 186–7, 190–6, 200, 202, 206
Tājik (Tāzik), 96, 98, 207
Tājikistān (Tājik SSR), 23, 25, 44, 50, 79, 100, 183, 207, 212, 219
takht, 239
Takht-i Sulaimān, 114
Talas, 200
Talas River, 50
Ṭalḥa b. Ṭāhir, 189, 190
Ṭalḥa b. ʿAbdallāh al-Khuzāʿī, 188
Ṭāliqān, 13, 51, 81, 95
Talmud, 18
tambūr, 239
Tamīm, 26, 61, 71, 75–8, 84–6, 92–4, 169, 199
Ṭamīs, 14
Tammīsha, 14
tanāsukh, 129
ṭanfasa, 240
Ṭʼang, 49, 182
Tang-i Azao, 138
Tanūkh, 24
Tapuri, 116
Ṭāq, 8
Ṭār, 49
Ṭarāz, 200, *see also* Talas
Tārīkh-i Sīstan, 199
Tarim Basin, 50
Tarkhān, 50–1
Ṭarkhūn (*trγwn*), 48, 80
Tāsh, 204
Tāshkent, 28, 36, 49, 50, 190
tasūq, 10
tasūḥ, 240
ṭassūj, 10, 108
tāʼwīl, 160
Tawwaj, 65
Tehran, 3
Termez (Tirmidh), 29, 30, 50, 77–8, 90, 181
Thaʿālibī, 25, 169, 202
Thābit b. Qurra, 164
Thābit b. Quṭba al-Khuzāʿī, 79
Thracian, 31
Tibetan, 49, 50
Tiflis, 114
Tigris, 24, 58
Tim, 207
Timotheos I, 137
Tīmūr, 235
Timurid, 223
Tirmidh, *see* Termez
Tokharian, 29, 31, 50
Tokhāristān, 29, 51, 81, 88, 90
Tolstov, Sergei, 29
Toprak kale, 29
Toramana, 38
Tortosa, 154
Transcaucasia, 115
Transoxiana, 49, 50, 67, 76, 81–3, 87, 89, 92–9, 100, 114–15, 120, 126, 128, 130, 150, 162, 166–8, 188, 198, 200, 203–4, 206, 214ff.
Tsentralnaya Aziya, 27
Tudun, 50
Ṭughril Beg, 226–7
Ṭughshāda, 81, 87, 90
Tulunid, 187
Tunisia, 187
Ṭūrān, 14, 31

Turbat-i Shaikh Jam, 144
Turfan, 50, 138
Türgesh, 49, 82, 91
Turkey, 181
Turk, 14, 37–9, 50, 68, 77–8, 80, 82, 87–9, 91–2, 115, 125, 128, 135, 137, 139, 142, 149, 184, 190, 200, 202–6, 213ff.
Turkī Shāhī, 120–1
Turkic, 14, 25, 39, 50, 236
Turkish, 4, 5, 35, 39, 40, 44, 47, 49, 50–1, 79, 81, 98, 120–1, 130, 142, 145, 203–5, 213ff.
Türkmen, 224–5
Ṭūs, 13, 67, 119, 216
Ṭūṣī, Naṣīr al-Dīn, 55, 160, 163
Tustar, 10, *see also* Shustar
twk'sp'δ'k, 48
twttk, 50
twspwn, 8

udabā' (*adīb*), 152, 173, 202, 222
Udabhanda, 121
Umaiya b. 'Abdallāh b. Khālid, 78
Umaiyad, 16, 26, 54, 68–9, 70, 72–8, 83, 84, 87, 90–3, 96–7, 100, 102–6, 114, 116–17, 119, 120, 124, 126–7, 132, 137–8, 141–2, 146–7, 151, 154, 166, 168, 178–9, 181, 188, 200, 217, 235
umma, 54
**uparisaina*, 44
Urmiya, 113–14, *see also* Reẓāiye
Ushnūya, 113
ustādh, 229
Ustrūshana (Ushrūsana), 28, 48, 91, 115, 189, 190, 201, 208
usṭuwāna, 240
Uzbek, 25
Uzbek SSR, 235

Vahrām-i Varjavand, 128
Vajda, 134
Varakhshā, 28, 40, 47, 181, 207
Varamīn, 172
Varāz, 8, 51
Varāz banda (Barāz), 51
Vardāna, 47
Vāspuhrākān, 11, 12
Veh Andiōkh Shāpūr, 10
Veh Ārdashīr, 112
Vēh āz Amīd Kavād, 10
vičīr, 18
vihāra, 51, 158
Viking, 26, 228
Volga, 28, 108, 167, 213
vuzurg framadār, 17, 18, 107

Wahabism, 234
Wakhsh Daryā, 29, 50
Wakī' b. Abī Sūd, 86
walī, 109
Walīd I, 82–3, 85, 102
Walīd II b. Yazīd, 91
Walkhon, 38
Wāmqubād, 10
wanj, 240
waqf, 17, 141, 216, 229
ward, 240
Wārdak, 45
wasaṭ, 128
Wāṣil b. 'Amr, 90
Wāsiṭ, 83
w'spwxlk'n, 11
Wāthiq, 190
wazīr, 18, 107, 151
Wellhausen, 68, 85, 103
Windād b. Hurmuz b. Qārin, 116
World War I, 224
Wushmgīr b. Mardawij, 209

xm'lkly, 17
xštr, 9
xvarenah, 8

yābghū, 51
Yaḥyā b. Adam al-Qurashī, 63
Yaḥya b. Asad, 200
Ya'qūb b. Aḥmad (Sāmānid), 200
Ya'qūb b. Laith, 45, 120–1, 143, 173, 191–2, 195–9, 200, 206
Ya'qūbī, 9, 64, 70, 80, 120
Yāqūt, 10, 15
Yarkand, 50
Yarmūk, 58
yātakgōv, 17
Yatīmat al-dahr, 169, 202
yazata, 140
Yazd, 10, 66, 113, 141, 145
Yazd-i Khwāst, 183
Yazdegird, 8, 42, 57–9, 66–7, 73–4, 89, 95, 97, 116, 140
Yazīd, 76
Yazīd II, 87–8, 93, 178
Yazīd III, 91
Yazīd b. Muffarigh, 171–2

Yazīd b. al-Muhallab, 79, 80, 86, 88, 95, 116
Yazīdī, 131
Yemen, 26, 57, 76, 137
Yemenite, 71, 76, 91, 144
Yudghan, 138
Yuhanna b. Masawaih, 164
Yusūf b. Dīvdād Abū Sāj, 208
Yūsuf b. Ibrahīm al-Barm, 129, 188
Yūsuf b. 'Umar, 91

Zābul, 46, 51
Zābulistān, 51, 77
Zādānfarrūkh, 84
Zagros, 58, 111
Zaidī Shī'ism, 117–18, 144, 191, 201, 208, 210–11
Zain al-'Ābidain, 140
Zajjāj, 150
zakāt, 54, 70, 87, 105
Zamakhsharī, 122, 169
Zamīndāwar, 77, 120
Zandana, 166
Zandanījī, 98, 166
zandaqa, 132–4
Zanj, 187
Zanjān, 208, 225
Zarafshān, 27, 44, 47–8, 87, 205
Zaranj (Zarang), 14, 77, 92–3, 119, 194–5, 199
Zari, 235
Zik, 7
zindiq, 132–4, 153
zīr, 240
Ziyād Abū Muḥammad, 88
Ziyād b. Abīhi, 64, 70, 72, 151, 154
Ziyārid, 204, 209, 220, 225
Zoroastrian, 1, 3, 8, 16–19, 20–2, 26, 34, 40, 42, 55, 66, 73–4, 84, 93, 96–7, 100, 105–6, 108–9, 110–14, 121, 126–9, 130, 132, 134–7, 139, 140–1, 143–8, 152, 154, 157–8, 172, 176, 183, 209, 210–12, 216
Zoroastrianism, 30, 41–3, 55, 73, 100–2, 110–11, 118, 126, 131, 133–134, 140, 142, 145, 155–7, 161, 177, 212
Zoroaster, 8, 29, 129, 131, 161
Zranka, 14
Zūn (Zhūn), 45–6, 77
zunbīl (*zhunbīl*), 51–2, 77, 81, 92–3, 120, 195
Zūr, 46
Zurvān, 46

Date Due			